Empowered Employees
become
Engaged Employees

Using Science to Solve the
Employee Engagement Crisis

**The Smart Way to Manage Emotions
and Increase Core Self-Evaluations, Psychological
Flexibility, Motivation, Emotional Intelligence,
Happiness, and Employee Engagement**

Also by Jeanine Joy

"*Trusting One's Emotional Guidance Builds Resilience*", Perspectives on Coping and Resilience. Ed. Venkat Pulla, Shane Warren, and Andrew Shatté. Laxmi Nagar: Authors Press, 2013. 254-279

True Prevention—Optimum Health: Remember Galileo

Prevent Suicide: The Smart Way

Is Punishment Ethical? The Fallacy of Good and Evil

Our Children Live in a War Zone, Use The Power of Resilience to Improve Their Lives, Applied Positive Psychology 2.1

Other books by Jeanine Joy: Coming Soon

Become More Resilient: The Smart Way, Be Ready for Life

Diversity Appreciation: Using Science to Transform the Paradigm

Bloom: The Keys to Happiness

Emotional Agility: The Smarter Way

Thrive More, Now Publishing

Empowered Employees become Engaged Employees
Using Science to Solve the Employee Engagement Crisis

The Smart Way to Manage Emotions
and Increase Core Self-Evaluations, Psychological Flexibility, Motivation, Emotional
Intelligence, Happiness, and Employee Engagement

A Thrive More Now Book

Published by
Thrive More, Now Publishing
Charlotte, North Carolina

ISBN-13: 978-0692546819
ISBN-10: 0692546812

Dedication

I dedicate this book to my wonderful husband, Phil.

When we met I was a Director. Now I'm an author, speaker, and trainer. It may be your fault for encouraging me to follow my dreams, for which I'm eternally grateful. Your encouragement, support, and love sustain me. You are the man I spent much of my life dreaming I'd find.

Love Always,

Your Lady J

Table of Contents

Table of Contents

Introduction

There are only three measurements that tell you nearly everything you need to know about your organization's overall performance: employee engagement, customer satisfaction, and cash flow. It goes without saying that no company, small or large, can win over the long run without energized employees who believe in the mission and understand how to achieve it.

Jack Welch

Humans are complex. A remark that thrills one employee may be upsetting to another. Work related situations are also complex because of diverse aspects of customers, employees, markets, and the speed of change. Can managers increase employee engagement in environments where the number of variables is infinite?

Yes, we can, but there isn't a single formulaic behavior a manager can follow that will increase engagement for all employees. Read any list of *3 fool proof ways to increase engagement* or *10 things you must do to increase employee engagement* or other articles that promise to increase engagement and there will be exceptions to nearly every piece of advice. That's because people are beautifully unique and what pleases one may irritate another.

We have to look deeper to find the solution to low engagement. We must begin in the mind of the employee. With the right knowledge this approach is easier and more effective than any other route. People interpret what they hear though a filtering process formed by past experiences, and most of the filters were created during childhood. All communication is translation.

Turnover is costly, but turnover of key staff can have devastating consequences to a business.

Get to know or *talk to staff* are common suggestions for improving employee engagement but not every employee wants to explore his own psyche, much less let a boss in on the secrets and fears that lurk just beneath the surface. Talking with and getting to know staff is a good thing, but a manager won't really know their employees if she doesn't understand:

1. What drives human behavior,
2. How to interpret the behavior,
3. And how to intuit an inspiring response on an individual basis.

All you have to do to know this is true is think about people in your personal life and decisions they've made that surprised you. It happens all the time. Someone decides to move away from their home and family, someone else gets involved in drugs, another person quits their job to go back to school, someone else cheats on their spouse when you would have bet they would never do that. The examples of behaviors that surprise us are endless and, for the most part, universal.

For many managers, the choices of individuals they know far better and longer than they know their staff are mysterious. Yet they are expected to understand and motivate their staff. The mystery dissolves when a manager understands the connections between emotional state and behavior,

Researchers estimate humans think between 60,000 – 80,000 thoughts and speak between 7,000 – 20,000 words each day. Each thought can contain many words. The contrast between those ranges of numbers is enough to illustrate that understanding how someone else perceives a situation by talking with him or her leaves significant gaps in your knowledge about what the person is thinking. There are other ways to communicate, including body language and facial expression. On the quantum level, our brains sync with one another but most people aren't aware that process occurs. Even when they know about mirror neurons, they seldom know what, exactly, their brains are syncing to or why or how to exert control over the process.

At the individual level it could take years to become aware enough of the nuances that motivate a single individual, much less one's entire staff unless you understand three things:

1. Factors that influence all human behavior,
2. Nuances associated with those factors, and
3. How to recognize and interpret employee's moods, attitudes, and work using a framework of evidence-based motivation and emotional intelligence data.

The purpose of this book is primarily to help managers understand how to improve employee engagement, but I begin by teaching them how to be happier, more resilient, emotionally intelligent, and psychologically flexible. In general (meaning there are exceptions), management already has greater levels of **employee engagement, resilience, emotional intelligence, self-efficacy,** and **psychological flexibility** than their staff.* It's usually the reason, over and above educational attainment, that they have the positions they have.

Although management have greater levels of those skills, the cause of those skills is still largely unknown to most managers—they've stumbled into habits of thought or learned them from parents or others who have influenced their habits of thought. Conscious awareness of how to deliberately cultivate the beneficial traits mentioned in the prior paragraph improves results in two ways:

1. It makes it easier for the manager to exert deliberate control over her own thoughts, words, and actions, and
2. It becomes very easy to understand others' decisions and behaviors.

Recognition of the reasons others behave as they do becomes so easy that most people would be appalled at what they are revealing to someone who understands the nuances of their words, actions, facial expressions, and body language. The key is not to reveal what you know, but to respond with compassion and communicate with them in ways that inspire them to believe they can become more of their potential.

One reason managers tend to have higher **core self-evaluations** is because higher self-efficacy beliefs lead to higher levels of achievement. Marilyn Gist, Associate Dean at Albers School of Business and Economics reported, "evidence shows that self-efficacy influences the goal level chosen on experimental tasks. Those high in initial self-efficacy tend to set higher goals than individuals who are low in self-efficacy. This finding has been validated in the training context. Goals, in turn, are widely known to influence performance. During **self-regulation**, goals direct attention and effort toward the task through a process that involves self-monitoring with respect to the goals and adjustment of effort to achieve desired outcome."[1] Essentially, higher self-efficacy leads to higher objectives to which one manages oneself.

Bobby Hoffman, an Associate Professor of Educational Psychology tells us:

*"Teachers and students with high mathematics anxiety, irrespective of ability, perceive they are **less competent** than individuals with lower mathematics anxiety . . . the uncomfortable feelings and worry associated with mathematics anxiety facilitates an intellectual paralysis, usurping precious working*

---

* Words emphasized with **this font** are included in a glossary in the Appendix.

memory resources, and diverting attention which might otherwise be directed to task processing." [2]
[Emphasis added]

His comment tells us an important, actually a critical truth, and that is that what we think does not reflect reality—it reflects our personal interpretation of reality. A person who is highly skilled may not believe they are highly skilled and, as a result, will not act with the confidence they could possess.

It does not make sense that a skilled person could believe they aren't skilled when the information is analyzed on the surface. It is necessary to go deeper, into the individual's beliefs about self and the thoughts they think. I am not, in any way, suggesting managers need to learn about employees at this level via dialogue. The information in this book will equip managers with sufficient knowledge and the ability to develop skills where they will be able to see beneath the surface without asking invasive questions. Insecurity, fear, guilt, resistance, and the perspectives that lead to frequent discord and low engagement can be easier to read.

It's not nearly as difficult as it sounds because numerous behaviors and emotional states move in tandem along a continuum. Imagine watching a group of line dancers moving on a crowded dance floor. If your eyes focus on a single dancer for a few moments, you still expect the rest of the group to be in similar positions when you change your focus to encompass the entire group. If you imagine each dancer represents one of the factors that move in tandem, identifying where one factor is gives you information about all the other factors. The movements can seem random unless someone understands the relationships between each one because there are so many variables.

The factors that move in tandem are determinants of human behavior. When managers learn about these factors and integrate them with their existing skills, they will be able to reliably increase employee engagement and inspire employees to perform at higher levels.

It is critical to understand that all communication is translation. There is translation of the words used, which may not mean the same thing to the people who are attempting to communicate even if they are both (or all) speakers of the same native language. Translation is also involved in facial expressions, body language, and tone of voice. Most workplace discord is the result of failure to translate clearly. Workplace discord has a significant negative effect on morale.

My goals for this book include:

- Demonstrate that traditional employee engagement methods aim at the wrong targets.
- Provide an **evidence-based method** of increasing employee engagement that begins at the **root cause**.
- Share information that is not commonly known that, when understood and applied, makes a significant difference in the physical, mental, and behavioral outcomes an individual experiences throughout life.
- Empower individuals with the ability to develop stronger relationships and experience greater success.
- Provide information about research on how beneficial happiness is.
- Demonstrate that stress can be lowered in a way that makes an employee's automatic stress response less stressful, and therefore, the chronic stress load lower.
- Employee engagement is positively related to happiness so higher happiness equates to higher employee engagement.
- Educate my readers about the negative impact of stress on every area of their life in an effort to help them decide to take steps to be happier (which is less stressful).
- Provide processes that individuals can use to feel better in any situation.
- Explain how the human mind works.
- Explain research demonstrating emotions are a sensory feedback loop

- Employee Engagement's connection to the big picture.

My intention is to share what I've learned about what helps humans get what they want—their personally defined goals and dreams.

In large part, psychology research ignores individual and situational differences in emotions and the physical (physiological) manifestations that result from various experiences.[3] Research tends to be structured as if two people experiencing the same event will have the same response on a mental and physical level. Nothing could be further from the truth. How an individual's mind appraises the initial response to an experience, or if the person reappraises, makes a tremendous difference in the amount of stress experienced. This is not a matter of intelligence as much as it is a set of learnable skills that even children can understand and utilize.

For fifty years we've been being told to reduce stress. Early recommendations told us to give up activities we were not required to do—which generally meant giving up the things that we loved, the things that nourished us. That advice was not taken. Then we were told to *Think Positive*, but not told **how** to change our habits of thought. This book tells you *how* to develop and maintain a positive mental attitude, which has been the missing piece.

Mindset is at the root of stress. The specific combination of mindset and metacognitive skills I teach was named *The Smart Way* because reducing stress in healthy ways is smarter than allowing stress to diminish one's physical and mental health. With practice, an individual can use *The Smart Way* to reduce how much stress any given situation causes them to experience. Some people are able to read a book and learn new skills by reading. Those individuals will find everything they need in these pages. Others learn better by being shown or hearing and would benefit greatly from my training programs.

We do not know the limits of human potential. In the last two decades scientists have made great strides in learning what adds to our ability to be successful, but application of that knowledge in the real world has been limited at best. Until core elements of the way we structure our society support the highest levels of **intrinsic motivation** we will not learn what humans at their best are capable of achieving.

Common sense does not work. Some things we think make *common* sense are counterproductive. For example, when someone establishes a personal goal to achieve something you also want them to achieve, offering extrinsic rewards to them if they achieve the goal reduces their intrinsic motivation. The level of positive energy the person feels about the task declines, even when the extrinsic reward is desirable. A boss who learns the employee has decided to learn a new skill who offers to reward the employee when the skill is mastered has just lowered the likelihood of the employee actually mastering the new skill.

The spouse who offers a mate who has set a weight loss goal a reward, such as new clothes or a weekend getaway to lose the weight, can decrease intrinsic motivation to achieve the goal.

These examples fly in the face of common sense, but the research has been replicated under many conditions. Intrinsic motivation is the most desirable type of motivation because it is the type that most often leads to sustained effort and achievement of goals. Why does adding extrinsic reasons to achieve a self-selected goal decrease intrinsic motivation? In most cases, the desire to feel autonomous is more powerful than the desire to achieve the goal. The attempt to exert extrinsic motivation can make achieving the goal feel less like a self-selected goal and more like one imposed by others, which often leads to feelings of rebellion.

Corporate wellness programs would do well to understand the interplay between **autonomy** and intrinsic motivation as they consider their carrots and sticks. Offering employees who are intrinsically motivated to achieve pro-health goals may lessen their intrinsic motivation. If this happens it can negatively impact employee engagement because it feels as if the employer is attempting to interfere with their free will (autonomy). Remember, most employees want to achieve pro-health goals like losing weight, eating well, and not smoking. It is more likely stress is impairing their efforts—not a lack of motivation or desire.

Adding extrinsic rewards to an intrinsically motivated goal can make the self-selected goal feel less autonomous. If managers don't understand how powerful the desire for autonomy is they can think they're being supportive while they trample the best sort of motivation into the ground. Neither the employee nor the manager wins if they don't understand the factors that are impacting motivation. An employee who understands why her level of motivation is decreasing can easily counteract the effects of a helpful but misguided manager. A manager who understands the factors that influence motivation can avoid decreasing employees' intrinsic motivation to achieve desirable goals.

Employees who come to work for you aren't all 100% well. In fact, these days, it is more likely that they are carrying some baggage and have sustained some damage to their psyche along the way. About 90% of adults have experienced a traumatic experience and many of those experiences happened when they were children.[4] As an employer it's not your job to fix their problems, but the more you're able to help (or at least not cause further harm), the better they'll be able to perform at their jobs and the less likely it is they will become disengaged and burnout.

Throughout this book are explanations and examples of why your employees psychological and emotional health are important to sustaining engagement and what you can do about it (short of sending everyone to therapy). You'll see why traditional methods of increasing engagement repeatedly fail to improve engagement and learn techniques that will work in your organization. Traditional employee engagement programs aren't even aiming at the right target—it's no wonder 70% of those collecting a paycheck aren't engaged.

Everything in life is really about relationships. The primary relationship everyone has is the one with their self. If they like their self they are different than they would be if they didn't like their self. It doesn't really matter if the relationship is with a parent, partner, friend, job, or home; relationships all reflect the primary relationship to some degree. Examples describing romantic relationships could easily be transformed to reflect one's relationship with their job or employer. All relationships are perceptual and all begin with one's relationship with self. One's **core self-evaluations** will determine the potential quality of all their other relationships.

1: Current State of Employee Engagement

US businesses lose $11 billion annually as a result of employee turnover.
Bureau of National Affairs

Employee engagement has been hovering at 30%, with 20% **actively disengaged** since the last economic downturn. There are a number of different measures that relate to employee engagement.

Emotional exhaustion is frequently a precursor to burnout. "When employees become emotional exhausted, they show declines in:

- Job performance,
- Organizational citizenship behavior,
- Customer service,
- Increases in absenteeism and turnover, and
- Increased physical health risks."[5]

The good news is that "employees' subjective perceptions and evaluations at work are likely to influence their feelings of emotional exhaustion in a wide range of occupations, including human services, education, clerical work, computer programming, military, and managerial roles."[6] It's good news for two reasons:

1. Employees want to feel better, they just don't know how to do it.
2. The book you're reading provides details that empowers employees with knowledge and skills that allows them to feel better without requiring circumstances to change.

Insecurity, low self-esteem, and consistently low emotional states contribute significantly to low employee engagement. Most people are far from fulfilling their potential to contribute to the world and far from enjoying life the way they could, and would, if they had a greater awareness of their own value and worth.

In this book you'll learn why pervasive beliefs that lead to feelings of inadequacy and doubts about self-worth make it impossible for traditional approaches to employee engagement to be effective. What we believe about ourselves determines:

1. How we feel about our work,
2. Our sense of connection to the work, and
3. Our level of employee engagement.

New research points to a solution that can solve the employee engagement problem by increasing employee's beliefs about their value and worth (self-efficacy and self-esteem) while simultaneously increasing their levels of happiness and resilience.

Teaching employees these skills equips them with powerful and effective tools that lead to and support beneficial changes in each of the following areas that researchers have identified are important to engagement, including:

- Relationships (social connection)
- Core Self-evaluations
- Happiness
- Psychological Flexibility
- Healthy Self-Esteem
- Autonomy

- Optimism
- Psychological Capital
- Positive Emotional State
- Positive Expectations
- Internal Locus of Control
- Growth Mindset

The new research also indicates needed revisions to Maslow's Hierarchy of Needs which, despite widespread acceptance, has failed efforts to be empirically validated. Many predominant belief systems in our society evolved based on popular opinion—not science. Approaching employee engagement from the standpoint of what cross-disciplinary science tells us about the causes of human behavior, group identity, and motivation is *The Smart Way*.

Evidence-based information may conflict with what you've believed for a long time and maybe even with positions you've argued for in the past. You have to be willing to have been incorrect in the past in order to be open to new information. Your mind is (literally) designed to reinforce your existing beliefs, even if they are wrong, and even if they do not contribute to outcomes you desire. When leaders let go of beating themself up about being wrong in the past and make being right today a higher priority, considering new ideas becomes easier.

This can be extremely difficult for individuals operating with a fixed mindset and easier for individuals with a growth mindset. You'll learn more about these two distinctions in mindset later. Let yourself off the hook for what happened in the past and focus on appreciating that you now know more—your ideas evolved. Appreciation is good for your physical, mental, and behavioral health. Guilt, resentment, and regret are not good for anything other than guiding future behavior and holding on to thoughts that evoke those emotions decreases your ability to function now.

Traditional methods of attempting to increase employee engagement have failed. Engagement numbers are hovering around 30%. That means 70% of the people who are collecting a paycheck are somewhat or highly disengaged. That's not success. The current conditions tell us that traditional methods aren't working. If traditional methods addressed the root cause of engagement the numbers would be much better.

Whatever you're thinking, it is your perspective, a valid perspective from your point of view. But whether it accurately reflects anyone else's perspective is unknown. Everything that happens at work elicits thoughts from your employees and their thoughts are all over the spectrum. That's why some employees will be upset by a change when others are happy about it.

Anticipating how changes will be perceived is a critical skill if one is to plan to respond in ways that promote engagement. Bosses who respond with comments such as "If you don't like it, there is the door" negatively impact morale in employees who could, with the right response, become strong supporters of changes that are taking place. Psychological flexibility allows a manager to anticipate a wider range of possible perceptions regarding an announcement which then provides an opportunity to structure the announcement in ways that address potential objections before they are voiced. Anticipating possible objections can stop those objections from gaining momentum.

How can you know how changes will be perceived at work? How will you know how different situations will be perceived? How do you know how you will be perceived?

While you can't know for sure, there is a guideline that is pretty accurate. Any given employee will perceive situations from their chronic emotional state and that will elicit in the employee emotional responses that match the employee's chronic emotional state. For example:

- If your employee is usually happy, she will usually focus on the positive aspects of a new situation
- If your employee is frequently frustrated, she will usually view aspects of the change as frustrating.
- If your employee is often insecure, he will usually view a new situation as threatening.
- If your employee is often angry, he will find aspects of a new situation to blame for his anger.

Simply asking yourself what could be perceived as frustrating or frightening about proposed changes can help identify potential objections or concerns.

Traditional methods of engagement charge management with managing employees' responses and helping them stay motivated. It was a daunting task. Remember, managers' emotions are all over the spectrum as well so you could have a manager who is frustrated by the changes attempting to soothe the ruffled feathers of an employee who is angry about the same changes. It's not a good plan. It hasn't worked and it won't work.

One reason it won't work is because it's too labor intensive. Every new situation has the potential to upset someone so the manager is constantly putting out fires—emotional fires. The manager is blamed for emotional responses that the manager had no idea how to control or change. Attempting to soothe every situation every time a change is made when change is traveling near the speed of light is like attempting to put out a forest fire with thimbles[†] filled with water.

The only sensible solution is to put employees in charge of their own emotional state and empower them with skills and knowledge that helps them feel better in a sustainable fashion. It is only because most people don't know how that they aren't all doing this. Everyone wants to feel better than they feel. It does not matter if they're depressed or frustrated or even happy—the prospect of feeling better is always attractive. The desire to feel better provides the ultimate intrinsic motivation because feeling better is the ultimate diver of human behavior.[7] You'll learn about the research supporting this statement in later chapters. The wisdom has always been known.

The reason we do anything we do is because we believe we will feel better doing it than not. When we dig deep into human behavior, the root of why we do everything is that we believe we will feel better by doing (or not doing) it. We go to work because we believe we will feel better than if we don't go to work. This can be true even if we hate our job. It's a complicated mental world. If we hate our job but love being able to feed our children we can love the job for what it provides while hating the actual work.

The individual who hates her work but loves being able to provide for her children can feed the negative emotions about hating the job or decide to feed the positive emotions she feels when she thinks about being able to feed her children. How she feels depends on which one she feeds, not the circumstances. She has a choice of feeling good or feeling bad. It is her choice.

[†] Since few people sew by hand these days, I'm not sure how common knowledge of a thimble remains. It's a small metal cup that is placed over one finger to protect it when pushing a sewing needle through fabric.

There is a story about a Cherokee elder was teaching his grandson about life. "A fight is going on inside me," he said to the boy.

"It is a terrible fight and it is between two wolves. One is evil – he is anger, envy, sorrow, regret, greed, arrogance, self-pity, guilt, resentment, inferiority, lies, false pride, superiority, and ego." He continued, "The other is good – he is joy, peace, love, hope, serenity, humility, kindness, benevolence, empathy, generosity, truth, compassion, and faith. The same fight is going on inside you – and inside every other person, too."

The grandson thought about it for a minute and then asked his grandfather, "Which wolf will win?"

The elder Cherokee simply replied, "The one you feed."

Feeding the wolf you want to feed takes skill if doing so is not consistent with your current habits of thought. Numerous practical and powerful techniques that help individuals feed the wolf that will lead to desired outcomes are provided in subsequent chapters.

The following examples of traditional approaches to improving employee engagement are provided to highlight flaws in the traditional approach.

Traditional Solutions

A leading global player in the engagement field offers this advice:

1. *Use the right employee engagement survey.*
2. *Focus on engagement at the local and organizational levels.*
3. *Select the right managers.*
4. *Coach managers and hold them accountable for their employees' engagement.*
5. *Define engagement goals in realistic, everyday terms.*

Two things about this advice are noteworthy:
1. Nowhere in the advice does it tell managers the *how* to increase engagement. It holds managers accountable for how employees feel, but does not tell them how to change how an employee feels, and
2. The global firm has been handing out employee engagement advice for a long time yet employee engagement remains at around 30%.

If traditional methods worked they'd be universal by now. *Entrepreneur* provided the following advice (**in bold**) and my commentary is in italics.
1. **Start at the top.** *I agree*
2. **Be transparent.** *When you can, I agree. However existing regulations make it difficult if not illegal to be completely transparent. Companies owned by stockholders are subject to many SEC and FINRA rules that are designed to CYA for the regulators and protect investors. Educating employees about restrictions may be a more workable alternative when regulatory restrictions preclude transparency.*
3. **Offer visibility.** *This came with the advice that "**management and C-suite must be accessible and visible around the office.**" In a global firm this is completely impractical. They also suggest public recognition which I agree motivates some employees, but there are employees who prefer to stay out of the limelight. Those employees might work hard to be sure they don't do something good enough to be publicly rewarded. I asked a Millennial who works in the IT field whether he would like public recognition at work. He said, "I've heard it might be a way to get ahead but I'd prefer it if it*

wasn't necessary."[8] *He went on to share that there have been times when he asked not to be recognized publicly for some of his work.*

4. **Say "thank you."** *This is just good manners.*

5. **Be authentic.** *This is good for engagement and good for health but many people have never been authentic, even within the confines of their own families—they may need some help becoming comfortable with being their wonderful, unique selves. Also, people in low emotional states often equate authenticity with being vocal about their negative viewpoints.*

6. **Be Flexible.** *I agree that whenever possible, the greater flexibility an employer can offer, the better it is. However, beware the broken window theory. Be clear on guidelines, too. In an interview (after telling an employee we offered flex-time which meant we had different starting time options) I once had a potential employee begin giving me her social schedule ecstatic that she would be able to come and go from the office to attend her weekly social events. This is a perfect example of all communication being translation.*

7. **Hire traits and behaviors.** *This hiring practice discriminates against minorities and low-income individuals who traditionally score lower on such tests. Also, every evidence-based measuring tool I've seen states that it does not meet US non-discrimination standards. Additionally, if you haven't always hired for traits like psychological flexibility, resilience, emotional intelligence, and* **positivity**, *the hiring managers are unlikely to be able to accurately identify them during the hiring process. Even if you give hiring managers a methodology that works and meets non-discrimination standards, if they don't have the skills they are likely to avoid hiring someone who does as they will perceive the person as a threat to their position.*

8. **Engage from day one.** *This refers to not having employees fill out a mountain of paperwork on their first day, but much of that paperwork is driven by regulations. I agree that making the first day a good one is important, but setting the expectation about the day may be more important when paper required by regulations will consume a considerable amount of the day. A hiring bonus and, if the person has been unemployed for a while, a first day bonus that may help them pay for lunches and commuting expenses until the first paycheck arrives may make a better first impression.*

9. **Volunteer together.** *This isn't a bad idea. It's very indirect. Opportunities that include families may be a good idea to make it easier on single parents and families where one parent is deployed or works out of town.*

10. **Play together.** *I agree. An environment where fun is not just tolerated, but welcomed, is a much better place to work.*

The article ended with the suggestion "***compassion, mutual respect, kindness and flexibility don't cost a thing.***"[9] This doesn't recognize the relationship between those attributes and the emotional state and beliefs of individuals, including managers. Compassion, mutual respect, kindness and flexibility are some of the behaviors that change in tandem with Emotional State (i.e. line dancers). Low employee engagement is not just a rank and file problem. It has infected employees all the way up to the C-suite. Compassion and kindness are very difficult for someone who is unhappy and someone who doesn't believe anyone respects them will misinterpret respect and still not be able to perceive that they are being respected. All communication is translation and the way the mind processes information makes individual beliefs and emotional state important for understanding and creating clear communication.

Business Collective offered this advice ""Meet with each of your employees once a week for thirty minutes. During this time, ask employees to raise concerns and provide feedback on their job satisfaction. Be honest and transparent in your answers. These conversations help employees feel engaged and empowered, and prevent team problems from sneaking up on you."[10] Twenty-four employees would mean 12 hours a week of one-on-one meetings, twelve hours of manager and employee time to monitor and ensure engagement. While this might be workable in some environments, I can't see it working in most employer situations. During the nearly six years I worked at Wachovia I don't think I had more than twenty hours of collective one-on-one time with the five bosses I had (they changed, my role always an expansion of my initial role). I asked a Millennial if a 30-minute meeting with her boss would increase her motivation. Her response was "I'd probably quit if I knew I had to do that every week."[11]

Notice that none of the traditional recommendations for increasing employee engagement address the "predisposition that individuals bring to the job" which has "long been claimed" to be a factor on which job satisfaction is contingent.[12] That is why they have failed to increase employee engagement. "The construct of core self-evaluations has been recognized as one of the most significant dispositional predictors of job satisfaction."[13]

In fact, an employee's core self-evaluations contribute more to their engagement level than any other factor. The leaders who recognize that healthy habits of thought lead to better outcomes for employees, employers, and society are the ones whose companies will achieve the competitive advantages of higher employee engagement. Everyone is intrinsically motivated to feel better and healthy habits of thought lead to immediate and long-term improvements in mood and behavior.

The old paradigm believed that personality traits, core self-evaluations, and emotional state were stable across the lifespan. New research reveals that they do change and that the reason change was slow in the past was because we lacked the knowledge of how to change them, which meant they were not being changed with deliberate intent.

The human mind and body strive toward optimal functioning. We have internal self-regulatory systems that correct problems without conscious attention. But Western science ignores the innate ability of the mind and body to seek wellness. Instead, we tend to leave malfunctioning or 'ill systems' as is and attempt to find work arounds. That tactic is akin to taking a car with a flat tire and attaching a sled to replace the wheel instead of fixing the flat. It is highly inefficient, requires constant maintenance, and can be dangerous in some situations.

For example, we know how low core self-evaluations increase the risk of employee burnout, but instead of attempting to fix the illness (low core self-evaluations) we see recommendations encouraging us to attempt to refocus employee's attention to the prosocial aspects of their work in the hope it will distract them from their low opinion of self. We don't recognize that low core self-evaluations is a form of malfunction—a flat tire—created by accepting false information as the truth and forming a belief that supports the inaccurate information.

For example, Grant and Sonnetag looked at the way "Doing good buffers against feeling bad" and write "By focusing employees' attention on how their actions facilitate positive outcomes for others, perceived prosocial impact may reduce the likelihood that they will dwell on their negative task and self-evaluations, protecting against emotional exhaustion."[14] This indicates an employer can dictate an employee's focus, which is not possible, and I question the ethics of attempting to do so. An employer can influence an employees' focus by highlighting the aspects they wish to promote, but that is no guarantee the employee will focus in the way an employer hopes they will. This also reinforces an external locus of control (employer directing the employee's focus to prosocial impacts of the work) instead of facilitating a change to a healthier internal locus of control.

An internal locus of control is a component of every high-level construct that increases employee engagement. Tactics that reinforce an external locus of control are counterproductive.

Focus is one of the easiest filters to adjust, but unless it is consciously adjusted, it will use default programming and highlight things that match the employees existing beliefs, expectations, and emotional state. An employee who is not generally in a state of appreciation will not easily maintain her focus on the best perspective about her work, which in this example would be the prosocial benefits to others. A second problem with this approach is that associating with a small in-group can lead to adverse consequences. Pool et al. found that learning your in-group supports an attitude that contrasts with one's own led to decreased self-esteem.[15]

Given Pool et al.'s findings, emphasizing the prosocial nature of the work instead of assisting the employee with developing healthy self-esteem could leave him vulnerable if an organizational leader is found to have acted in unethical ways which would essentially knock the legs out from under the employee who has based his self-worth on the prosocial elements of the company. For an individual with low enough self-esteem and heavy enough reliance on the company for his value and worth, unethical behavior of senior leaders could have devastating psychological consequences.

Additionally, low self-esteem could, at very low levels, cause an employee to be unable to respect an employer 'that was fooled into hiring them because no good company would hire someone of their low worth.'

Perhaps employers think they can't change low core self-evaluations, but that ignores the power of self-correcting systems that continually strive to feel better. Give an employee a method that helps them overcome a low core self-evaluation and it will be used as soon as they believe it has a chance of helping them feel better. The new science in the next chapter demonstrates we can facilitate higher core self-evaluations in employees and it is easier than using work arounds and it is more reliable.

2: Emotional Guidance: New Science That Matters

The best leaders are readers of people. They have the intuitive ability to understand others by discerning how they feel and recognizing what they sense.
John C. Maxwell

New research demonstrates that emotions are a sensory feedback system designed to guide us toward self-actualization and away from danger. Self-actualization as intended here refers to movement toward the full development of one's abilities and talents. It is toward, rather than the fulfillment of, because as we achieve more, our ability to achieve expands—there is no end to what can be accomplished by an individual who continually moves in the direction of self-actualization. The goals our Emotional Guidance guides us toward are what we want—not what another person wants. I will break it down for you.

We make decisions about our behavior based on what we believe will make us feel the best. This can be doing something we believe will make us feel better or not doing something that we believe would make us feel worse.

We have information about how we believe it will feel because emotions respond to our thoughts about doing (or not doing) the thing we're thinking about doing.

We use how we believe we will feel to regulate our actions.

For example, let's say your boss is being an arrogant jerk and really pushes your buttons. You want to lash out at him verbally; you may even want to punch him. But you take a moment to consider the consequences of your actions and you decide it's better to have a steady paycheck than to face your wife after being fired for insubordination or jailed for assault. It feels better not to act on the impulse that would lead to those outcomes.

What you've done is had a thought that felt better. It feels better to stand your ground and attack (verbally or physically) someone who is being as mean-spirited as your boss is being. But it feels even better not to have to explain to your wife why you were fired than it does to lash out at your boss. Restraint wins. You self-regulate your behavior. Now, you still have anger at your boss. If you're the common man, you'll take it out on someone else or dim the emotions using alcohol or drugs. You may go to the gym and spend some time pretending the punching bag is your boss. You may go golfing and imagine the ball is your boss's head (this can result in a good round of golf). You may go home and pick a fight with your spouse or child.

But what you could do is soothe the anger using your mind which is the choice that leads to the best outcomes. You can remember that your boss has a lot of demands on his time that sometimes make him more thoughtless when he interacts with others. You may remember calmer times when your boss showed you a different, kinder and gentler, side of himself. You may remember that you're going to finish obtaining a degree or a professional certification soon that will open up new job or promotional opportunities for you. You can remember that you've seen other bosses like this who enjoy their power for a brief time and then create their own downfall— that the company does not want that type of boss. You can refocus your commitment to continuous self-improvement to prepare yourself to step into your bosses shoes after he self-destructs and enjoy the thought that he is making it easy for the person who follows him into that position to shine.

Those are just a few thoughts that would feel better without requiring any action before the employee can feel better. Merely planning action or finding a better-feeling perspective can improve the emotional experience. Perceiving the situation from a more general or broader viewpoint instead of focusing on today's specific incident, changes the emotional response. Each person is in charge of their thoughts and the perspective they take about a situation. The boss has no control over that. People who know how to do it will choose the perspective that feels best to them. All the manager has to do is provide information that empowers employees to recognize their ability to choose and techniques that help them overcome habitual patterns of thought that aren't serving the employee's highest good.

The manger does not need to dictate what habits of thought to change or what the employee should think. Emotional Guidance does that in response to every thought by providing feedback in the form of emotions.

Both scientific circles and laypeople commonly believe emotions are unreliable and that emotions directly cause behavior. In 2007, Roy F. Baumeister et al. presented a new theory of *How Emotion Shapes Behavior: Feedback, Anticipation, and Reflection, Rather Than Direct Causation* in which they conclude "the direct causation theory should be converted from a standard assumption to a questionable hypothesis." Their thorough analysis of current research lends support to the theory that the purpose of emotion is to guide behavior. This series of quotes from their extensive work reflects a small portion of the support it contains for the concept that emotions are guidance:

*Anticipation of emotional outcomes is an important aspect of the feedback theory. As people learn to anticipate feedback, they may alter their behavior (constructively) to pursue the feedback that they like. Emotion is ideally suited for this because of its **hedonic** power: Behavioral choices could well be swayed by the anticipation of feeling good or bad thereafter.*

*The resistance of emotion to direct control is, in short, a puzzle to self-regulation researchers. Why did the human self-regulatory capacity evolve so as to be able to exert direct control over actions and thoughts but not emotions? The answer, we think, is that **you cannot control your emotions because the purpose of emotions is to control you**. Emotions are a feedback system for facilitating behavioral learning and control. If they were themselves controllable, they would lose that crucial function.* **[Emphasis added]**

In sum, the human emotional apparatus may shape behavior by providing a feedback system that may be useful for sophisticated goal pursuit and learning to behave effectively in complex social and cultural situations. Conscious emotions provide feedback about behavior, stimulate cognitive analysis, and promote revisions of the programming on which people react to events. Conscious emotions can also be anticipated and so people behave in ways that will pursue desired emotional outcomes.

. . . the reality is that behavior pursues emotional outcomes. . .

*. . .much prosocial behavior turns out to be informed by anticipation of possible mood changes. Other research supports the notion that whether people give **mood-congruent** or **mood-incongruent** responses depends on their beliefs about the power of the stimulus to enhance their mood.*

. . . one could entertain a view of human behavior as fundamentally and pervasively guided by the quest to regulate one's emotions. A person could certainly do far worse, and arguably not much better, than to go through life making all decisions so as to maximize positive emotions (especially in a long-term perspective) and minimize negative ones.

. . . there is a fair amount of evidence that anticipated emotion does lead to adaptive, beneficial, socially and personally desirable behaviors, especially insofar as these take the form of choosing a safe, readily defensible option.

Before Baumeister et al.'s paper, the old belief about emotions had been the central accepted belief in the scientific world for eighty years. The belief that we act at the whim of our emotions, without conscious cognition between feeling the emotion and action, has created a society filled with mental health problems. Between 20 – 25% of the population suffers from a form of mental illness every year. Diagnoses from depression, anxiety, bulimia, anorexia, OCD, and more can be prevented through an understanding of one's Emotional Guidance. Some of the people I worked with when I first began teaching Emotional Guidance had suffered chronic bouts of depression for decades and have now been free of depression for eight years. I can't guarantee that everyone will achieve these results, but I believe that anyone who really understands their Emotional Guidance has a very low risk of depression and has the ability to recover if something should cause them to become depressed.

I used to suffer from periodic bouts of depression with suicide ideation and have been completely free of such episodes for a decade because of the tools and knowledge in these pages. I no longer worry that something will upset me and throw me back into a depressed state. The person I was when I was suffering in that way is so different from who I've become that the memories seem to be of another person or another life. I am no longer who I was when I had those problems. I am stronger, more resilient, more confident, and more sure that I can handle whatever life brings me.

And it's not a strength born of **willpower**. I used that type of strength in the past. . . to keep going when I wanted to stop . . . to put an acceptable face on at work and pretend everything was okay. Using willpower drains you so that when you are finally where you can stop pretending everything is alright you have nothing left to give to your family, yourself, your community, or your world.

The strength understanding your Emotional Guidance gives you comes from your core and does not require willpower. It is who you have become. It's unshakable and deep.

EGS refers to our Emotional Guidance System. EGSc refers to the Emotional Guidance Scale. The scale is included in the Appendix I. Take a look now and note the Zones. You may want to mark the page so it is easy to flip to as I reference the EGSc throughout the book.

Several other researchers have added to Baumeister et al.'s work since 2007. Katherine Peil demonstrates that our emotions are a sensory feedback system in *Emotion: A Self-regulatory Sense*.[16] Her position is that emotion is our oldest sense, and she uses molecular biology and the biophysical processes of living systems to lead us on a step-by-step exploration of this idea. In her work and our discussions, Peil has explained that the function of the basic negative emotions is to provide information that helps us keep our bodies safe. The function of positive emotions is to point us toward self-development and well-being. Peil states we derive no benefits from ignoring the output from our emotional system and that our guidance provides information that will improve our lives if we act upon it appropriately.

Humans tend to override the feedback from their emotional sense with rational thought. Yet, filters (biases) in our minds distort our perception of reality. Our emotional feedback by-passes the filters and provides feedback that contains greater clarity and accuracy.

Only a small amount of the information gathered by our senses comes to our conscious awareness. The information that we do become aware of is not reality, it is filtered based on our emotional state, expectations, beliefs, and focus. Psychologists call these filters biases. Our emotions do not lead us astray—a common and false belief. Faulty thinking stemming from emotional distress can lead to self-defeating behavior, but the behavior is the result of the desire to feel better by someone who lacks skills that empower him/her to feel better in the circumstances being perceived. Misinterpreting the meaning and best response to negative emotions can exacerbate difficult situations.

Emotions are far more valuable and accurate than most people understand. It is not the inaccuracy of emotions, but humanity's lack of understanding of the language they use and their meaning that makes them seem irrational.

> *Inaccurately interpreting what our emotions mean is what leads us to actions that do not support our highest good.*

Most people think emotion validates the accuracy of their perception when it is really a road sign that indicates "keep going" with positive emotion and "go another way" with negative emotion. While science misunderstood emotions for eighty years, leading us even further from *trusting our instincts* and *gut reactions*, it's no wonder so many are suffering so much. Dr. Dan Siegel shares:

"We now know that the intestines, our gut, have a set of neural net processors that function like sophisticated computers. The computers we have at home are linear processors, and they can do all sorts of fancy things quickly, but the really sophisticated computers are those that are in a spider web like network called parallel distributed processing. We have these parallel processors in our intestines and also around our heart. So the heartfelt feelings that we have are not just poetic metaphors of the gut instinct and heartfelt feelings but instead are really sophisticated processors. Now, it's not rational—meaning it's not a logical thing where you could say, 'A went to B went to C.' But it is a very important way in which our whole being is processing information, and often this source of bodily wisdom is very useful when contemplating an organization's direction." [17]

It is critical that you allow yourself permission to feel whatever you feel. If you feel guilty about how you feel, guilt is low on the EGSc. You can't move to great feeling Zones if you feel guilty. You feel what you feel. What you feel is valid, from your current perspective. From your current perspective, what you feel is the appropriate response. From your current perspective, what you feel is what you can feel. You cannot change how you feel about the situation without changing your perspective. Suppressing emotion leads to physical and mental illnesses.

Veilleux, Skinner, Reese, and Shaver found that "Drinking [alcohol] to cope with negative emotions is the drinking motive most predictive of problematic drinking." [18] They also reported the tendency to focus on negative emotions is a "risk factor for the onset and maintenance of alcohol use disorders." [19] Both the absence of strategies for dealing with negative emotion and lack of skill at identifying emotions are highly correlated with drinking to cope.

There are numerous ways to cope with negative emotions in constructive ways. Understanding that emotions are guidance and the Emotional Guidance Scale (EGSc) (see Appendix I) will help individuals recognize how they are feeling so they can proactively manage their cognitive processes and experience more positive emotions.

In a study of men seeking treatment for alcohol addiction Petit et al. found "that abstinence is associated with a shift toward more adaptive emotion regulation patterns, and inefficient regulation strategies may lead to craving and the maintenance of alcohol use." [20] Berking found "enhancement of general emotion-regulation skills . . . is an important target in the treatment of alcohol dependence."[21] Employers should be concerned about helping employees prevent the development of, and overcoming, alcohol use disorder.

In 2015, *JAMA Psychiatry* reported that "Twelve-month and lifetime prevalence of Alcohol Use Disorder were 13.9% and 29.1%, respectively" following interviews of over 36,000 individuals.[22] That's significant risk to any company from hung over or intoxicated employees operating machinery, driving on company business, or even interacting with customers while impaired. The consequences are real. A friend of mine lost his arm (and nearly his life) because his co-worker was drunk and did not hit the safety switch when his glove caught in machinery even though that was his only job during the procedure.

We live in the best time ever to solve society's most pressing problems—poverty, crime, racism, war, disparate outcomes, addictions, and chronic mental and physical diseases because all are rooted in misinterpretation of emotions. This book is designed to demonstrate not only why Emotional Guidance is the best resource we have to improve employee engagement, but also to empower all people with its benefits. Information about the purpose and use of emotions must be integrated with other knowledge and skills to become a resource employees can use. It is a major factor that determines success or failure.

Emotional state is used two different ways. One is the emotional stance or state in any given moment—how an individual feels in that single space in time. The other is their chronic emotional stance. Both impact behavior and how an individual perceives the world. For example, if you're annoyed often, it's a habit of thought and may not reflect your best possible reality. Any emotion that is not pleasant can be substituted for annoyed in the above sentence.

Emotional Guidance directs us to positive viewpoints but it will tell us of danger. In fact, one of the first ways I learned to trust my EGS was because of what I termed my *creep alert*. Back then, I was like most of humanity, trained away from my guidance by parents and a society that did not understand anything about emotions. I was taught to trust my *rational mind*. Someone came into my experience and I had a strong and immediate negative reaction to him. Because at that point in my life I had no rational explanation for my intense negative response to the particular individual, I talked myself out of it.

From that experience, I learned that my *creep alert* as I termed it was an accurate predictor of undesired behaviors. I did not know why it worked, but I began listening to it. Later, when I learned more about the EGS, I understood it was just strong Emotional Guidance. I am able to maintain a positive outlook because I have developed that habit of looking at life. It does not mean I will not know about danger, or take appropriate action. In fact, I have had experiences where my *creep alert* has let me know about danger and I have been able to take evasive actions. My focus in those situations is far more on appreciation for having my guidance than in seeing the world as an evil place full of trouble.

Emotional Guidance really is much easier to understand as you consciously experience it. There is a level of energy below what we can measure, on the level of Quantum Physics. We feel things from that level. The more we pay attention to how things feel, the more sensitive we become to our own guidance. In many ways, guidance is like our other senses. Our eyes interpret light waves that are translated into what we see. Our ears interpret sound waves that we cannot see. We do not doubt our ears—even though we cannot see the sound waves. Our taste buds translate molecules into specific tastes. Our nose translates the vibration of scents we cannot see, enabling us to smell. Do we ask our nose if the smell we enjoy is real? We were trained to trust those senses so we do not question them. Our emotions are also sensory feedback. We question them only because we were trained to disregard them. We were trained to believe emotions are unreliable and irrational. We were trained to believe that our *rational minds* are the source of intelligent decisions.

Most people still believe that. They do not know the real function of the *rational mind* is to prove our own beliefs to us.

Artists and musicians show us that using a sense increases the individuals abilities. The artist does not paint his best picture the first time he holds a brush. As he practices seeing from an artist's perspective, his ability to create the image he sees increases. The musician does not have perfect pitch the first time he picks up a guitar. Practice enhances the ability of his mind to translate what his ears hear and fine tune sounds in ways he could not have done before he practiced for many hours. As you use your Emotional Guidance it becomes easier for you to do so.

Our *rational mind* does not consider what is best for us. It trusts that we have established beliefs that serve us. Unfortunately, society did not train us to do that. Society trained us to establish beliefs that were similar to those around us. For the most part, beliefs are passed from parent to child with little change. Teachers pass on their beliefs, not realizing that many of the beliefs they share have the opposite effect of what they truly desire—which is helping their students live a better life.

> *Acting on the basis of current, intense emotion is generally not a good idea—and we deliberately chose that colloquial phrase because it expresses the point that cognition (ideas) rather than emotion should be the proximal influence on behavior. At least, that is how we think the system is designed. To be sure, emotion may occasionally bypass rational analysis to influence behavior directly, sometimes with dire consequences. Still, the fact that the heat of emotion may cause irrational behaviors is not a problem for this view because the benefits of emotion depend on their long-term benefits, and occasional short-term costs might be outweighed.* [23]

The EGS appears to consider information available on the quantum level of physicality. There was a show that I saw part of in which a man could predict the probability of future events with precision. That is what our EGS does. It knows what we want and the fastest way for us to get there from where we are. It's much like a GPS in your car can tell you how to get where you tell it you want to go from where you are. But our EGS is much more sophisticated. We don't have to tell it what we want—it's been collecting that information our entire lives, including every tweak and amendment we make to our desires. It knows where we are and the shortest path to get us where we want to go.

Our EGS is very creative and it understands us. It knows what will help us move toward something and will use that something as a detour if it is the easiest way to move us toward our goals. It doesn't use only emotions—it uses our likes and dislikes and our preferences to guide us.

The EGS bypasses filters that distort information our conscious mind receives from our other senses. **The only reason humanity is not thriving is because we have been taught to misinterpret the feedback from our guidance.** I do mean the *only* reason. Everything else anyone might point to as a reason is a symptom of this root cause.

The actual job of the rational mind, as you'll learn in the next chapter, is to prove our personal beliefs to us and create meaning from our experiences. This would be fine if the beliefs were deliberately crafted in a society that understands the impact of beliefs and nurtures beliefs that lead to thriving. We do not have that luxury. Many common beliefs diminish thriving yet our rational minds trap us into lives that repeatedly prove those realities to us.

The desire to feel happy or joyful is strong, but when we are at the lower end of the EGSc attempting to reach those emotions will typically result in failure if we attempt to get there in one step. The most successful method is to simply reach for a better feeling thought, which provides a sense of relief from the tension (stress) being felt.

The scale is very beneficial because it is easiest to move up one emotional level at a time—and certainly not more than one Zone at a time. That does not mean we have to remain in a lower emotional state for a long time. Generally, an individual who has some experience shifting perspectives can feel better rapidly—one step at a time. The definition of rapidly varies depending on the circumstances and level of experience. It can mean as little as less than a minute to a day or two or three.

That may not sound fast but compared to the typical experience, where movement only occurs when circumstances change and some people remain in lower emotional states for years (or life), even a week is fast. Early in my own journey, I went from feeling so devastated by the end of a relationship that I could not talk about it without choking sobs to feeling ready to move on with my life in one weekend. A few years later, at the end of another relationship, I did not suffer the feelings of emotional devastation. The difference was that by then I knew there was a silver lining, so within minutes I was reaching for the better-feeling thoughts that come with knowing there was an upside.

The same is true of a lay-off. It is possible to feel excited anticipation about what is coming when you're in the middle of being laid off. It is also possible to hold onto anger about a lay-off for years and allow it to diminish your enjoyment of life the entire time.

Things turn out best for people who make the best of the way things turn out.
John Wooden

Humans often ignore or suppress their emotions and suffer the negative consequences of doing so by living lives that are less robust than they could be.[24] Ignoring negative emotional output is no different from ignoring pain from one's sense of touch. Emotional pain should be responded to in much the same way physical pain is managed. When emotional pain is ignored or suppressed, it can be as harmful to our well-being as leaving a burning hand on a hot stove.

Learning to follow the guidance from our EGS may conflict with instructions received throughout life, for example, the opinions, expectations, and desires of others. In a world that does not currently understand the EGS, it is common for others to want you to behave in ways that make them happy. On the surface, it sounds very selfish to follow one's own guidance over what others may desire from you. But turn it around, why do others want you to do what they want you to do instead of doing what you want to do? Is it not their selfishness that leads to a perspective where you are called selfish for not seeing the world through their perspective?

This misinterpretation of selfishness has led to inaccurate conclusions. Donald Campbell, president of the American Psychological Association in the mid–1970's argued for the notion of a genetic predisposition of selfishness in humans which leads to a "social personality of self-serving opportunism," and that "socialization and culture … are necessary to counter this disposition."[25]

Perhaps socialization and culture aid the process, but not when they convict selfishness of being misguided. When socialization and culture point each person to their own Emotional Guidance, where feeling good causes us to do good, we will be on the right track.

> *Emotions are information designed to guide us.*

Consider that when we are happy uplifting others feels good to us. By setting goals that include being loving, respectful to others, or to have good relationships, the EGS will provide guidance that considers these goals. Emotional Guidance opens the door to a path to resilience that is simple and sure.

By heeding the guidance emotions provide, one increases their level of resilience.[26] Emotions provide information about whether we are moving toward or away from our best interests. While people have labeled emotions that feel bad as *negative* and those that feel good as *positive*, all emotions are good because they are providing guidance, whether the receiver understands the message or the appropriate response to the message, or not. Emotions that do not feel good indicate action should be taken to feel better; action can be actual physical action or may consist of changing the perception that is causing the emotion that does not feel good.

Researchers have made it clear that we have more to give to others when we are happy. Our EGS guides us to happier states. The increased resilience we gain from following our guidance can greatly benefit our families, employers, and communities.

In Peil's groundbreaking paper she clearly demonstrates the importance of heeding the messages from the emotional sensory system. The paper also points to the true nature of humans and of the simplicity of following the Emotional Guidance System. Humans are good at the core of who they really are. However, it is only when they follow their Emotional Guidance that this is demonstrated consistently. When they do not follow their Emotional Guidance, behaviors that society does not favor can be the result.

Peil's theory expands the responses to negative emotion from Fight, Flight, or Freeze to include Right Responses. Right Responses (RRs) should be the first response to most of the negative emotion experienced in modern life. There are different types of Right Responses, one is:

> "*...to affect the internal environment in the personal mindscape, in conscious knowledge acquisition, in an act of deliberate learning and personal mental tactic to invoke optimal belief structures to reappraise.*"[27]

In other words, reach for a different perspective about the situation, one that feels better, and adopt that perspective because it serves your highest good to do so. Peil elaborates and clarifies the difference between a RR and suppressing emotions:

> "*There is a vast difference between a RR and* **suppressive emotion regulation**, *as the corrective action itself is informed by the specific emotional message, is consciously undertaken and it self-preserves through open, approach behavior, adaptive development and social cooperation. In short, the RR is a self-developmental response more indicative of the neurally well-endowed, culturally creative human being.*"[28]

The knowledge and skills necessary to become adept at utilizing Right Responses are easily learned. The skills increase the level of positive emotions experienced by individuals—daily and over time—thus reducing stress and increasing their level of resilience.[29] The main direct impact of emotion is to stimulate cognitive processing, not behavior.[30]

Teaching someone, even a child, to follow her own Emotional Guidance is simple.

If you have ever had a *Hell Yes* experience, it was your guidance shouting encouragement. Yes, your guidance could have told you that someone you are now divorced from was a *Hell Yes* to marry. I know that from our perspective that seems wrong but sometimes the shortest path to where you really want to go involves what appears to be a wrong turn. The key is to take the good, the silver lining, and leave the unpleasant parts out. If you felt the *Hell Yes*, it was on your best path to what you wanted (or helping you avoid a worse path).

Sometimes you can see what that was—or at least make a guess that feels right (which to me is the same thing). Sometimes you will never know. I was on an Alaskan cruise a few years ago. After the cruise, I planned to spend a few extra days in Seattle. Mid-way through the cruise I began having a strong urge to go home as soon as the cruise was over. I changed my flight and went home early. I have never learned why my guidance encouraged the change of plans, but I trust that it was the right path at that time.

Other times, I have known why. For instance, a few years later my fiancée and I were booked for a cruise and months before the trip we both began feeling we should not take the trip. We cancelled and later my Fiancée's father died when we would have been on the trip. I enjoy several vacations each year and that is the only one I have ever cancelled after it was booked.

Truly, the best way to understand how strong one's trust can be is to consider how strong our belief is when another sense has convinced us of its truth. If we see something, we tend to believe it. If we hear something, we tend to believe we heard it. If we touch something, we tend to believe what our sense of touch tells us about it. If we smell something, we believe it smells the way our nose interprets it.

Emotions are sensory feedback from our oldest sense. The only reason we do not trust them as much as our eyes, ears, nose and touch is that we have been trained not to trust them. Yet, when interpreted accurately, emotional feedback is the most accurate sense.

The myth that negative emotion means something outside ourselves is bad is commonly believed. It is responsible for significant amounts of unnecessary stress every day. Negative emotion means we are looking at something from a perspective that is less than ideal, or that we should focus elsewhere.

Let's look at a difficult situation for an example of alternative ways to perceive an event. Imagine a law enforcement officer working a murder investigation. If the job required the officer to focus on the loss felt by loved ones, the experiences the victim will miss in the future, and other aspects that feel awful, the negative emotion would quickly prostrate the officer. I am not saying officers do not think about these things, I am saying their job does not require them to focus on these aspects.

The job requires a problem-solving attitude. When gruesome details are the focus, the perspective is in relationship to answering the question, "What will this tell me that will help solve this case?" The focus on future action feels better in comparison to focusing on an unchangeable past event. The focus on solving the mystery feels better than a focus on a life ended too soon. The focus on providing answers to the family feels better than thinking about all the times the family will miss their loved one in the future.

The negative emotion is not saying the situation is bad. Nor is it saying it is good. The negative emotion is communicating that there is a way to perceive the situation that is more in alignment with our personal goals. A law enforcement officer choosing to focus on the aspects of a case that feel the worse will not be able to achieve the goal of solving the case. Her cognitive function will be impaired and her immune system will be depressed. Choosing the worse feeling perception will not advance the goal of solving the case. A mental stance of hopefulness that a case will be solved supports the cognitive function required to accomplish the task—and is accompanied by better feeling emotional responses.

Any law enforcement officer or combat veteran will already know that sometimes he or she just knew. They may not have the language to describe how they knew, but they did. You probably do too in some situations. Think about a time when you knew something but you didn't know how you knew it. It could be as simple as knowing who did it in a mystery book or television show or knowing that two friends would hit it off if they met. It could be KNOWing that something was going on between two people with no reason to believe it was true. It could be the instinct that led you to go into your child's room and find something you needed to know about. It could be when you picked up the phone to call a friend who needed you or you know who was calling before you looked at your phone, even when the call was unexpected.

When I am speaking I often ask for a show of hands from individuals who recognize that sometimes they change lanes based on a gut instinct or other subtle urge and then observe a reason they are very glad they changed lanes. Sometimes it involves debris in the roadway that was not yet visible in the lane they were in. Other times it is watching someone swerve into the lane where you would have been. More than half the people in the room usually raise their hand to acknowledge they've noticed experiencing this type of guidance.

It's the tension you feel in the air when you walk in a room. It's the sureness you have with no reason. It's KNOWing that you'll find the parking space if you turn left. It's catching the thing that falls out of the cupboard that you anticipated falling before you opened the cabinet without knowing why. Sometimes I write KNOWing in all caps to differentiate it from rational knowing.

Now that you've read about this you'll be more aware of such incidents over the next few days. As that happens, celebrate recognizing the times when you just KNOW and pay attention to the subtle energy you can feel that are associated with KNOWing. The more you tune your mind to pay attention, the more often you'll recognize that you just KNOW.

We have the ability to choose the way we perceive any event. Our EGS guides us to the perspective that gives us the best chance of achieving our goals.

With practice we can learn to trust our Emotional Guidance as much as, or more than, our other senses. Once that level of trust develops, life improves immeasurably. This is because our emotions take into consideration information available on the quantum level that our other senses cannot consider and is not subject to the biases (filters) information flowing from the rational mind pass through.

Biofield science is an emerging field of research that is exploring "the idea that living systems generate and respond to energy fields as integral aspects of **physiological regulation** . . ." It is based on a foundation formed from "advances in biophysics, biology, psychology, and the developing fields of mind-body research such as **psychoneuroimmunology** and **psychosocial genomics** . . . which have been combined to form a foundation for this expanded integrative medical model."[31] A growing body of scientific literature suggests "the existence of a more subtle level of **bioinformation transduction** operating at extremely low energies . . . contemporary **biophotons** research and cell to cell communication via coherent biophotons emissions has been demonstrated in several studies . . . suggesting a new paradigm wherein the concept of regulation via a **biofield** of dynamic information transfer may become central to biology."[32]

For example, our EGS considers others' intentions. While our eyes might catch a glimmer of intent through body language, accurately interpreting body language is a science that few have mastered. Likewise, our ears might sense something in the tone of voice, but unless we are experts, we may not trust our interpretation. If we were experts at determining truth from lies in the spoken word, we would not need a machine to detect lies. Interpreting and trusting our EGS is far easier than becoming an expert in body language and the nuances contained in various tones of voice.

For example, this morning a young couple had an interaction during which it sounded as if Fern was upset at Bob when he asked if she would join him in an activity they both enjoy. Bob interpreted it as if Fern was upset with him for asking and his feelings were somewhat hurt. He had no idea why she was being prickly. Fern declined his invitation because she had responsibilities to take care of. She was not upset with Bob, but with the fact that her duties made it necessary to forgo the desired activity with him. Her reason was almost polar opposite to the reason he perceived (upset with him) whereas she was upset she could not accept his invitation.

Utilizing my guidance to interpret what was really going on, I was able to KNOW, with certainty, that there had been a miscommunication. I let them know how it was misinterpreted and clarified Fern's intent. I then asked each of them to correct me if I was in any way wrong. "Nope, you nailed it," was the reply.

How many times a day do misunderstandings like this interfere with the smooth functioning of a work environment? How much more productive would it be if employees could use their guidance to check on the others' intent. Even better, if employees understood that even if someone intended to be rude, their behavior has far more to do with their own emotional state than it does with anyone they are interacting with, they just wouldn't take it personally. After all, it is not personal. If the co-worker were happy, he would not be rude.

If he understood how to interpret his Emotional Guidance, the negative emotion would have informed Bob that the perspective he took was not the best one he could find. He could have then asked for clarification and been certain (KNOWN) that the explanation would feel better than the **back story** his mind had created. He could have refuted the back story. If he did, his Emotional Guidance would have provided positive emotion in response to refuting the idea that Fern responded the way she did because she was upset he asked her to go with him.

Believing negative emotion validated the way he interpreted her response as an accurate interpretation felt awful. On the other hand, Fern could have reappraised the situation and responded in a nicer way. She was focused on what she wanted and couldn't have. She could have just as easily chosen to be happy he asked or even be happy she had a lot of work to do which equated to job security in those particular circumstances. Many people would argue that the reactions were aspects of Bob and Fern's personalities but they are indicators of emotional state, not of fixed personality traits.

The lack of knowledge of the EGS and thus society's failure to use it leads to many problems, from simple misunderstandings to wars between nations. In more traditional relationships and lifestyles, the desire to have ones choices validated by others is evidenced by disagreements that often become divisive.

Regardless of the choices a person makes, there are usually people who disagree with the choice. We are surrounded by examples of variety in what people think are the best choices including single Mom, working Mom, stay-at-home Dad, public school, private school, structured activities or free play, make your bed every day, don't make your bed every day, mow your grass to 2" or mow it to 4", eat meat, don't eat meat, and more. Having choices is good, but expecting everyone else to make the same choice we make creates conflict.

The root of it all is a defensiveness born of insecurity. Because they do not understand or use their guidance, people feel an unsatisfied desire to have their decisions validated. The desire for validation is natural. We are born with guidance that provides validation. When we have a *Hell Yes* experience, we are receiving loud and clear validation. When we do not receive the validation, we can become quite upset—because we inherently feel that our choices should be validated. We have been looking in the wrong place for validation. Our guidance is where that need should be satisfied. Our guidance validates our choices when they are correct for us and lets us know when they differ from our best path by how they feel. But if we do not recognize the guidance for what it is we do not gain the satisfaction of feeling validated.

> *There's no such thing as insecurity……it's only thought.*
> *Unknown*

This discord is seen in every area of life. It is common in religion, politics, and even music. A great deal of time, effort, and stress results from attempting to demand conformity. Actions that someone with a belief that the world is a good place would interpret one way, someone who believes they live in an evil world will interpret extremely differently.

This points to another reason there are so many conflicts, and why it could be so hard to convince people of something that others could see clearly. People are taught that their minds are rational. They are encouraged to trust their mind over their emotions.

With most people, unbelief in one thing....is founded upon blind belief in another.
Georg Christoph Lichtenberg

Emotional Guidance is not filtered by ones beliefs. It is often difficult to understand its messages once one has been trained to believe the rational mind is the better source of decision-making. But, it is not hard to straighten out with a little bit of effort and practice.

Using a dual system for decision-making, by using both the rational brain and Emotional Guidance for the same decisions and giving their EGS more weight in areas that do not seem important develops confidence. By beginning in this way, it soon becomes clear that the guidance from the EGS leads to better outcomes. Many people quickly begin giving greater weight to the EGS.

Our society does not give emotions the credit they deserve. We are taught to give our *rational minds* and thought processes the credit for our intelligence. This is another false premise. Researchers have worked with individuals who have lost part of their brains, the part that recognizes emotions, to disease or injury. Many people would assume that not having emotions would create a person who was very good at decision-making; they might even envision someone like Spock from Star Trek. If you get an opportunity to take that bet, bet the farm.

What the researchers found is that rationality depends critically on sophisticated emotionality. Our emotional process works so well that we do not even know much of what it is doing. It provides instant and automatic appraisal of tremendous amounts of data that we never have to consider consciously. Robbed of this function, individuals find it almost impossible to make even simple decisions such as choosing what to eat.[33]

What are some of the ways we are taught to misinterpret our Emotional Guidance? From young ages, many of us are taught to ignore or suppress our guidance. When we were two and our brother took our toy away, Mom did not show us how to feel better using our guidance. She distracted us by giving us another toy. Or she told us, "Don't cry. You're alright." While those may not be considered bad ways to parent, and they are certainly superior to the angry parent who smacks her child for crying, they ignore the guidance the child was born with. The first technique teaches the child the parent will make him feel better when he is upset. The lesson the child learns is: *"Finding a way to feel better is not your job. Mom will do it for you."* In the second example, the message is: *"Expressing your emotions is not good behavior. Suppress them."* Emotions become bothersome things that we have to deal with instead of the valuable tool they are.

Emotions are our friend. We should understand emotions as messages letting us know if we are moving in the direction we want to go. We should understand our power to change our emotional stance by changing our perception of any situation. When I say *any situation*, many people argue that some situations are just so awful that there is no way to find a better feeling perception. As long as someone has that belief, they won't find it. In his book *Infinite Love and Gratitude*, Dr.

Darrell Weismann writes about how he found a better perspective about his daughter's death and how doing so helped the wound heal.

I agree that one would wish for awful situations but many live through them. A book I found especially helpful after my first miscarriage was, *Ho for California!: Pioneer Women and Their Quilts* by Jean Ray Laury and the California Heritage Quilt Project. The book chronicles quilts that came to California, by wagon train, around the horn and, if memory serves, by train. The great value I found in it was the strength of the women, some of whom birthed a dozen children and lost over half of them before they reached adulthood. That women could suffer losses like that and still function, much less leave a lasting legacy in the form of a quilt, helped me see the potential for resilience in each of us.

Once something happens that must be lived through, there is a choice. Live through it and celebrate your life, perhaps giving greater meaning to your child's life, or choose a path of suffering. Another example of a parent who brought meaning to her daughter's death is the founder of MADD, Cindy Lightner. Although I am sure no parent would ever choose to sacrifice their child, the fact that MADD has been instrumental in decreasing DUI fatalities by about 50%, saving 12,000 lives each year must bring some solace and meaning to her loss.

There is a way for anyone, in any circumstances, to move forward. If you are currently suffering, I do not know your path forward—but your EGS does know. It is with you 24/7 providing feedback in response to your every thought. Find a thought that feels better. Soak it in until you feel stable in holding that thought and then reach for one that feels even better.

I've met many people in my life who are actually afraid of what they will find if they explore their inner world. Somewhere along the way they have been convinced of the possibility (or probability) evil could be hiding inside them. Peil's paper suggests the true nature of humans: they are good at the core of who they really are. Seligman echoes this argument in *Flourish* and Dacher Keltner reinforces it in *Born to be Good*.

However, only when Emotional Guidance is followed consistently is our true nature demonstrated. Frequent positive emotions lead to pro-social behaviors. Prolonged negative emotions that result can lead to undesirable behaviors. We feel emotions in response to thoughts. In a world with 24/7 news scouring the planet and looking for every awful thing that has happened around the world stress management skills are important.[34] Ignoring Emotional Guidance is done at the individual's peril.

Far more goes right in the world, every day, than goes wrong. If we put the worlds' troubles in the perspective of our body with the bad things in proportion to the good, the world has a hangnail. I am not saying awful things aren't happening. I am saying that filing your head with them as you begin your evening and/or as you head to bed is not healthy for you. It does not solve the problem. In almost every situation, there is nothing you can do. But what do most people do? They feel fear. Look at where fear is on the EGSc. Fear is even higher when loved ones, especially teenagers and young adults, are out or away at college.

The 24/7 negative news can prime us to be afraid of this beautiful world we live in. Many will argue that they have to be realistic. Viewing a minute percentage of the things happening on the planet is not at all realistic—it is a view with a major negative bias. If the 24/7 news channels reported good news and bad news in proportion to their occurrence, the bad news would last less than a minute each day. In *Bias*,[35] the following facts are clear:

1. The job of the news media is to get ratings,
2. Research consistently shows that more people watch the news when they are afraid,
3. Their job is not to inform us

If you are feeling you live in a bad world, I encourage you to shift your focus to one that is more realistic. Start with the big picture and get as specific as you can while still feeling good. The sun came up today. Even if it was on the other side of clouds, the sun rose today. The atmosphere is filled with air I can breathe. Wow! Two huge, necessary hurdles done! Are the birds singing? Are the plants growing? Is the sun feeding the plants? Are the clouds watering the plants? Did people fall in love today? Did people hold hands today? Were any babies born today? I have two eyes that see, two ears that hear, one nose, two arms, two legs complete with feet. I have family I love, who love me. I have friends I love, who love me. I have a bed and a kitchen and windows. I have guidance that responds to every thought I think. I could go on like this for an entire book so I'll stop now. You get the idea. The amount of wonderful going on, every day is enormous. So be realistic, think positive—now that you know how.

By deliberately choosing a different perspective, our thoughts change and better-feeling emotions can be deliberately cultivated.[36] Thoughts actually create meaning for events in life.[37]

It is really as simple as understanding that better feeling thoughts are guiding us toward our desires and thoughts that feel worse are advising us that we are moving away from our desires. Some clarity regarding desires is required. There is a difference between short-term and long-term desires. Although all desires contain the characteristic that we believe we will feel better in the attaining of them, some desires relate to immediate gratification; a response to current conditions without consideration for the long term. Desires for some foods, drugs, alcohol, and other addictions are fueled by these types of desires. Short-term desires are often accompanied by conflicting emotions caused by conflicts with longer term desires. For example, a desire to feel better right now may be satisfied by enjoyment of a piece of chocolate cake but the desire to maintain a comfortable weight in the long-term may be in direct conflict with that desire.

There is an inherent desire to feel better. Many *desires* are not beneficial in the long term. Without knowledge of techniques to change thoughts, endless loops can result—sugary foods, alcohol, drugs, shopping and more can temporarily improve mood, but do not build long-term resilience. To build long-term resilience one must reach for better feeling thoughts. The more attention that is given to long term goals, the more they will be considered in the emotional response you receive when a short-term goal conflicts with the long-term goals.

For example, in an upsetting situation it is not uncommon for individuals to reach for alcohol to provide relief from their negative emotions. Unfortunately, alcohol provides only a temporary dulling of the pain (or lessening of the focus on the painful thoughts) and can lead to even greater problems. A more permanent method of approaching an upsetting situation is to reframe ones perception of the event in a way that feels better.[38] With practice, finding better feeling thoughts becomes the easier choice.

It is possible to maintain a positive bias about life when circumstances are not ideal. This has been proven by many in very adverse circumstances. There are many accounts; one of the direst is the story of Viktor Frankl, documented in his book, *Man's Search for Meaning*, about his experiences in a Nazi concentration camp. In the worst of circumstances he discovered the importance of finding meaning in all forms of existence, which made his current circumstances, even though unchanged and reprehensible, feel better and provided a reason to continue living. This is an example of a RR, where the individual found better-feeling thoughts. Although the thoughts he found were philosophical in nature, any thoughts that felt better and thus made the situation more tolerable would be considered RRs. Philosophical thoughts are often the easiest way to feel better fast.

Science has tended to study various aspects of humanity in isolation (Psychology, biochemistry, medical, neurological, consciousness, behavioral, sociology, criminology, genetics, physics, etc.). These areas of science are often subdivided into specialties, such as addiction, immunology, cardiovascular disease, beliefs, epigenetics, and more. It is all interrelated. Root cause solutions require an understanding of the larger picture. Thoughts create the emotional feedback. The emotional stance affects body chemistry, bodily processes, behaviors/actions, and ultimate outcomes.

Circumstances do not create the emotion. There is evidence from individuals who live in far less advantageous circumstances who are happy with their lives and receive the benefits of **positivity**. Research into disparate outcomes in situations with **homogenous incomes** vs. situations with greater differences reflects that it is not actual circumstances, but perception thereof that matters.[39]

Likewise, there are many stories of cancer survivors who claim that being diagnosed with cancer was the best thing that ever happened to them. The reasons vary, but most of the individuals learned to live more consciously instead of being content with an **autopilot life**.[40] where they merely react to their circumstances without any knowledge that they can control how they respond to events. "With the cancer diagnosis, my priorities changed in an instant. The list of what was truly important got real short, real quick. Decision-making became easier. I became more motivated to do things I had been putting off. The old phrase about not sweating the small stuff became crystal clear."[41]

Human societies train people to *keep a stiff upper lip* and to *be strong* by which they mean endure negative emotions instead of finding better-feeling thoughts. A better solution is to use metacognitive processes to think about what we're thinking and consider alternatives while noticing how each alternative feels.

A change of perception changes everything. Each mind interprets the world according to factors specific to the individual,[42] including beliefs, expectations, emotional stance, and focus. These factors create a filtering system in the brain that determines the sensory input that is communicated to the conscious mind. People project their thoughts onto what they see and experience in the world. When you change your thoughts, your world changes. You give thoughts power when you accept them as true. Everyone has a choice. Right Responses involve deliberately changing perspectives, beliefs, expectations, and focus.

Marketers are skilled at changing consumers' perspectives. It really isn't difficult to do with people who aren't mindful about what is happening. In a study that looked at the importance of perspective the participants were all told that a teacher had scored 70% on a teacher competency exam while half were told that the passing grade was 65% and half were told the passing grade was 75%. The group that were told passing was 75% and therefore thought the teacher failed the test judged the teacher as less competent than those who thought the teacher passed the test, even though the score was still only 70%.[43]

Several branches of science have been studying human thriving. The compiled results point to the fact that people thrive when they feel emotionally good and suffer when they do not.[44]

I am often asked to explain the source of the guidance. Realistically—it does not matter. Our guidance guides us toward our individual goals and toward our highest good. Experimenting with your guidance makes it clear it guides us around obstacles and toward goals. Sometimes faith is required because the path the mind wants us to take seems more logical but when our guidance is followed we usually, eventually, learn why the straightest path is where our guidance feels best. Our guidance helps us be more of who we want to be. Conforming to other's desires instead of our EGS confuses us.

Where it comes from is another matter. Quantum physics provides many of the answers. The research into biophotons and cellular communication using light are illuminating.

"Experiments are showing that biophotons can be captured and stored inside of cells and can even travel through our nervous system; suggesting that biophotons might provide a way for cells to transfer energy and communicate information."[45]

Light carries information through our brain, nervous system, and even our DNA."[46] We have the ability to affect light with our thoughts. Study participants in a dark room who visualized a bright light increased their levels of biophotons emissions significantly, revealing that our intentions influenced light.[47] There is much that is not known yet. I strongly encourage readers to experiment with their own EGS because experience is the only way to personally know that the guidance is beneficial, accurate, and always present.

In a peer-reviewed textbook I contributed to, *Perspectives on Coping and Resilience*, I detail my research into whether common religions including Buddhist, Christianity, Islam, Hindu, and Confucius support guidance. More than 90% of humanity has a worldview that is influenced by religious and/or spiritual beliefs. It is important to understand if they those views support the science and if the science supports them. In every religion I researched, passages that support the existence of guidance that dovetail with what science now understands about the purpose of our emotions were present.

Positive emotions are immensely beneficial for us—increasing our resilience, reducing the risks from negative life events, decreasing the risk of all types of major illnesses and improving relationships. We have an EGS that helps us enjoy better-feeling emotions. It makes sense to understand and use the guidance available to us.

Negative emotional states are harmful to our bodies, minds, relationships, and choices. Depressed individuals will participate in riskier behaviors than individuals at higher emotional states.[48]

After regular practice using metacognitive processes and Emotional Guidance, it becomes possible to find equanimity in the middle of a crisis or other event that would have previously derailed an employee's emotional state. The best solution is not to wait until the middle of a problem to begin—that would be like trying to stop a freight train with broken brakes. Regular practice keeps the brakes in good repair.

Resilience can build upon prior success at navigating life's obstacles. However, someone with high optimism, internal locus of control, and healthy self-esteem who has led a relatively mild life can be resilient in the face of adversity. Someone who lacks one of those three factors is not likely to fare as well in the face of their first real adversity.

<<<-- Away from self-actualization

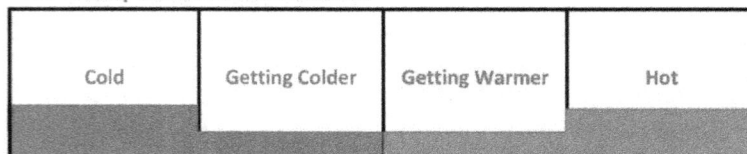

Cold	Getting Colder	Getting Warmer	Hot

Toward self-actualization -->>>

Emotional Guidance works just like the child's game, *Hot* or *Cold*. While it does feel different to move from despair to anger than from anger to frustration, or from hope to passion, each of these steps is a step in the right direction; each is *getting warmer* and each is associated with a feeling of relief.

The common element of any mental change in the right direction is that a feeling of relief (a releasing of tension or stress) is felt. The emotion that is in the *warmer* direction always feels better than emotions that are *getting colder*.

From neutral, any change in the wrong direction feels worse. Some would describe it as heavier, like picking up a burden. The steps involved in understanding Emotional Guidance are easy. Humans have received feedback in the form of emotions their entire life. The only reason anyone is off-track is because our society tends to teach us to interpret and respond to the feedback incorrectly. The steps are:

- The first step is an awareness that guidance exists.
- The second is setting an intention to hear its messages.
- The third is listening to the messages—they are often subtle.
- Correctly interpreting your guidance

In the beginning, individuals may only recognize that they received guidance in hindsight after they did not act upon it. The key here is not to beat themselves up for failing to recognize it—that does not serve anyone. Recognizing they had guidance and did not heed it is a gift. It allows them to recognize and remember how it felt which helps recognize guidance in the future.

Emotions are responses to thoughts. Thinking about something pleasing (past, present, or future) will create *getting warmer* Emotional Guidance. Thinking about something unpleasant (past, present, or future) will create *getting colder* Emotional Guidance. Everyone has the ability to make the choice to think about someone or something and focus on an aspect that feels good or an aspect

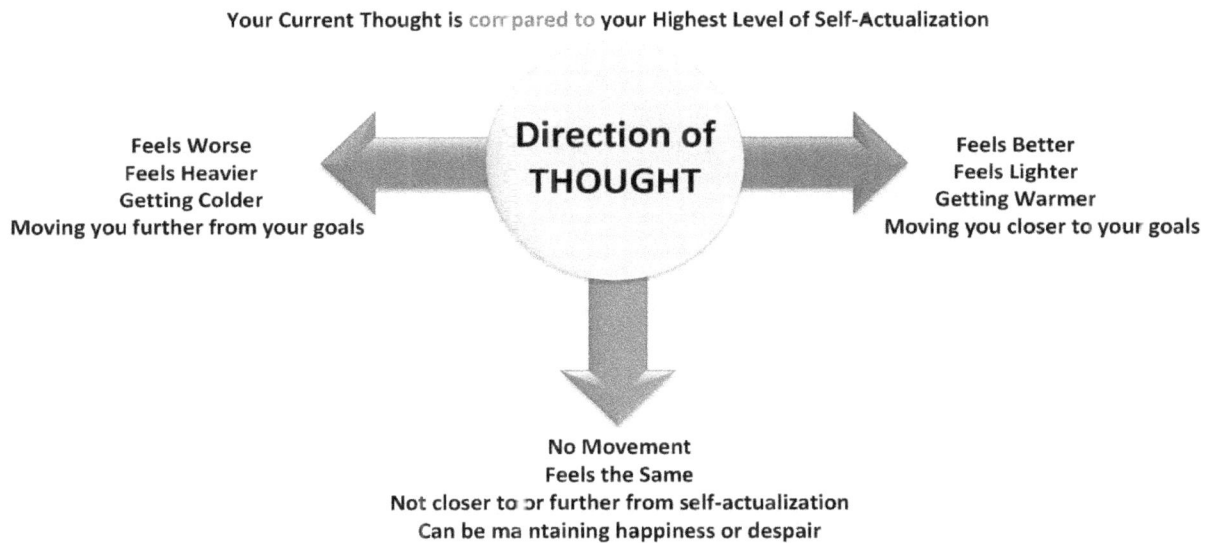

Your Current Thought is compared to your Highest Level of Self-Actualization

Feels Worse
Feels Heavier
Getting Colder
Moving you further from your goals

Direction of THOUGHT

Feels Better
Feels Lighter
Getting Warmer
Moving you closer to your goals

No Movement
Feels the Same
Not closer to or further from self-actualization
Can be maintaining happiness or despair

that feels bad. The Emotional Guidance feedback system provides feedback in response to each thought:

- Thoughts that elicit emotions that feel good are moving in the desired direction.
- Thoughts that elicit emotions that feel bad are moving away from the desired goal.
- Thoughts that elicit the same emotion the person felt at the preceding thought are not moving from where the last thought was—whether good or bad.
- A thought can still feel bad, but be better than the thought that preceded it, which means it is shifting toward a better direction.

Many people don't think about their thinking (**metacognition**). But it is easy to train people to do so and to understand the real purpose and function of their emotions.

Emotional state is primarily the result of whether one is moving toward or away from self-actualization. Emotional Guidance provides information that lets each person know the best thoughts, words, and actions to use in order to move toward self-actualization by providing positive emotion when thoughts are moving toward fulfilling more potential. As an individual becomes more, their fully self-actualized self becomes more so they never become fully self-actualized.

Emotional Guidance seems to know the unique personal goals for every person, even when the person has forgotten something they decided was personally important. It does not matter what those goals are. They could be to become the richest person on the planet or to become a stay-at-home Mom who has time for bubble baths each day or simply someone who has time to get enough sleep or the ability to get enough food for one day, or any other goals that are meaningful to the individual. If he's moving in the direction of his goals, he feels much better than if he's moving away from them. If he's not moving in either direction, his emotion varies by how long he's been there, whether he believes he'll ever get there, and with how specific or general his thoughts are about the subject he is thinking about, and whether where his current emotional state feels good.

Barbara L. Fredrickson found that using skills to increase the level of positive emotions experienced by individuals—daily and over time—reduces stress and increases their level of resilience.

When individuals know they have Emotional Guidance and practice using it they also know that no matter how bad their current circumstances may seem they can find ways to feel better. Hope, a belief that a positive or desired outcome is possible, is a key emotional state for resilience. Peil affirms that just knowing that guidance exists builds a firm foundation for hopefulness. Martin E. P. Seligman, the Father of Positive Psychology, tells us that without accurate knowledge about the purpose and meaning of emotions, it is easier to feel hopeless, which can lead to inertia or giving up.

Positive Psychologists tell us "we have more control over our own emotional well-being than previously believed."[49] Repeatedly using metacognitive processes to improve one's emotional state forms new neuropathways that lead to habits of thought that support positive emotions and, eventually, better automatic responses to stimulus. Once an individual trains their brain they automatically have less stressful reactions in new situations. Todd Kashdan and Jonathan Rottenberg reported that "Well-practiced behaviors easily become automated wherein conscious intentions are no longer a prerequisite to perform an act. That is, by repetition, a person can act without conscious thought to guide and monitor every behavior."[50]

The research is clear that individuals and employees have more to give to others when they are happy. The purpose of Emotional Guidance is to guide individuals to happier emotional states, which is the same as saying Emotional Guidance points us towards thoughts that increase our ability to become self-actualized.

Unfortunately, much like Maslow's Hierarchy of Needs, simple concepts quickly gain ground without validation. Several years ago a couple of psychologists did some studies and reported that it took 2.9013 positive comments to offset one negative comment. When I first read this, I thought it was a joke. There is no way to estimate how many positive comments a specific person needs to offset one negative comment. An employee with low self-esteem may receive 100 positive comments and those comments sill still not offset the detrimental impact of a single negative comment that affirms a belief that the employee will never amount to anything. If a manager does not understand the matrix formed by beliefs, emotional state, and behavior, they won't understand how to help the employee. Another employee with higher self-esteem, or one who understands negativity comes from someone in a negative emotional state, may not need a single positive statement to recover because the negative comment does not injure their self-esteem or ego. The 2.9013 ratio has been refuted but it is still sometimes referenced in new articles as if it is valid.

Self-esteem has been considered:

1. The strongest core self-evaluation predictor of job performance.[51]
2. The most difficult factor to change.

Emotional guidance provides the perfect tool with which to increase healthy self-esteem. Once an individual begins to trust his guidance he can begin thinking about his appraisal of self and when the emotional response to self-appraisal is negative, apply metacognitive processes to find thoughts that feel better. For many individuals, improving self-esteem is one of the most difficult hurdles to attaining and maintaining sustainable **True Happiness**, but Emotional Guidance makes it easier. If an individual has habitually always thought negatively about self it is often best to use another subject to feel good and then deliberately switch to thoughts about oneself.

In that way, glimpses of positive thoughts about self will be available. Through repetition of the process, the old negative habits of thought will be re-wired to more positive thoughts. Just knowing that the negative thoughts are merely the result of repeated negative thoughts and not some form of condemnation that affirms one is a bad person can provide significant relief. After one success, additional efforts are intrinsically motivated because of the powerful and natural desire to feel better that underlies all our choices.

Each person's Emotional Guidance System directs them toward their personal goals and desires. What you want is part of the programming. In fact, it's such a big part of the programming that it may seem you've been given faulty guidance if you look at too small of a picture.

Charles S. Carver is one of the most respected names in psychology. He is the editor of the *Personality Processes and Individual Differences* section of the *Journal of Personality and Social Psychology*. I have read many of his research papers on optimism vs pessimism, self-regulation theory, coping, and more. His work as a professor at the University of Miami has helped shape my positions and I was delighted when he recently published a paper supporting my position that the purpose of emotions is to provide moment-by-moment guidance to us about our behavior.[52]

My stance goes deeper as I believe that emotions provide moment-by-moment guidance to let us know whether our very thoughts are helping us move toward our self-defined goals or away from them. It is still satisfying to see that he has reached the conclusion that emotions are part of a feedback loop, "managing rate of progress at goal attainment or threat avoidance" and that he went on to say that "given multiple simultaneous goals, these functions assist in moment-to-moment priority management, facilitating attainment of all."[53]

I'll give you an example that may be familiar. You may have experienced or know of someone who has. Someone is in a relationship that isn't serving their highest good but they are clinging to the unhealthy relationship. It could be a relationship with another person, with a job, or even with a place to live. Then something happens that increases their motivation to move. A woman in a relationship with the wrong man may find that an old flame shows up on the scene and she is strongly drawn back to him. But after she has left the unhealthy relationship, the heat from the new flame quickly dies.

What often happens in this situation is the woman begins questioning her judgment, or her decision to leave the unhealthy relationship. But if she understood her Emotional Guidance she would quickly realize that the desire to reunite with the old flame was simply what I'll call the *path of least resistance* to what she really wants. Your guidance seems to know the best possible path to get you on the road to what you want. When she was in the unhealthy relationship she needed a stronger emotional pull to motivate her to leave the relationship. Once she was clear of that relationship, the new relationship, which was only needed to motivate her to leave the relationship she was clinging to, is no longer serving her and it is no longer on the path toward what she really wants so the energy supporting it subsides. The other person is not a tool. The relationship served him in some way as well. Such relationships are often the result of putting short-term priorities above long-term priorities, such as "I want a job (or relationship/home) and I want it now. A goal that focuses on wanting a job that best suits my short and long-term needs and desires would serve both the employee and employer better.

When I speak about being fired or a lay-off, people frequently share that they've realized it was actually good for them. The sooner a person realizes the potential for a silver lining exists, the sooner they will look for it. The sooner they look for the silver lining, the sooner they will feel better. When they feel better they will have access to greater resources with the most important resource being their own cognitive capacity not being diminished by high stress. It is possible to find the silver lining in moments or even before the event. By establishing an expectation that being laid off always works out well for you before it happens, it is possible to feel anticipation of good things to come when you are notified you're being displaced.

Affirmations like the following can help an employee avoid fear of a layoff and are especially helpful for maintaining ones' focus during economic downturns:

If I am laid off I will find a better job that pays more money quickly.

I am my job security. I continuously improve my knowledge and skills. My employer is not the source of my job security. I create my job security by continuously becoming more of my potential.

I'll give you an example of how my guidance helped me find a book. I don't have a library in my home, but I have bookcases in every room. As a result I sometimes have to search when I want a specific book. I knew a particular book had a passage I wanted to quote and I looked all over the house for it, scanning every bookcase without success. When I passed the dining room after looking upstairs I noticed that a case of Malbec my husband ordered from Argentina was on the table. It had been delivered the day before. I felt a sudden urge to put it in the wine rack. I wasn't thinking about the book, I simply felt an urge to put the wine away. The idea of doing something nice for my hubby felt good. There is a small bookcase next to one of the wine racks in the dining room. I'd already looked for the book there. It wasn't until I bent over to put a bottle in the bottom of the rack that I spotted the book. It was in a horizontal stack and the book above it was slightly larger so the book was not visible from above.

I immediately recognized that the urge I'd felt to stop and put the wine away during the workday was my guidance knowing the *path of least resistance* to get my head in the right position to see the book I was searching for. When you become aware of your guidance you begin noticing synchronicities like this every day. The source of my guidance knew where the book was and the easiest way to get me to find it was to bend over far enough to see it beneath the larger book.

When you begin using your guidance you feel emotion and urges in a stronger way. Before I understood my guidance I would have felt the urge and ignored it because it was the workday. I wanted that book enough that I might have ordered a new copy, perhaps assuming a friend had borrowed it and not returned it. I would probably not have found it because I usually leave my husband's wine for him to take care of as he's something of a connoisseur.

The woman whose guidance encourages her to leave the relationship that isn't serving her who understands her guidance can view her actions and emotions from a larger perspective. She is far more likely to reach the conclusion that she is on her way to the relationship she wants than to mourn the one she left. She can even learn from the situation by paying attention to how she felt in the relationship she left (not the new one) and realize that if she ever feels that way in the future it might be best if she did not cling to a relationship that was obviously not serving her highest good. When the energy and emotion that pulled her toward the new one stops calling her in that direction she can quickly recognize that it was merely the *path of least resistance* and move on.

The woman who does not know she has guidance has all sorts of pitfalls and traps in this scenario. When the energy supporting the new relationship drops she may think she made a mistake and attempt to return to the relationship she left. Or she may cling to the new relationship because she gave up the old relationship so she could be in the new one. Not understanding that you have guidance and how it works can make life seem as if you are in a rudderless boat being tossed on stormy seas. I can't tell you how many conversations I've had over the years where someone is questioning (second guessing) their choices.

The same basic scenario can play out when a job is not serving your highest good. Your guidance can begin making some aspect of the job distasteful. It can be the work itself, a co-worker, the commute or any other aspect of the job. It can direct your attention with encouraging emotions toward other jobs, locations, or industries. It can give you an urge to click on a link that takes you to information about a better job even before you've consciously decided to look around. It can also help you identify better-feeling thoughts about the existing job. Sometimes you've just gotten out of sorts and nothing will feel good until you focus in a new way.

The person whose guidance is encouraging him to relocate to a new home can either begin highlighting aspects of the current home that aren't as he'd like them to be in order to decrease his satisfaction with the current home or increase his awareness of aspects of other homes that his current home doesn't have thus increasing his desire for a new home. Guidance can even lead him into a conversation where he learns something that helps him decide he can or should move. The best way is the one that feels best. Appreciation for what the home offered and provided and appreciating that there are homes that will fulfill the newer desires just as well.

At one point in the past one of my friend's credit was destroyed while she was in the process of getting a divorce. Two years later, she was very unhappy with her landlord because he was not doing repairs that needed to be done for her to be able to enjoy the home she was renting. She felt stuck and frustrated but she did not believe she had done enough to repair her credit to be able to buy a home of her own. Because she had the belief that she could not get a mortgage, she had not taken any steps to try to find out if she could. She already believed she couldn't do it so trying didn't make rational sense to her.

When we talked I disrupted her inertia by simply asking her what the worst that could happen would be if she did try—they could say no and she'd be right where she was now—not any worse off. I didn't know if she could buy a house, but I thought she might be able to. As a result, my cognitive process gave me thoughts hers did not have access to. She tried to buy a house as the result of that conversation and was successful. She thought her credit score was standing in her way, but it was her belief about her credit score, not her credit score, that was stopping her from doing what she wanted.

For a woman in my generation, buying a house on your own for the first time is a very empowering event. I remember the first time I did it. I watched my friend's confidence in herself surge after she bought the house. That surge in her confidence extended to other areas of her life and her career began advancing faster than it had in the past. When you feel empowered others perceive you differently.

"Metacognition refers to awareness of one's own knowledge—what one does and doesn't know—and one's ability to understand, control, and manipulate one's cognitive processes. It includes knowing when and where to use particular strategies for learning and problem solving as well as how and why to use specific strategies." Teacher Excellence in Adult Education (TEAL)

Metacognition is defined in a variety of ways in the scientific literature. The way I mean it involves the conscious overseeing and regulation of cognitive processes. Instead of just letting thoughts come and go without thinking about why you're thinking the thoughts you're thinking, or about alternative thoughts you could think, or how the thoughts you're thinking are affecting your experience, metacognition involves conscious awareness and exertion of some control over the process. It does not mean you have to control every thought. Using a combination of meta-cognition and Emotional Guidance is the best way to improve your life experience. Your Emotional Guidance provides you with information that helps you know which thoughts you may want to adjust (feels bad), which it would serve you to give more air time in your mind (feels good), and which aren't serving your highest good.

Thoughts you might want to adjust would be ones where you can find a better feeling perspective. Thoughts you want to give more air time in your mind (or by talking and/or writing about them) are the thoughts that feel good when you think them.

How your emotional sense feels when you think the thought lets you know if it is serving your highest good (feels good or better than prior thought) or not serving your highest good (feels worse than your prior thought, or, if the prior thought felt bad, it feels the same).

If you're aware you have Emotional Guidance and how to accurately interpret its meanings, you can think about what you're thinking in a more intelligent way.
You are fully capable of knowing what is best for you.

Learning to be conscious about reappraising one's emotional state lowers negative rumination and increases positive reappraisals. The ability to identify the silver lining quickly during an adverse situation increases resilience and lessens the negative emotions the situation elicits. Emotional Guidance is an effective way to reinforce statements used to refute cognitions that lead to negative emotional responses.

The emotional state an individual is experiencing dictates which process(es) will be of the most benefit in improving emotional state using the right process is important. If a process makes you feel worse, it is not right at that time.

Positive Affirmations

Positive Affirmations are scientifically proven to reduce stress, when they are used correctly.[54] Used incorrectly, they are probably the most damaging commonly used technique. It is important to know how to use them correctly.

Positive Affirmations are recommended as long as the affirmation is for the current emotional stance reaching for no more than one Zone higher than the current emotional stance.[‡] Basically, you can do affirmations from any emotional stance as long as the affirmation is believable from your current position. Positive affirmations are one of the most widely taught techniques and they probably cause the most harm. They cause harm, not because the process is bad or defective, but because most teachers do not differentiate between when Positive Affirmations are beneficial and when they are inappropriate or counterproductive.

Positive affirmations have been scientifically shown to be counter-productive when the individual does not believe the affirmation.[55] The person can say the positive affirmation, but internally the mind refutes it, which makes the underlying negative belief stronger. Positive affirmations should only be used when they do not create this mental backlash. In other words, make adjustments that are not huge stretches from the existing belief on the specific topic. For

---

‡ Refer to the Emotional Guidance Scale (EGSc) in Appendix I for details on the Zones.

example, affirming you love your job when you hate it just reinforces the aspects of the job you do not enjoy.

The researchers who found that Positive Affirmations were counterproductive for some associated it to low self-esteem. But the low self-esteem was not the root issue. The low self-esteem led to less favorable beliefs about the self (or was the result of less favorable beliefs about the self). It is not that individuals with low self-esteem can't benefit, they just can't begin with the same affirmations someone who has higher self-esteem can use. It does not mean that they can't get to those more affirming affirmations; it just means they can't do them today.

By affirming beliefs that are only slightly better than what is already believed new, more positive beliefs develope. Once that step is done, it can be repeated with new affirmations that are slightly better than the new beliefs. This can be done repeatedly. The person's life will improve each step of the way. It is not a situation where you have to reach the ultimate destination to benefit from the journey. If your mind refutes an affirmation, you're reaching too far. Take a smaller step. Using the process described in General to Specific (See Developing **Psychological Flexibility** chapter) can be very beneficial in identifying affirmations that move in the right direction.

Positive affirmations can be especially useful when involved in a situation where one faces a challenging message and has been shown to "release participants from concern over the evaluative threat posed by a challenging message."[56] For example, someone who has connected laziness with obesity in their own mind might feel shame if they gain weight. Obesity has more to do with stress and diet than with laziness. In fact, I've been forming a hypothesis that looks at laziness as a symptom of low emotional state, not an actual trait, but that's a story for another time.

If the person with this belief goes to the doctor and is admonished for gaining weight, she could affirm important personal values and beliefs about herself to help her recover her self-esteem. She might reflect that a contributing factor to the weight gain was working long hours that have resulted in her receiving a nice promotion and salary increase, or looked at from another angle, made her better able to care for her family's needs and increased her skills so her employability is more stable, even if the economy takes a dive.

The key to using Positive Affirmations is to lean in direction of the desired emotion. This approach, applied consistently over time, results in amazing and delightful changes. If your emotional stance is in the Drama Zone, reach for another emotion in the same Zone that feels slightly better or for one in the Blah Zone. If you attempt to affirm a thought that would be in the Hopeful Zone you're likely to have pushback in your own mind. Move to the Blah Zone and stabilize there by affirming thoughts you believe in the Blah Zone. Once you are stable, move to new thoughts that feel even better.

It is always the underlying mental attitude that determines whether something is counterproductive. For example, knowing that exercise makes one feel better is helpful when we actually exercise. When we feel bad and don't take the physical action of exercising, there is a tendency to add guilt for not exercising to the existing negative emotion—perhaps starting a **downward spiral**. When we understand how to adjust our perceptions to feel better, we can counter any guilt we begin to feel before it adds to our emotional burden.

Here is an example of trying to move too far, too quickly. The person is afraid of public speaking and shy about interacting with strangers.

Affirmation: *I am a charismatic public speaker.*

Internal dialogue: *"Who are you trying to fool? You couldn't talk your way out of a paper bag. If you get up on the stage they'll laugh you right off."*

Affirmation: *I am a charismatic public speaker.*

Internal dialogue: *"Still trying to convince yourself of that? You can try forever; you don't have what it takes to be on stage."*

Instead of leaping from the current belief (I am not even good at interpersonal communication. There is no way I can speak on stage in front of hundreds of people.) all the way to the desired belief, take a baby step.

Affirmation: *Today I will speak to a stranger, even if I am afraid. The worse that can happen is I'll look foolish.*

Internal dialogue: *"There is someone. Oh, this is scary."*

Action: Walking toward the stranger.

Internal dialogue: *"Just say hello. Or ask him what time it is."*

Internal dialogue: *"I can do this."*

Action: "Hi, isn't it a pretty day?"

Internal dialogue: *"Wow. I got that out without tripping over my tongue. I can do this. What should I do next?"*

Internal dialogue: *"Tomorrow I'll speak to two strangers."*

You can feel your progress as your belief shifts. Each shift, however slight, is positive motion forward. Affirming your progress serves two purposes. First, it is actually an affirmation of your personal power to change yourself. It reinforces an internal locus of control. Internal locus of control is associated with resilience and a healthy mental attitude. It also helps you stabilize yourself in the new place. This provides a firmer foundation for further progress. Affirming your progress helps maintain the better self-image and can increase your satisfaction with life.[57]

Positive affirmations that reach too far cement undesired beliefs more firmly in our minds. Remember, it is possible to feel hopeful that you will actually be able to have two conversations with strangers tomorrow and frightened about the idea of being on stage talking to a room full of strangers.

Pay attention to the internal dialogue. If your inner critic is responding, you have two choices. The easiest is to take a smaller step that your critic won't attack. The long-term solution is to kill your inner critic. You can also use your guidance, if saying the affirmation feels good, it's working. If it feels bad, you're taking too big of a step. Take a smaller step.

The Chart on the following page provides some guidance about which process will be the most useful based on the emotional state an individual is in when they use the process. Some mindsets diminish one's ability to thrive. The processes in the column on the far right reflect specific ways to reprogram one's mindset, thus allowing the individual to achieve more success in any area of their life.

When Feeling	Reach for	Process(es)[1]
Disempowered	→ A more Empowered perspective	See EGSc
Problems are unsolvable	→ More general thoughts	Go General
Victim Mindset	→ What steps can you take	Too many to list
Blames	→ Take responsibility	See EGSc, Forgiving, etc.
Feels fearful	→ Belief in self	Refute
Feels helpless	→ What steps can you take	Role Models, Refute, Go General, See the potential in other, etc.
Emotionally out of control	→ Any thought that feel better, long-term goals, more general thoughts	Go General, Forgiving, Set Intentions
Rigid Thinking	→ Ask self if there is another valid perspective	Remember how your brain works
Clinging to anger	→ Remember that anger hurts you	Forgiving, Reframe
Resistance to new ideas	→ Confidence that you can learn, remember that your brain is trying to prove your existing beliefs to you—even if they do not serve your highest good	Humor, Use Big Picture
Negative emotional bias	→ Begin leaning more positive	See Positive Affirmations
Hopeless	→ Remember you have skills to feel better and/or perceive differently	Go General—you'll have better ideas
The worse will happen	→ Ca sera sera (What will be, will be)	Refute, Stop Catastrophizing
Tendency to attack oneself	→ Refute the negative voice	End self-criticism
Holds onto guilt	→ Realize you've learned	Forgiving
Feelings of shame	→ Why were you taught to feel that way about the subject? Who benefited? Let it go.	Refute (shame is a construct of man)
Long-term worry and anxiety	→ Set an intention to change	Think Positive, Focus Shift
Being "right" is highest goal	→ You have nothing to prove, develop growth mindset	Stop self-criticism
Feels life "just happens"	→ Use control over perspective	Set Intentions
Seeing obstacles as enemies	→ See obstacles as challenges (opportunities)	See the potential

---

[1] Not all Jeanine Joy's books include **all** the processes. *Our Children Live in a War Zone: Use the Power of Resilience to Improve Their Lives, Applied Positive Psychology 2.1* contains the most complete set as of 2016. The right process depends on your current emotional state as some processes are counterproductive when used while in an emotional state out of their effective range.

There are many things that move along a continuum in lockstep (tandem) with each other. It may not be a perfect lockstep, but for illustrative purposes, it works to explain the research. At one end of the continuum, you have:

- Low stress
- Sense of empowerment
- Healthy immune function
- Best possible cognitive function
- Best relationships

- Happiness
- Internal Locus of Control
- Healthy digestive function
- Best pro-health behaviors
- Best pro-social behaviors

At the opposite end of the continuum, you have:

- High stress
- Sense of disempowerment
- Diminished immune function
- Restricted cognitive function
- More relationship trouble
- Increased risky behaviors

- Low emotional states (depression, despair, learned helplessness, grief, hopelessness)
- External locus of control
- Impaired digestive function
- Poor pro-health choices
- Low level pro-social behaviors
- Increased addictions

When metacognitive processes are used to reduce stress, everything shifts. So even with a bad manager an employee who uses skills to manage his or her own emotional state can remain engaged and feel low stress—especially when compared to the employee whose emotional state is based on observation with no deliberate metacognition.
Emotional state is one of the filters that determine perception. An employee with low self-esteem, for example, may negate a manager's compliments so that the compliment is not actually received.

Example: Manager says "Good job, Jeanine."
But if my self-esteem is such that I don't believe I can do a good job or that I don't deserve such praise, instead of receiving the compliment I will reject it and think something like, "What does he want from me now? The only reason he'd say that is because he wants me to do something and he's trying to butter me up."

There would be no sense that a real compliment was ever made. It won't be remembered as praise--it will be remembered as another attempt to manipulate a *yes* to something unwanted—even if it was meant sincerely. The emotional state of the employee and the beliefs of the employee affect the way a sincere compliment is received. It's a personal responsibility to manage one's own emotional state, but we're living in a time when science had the purpose of emotions wrong for 80 years and most people don't understand how to use them to their advantage.

Don't give other people permission to ruin your day.

The following chart shows some of the factors that research has demonstrated change as emotional state changes. Additional relationships are described in the Business Case chapter. In the

Hopeful and Sweet Zones an individual will exhibit the characteristics in the higher grouping. As emotional state decreases, the lower grouping of characteristics will be demonstrated.

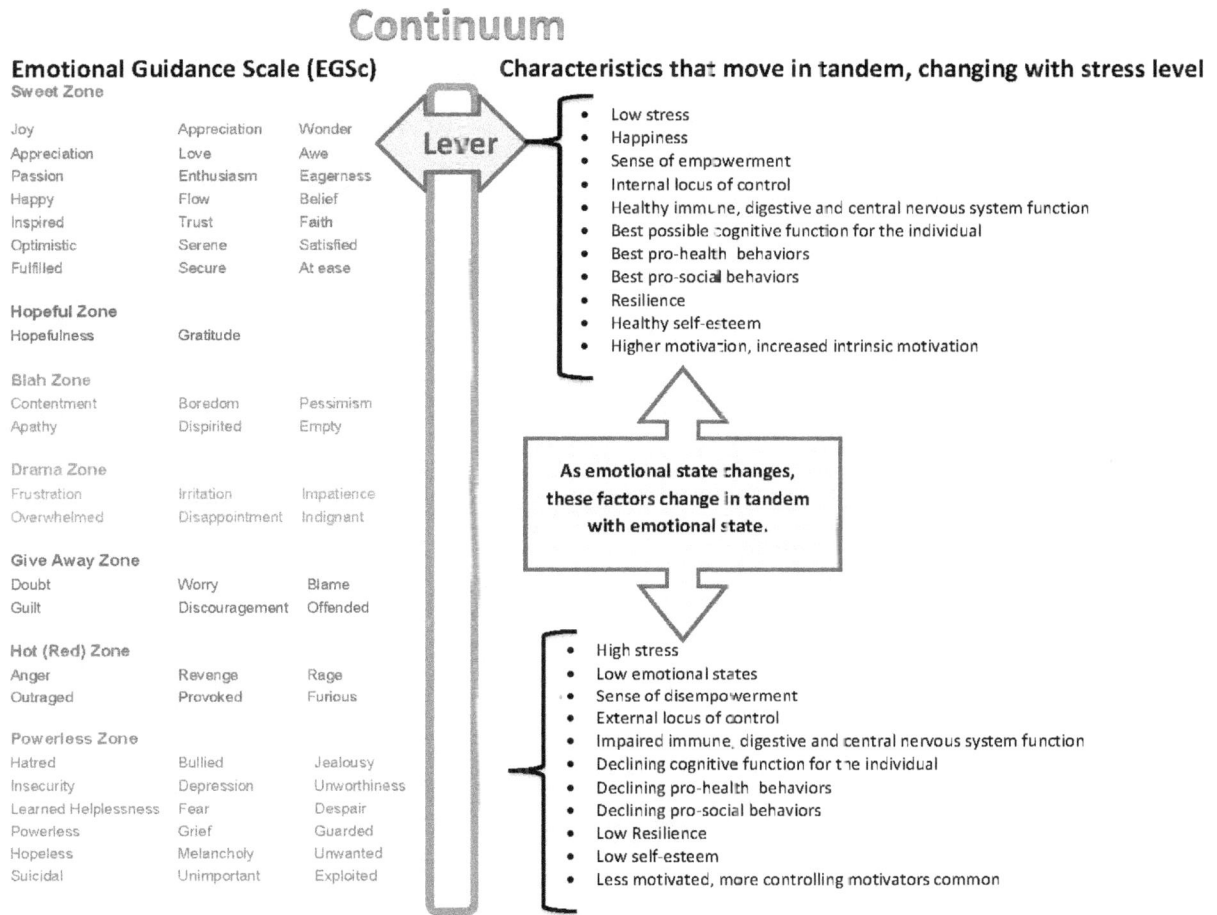

Continuum

Emotional Guidance Scale (EGSc)

Characteristics that move in tandem, changing with stress level

Lever

Sweet Zone

Joy	Appreciation	Wonder
Appreciation	Love	Awe
Passion	Enthusiasm	Eagerness
Happy	Flow	Belief
Inspired	Trust	Faith
Optimistic	Serene	Satisfied
Fulfilled	Secure	At ease

Hopeful Zone

Hopefulness	Gratitude

Blah Zone

Contentment	Boredom	Pessimism
Apathy	Dispirited	Empty

Drama Zone

Frustration	Irritation	Impatience
Overwhelmed	Disappointment	Indignant

Give Away Zone

Doubt	Worry	Blame
Guilt	Discouragement	Offended

Hot (Red) Zone

Anger	Revenge	Rage
Outraged	Provoked	Furious

Powerless Zone

Hatred	Bullied	Jealousy
Insecurity	Depression	Unworthiness
Learned Helplessness	Fear	Despair
Powerless	Grief	Guarded
Hopeless	Melancholy	Unwanted
Suicidal	Unimportant	Exploited

Top grouping:
- Low stress
- Happiness
- Sense of empowerment
- Internal locus of control
- Healthy immune, digestive and central nervous system function
- Best possible cognitive function for the individual
- Best pro-health behaviors
- Best pro-social behaviors
- Resilience
- Healthy self-esteem
- Higher motivation, increased intrinsic motivation

As emotional state changes, these factors change in tandem with emotional state.

Bottom grouping:
- High stress
- Low emotional states
- Sense of disempowerment
- External locus of control
- Impaired immune, digestive and central nervous system function
- Declining cognitive function for the individual
- Declining pro-health behaviors
- Declining pro-social behaviors
- Low Resilience
- Low self-esteem
- Less motivated, more controlling motivators common

Because the characteristics move in tandem, you only have to recognize where one characteristic is in order to know the other factors are in the same vicinity. Imagine the lever sliding up and down and see the emotional state it points to on the left and the corresponding behaviors and Psycho-bio-social changes that correspond with the emotional state on the right.

3: Coherent Thought

Quantum theory provides us with a striking illustration of the fact that we can fully understand a connection though we can only speak of it in images and parables.
Werner Heisenberg

In quantum physics, **quantum coherence** means that **subatomic** particles are able to cooperate. Subatomic waves, or particles, can communicate with each other because they are highly interlinked by bands of common electromagnetic fields.

If you've never heard of quantum physics, don't be intimidated. When I was in school I was taught that an atom was the smallest building block of humans and other things. Now we know there are smaller building blocks than atoms. We can measure some of these smaller things, much like we can see cells through a microscope. There are other things we can't see yet, but scientists are aware they exist because of the effect they have on other things. Atomic merely means at the level where matter (i.e. cells) are built. Subatomic is smaller than atoms.

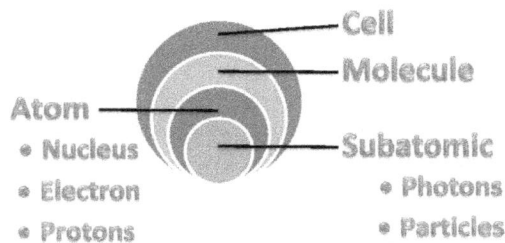

All physical matter (atoms and larger) are said to behave in ways described in **Classic Physics**. But unlike atoms and large physical objects, subatomic particles don't behave the same way. They can have patterns, either waves or streams. There is evidence that observation of subatomic particles can change the particle.

There is more that we just don't know because we have not discovered all there is to discover and do not yet have the ability to measure things that are even smaller. To think any other way is to risk slowing progress.

Physics dealing with the subatomic level is called Quantum Physics. They needed a different name because rules that work with Classic Physics don't explain what has been observed with subatomic particles.

The following information is provided to help you understand why *what we think* is important by shedding light on the relationship between your thoughts and the outcomes you experience every day. If thinking that small, invisible things can have a significant effect on your life feels like a stretch of the imagination, consider the power of viruses, germs, and bacteria.

Think about how much damage something that tiny can do to your body or mind. Also think about how beneficial tiny things are for you. If you're squeamish about the fact that your body is actually an entire ecosystem and not just you, skip the next two paragraphs.

Microorganisms inhabit our body, live on our skin, and in our intestines. Although no one has actually counted how many cells exist in our bodies or how many microbiotas[§] inhabit our bodies and live on our skin, the general consensus of the Human Microbiome Project is that what we think of as our bodies are composed of 10 times more microbiota than human cells. The microbiota cells are much smaller than human cells, so even though there are more of them, in size/weight current researchers estimate human cells still make up about 97% of our mass. In

---

[§] Formerly called normal flora

healthy individuals, the relationship between our bodies and microbiota is symbiotic, a harmonious and mutually beneficial partnership. Neither humans, nor the microbiotas that live on and in us could survive without the other. Microbiotas aid the digestive process and may even help to remove dead skin from our faces.

It is clear that humans cannot live without the healthy relationship with microbiota. Microbiotas help us digest carbohydrates and extract nutrients from our food so our blood can deliver it to our cells. The Microbiota work with and may even train our immune system to recognize intruders.

A sense of coherence between one's life and personal values has a positive influence on health because there are more waves with Constructive Interference arising from their thoughts. Generally, individuals who have significant adverse events during their lives have negative health impacts, but developing a positive mental attitude can offset the negative impact of adverse life events. For example, researchers who followed Israeli women who stayed healthy despite experiences in concentration camps during WWII referred to this sense of coherence as **salutogenesis**.[58]

The way I think of the quantum level of reality, including subatomic particles, is that they respond to subtler energy than atoms. Fritz-Albert Popp researched both healthy and unhealthy subjects and eventually concluded good health was a state of perfect subatomic communication (coherence) and ill health was a state where communication breaks down. We are ill when our waves are out of sync. Our emotions let us know whether our waves are in sync. When we have Constructive Interference toward something we desire, we're feeling joyful. When we have Destructive interference, we're feeling stressed and our emotions are in lower Zones on the EGSc.

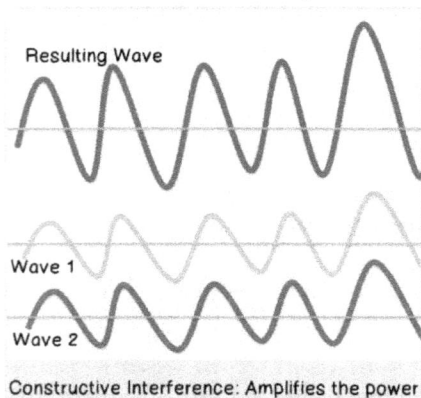

Resulting Wave

Wave 1

Wave 2

Constructive Interference: Amplifies the power

When the waves are in sync, they begin acting like one giant wave and one giant subatomic particle. Coherence creates the ability to communicate, like a highly sophisticated computer system.

In Quantum Physics, waves are encoders and carriers of information. When two waves are in phase (sync), and overlap each other (technically referred to as *interference*) the combined amplitude of the waves is greater than the combined amplitude of the separate waves; there is a compounding effect.

Now, think of thoughts as a pattern of energy with the ability to affect subatomic particles. Imagine that a thought is wave 1 and a desire is wave 2. In this case, the waves are in sync (thoughts and desires are in sync). The individual in this situation would not be stressed about this subject—waves in sync do not create tension. The resulting outcome is positive. Popp found that individuals whose waves were in-sync were healthy.

This is consistent with research indicating that positive and optimistic individuals enjoy significantly better health[59] and greater success.[60] A pilot study by The HeartMath Institute achieved a 36% reduction in pain ratings by increasing **heart coherence** in a group that had moderate to severe perceived pain. The same technique reduced negative emotions by 49% and perceived stress by 16% while physical limitations decreased by 42%. The control group was unchanged.[61] This successful intervention included instructions to be more aware of their feelings and emotions and use self-regulatory techniques to shift into a more coherent state of mind to achieve heart coherence.[62]

Constructive Interference could be represented by the desire "I want a job where I make enough to take good care of my family" amplified by the belief "I am well prepared to find a good job." The math we are taught in elementary school relates to Classic Physics. The same math does not work in Quantum Physics.

When what you want and what you believe you can achieve don't conflict your thoughts are in-sync (Constructive Interference) and energy on the quantum level is working in your favor. Everything from the function of your cells (immune, digestive, cognitive, and central nervous system), to the thoughts you think and the words you speak are supportive of achieving your desire. There is power in Constructive Interference as illustrated by the compounding effect seen in the amplification of the wave in the diagram.

The amount of energy it takes to shift thought into alignment with desires is far less than the energy required to make an equal change in the world of Classic Physics where:

Work = Force x Distance
Force = Mass X Acceleration

I'm not Einstein, but I've come up with a way to attempt to explain Interference mathematically. Constructive Interference acts as a multiplier because it increases power and Destructive Interference acts as a divider because it decreases power. Begin with the following equation:

Interference = Desire x Belief = Power (multiplier/strength/energy)

With a belief that one can accomplish a desire, Constructive Interference increases the power the individual has to achieve the desired goal.

Constructive Interference = Desire x 100 (belief = "I can")

With an "I want it but I believe it is possible" belief, Destructive Interference decreases the power the individual has to achieve the desired goal.

Destructive Interference = Desire x 0 (belief = "I can't")

I created the following chart to illustrate a few of the mindsets and how they would affect the power or energy to achieve the desired goal. Fractions or percentages would be used as the multiplier between 0 and 1.

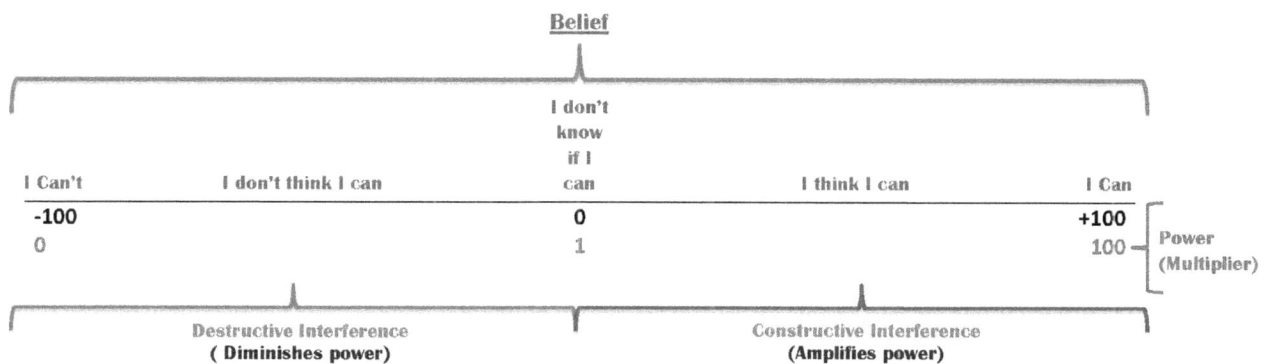

Belief

I Can't	I don't think I can	I don't know if I can	I think I can	I Can
-100		0		+100
0		1		100

Power (Multiplier)

| Destructive Interference (Diminishes power) | Constructive Interference (Amplifies power) |

This next example is not yet explainable using modern science, but anyone who has deliberately attained and sustained a positive mental attitude will tell you they've observed this effect. It is also documented in Carl Jung's work in synchronicity.

Published research reports about (currently) inexplicable things are common. Experiments in quantum entanglement and quantum coherence in biological molecules is considered proved at experimental levels. [63] In replicated experiments, researchers have been able to measure changes in the brains of individuals who are separated by distance where changes to one affected the other while at a distance. [64] Also currently unexplainable but documented are incidents where a loved one experiences symptoms of physical distress at the same time a loved on suffers an actual injury. In one instance, a nurse who did not regularly experience headaches was suddenly in severe pain from a headache centered in the back of her head. [65] After going home and taking pain pills to help her headache she learned her brother had been shot in the back of the head at the same time she developed the headache.

Some people are reticent to share examples of such events in their own lives. I'd love to have your stories. Because we cannot yet explain how they happen, old superstitious ideas and stigmas can be associated with anyone who claims such experiences. But in groups where folks are more open-minded and less concerned with being adversely judged, it is my experience that almost everyone has stories of synchronicities that, while fortunately not as tragic as the nurse's story, are nonetheless compelling. It is often difficult to verify such stories. I've had numerous times in my life that made me a believer. Or, perhaps it would be more accurate to say, events that kept me believing. The earliest incident I remember was when I was under 10-years old and I woke up and told my Mom that her brother and his wife and their three children were going to come for a visit the following summer. Mom and I were in the midst of arguing about how many children my uncle had, with her maintaining that he only had two and my insisting he had three, when the phone rang and it was my uncle who rarely called. He was calling to tell us that he and his wife were expecting and that they wanted to come from Michigan to California to visit us the following summer.

I still remember my mom questioning me after the call. She was convinced that my uncle had called the day before and spoken with me because there was no way she could conceive of for me to know they had a baby on the way. I had dreamed it and was sure the dream gave me accurate information. I was too young to *know* we shouldn't **know** things in that way. I have continued to experience synchronicities throughout my life. What sort of synchronicities have you experienced?

The writings of many of the greatest business minds tell stories about synchronicities that occurred after they believed they could succeed and decided they would find a way to do so but did not know what that way would be. Soon after they made the decision they'd go somewhere and be introduced to or meet (by happenstance) exactly the right person to move their goal forward. If you read biographies of men like Henry Ford, Napoleon Hill, and Joseph Murphy they are filled with such stories. This is not luck. Decisions have power.

Two of my favorite quotes are from philosophers who wrote about the power of decisions.

The German philosopher Johann von Goethe wrote:

Until one is committed, there is hesitancy, the chance to draw back; always ineffectiveness. Concerning all acts of initiative and creation there is one elementary truth, the ignorance of which kills countless ideas and splendid plans; that the moment one definitely commits oneself, then Providence moves too. All sorts of things occur to help one that would never otherwise have occurred. A whole stream of events issues from the decision raising in one's favor all manner of unforeseen incidents and meetings and material assistance which no one could have dreamed would come his way.

Once you make a decision, the universe conspires to make it happen.
Ralph Waldo Emerson

Remember: Not making a decision is a decision. **Make Decisions** that feel good for long-term goals. Short-term goals can de-rail your long-term goals (i.e. drugs and alcohol). Drug and alcohol problems begin because a person wants to feel better and does not have skills to do feel better in a healthier way.

We may not know exactly how it occurs, although it is not a difficult jump to see the link between the compounding effect of Coherent Interference and the synchronicities that are commonly reported. The Harvard Men's Study, (formally the Grant Study) began in the 1930's followed 268 Harvard men for the rest of their lives. Individuals who were positively focused, which includes positive self-regard and belief in one's abilities, were far more successful than those who were not positively focused, despite all of them having the advantage of a Harvard education.

Individual positivity or negativity had a great impact on success in all areas of life including business, marriage, and health. The correlation between a positive attitude and Coherent Interference is obvious. You must believe you can (have positive expectations) before you can achieve Coherent Interference.

> *The absence of negative emotions is not the same as the presence of positive emotions.*

Herbert Fröhlich, of the University of Liverpool, was one of the first to introduce the idea that some sort of collective vibration is responsible for getting proteins to cooperate with each other (in our bodies) and carry out instructions of DNA and cellular proteins. Waves (at the quantum level) synchronize activities for the living system. Positive thinking creates Constructive Interference, allowing clear communication between the cells of the body.

Negative thinking creates Destructive Interference that interferes with communication between the cells of the body. Desires are always about positive emotion and positive motion forward. Negative thinking, by definition, is in opposition to goals and positive motion forward. Anything less than positive thinking loses the beneficial impact of Coherent Interference.

Researchers at Harvard found that positive emotions reduce the risk of developing heart disease by 50%.[66] Heart disease is the number one cause of death, responsible for about 33% of all deaths. Boehm's research report clearly stated that the absence of negative emotions was not the same as the presence of positive emotions. Positive emotions are required to obtain the health benefits. This fits the theory that positive emotions create clear communication between our cells, evinced by (or supported by) Coherent Interference while neutral emotions and negative emotions do not create Coherent Interference.

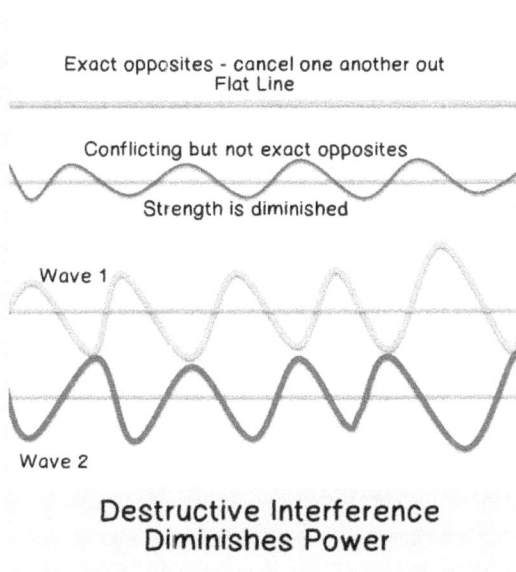

Destructive Interference Diminishes Power

Negative emotions create Destructive Interference. The flat line at the top of the chart is indicative of someone who wants something but whose belief is opposite the desire. For example, the desire "I want a job where I make enough to take good care of my family" contrasted with the belief "It is impossible to find a good job in this economy" would be a flat line.

The lower power wave (conflicting thought) indicate the same desire combined with a less pessimistic (but still not positive) belief "It will take a long time to find a good job in this economy."

Mathematically,

$$1 \times .5 = 50\% \text{ power}$$

Can you feel how conflict between the belief and the desire create tension or stress? This stress exists at the quantum level, which is why it is the root cause of ill health. When our thoughts and beliefs are in sync, tension (stress) is lower.

Although many people try, I have not found evidence of a way to pull back our desires and maintain positive emotions. I have found ways to shift our beliefs to be more coherent with our desires. Increasing Constructive Interference on the quantum level magnifies our success and our health. Better cellular communication could explain the greater cognitive abilities that are documented when people are in positive emotional states. Improved immune and digestive function could have similar explanations.

Imagine that our thoughts are waves. A healthy, positively focused individual will have more coherent and positive thoughts. In other words, their thoughts will be consistently looking for solutions and believing they exist, their thoughts will reflect a belief that they will get through whatever hardship or turmoil they are surrounded by and be able to move forward. Or, if their life is going well, that it will continue to do so. Their waves are in sync, combining and amplifying one another. Communication with the body is consistent and clear. The level of stress is low.

On the other hand, someone who is experiencing illness will want the same things, they will want to get through it and move on, and they will want to believe things will turn out all right, but their negative bias will create Destructive Interference with the desires, thereby leaving the positive desires without enough power to manifest. Someone whose life is going well but who believes that it will not continue to do so creates Destructive Interference with continued wellbeing which eventually manifests in their reality.

When we think a thought, an "electrical charge occurs in our brain that causes the synapses to grow closer together in order to decrease the distance the electrical charge has to cross . . . the brain is rewiring its own circuitry, physically changing itself, to make it easier and more likely that the proper synapses will spark together—in essence, making it easier for the thought to be triggered."[67] In essence, once you think a thought it is easier for you to think the thought again. If you repeatedly think the thought it begins acting like a belief. A belief is a thought you've thought repeatedly, which your brain then uses as a filter to interpret reality.

During my life time, we've shifted from a view of cellular communication that was the equivalent of a key being able to find its own keyhole to one that involves biophotons that move at the speed of light and vibration.[68] Science does not have all the answers yet, but this new direction answers more questions. It is clear that a lot is going on that we have been unaware of because it occurs on a subtler level than our *vivid senses* allow us to observe. We can deliberately cultivate awareness of the subtler sensory feedback. We have sensory feedback that informs us about our state of coherence but most humans are taught not to trust it or to trust it less than their *vivid senses*.

Imagine holding a meeting with hundreds of people in a room. You cannot hear the hum of the air conditioner. When you sit quietly in the same room when it is empty, you are able to discern the hum of the air conditioner.

In our normal state, input from our *five vivid senses* is much like the meeting room with hundreds of people. The input from those senses is so clear and strong, the ability to perceive the subtler aspects of our environment is muted. We have far more than five senses. They are more accurately categorized as the five *vivid senses*. We know that when one of the five *vivid senses* is muted, as in someone who is deaf or blind, the perceptual ability of the remaining senses increases.

Three examples of thoughts and their coherence (or lack thereof) are shown below. The first example is of someone who lacks resilience and is in a low emotional state. Their thoughts oppose their desires leading to Destructive Coherence because of the negative thought patterns, which can cause a downward spiral. Notice the negative self-criticism. In each example, Emotional Guidance would let the person know when thoughts were not productive.

Thoughts	*Power Multiplier*	*Direction*
I can't believe this is falling apart. Nothing ever works out for me.	*0*	⬇
Every time I think something is finally working out it crashes.	*0*	⬇
If I wasn't stupid I might be able to find someone who loves me.	*0*	⬇
No one is going to hire someone my age.	*0*	⬇
I can't remember the last time something worked out really well for me.	*0*	⬇
I might as well stop trying. It never works out for me.	*0*	⬇
I must be cursed. What is the point?	*0*	⬇
I don't know what to do. I can't do anything well.	*0*	⬇
Life is awful and then you die.	*0*	⬇
I'm a loser.	*0*	⬇

In the next example, the random and unfocused thoughts of someone whose thoughts are inconsistent cancel one another out. The person has some positive thoughts, but not enough to cause thriving. If the thoughts continue to be more negative than positive, a **downward spiral** is a possibility.

Thoughts	*Power Multiplier*	*Direction*
I really hope this will turn out OK (without any real feeling of hope)	*0*	⬇
Sometimes things turn out OK	*100*	⬆
Maybe my brother will help me out (hopeful but no real faith)	*.79*	⬈
Bad things happen in three's; what is next?	*0*	⬇
At least I have people in my life who will always love me no matter what	*100*	⬆
I hope Joe never hears about this; he will never let me live it down	*.25*	⬋
Every time I think things are going well something bad happens	*0*	⬇
I've been in worse situations. I can probably find my way out of this	*.75*	⬈

Deliberately choosing to focus on better feeling thoughts could turn the situation around and create the far more desirable **upward spiral**. Most people's thought patterns are a lot like the second example. If they understood the importance of focusing on what they want with positive expectation, they would make a greater effort to think more thoughts that would benefit them.

Each one of the thoughts that has a multiplier of less than 100 could be improved using metacognition and reappraisal. For example, worrying Joe will hear you've had a hard time is giving Joe's opinion of us power. That thought could be reappraised by focusing on the fact that if Joe is in a state of appreciation he will probably feel compassion toward our situation and that if Joe ridicules our situation it would be a reflection of Joe's own low emotional state.

The concern about Joe finding out could also be reappraised with the concept that by the time Joe finds out the situation will be solved and Joe (if we insist on making his opinion important) will be impressed at our resilience while we dealt with a tough situation. Research shows that we typically underestimate other people's opinions of us and this is especially true when our own self-esteem is low.

Constructive Interference is at the root of why businesses have taught goal setting and other techniques that have proven successful, even if they didn't know about Constructive Interference. Setting goals creates greater coherence and amplifies the ability to achieve them. In the third example, of thoughts from a positively focused and optimistic mindset, the coherence of thoughts that support the individual's underlying desires increase wellbeing in all areas of life where this thought pattern is present.

Thoughts	Power Multiplier	Direction
Every time I think something bad has happened to me it turns out to be good when I get a clearer view of it	100	↑
I wonder what the silver lining will be here?	100	↑
I know there is a solution. There always is. I wonder what it is.	100	⇑
Things always work out well for me. I don't have to know the ending to know this will work out well, too.	100	↑
I wonder what new things I will learn because of this?	100	↑
It is fun to solve problems.	.75	↗
I have lots of people who will help me if I need help.	100	↑
I am really blessed. My life is going well.	100	↑

When comparing the above examples of thoughts, the scattered, powerless nature of the middle example, the destructive power in the first, and the amplifying power in the third example can be felt. On the quantum level, we understand that as coherent thoughts and desires overlay one another, the combined strength is amplified. The last example is indicative of individuals whose situations are changing because the Constructive Interference of their thoughts have amplified power.

The middle example is a more common thought-pattern, characteristic of a person who seems to be moving in circles or chasing his own tail, so to speak. He moves around a little bit but often ends up back where he began.

He may change jobs only to find that six months later he has an equal number of similar problems in the new position as those he was experiencing in the role he left. Until he changes something about himself he will continue thinking in ways that lead to the same outcomes.

Momentum of desire increases —>

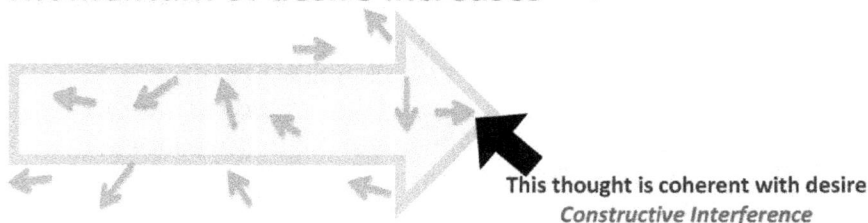

This thought is coherent with desire
Constructive Interference

Small arrows are thoughts

Sometimes an event in one's life causes a temporary decrease in one's perception of worthiness. This results in a decrease in wellbeing in areas that may have previously evinced a strong coherent pattern of thought toward their desires.

In essence, the emotional stance decreases. For individuals who live in the public eye, such as Donald Trump and Tiger Woods, it is possible to see the dip in their financial success while the emotional stance is lower. In the case of both of these men, it was trouble in their marriages that led to the lower emotional state which then impacted their financial success. Eventually, they return to their original chronic emotional stance and their finances improve. It is possible to shorten the duration of the downturns using the techniques outlined in this book. The same dips occur in the lives of people who do not live under the microscope of public opinion. If you think about your own life, you will see evidence of this. People who are more deliberate about their thoughts and use metacognitive processes are able to reduce the volatility even when some areas of their lives aren't as desired. Everyone has that power.

Someone can have cohesive positive thoughts about one area of life and destructive interference in another area of life. Some factors create spillover into many areas of life. Self-esteem, or worthiness, is one of the areas that will have an effect across the board. Other factors may only affect one aspect of life or an even narrower topic, such as a single relationship or goal.

Once you desire something, you won't be in-sync with your desire unless and until your thoughts are consistent with your ability to have the desire.

> ***Want it + Don't believe you can have it = stress/discord/Destructive Interference***
>
> ***Want it + Believe you can have it now = Constructive Interference/harmony/low stress***

Once you want something you cannot stop wanting it. But to fully understand what that means you have to understand that what you want is not the specific thing that you think it is. If you fall in love with someone, you can stop wanting that particular person because what you really want is the way that person makes you feel when you're in love. If you want a new sofa, it is the way you believe you will feel when you have that new sofa that is the real desire—the sofa is just the excuse you're using to feel that the way you want to feel.

Thoughts are a pattern of energy with the ability to affect subatomic particles. Your EGS will guide you toward greater positive (Constructive) coherence. Your heart is always in a positive, loving, appreciating, hopeful state. When you attempt to be other than that you can feel heartache. The more you bring your mind into alignment with your heart, the better you will feel and the better your life will become.

The HeartMath Institute has been studying Heart Rate Variability for a couple of decades. They define coherence as, "Coherence is the state when the heart, mind, and emotions are in energetic alignment and cooperation . . . it is a state that builds resiliency—personal energy is accumulated, not wasted—leaving more energy to manifest intentions and harmonious outcomes . . . . When the physiological coherence mode is driven by a positive emotional state, we call it psychophysiological coherence. This state is associated with sustained positive emotion and a high degree of mental and emotional stability."[63] They could just as easily be discussing the results of using *The Smart Way*. I remember my former boss asking how I could display so much equanimity while being laid-off about six years ago. Our potential for **equanimity** is so great; it can remain stable in the midst of a lay-off that occurs during a bad economy.

Write one of your goals or desires at the top of the blank chart. Use the chart to record your own thoughts. Add arrows to indicate the whether your thought patterns are consistent or inconsistent with your goal. Nuances do matter. "I can" is not equal to "I think I can," use your EGS to feel for the difference between the two thoughts.

If your thoughts do not currently support your goals, use the metacognitive processes described in this book to shift your thoughts to ones that support your goals. A separate chart for each topic can be beneficial. However, the goal is not to complete a lot of charts. The goal is to pay attention and recognize how the emotional discord feels and then adjust your perception to one that feels better.

Do you need some help coming up with ideas for your topics? Do you have a co-worker who tends to be irritating to you? Are you happy with the current political climate? Are all your relationships as good as you want them to be? Do you have a health condition that is not as good as what you would like it to be? See if your thoughts are in alignment on these topics.

If you enjoy good health, you can use the way you feel when you are ill—such as when it feels like a cold is starting. Another alternative is to think about how you think about an illness someone you care about is experiencing. Remember mirror neurons and the influence of expectation.

Thoughts Worksheet	*Power Multiplier*	*Direction*

Another way to use the chart is to ask your friends about things you say on a regular basis. One example is "I can gain weight just from smelling the cakes in the bakery."

Because our society currently operates as if the quantum level does not exist or matter many common beliefs and phrases that do not serve our highest good are in common usage. I used to think such thoughts could not really matter. However, after consistently feeling for how different thoughts felt, I began to feel the discord of unsupportive thoughts in a stronger way. When that happened, I shifted my mindset away from unsupportive thoughts and my results changed.

Here are some more examples of common unproductive expressions:

- *A good man is hard to find.*
- *I always choose the slowest line at the checkout counter.*
- *I can never (fill in the blank). i.e. find my keys*
- *I always (fill in the blank). i.e. anything you don't want*

- *Nothing good lasts forever.*
- *I am always a day late and a dollar short.*
- *He does not respect me.*
- *I can't (fill in the blank) i.e. anything you want to do*
- *(fill in the blank) is too expensive for me to do.*
- *It's a once in a lifetime experience. (unless you only want to do it once)*

Just realizing you have more ability to exert control over how you feel by changing your perspective (and therefore your thoughts) about a subject reduces stress significantly.

Exercise

Create revised statements that are more empowering than the ones listed above. Can you think of expressions you think or say that may be creating Destructive Interference with your ability to achieve your goals?

Don't be afraid of your thoughts. Occasional negative thoughts won't kill you. The accumulation of your thoughts creates momentum. You just want your momentum to be more positive than negative. The more positive outweighs the negative, the better life feels, but any step in the direction of feeling better is good. This is not something you should, must, or ought to do. This is something you do because it feels better to do than not do. The benefits of doing it are secondary.

4: Perception

Because, you know, resilience - if you think of it in terms of the Gold Rush, then you'd be pretty depressed right now because the last nugget of gold would be gone. But the good thing is, with innovation, there isn't a last nugget. Every new thing creates two new questions and two new opportunities.
Jeff Bezos

It is the way we perceive work, not the actual work that creates and supports our mental attitude. Our consciousness does not perceive an actual reality.[70] The reality our minds perceive is filtered.[71] This chapter will explain the main filters that impact our perception of reality.

Everyone has noticed that two people in like circumstances do not experience the same amount of stress. It's not circumstances that determine stress load. Mindset (current emotional state, expectations, beliefs, focus, and experience) is where it begins. When something stimulates a thought the brain filters the stimulus before conscious awareness and what comes out is a personal perspective of the situation based on the individual's mindset.

That perspective elicits an emotional response. The emotion is feedback from a sensory feedback system designed to work together with cognitive processes to let the individual know whether the thought supports or detracts from goals and desires.

How individuals perceive a situation is processed within their minds using programming that was created by influences during their youth including family, religion, school, and environment. This programming establishes beliefs, which were largely formed by age 6. Two people do not perceive the same circumstances exactly the same way because of the way the mind makes sense of stimuli. Most people are not consciously aware their minds are creating their personal reality. This causes them to cling to their way of perceiving situations and, when their programming is not self-supportive, it causes their lives to be far less fulfilling than they could be.

James Farr indicated that individuals who perceive the world while operating on auto-pilot tend to be rigid and inflexible in their views and resist change.[72] When employees are asked why they believe what they believe they can feel challenged and usually cannot provide rational reasons for their position when the position is based on beliefs they absorbed as children. This is evident in many biases, such as racism and insisting on narrowly defined roles based on manmade labels. They accepted beliefs without questioning the basis of those beliefs, so they are unable to substantiate their position. People who are unaware their perceptions are based on programming may feel as if their value and worth as a person is being challenged when their beliefs are challenged because they perceive their beliefs as being a part of what makes them who they are.

The biggest barriers to strategic renewal are almost always top management's unexamined beliefs.
Gary Hamel

Other people realize that the way they perceive any situation is only one way out of many possible ways of perceiving the situation. When a person realizes this, they increase their ability to be psychological flexible and to adjust their perception of situations to improve their emotional state. Psychological flexibility was recently recognized as a key factor in the ability to be successful.

It's easy to see why psychological flexibly is so important. This is a time of enormous and frequent changes in social values, technology, and economy. Individuals who do not have psychological flexibility can become rigid in their perception of situations, leading to sustained negative emotional states.

Ben-Itzhak and Bluvstein tell us:

"Psychological flexibility refers to the ability to be open, present-focused, and to change or persist in behavior according to changing internal and external circumstances. It is a complex psychological construct encompassing emotional, cognitive and behavioral aspects. Psychological flexibility has demonstrated longitude and cross-sectional connections to mental health and resilience, while a lack of psychological flexibility is associated with psychopathology . . . Psychological flexibility is simultaneously intrapersonal as well as interpersonal and enables adaptation to ever-changing circumstances. It is a way of expressing the individual's wish to experience a variety of conditions in the real world, while staying tuned to the variety of "inner voices". For an individual with a higher level of psychological flexibility, the quest for divergence and changes is an active one, and is perceived as a positive experience." [73]

"Kashdan and Rottenberg define psychological flexibility as the ability to "recognize and adapt to various situational demands; shift mindsets or behavioral repertoires when these strategies compromise personal or social functioning; maintain balance among important life domains; and be aware, open, and committed to behaviors that are congruent with deeply held values." [74]

Ben-Itzhak and Bluvstein tell us "Their [Kashdan and Rottenberg's] definition captures two significant points about psychological flexibility: that it is a multifaceted trait, manifesting across many life domains, and that it is a dynamic that expresses itself through "repeated transactions between people and their environmental contexts" . . . The concept of psychological flexibility signals a move from "simple, universal accounts or theories of positive versus negative emotions" to a more contextual assessment of the functionality of a specific emotion or coping style. "Indeed, one might question whether any regulatory strategy provides universal benefits, as opposed to contingent benefits that hinge on the situation and the values and goals that we import." [75]

Dukudraw 1

Every aspect of what an individual perceives as reality—including what they see, smell, taste, touch, and hear—is not only subjective and unique, it is also filtered by their beliefs, expectations, emotional stance, experience, and focus. When this is understood, the individual learns to see that different conclusions are true from different perspectives.

The parable of the blind men who argued over the nature of an elephant after each felt a different part reminds us that perception is based on unique individual experiences.

One of the reasons so few people are thriving is that fundamental ways they are taught to look at the world are inaccurate. To some degree, many premises humanity bases their opinions and decisions upon are not absolutes. But people typically do not apply that knowledge to things their senses make them believe are real. It is important to remember that physical senses do not *report* reality—they *interpret* reality.

James Farr uses the analogy of a radio transmission to discuss the programming that determines our perception:

> *"Like a radio, the mind is the instrument that brings the outside world into a consciousness. The mind receives external stimuli which range from auditory to visual to tactile. These stimuli prompt us to think or judge or react in a great many ways, which are almost always congruent with the mindsets we create through our educations, social, and moral conditioning. Our mind receives the stimuli, then processes them through our mindsets (programs or mental models). The result is the world as the mind perceives it—not necessarily as it may actually be. We have the same reality but two different perceptions of that reality. What is more, each mind triggers reactions in accord with those differing perceptions."* [76]

Failing to recognize that perceived reality is an interpretation and that there are numerous accurate ways to perceive the same situation (some more stressful and some less so) increases the level of stress in many lives. Recognizing that a perspective that creates less stress can be chosen and be an accurate assessment of a situation allows individual's to reduce stress without requiring circumstances to change. Chronic Stress is very detrimental to physical, mental, and behavioral health and to relationships and success in all areas of life. Chronically stressed individuals are not engaged employees.

The "consequences of false beliefs about stress is that many employees have been misled into blaming their working conditions for their feelings of distress." [77] This is primarily an external locus of control so it reduces the likelihood that an employee will deliberately seek out ways to increase personal resilience in order to reduce the strain. It is possible to change their perception.

Visser tells us "Aronson et al. did a workshop with students and noticed how this led to an important change in how these students viewed school. Before the workshop, many students saw school as a place where you, as a student have to perform, and where the teachers judge you. After the workshop they saw school more as a place where you learn, with the help of the teachers, things that make you smarter. Also, they said that, while they were learning, they imagine how new connections in their brain were forming." [78]

There are myriad instances where most adults are aware that what their brains show them about reality is not accurate, but almost no one consciously extends that awareness to a deeper understanding.

Arguments about colors, tastes, sounds, and even intentions, actions, and words are not about the actual color, taste, sound, intentions, actions, or words

because people are not able to perceive any of those things in the exact way another person perceives them. For example, someone who believes the world is good interprets words and actions differently than someone who believes the world is full of evil. People tend to believe they perceive an actual reality, but they do not. What they perceive with their eyes, ears, nose, taste, and touch are perceived using senses that are not identical to the sensors others' use. Once stimuli are sensed, it goes through a filtering process that distorts perception in significant ways.

The ability to perceive a single situation from multiple perspectives is psychological flexibility. Psychological flexibility leads to emotional flexibility, or, the ability to have greater control over one's emotional state.

Perception is malleable. The mind can make things up and the perceiver doesn't know if they are true or not. Sometimes illusions are functional and helpful. At other times, they are highly dysfunctional. For example, a disorder named Capgras Delusion occurs when someone believes a friend or family member has been replaced by an identical-looking imposter. The mind has an amazing ability to *create* a unique reality. Teaching employee's psychological flexibility skills helps them manage their emotional state and reduce their daily stress level.

Life is a combination of events and experiences that pass through filters (which individuals can learn to adjust). Emotional experience is the result of the thoughts a person has about what is perceived. Our brains create stories that help us make meaning from our experiences. In *Learned Optimism*, Martin Seligman called the stories people create *back stories*. In many ways they suppress cognition by not bringing our attention to things that don't make sense (because they create a bridge between what we believe and new stimuli) that makes it appear to make sense with our existing worldviews even when it doesn't. The creation of back stories is probably necessary to give us the sense that life makes sense and continues in an orderly manner. Back stories are created below conscious awareness and are designed to fit what the person believes are the facts together in a way that provides consistency and seamlessly fit with the rest of their perceptions about reality.

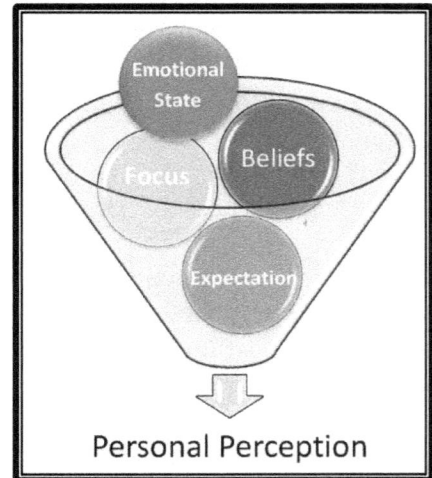

When a perspective changes, the thoughts evoked change. When an employee thinks a different thought, her emotional response changes.

People translate sound and light waves throughout their life—they're so good at it that they don't even realize they're doing it, much as they don't have to think *put one foot in front of the other* when they walk. They simply walk. They're good at it if their bodies are normal and healthy. The mind is designed to make people believe what they sense is reality. Grasping the concept that what the *vivid senses* reveal is merely an interpretation is critical to the ability to increase thriving to optimum levels. The more psychological flexibility individuals develop, the better their ability to find perspectives about situations that serve their highest good can be developed.

Appreciative Inquiry addresses organizational change from a strengths perspective. In many ways, learning how to use metacognitive skills and Emotional Guidance facilitates a type of personal appreciative inquiry. Following the trail of thoughts that evoke better feeling emotions using Emotional Guidance leads to better perspectives about self and about others. Diana Whitney and Amanda Trosten-Bloom say "Appreciative Inquiry works because it liberates power. It unleashes both individual and organizational power. It brings out the best of people, encourages them to see and support the best of others, and generates unprecedented cooperation and innovation."[79]

Learning metacognitive skills and combining them with Emotional Guidance unleashes even more power at the individual level because of the continual and reliable positive feedback loop provided when Emotional Guidance is interpreted accurately.

Unique perspectives create unique desires. Society's lack of understanding that everyone does not perceive reality in the same creates unnecessary conflict. That conflict is completely avoidable by making an effort to be more conscious that perception of reality is unique. Much workplace discord originates because of differences in the way individuals perceive situations.

Optical illusions may be only a cool phenomenon when viewed as something that tricks the mind. Considered from the perspective of "Is my mind showing me an actual reality?" the illusion gains greater meaning and provides insights that surface thinking does not begin to consider.

Surface thinking is thinking that does not look beneath the surface. It sees only what is perceived through the filters our brains use to determine what information is important to us. *Surface thinking* does not acknowledge that our perceptions are unique interpretations of reality. *Surface thinking* does not acknowledge that our very thoughts are the product of filters between our unconscious and conscious mind.

What is perceived is based on many personal factors. In truth, no two individuals experience exactly the same reality. Each person is creating their own version of reality from the information that exists.

Influencers who can facilitate change in an individual's beliefs or self-concept about identity will have the greatest impact on outcome, regardless of circumstances. If influencers reinforce autonomy, an internal locus of control, optimism, and healthy self-esteem, they will contribute to resilience and improve outcomes. If influencers reinforce neediness, diminish autonomy, create or reinforce an external locus of control or negative expectations, they will diminish resilience and outcomes.

James Farr explains it this way:

> "We end up inventing much of the "out-there" reality to fit the perceptions we have put in place to screen and react to incoming stimuli. Thus, for example, if we enter a situation and "see" it as threatening, our mind will cause us to react defensively and perhaps aggressively. In turn, that defensive, aggressive behavior will cause people to incline toward being unfriendly and difficult with us, thereby creating a hostile and aggressive experience—just as we perceived it in the first place. On the other hand, had we seen the situation as friendly and acted accordingly, the environment may very well have presented itself to us as friendly and satisfying."[80]

Beliefs

For example, if someone believes they are the best at something, but someone else wins, their mind will create a back story that explains the other person's win without shattering their belief. The back story might give credit to something that seems unfair or dishonest to protect their belief that they are the best—even without evidence to support the conclusion. The mere fact that someone beat them when *they're the best* is sufficient evidence for the subconscious mind to create such a back story. The back story provides a way to continue a belief that is not accurate. The mind is not interested in accuracy so much as it is interested in consistency and reinforcing existing

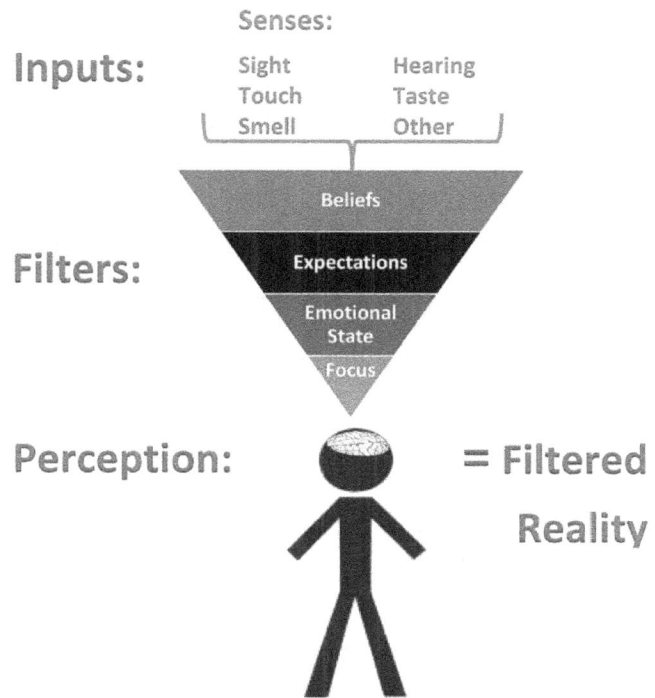

beliefs, even when they are ill-founded and interfere with one's ability to achieve strongly desired goals.

In 1991, Talbot told us that thoughts actually create meaning for events in life. For example, if someone cancels an appointment the individual who is told the meeting will not occur is free to

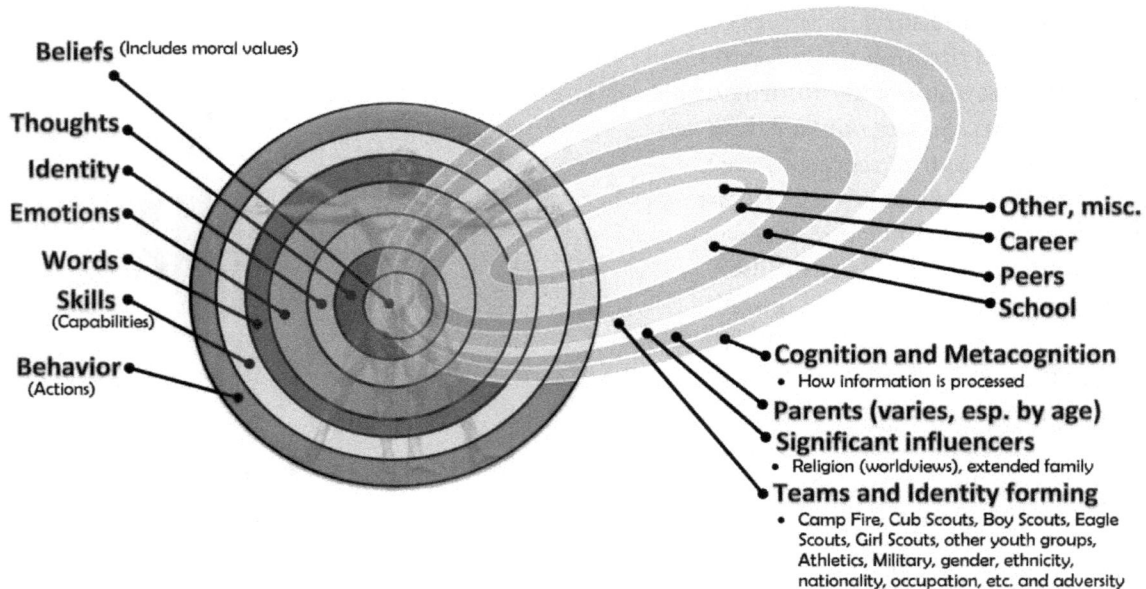

Beliefs (Includes moral values)

Thoughts

Identity

Emotions

Words

Skills
(Capabilities)

Behavior
(Actions)

Other, misc.
Career
Peers
School

Cognition and Metacognition
• How information is processed

Parents (varies, esp. by age)
Significant influencers
• Religion (worldviews), extended family

Teams and Identity forming
• Camp Fire, Cub Scouts, Boy Scouts, Eagle Scouts, Girl Scouts, other youth groups, Athletics, Military, gender, ethnicity, nationality, occupation, etc. and adversity

assign meaning to the event. Even when a reason is given, the reason may or may not be accepted by the receiver. If the reason is not accepted, the individual will create a reason to explain the event to himself. That explanation may be one that feels good or one that feels bad. Whichever is chosen, the event will be experienced (felt emotionally) by the individual as if the assigned reason is true.

Stories from individuals who learned how the mind works to create illusions often refer to the time before they knew as before they were awake. That story provides a bridge over the gap between the worldviews. Significant shifts in worldviews require a bridge for the mind to make sense of the situation in order to maintain mental health.

Our mind has a variety of layers, as indicated in the diagram.
- Changes at inner levels affect every larger layer
- Changes at larger layers can have an impact on inner layers, but it is the more difficult path to change
- Changing the outer levels without changing the inner layers creates conflict that the inner layer will eventually win
- Changes made at outer layers that are assimilated into the inner layer can become permanent

For example, using willpower to force daily exercise can lead to an identity change regarding exercise but most people fail before they achieve an identity change. Defining oneself as an exerciser uses less willpower because over time it creates a belief about self that is then supported by the individuals thoughts and therefore no longer results in resource depletion along the way.

A couple of keys are to recognize, in yourself, when you believe something is true for you but not for others. Remember, beliefs are able to help or hinder. They are not all good or all bad. Most importantly, the brain does not differentiate between those that serve our higher good, and those that thwart it. The mind *irrationally* attempts to support whatever we have decided to believe.

Actually, *irrationally attempts to support* what we have decided to believe is probably too harsh. I believe the brain is designed as if we understand the impact our beliefs have on our experience, so when we have a belief it acts as if we have deliberately chosen that belief and understand the ramifications of it. Unfortunately, most people have no idea how their beliefs affect their thinking and experiences.

A couple of things may help you identify beliefs that are not serving you. If you find yourself saying, 'I want to but,' you are pointing out a belief that limits you. The second is when you believe that another has it better than you and have an excuse or explanation for why that is. In 2010, the American Psychological Association reported that "willpower is the most commonly cited barrier to making lifestyle changes. 32% of Americans say a lack of willpower prevented them from making a change."[81] The need for a new view of how to effectively make desired changes is evident in the fact that so many struggle to make changes using willpower. If they would change their beliefs first, the behavioral changes would be much easier to implement.

Willpower is required when there is a struggle between self-concept (beliefs) and desired behavior. In the illustration, the elephant represents a belief. The people tugging on the rope represent good reasons to change and the desire to change a habit. Because beliefs lead to thoughts which then lead to words and actions, willpower fights a losing battle against underlying beliefs. The battle will continue until the belief is changed or the individual gives up the attempt to change behavior with willpower alone. No willpower is required when beliefs are changed first because willpower is essentially a fight between beliefs and desired actions.

Baumeister, Vohs, and Tice reported that "Inadequate self-control has been linked to behavioral and impulse-control problems, including overeating, alcohol and drug abuse, crime and violence, overspending, sexually impulsive behavior, unwanted pregnancy, and smoking . . . and it may also be linked to emotional problems, school underachievement, lack of persistence, various failures at task performance, relationship problems, and dissolution and more."[82]

When an action is consistent with one's beliefs, it feels natural and does not deplete the energy required for self-control. When the action conflicts with one's beliefs about the self or world, self-control is required and the energy required for self-control can become depleted, leading to a decreased ability to control one's own behavior. For example, non-smokers don't need willpower to prevent them from smoking whereas an x-smoker will (at last occasionally) require willpower in order not to succumb to the urge to smoke.

"A match between implicit (beliefs) and explicit (conscious desire) in goal achievement is associated with adaptive outcomes."[83] When our beliefs and our desired behaviors conflict, beliefs win. Beliefs are simply neuropathways created by repeatedly thinking a thought. New beliefs can be created by reinforcing thoughts the individual wants to believe.

Just as a fiction writer creates a character who then writes their own dialogue, individuals create the character that is themself, and the outer *accoutrements* fill in thoughts, words, action, health, wealth, and love.

Not only can an employee choose to define himself, he can choose how. By doing so, his definition of self changes the way he thinks about himself. His definition of self equates to his beliefs about himself. When an employee defines himself with deliberate intent about how he wants to show up in the world, he recognizes quickly when he begins to stumble into something that is contrary to his definition of self because he will feel the discord via Emotional Guidance and can make in-the-moment course corrections in the early stages while they are still easy.

Until we consciously define ourself as the person we want to be, complete with the characteristics and qualities we wish to possess, we are vulnerable. We allow others' opinions and treatment of us to affect how we feel, to devalue us and our sense of worth. We leave the door to our self-esteem not only unlocked, but open to undesired intrusions. We feel defensive. Before we even arrive at the office we may have had dozens of fearful thoughts hoping that our boss does not criticize us or that our co-workers include us in conversations or lunch invitations lest we feel demeaned or left out (unwanted). We may have lost sleep worrying that a co-worker was still working on a project while we slumbered and might get ahead of us because of their greater dedication or fewer non-work obligations.

When an employee changes her beliefs to align with her goals and desires, she does not need willpower to force herself to comply because doing things that support her motion forward feels good. The same is true of actions she refrains from doing because not doing them is consistent with her definition of self.

When willpower is the primary method of change, Baumeister says people "have to resist many desires and impulses and must control themselves in other ways, and so over the course of a typical day many people gradually become ego-depleted. The result is that they become increasingly likely to give in to impulses and desires that they would have resisted successfully earlier in the day. . . During the state of ego-depletion, people become less helpful and more aggressive, prone to overeat, misbehave sexually, express more prejudice, and in other ways do things that they may later regret."[84]

For example, after numerous unsuccessful attempts to quit smoking in the 80's, I decided to become a non-smoker. I spent six weeks changing my beliefs about myself with no attempt to change my behavior. In fact, I began wanting to change my behavior before the date I was going to be a non-smoker and had to use willpower to continue smoking until the day I had selected for my transformation to a non-smoker. I went from being a 2-pack-a-day Marlboro girl to a non-smoker and after the first three days of nicotine withdrawal, there was no struggle and no need for willpower. I had successfully convinced my mind that as of that date I would be a non-smoker so my beliefs supported my new status. My thoughts followed my beliefs. I did not have to fight them using willpower.

Recognizing the settings of one's belief filter is the one that is the most difficult to determine alone because an individuals' reality is perceived as if the beliefs are true. We simply believe it is reality—not belief. It is often easier for someone else to see beliefs that may be hindering another person's ability to thrive. Today, our society tends to reject observations that could be extremely helpful. The story I shared earlier about my girlfriend who was not taking action on buying a house because she believed she couldn't get a loan is an example of this. She took no action because her mind would not present her with ideas that would lead to those actions as long as her belief was that she could not do it. If she had understood her emotional guidance, the negative emotion she felt when she thought about not being able to buy a new home would have let to her reappraising the thought and she would have decided to try without needing someone else to encourage her to do so.

This is not a matter of intelligence. That same girlfriend is now a senior vice president at a Fortune 100 company. However, beliefs about intelligence can limit intelligence. If someone believes they are dumb they will not do things that smart people do such as read books smart people would read or even pursue educational goals or careers that they associate with smart people.

One way to identify beliefs is to look for things where you believe something is true for you but it is clearly not true for others. If you believe you can't do something that others are able to do, it's probably a belief, not reality. Many people will argue for their own limitations, but if they've learned to interpret their emotions accurately they will recognize the discord they feel and the energy drain they experience when they do.

Expectations

An individual's expectations are one of the filters the mind uses to determine what unconscious information the conscious mind will be made aware of. The expectation filter plays a massive role in success. If an individual expects exceptional opportunities, he is far more likely to spot them. If he does not expect much, the opportunity could be right in front of him, and he will not recognize it. The brain will not pass information that contradicts or exceeds expectations to the conscious mind, even when the information is right in front of the person.

For example, Jerry Rice is a veteran of twenty seasons in the NFL and is "widely considered to be the greatest wide receiver in NFL history and among the greatest NFL players overall." He won three Super Bowl rings playing for the San Francisco 49ers. The day before Super Bowl 2016 a news report showed a man who had hired an Uber driver to take him somewhere and, from a hidden camera, recorded the driver asking the passenger (who was in the front seat) which team he supported. The passenger said he was a lifelong 49ers fan because he was born and raised in San Francisco. A lifelong 49er fan was being driven by Jerry Rice and did not recognize his driver until Rice introduced himself. Football fans know that the most popular players are interviewed frequently. This man would have seen Jerry Rice without his helmet hundreds of time and still didn't recognize his face or voice—because he did not expect Jerry Rice to be his Uber driver.

Expectations greatly impact accomplishments. Learning to use the power of expectation in your life, and in the lives of others, leads to significant improvements. Researchers have repeatedly shown that expectations create a self-fulfilling prophecy. The prophecy can be about our own accomplishments or about another's accomplishments. Expectations influence outcomes bi-directionally. High expectations improve outcomes. Low expectations decrease outcomes. Emotional Guidance will provide positive feedback supporting high expectations. Bosses who understood their Emotional Guidance could overcome subconscious biases that cause negative expectations of underprivileged workers. Without conscious interference, low expectations often become self-fulfilling prophecies.

A bias toward optimism or pessimism influences assumptions individuals make about the future, as do people's past experiences. An experience in the past that resembles a current situation may cause the brain to interpret it as the same even when there are significant differences. One way to ensure one's expectations are serving one's highest good is to think more deeply about why the person views things the way he does. Emotional Guidance is of great value in helping discern better ways to perceive our environment; it contains more wisdom than the brain.[85]

There are also many examples of the way humans do not do things considered impossible but once one person accomplishes it, whether it is learning to walk again after a spinal cord injury or running the first 4-minute mile, others who hear of it become able to do the same. Lack of belief in one's ability to accomplish something plays an important role in whether or not we even try.

When someone uses what others have accomplished to decide what is possible, they limit themselves to the successes of their predecessors. Emotional Guidance reinforces the belief that a goal is attainable even when it has never been done before. Individuals who have practiced using their guidance and trust it will know that hope is not misplaced and that there is a way. Hope opens up possibilities that do not exist when one believes a situation is hopeless.

Developing familiarity with one's own guidance system to the point where trust is established can provide as much advantage as knowing someone else has accomplished a goal. It opens the possibility of not needing anyone else to do it first before someone can believe it is possible. Stories about walking after spinal cord injuries are a good example. When it was believed hopeless, it was unheard of for someone to recover the ability to walk. Today there are frequent stories. Some are the result of new techniques, but one has to ask, would anyone have developed those techniques if they believed it was hopeless, or did having hope stimulate new research? Much of what people believe they *can't* do is the result of a belief that they can't.

In a classic *Harvard Business Review* article, J. Sterling Livingston wrote "What has long been recognized by teachers, physicians, and behavioral scientists holds true for management: One person's expectations shape another person's behavior. When a manager has high expectations, employees are likely to excel; if expectations are low, employees will likely respond with poor performance."[86]

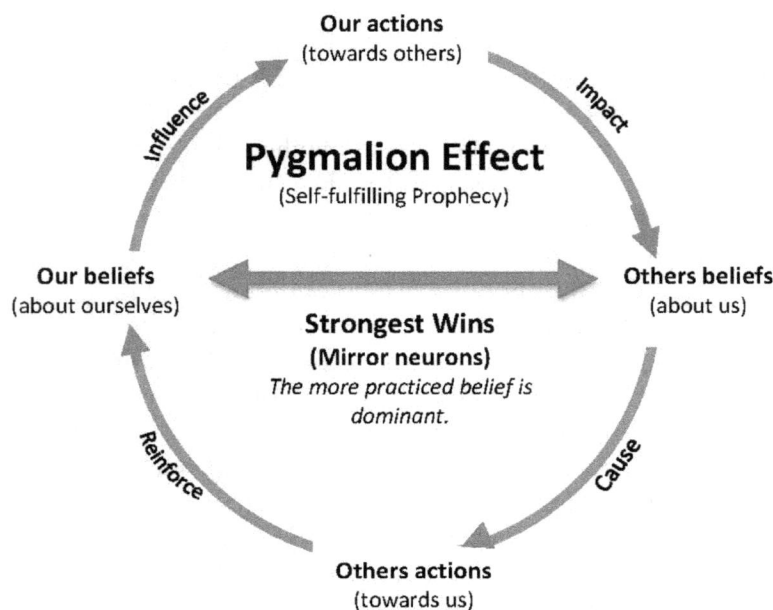

People want to control others, often because they have low expectations of them or don't trust them to do what they agreed to do. Expectations influence the outcome. In a study by Rosenthal and Jacobson an elementary teacher was told that two of her incoming students were exceptionally bright. The person who advised her of this did not have firsthand knowledge—he was merely the messenger. The two students were actually performing very poorly.

At the end of the year, the two previously poorly performing students were performing exceptionally well. A possible explanation exists in quantum physics where they have discovered mirror

Pygmalion Effect
(Self-fulfilling Prophecy)

Our actions (towards others)

Influence

Impact

Our beliefs (about ourselves)

Others beliefs (about us)

Strongest Wins
(Mirror neurons)
The more practiced belief is dominant.

Reinforce

Cause

Others actions (towards us)

Adapted from an illustration by Gregg Swanston.
Mirror Neurons is my addition.

neurons, which Alexandra Bruce tells us explain how others' high or low expectations influence another's' behavior. Our brains sync with one another. The brain that is sync'd to has the most stable belief. If an employee's self-esteem is solid, someone else's low opinion of him won't disturb his sense of self because the other person hasn't thought about him nearly as much as he has thought about himself. But if he hasn't practiced a self-supportive belief about himself and someone else comes along with a negative one, he is vulnerable.

They don't even have to have thought about him personally to have more stable beliefs about him because beliefs may be based on a label that the person attaches to him. The *label* doesn't even have to be accurate. They could have negative stereotypical beliefs that they believe fit him based on their perception of him. That belief about him will fight with his unstable belief about self and theirs will win if it is more stable than his beliefs about himself.

The same thing that happens with students happens in the working world. Bosses with low expectations of an employee or group of employees get what they expect. An early study at the Massachusetts Institute of Technology by David E. Berlew and Douglas T. Hall concluded that:

"The results indicate that the amount individuals contribute to an organization accounts for 52 percent of the variance in their success at the end of five years, those contributions being influenced both by what the company expects, particularly in the first year, and to a lesser extent by personality factors."[87]

But that doesn't have to be the case. J. Sterling Livingston identified a group of sales staff where the manager's expectations of the group were average, but the assistant manager strongly believed the group could perform at the level of another group that was considered *superstaff*. The assistant manager's belief in the group's ability to succeed was greater than the manager's belief that they were average, and they achieved results that far exceeded expectations for the group.

Any manager can cultivate within herself high expectations of her employees. Any individual can cultivate within himself high personal expectations which will override any lower expectations as long as they maintain their belief in their ability to achieve them. In both cases, Emotional Guidance will reinforce self-actualizing thoughts, words, and actions with positive emotions and support healthy self-esteem by reinforcing affirmations that include high self-regard and high regard for others.

Seeing others for their potential rather than their current state helps them achieve more of their potential. This is true whether they ever speak a word about it to them. The best way to help others is to create strong positive impressions of their potential in the privacy of your mind when you are not with them. This practice works with family and with students, employees, and even bosses.

The Pygmalion Effect (or Rosenthal as it is sometimes called) is well-documented beginning with Rosenthal's experiments in the mid-1960's and has been confirmed repeatedly including research in 2011 by Jie Chang.[88] Unfortunately, knowledge is not sufficient to prevent teachers from impacting minority and low-income students with negative expectations. Rubie-Davies, Hattie, and Hamilton confirmed that high or low teacher expectations of students affect the outcome of the students and found significant evidence that low teacher expectations negatively impact the outcome of many Black and Maori children in New Zealand.[89]

Educating teachers about the Pygmalion Effect is not enough. A district-level school administrator relayed to me that her teachers understand the Pygmalion Effect intellectually, but still (unfairly) perceive students from poor families as having less potential.

An awareness that minority and low-income students may not have lived up to their potential because of low expectations may help employer's recognize and benefit from the untapped potential of individuals whose past performance was far below their potential. Coaching and positive expectation can bring out a lot of hidden potential and win significant loyalty.

Surprisingly, even rats respond to experimenter expectations. Students were told that some lab rats were bred to be smart and would run the maze faster than other rats that were not as intelligent. The rats were actually no different in terms of breeding. The rats the students believed would learn faster did learn faster. This points to a quantum level explanation because nothing in Classic Physics accounts for human beliefs affecting rodent behavior.

Emotional Guidance supports the development and maintenance of healthy self-esteem. Self-concept is simply one's beliefs about oneself and the thoughts that they think because of those beliefs. When beliefs change, thoughts change. Once someone has used their Emotional Guidance for a month or two, they develop a high degree of trust in its guidance that can help them feel confident refuting life-long negative perceptions of self.

Self-concept is critical to employee engagement. Repeated studies point to core self-evaluations as the primary factor impacting employee engagement. Who a person perceives themself to be is part of their self-concept. If they see themselves as someone who messes up, it leads to more mistakes. If they see ourself as capable, they will display greater levels of confidence.

291 9th graders in a predominantly Latino high school participated in a study about the relationship between behavioral self-concept and alcohol use. Students with low versus high self-concept had a predicted probability 50 – 350% higher for adverse drinking behaviors.[90] Self-concept directly affects behavior, first in our thoughts, then in our words and actions.

In 2014, Khanlou and Wray conducted a review of the existing literature on resilience from a public health perspective. They stated "Resilience is seen as an important element to maintaining and promoting child and youth mental health, and as a life-long buffer to potential threats to wellbeing over time and transition."[91]

I first learned about the brain's **plasticity** when I read David Shenk's book, *The Genius in All of Us,* and found the fact that age would not decrease my ability to learn liberating. In *Mindsight,* Dan Siegel wrote, "The brain changes physically in response to experience, and new mental skills can be acquired with intentional effort, with focused awareness and concentration" or, more simply, "Neurons that fire together wire together."[92]

Beliefs about self and the world have an effect on the thoughts the person thinks.

Existing habits of thought determine what new beliefs and self-image arises as the result of an adverse life event. The habits of thought also determine the actions that follow.

- A belief that one just has to live with the debilitating emotional pain of loss following a trauma makes it unlikely that the person will reach out to a professional for help or even search the self-help aisles of the local bookstore or library.
- A believe that a professional can help but that the help would adversely impact one's career makes it unlikely the person will reach out to a professional for help, although this person might try to find a book that will help him deal with the situation. I have memories of not wanting other people to see the books I was buying and even of buying books to carry on top that I considered more appropriate or less stigmatizing.
- A belief that a professional can help but that society might ridicule her for obtaining counseling makes it unlikely the person will reach out to a professional for help.
- A belief that a professional will be of benefit and that it is worth the price (financially, career-wise, or stigma-risk) would be present in an individual who reaches out to a professional for help.

The event itself has an impact. A violent rape, car accident, domestic violence, or repeated exposure to violence and death in a war zone or as a first responder can all lead to adverse outcomes. But in each type of situation there are those whose suffering continues endlessly and those who seem to recover and live lives that they enjoy. It is mindset more than the event itself that leads to the outcome. "The mental construction of our daily activities, more than the activity itself, defines our reality."[93] A negative mental attitude is a self-imposed handicap. It makes a person more susceptible to adverse outcomes from traumatic events.

If scientists would study the connection between mindset and habits of thought as I did, they would discover that it is mindset more than the event itself that leads to the outcome.

Emotional State

There are thousands of variations of beliefs individuals can hold on any topic. All of them affect the outcome. Individuals who think the first three thoughts (above) will feel negative emotion. That negative emotion is telling them there is a different thought they could find and believe about the same subject that would serve their highest good better than the thought they are thinking.

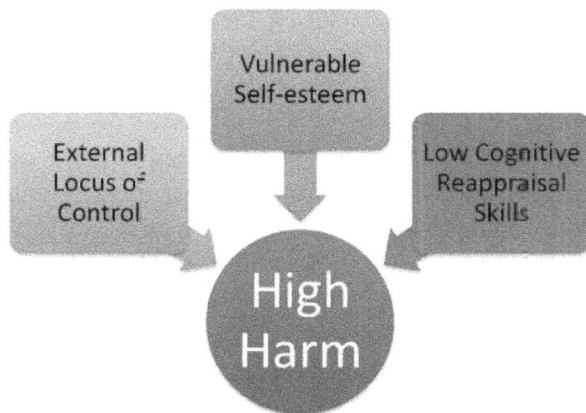

Negative emotion does not validate the thought that brings it forth. Negative emotion indicates that the thought the employee is thinking is not the best thought she could have about that subject. Yes, from the perspective she's viewing it, the emotion she feels is valid. But in most cases, negative emotion means: "Find another perspective; there is one that would help you feel better right now."

A traumatic event affects different people differently. Individuals who have one or a combination of factors that include an external locus of control, vulnerable self-esteem, or low cognitive reappraisal skills are more likely to experience significant harm with lasting adverse effects. An individual who has an internal locus of control, stable self-esteem, and cognitive reappraisal skills is less likely to experience low or no psychological harm from the same event.

One of the reasons employee engagement is so low (and that the political climate is reflecting so much anger) is because of the Emotional State filter. The way the mind works is it assumes people are focusing in ways that bring about the emotions they want to experience. It acts as if we know that how we focus determines how we feel and wants to help us maintain our chronic emotional state. Since most people are completely unaware of this, it does more harm than good in our current environment. Understanding how the mind makes decisions about what information it makes our conscious mind aware of increase the employee's ability to actively change her emotional state.

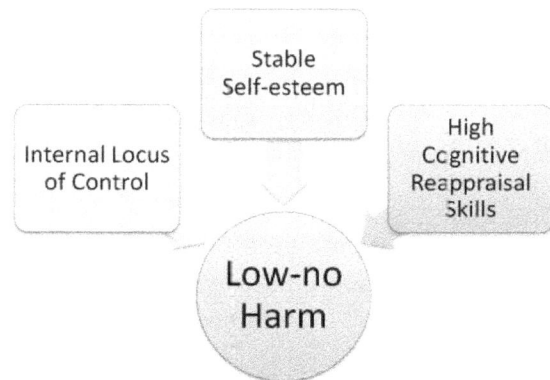

The economic downturn made life harder for many people and it made life seem harder for most people. The 24/7 negative news media exacerbated the problem like never before. Research shows that people who are afraid will watch the news more often. This led to chronic states of financial fear that set the filters in the minds of many people on the fear setting. Now their minds are doing much as the news media does, scouring their world for things that match their fearful emotional state.

Their minds will ignore good things and focus on things that elicit more of their chronic emotional state—even though that state is very unpleasant. They simply do not know how their minds work. If they did, they could deliberately refocus on things that feel better and after a while their filter would help them do that. This is not explaining the left or the right—it explains the strength of the division. Both are blaming others for their problems. Both are seeing the worst of times even when there is much that is good in the world.

Focusing on problems narrows cognitive function and decreases pro-social behaviors.

It is a good idea to create a personal barometer to see how your mind is focusing. You can use your Emotional Guidance, but I find an external barometer useful. A barometer will act as a reminder by helping you recognize when you've moved away from the emotional state you prefer. I check my barometer every time I leave my neighborhood. If I am noticing my neighbors' weeds as I drive out of the neighborhood, I'm not focused in the best possible way. If I am noticing their flowers, I'm golden.

Paul and Moser conducted a meta-analysis of 237 cross-sectional and 87 longitudinal studies, finding that psychological problems affected 34% of the unemployed compared to 16% of employed individuals. They were also able to determine that unemployment is not only correlated to mental distress, it causes it. Early researchers assumed that mental health problems led to unemployment and while that is also true in some instances, Paul and Moser found the negative mental impact of unemployment is significant absent pre-existing mental health issues and "Intervention programs have positive effects on mental health among continuously unemployed people. The effect was of medium size."[94] The risk of mental health problems rises during the first nine months of unemployment and affects male blue collar workers the most. The study concluded that "The result is a clear and unequivocal warning that unemployment is a severe risk for public mental health that must be fought with all possible means."[95]

Because thoughts are largely due to habits of thought, re-employment won't necessarily cure mental illnesses that develop during unemployment. This could subsequently be a factor in low engagement. Managers who do not understand the matrix between thoughts, behavior, and emotional state may feel an employee who was hired when unemployed should feel gratitude for the position that is not being demonstrated and resent the employee's lack of gratitude.

Employee engagement is significantly affected by the employee's emotional state, self-esteem, locus of control, and the ability of the role to elicit both a sense of autonomy and a bond with the organization. Employees bring a lot of emotional baggage to work with them. Much of it lingers because our educational system and society do not teach skills and processes that help us manage life's upheavals. It's been a decade since researchers discovered the purpose of emotions that has been taught for eight decades was based on an erroneous hypothesis, yet our schools have not yet adjusted their curriculums to reflect the updated understanding.

Focus

For example, shortly before I left corporate America to start my own firm one of my employees was complimentary toward me in the exit interview but uncomplimentary about my boss. This was not the first employee to lambast his management style in an exit interview and after he was called on the carpet for it, he was upset with me because it was my employee who gave the negative feedback about him. He demanded that I not allow it to happen again.

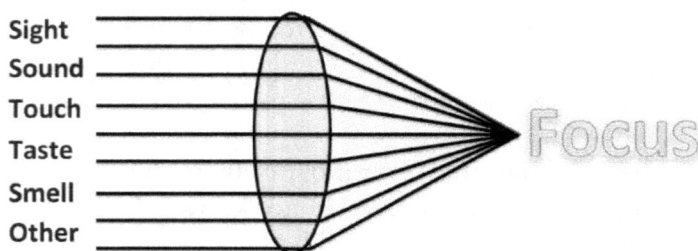

Now, to be honest, he was one of my all-time favorite bosses. But it was a small company and he (the CEO) had far more contact with the employees in lower positions than most CEOs. If he was preoccupied, he could walk past an employee and not speak. Some of the lower echelon employees felt as if they weren't valued or respected when he did that, but that interpretation reflected their own insecurity about their value and worth—not what he intended to communicate. He wouldn't have kept anyone on board if he felt they did not add value to the organization.

He wanted me to be responsible for how my employee viewed him. If I'd had the freedom to teach them how to increase their emotional state I would have had the ability to have a positive influence. But it is unrealistic for a company to expect good reviews of management after an involuntary termination even when it is a layoff. It is extremely difficult to be unbiased in those circumstances.

Focus is the fourth main filter. It is the easiest to adjust. Simply shifting our attention to a different subject can change our emotional state. We can also plan to focus more on one aspect of our lives than another by setting goals.

Generally, successful people are better at focusing than less successful people. After all, the ability to focus is essential if one is to achieve one's goals. Employees in lower positions would be much better off if they asked themselves why he might not have acknowledged them instead of assuming his lack of acknowledgment of their presence was personal. The ability to recognize that there is more than one possible explanation for something is an aspect of psychological flexibility. If the employee understood how to accurately interpret his Emotional Guidance he would have known the negative emotion he felt when he observed the boss's lack of recognition meant he perceived the situation in a way that was moving in opposition to that where his self-actualized self would be found.

5: Factors that Impact Employee Engagement

Responsibility equals accountability equals ownership. And a sense of ownership is the most powerful weapon a team or organization can have.
Pat Summitt

Many factors that impact employee engagement deserve mention. Factors that do not have their own chapter will be found in this section. The key to understanding how to improve employee engagement is recognizing that humans always attempt to maximize positive emotions. How we believe we will feel if we do something informs our decision-making process. Most people don't recognize consciously how large a factor feeling good is to their decision-making process. They may believe they are very logical.

Research has demonstrated that we make emotional decisions and then rationalize the decision using logic but the actual decision is made using emotion. People make choices that will optimize their positive emotions. Sometimes those choices are to forgo things they want because the emotional price doesn't adequately offset the anticipated pleasure.

The process is also heavily influenced by focus. One aspect of that focus is one's goals and whether short-term or long-term goals have been given more prominence in the individual's thoughts. Since many people don't make long-term plans they are ruled by short-term goals, which are usually less useful in the long term. Developing a habit of making long-term plans serves individuals well although balance is also important.

I'll share an example of a decision I made early in my career that was influenced by my tendency to make long-term plans. A woman I'd worked with and spent some time with after-hours had been fired and went on welfare. I learned she was being paid more on welfare than I was making by working 40-hours a week. I was 18-years old, on my own, and going to college part-time at night. I remember wondering why I was working when I could have more money by not working. The thought process didn't take long but I've always vividly remembered it.

When I thought out into the future I realized that by working my future would be better and hers would be the same, my decision was clear. I never again contemplated whether it would be better to go on welfare because doing so would not support my long-term plans. I shudder to think what I might have decided if I had not already developed the habit of making 1, 3, 5, 10 and 20-year plans.

On the flip side, too much of a long-term planning focus can rob the present of its potential for fun and joy. A mix of long-term and short-term goals is best. In fact, my focus in my 20's was heavily weighted toward long-term goals. I often tell the story of learning how to have fun in my mid-30's because I didn't know how to play. I even decided to have my babies close together because I recognized my inability to play. At the time I thought it was just my personality.

A number of different high-level constructs are used to explain how to increase employee engagement which can make understanding unnecessarily complicated. When you break the high-level constructs down into their component parts, it becomes easy to see that the high-level constructs share many common factors as illustrated in the chart on the next page. Citations in the chart can be found in Appendix IV.

High Core Self-Evaluations (CSE)	Resilience	Psychological Capital (PsyCap)	Growth Mindset	Happiness	Psychological Flexibility
Internal Locus of Control Healthy Self-esteem Self-efficacy (task & general) Emotional Stability	Internal Locus of Control Healthy Self-esteem Optimism	Hope Optimism Self-efficacy* Resilience*	Internal Locus of Control	Internal Locus of Control Healthy self-esteem Optimism Metacognitive skills Hope or better Priority = happy Positive habits of thought Self-awareness	Internal Locus of Control Metacognitive skills
Outcomes:	**Outcomes:**	**Outcomes:**	**Outcomes:**	**Outcomes:**	**Outcomes:**
Higher motivation[1]	Greater task persistence[2]	Manager rated performance[3]	Sets higher goals[4]	Better cognitive abilities[5,6,7,8,9]	Increased Resilience[10]
Greater task persistence[11]		Job Satisfaction[12]	Open to learning[13]	Long-term success[14,15]	
Higher work engagement[16]		Trust[17]		Manager rated performance[18]	
Higher commitment[19]		Higher work engagement[20]		Job Satisfaction[21]	
		Higher commitment[22]		Trust[23]	
		Lower absenteeism[24]		Higher work engagement[25]	
				Higher commitment[26]	
				Lower absenteeism[27]	
				Better pregnancy outcomes[28,29]	
				Better negotiation outcomes[30]	
				Lower crime[31]	
				Better Relationships[32]	
				Better goal attainment[33]	
				Higher Emotional Intelligence	
				Lower stress[55,56,57,58]	

Outcomes that are the same for all high-level constructs:

Better physical health[34,35,36,37,38,39,40,41,42]
Better mental health[43,44,45,46,47,48,49,50]
Better behavioral health[51,52]
Better pro-health choices[53,54]

* The literature for PsyCap treats resilience as a single construct when it is really another high-level construct, resulting in duplication of optimism because PsyCap literature mentions optimism, but not the other components of resilience, healthy self-esteem and an internal locus of control. PsyCap is essentially Resilience plus hope and self-efficacy. Optimism and hope are not identical.

Lyubomirsky, King, and Diener are prominent positive psychologists. They "extend the earlier work in predicting that chronically happy people are in general more successful, and that their success is in large part a consequence of their happiness and frequent experience of positive affect [good-feeling emotions]. Although the vast majority of research on emotions has been on negative states, a body of literature has now accumulated that highlights the importance of positive emotions in people's long-term flourishing."[96]

There are many moving parts when it comes to the underlying cause of employee engagement. Researchers have documented so many of the behaviors and traits that increase engagement that understanding all of them feels overwhelming to some and cumbersome to most. Working at the level of the factors can cause frustration and, as the consistent low engagement numbers demonstrate, stall progress and in some cases lead to unproductive strategies. Counterproductive strategies can occur in two ways. One is when the manager thinks he understands the concept and doesn't, therefore misapplying misunderstood information in the real world. The second is when a manager understands a concept and applies it correctly but does not understand the unique traits of the employee she's interacting with and the strategy is not productive with that person.

There is a way to simplify the engagement discussion. It requires a deeper dive in order to understand what people ultimately want and why they want it. When the pieces of the puzzle at that level are understood, the higher order concepts can be easily understood and seen for what they are—human attempts to create labels that hope to explain human behavior. The problem with labels is there are always exceptions to the label that mandate yet another label.

For example, when I was a child there were two generally recognized gender categories, male and female. Today a popular social media site recognizes 58 gender categories. I'm not saying it's wrong to have more categories, only that it is complicated and makes understanding difficult. In the same way, employee engagement experts create definitions that managers have to learn and they seldom compare their high-level definition to another one that is nearly the same. Managers can come away thinking things are far more complex than they are when they don't understand the overlap between the constructs. In this chapter, many of the commonly used terms relating to employee engagement will be defined. More detailed discussions of some high-level constructs have their own chapter.

The following diagrams illustrate the factors that lead to engagement using the categories from scientific literature used in the chart at the beginning of the chapter. Through a series of reductions, the roots of employee engagement can be simplified to one concept.

Diagram1 reflects the major factors the scientific literature suggests are required

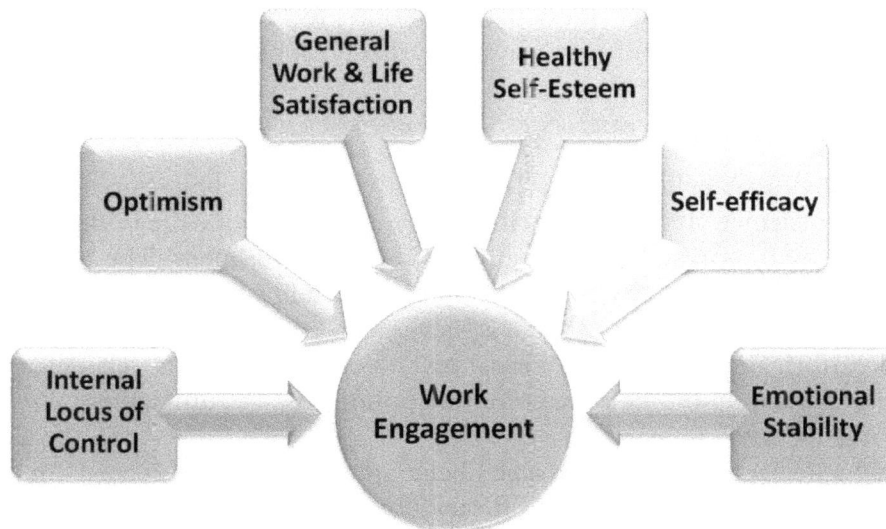

Diagram 1

for engagement.

Optimism

Optimism is loosely related to hope and includes confidence or a belief (faith/trust) that the future will be good or successful. Parashar tells us that "optimism is correlated with many positive life outcomes including increased life expectancy, general health, better mental health, increased success in sports and work, greater recovery rates from heart operations and better coping strategies when faced with adversity."[97] A historical view of optimism as delusional and Pollyannaish is still believed by many individuals today. Although popularized by both Voltaire with his *Candide* essay and Freud, who "decided that optimism was widespread but illusory . . . Sophocles and Nietzsche argued that it [optimism] prolongs human suffering: better to face the hard facts of reality."[98] But later evidence revealed "that psychologically healthy people in particular showed the positivity bias."[99] The evidence supporting the benefits of optimism soundly refutes those historic views. It is still easy to find people who believe the early views and education is the only way to change their mind about optimism.

Seligman developed a program to teach children optimism that protected them from depression for two years, but without boosters the protective factor faded.[100] When you add Emotional Guidance to the equation there is continuous positive reinforcement that acts to provide boosters at no costs.

The obituary of a North Carolina icon, Ralph Ketner, repeated the forward to his book, *Five Fast Pennies*, "Throughout my life, I faced an uncommon number of obstacles – orphan, child of the depression, no money. But I was blessed with an 'attitude,' a point of view. I saw 'problems' as opportunities in disguise.' I saw a 'lemon' and made 'lemonade." I started 'thinking' before 'starting to work [at age 9].' I have never had ambitious goals for myself, but have always done my very best on each job." For early investors in Mr. Ketner's Food Lion, every $28 returned a cool million.

I met Mr. Ketner shortly after founding Happiness 1st Institute and after enthusiastically telling him about the benefits of happiness to employers and my plans to build a nationwide company he encouraged me to take the company international. He was 90-years-old and had just given an hour long speech when he encouraged me to think bigger. His encouragement inspired me and his optimism affirmed my own.

General Work and Life Satisfaction is an overall evaluation of one's feelings and attitudes about their life at a particular point in time. It is one of many ways to evaluate happiness, or a thereof. Happiness has its own chapter.

Self-Efficacy

"Self-efficacy refers to an individual's belief in his or her capacity to execute behaviors necessary to produce specific performance attainments. Self-efficacy reflects confidence in the ability to exert control over one's own motivation, behavior, and social environment. These cognitive self-evaluations influence all manner of human experience, including the goals for which people strive, the amount of energy expended toward goal achievement, and likelihood of attaining particular levels of behavioral performance. Unlike traditional psychological constructs, self-efficacy beliefs are hypothesized to vary depending on the domain of functioning and circumstances surrounding the occurrence of behavior."[101]

Psychologist Albert Bandura defines self-efficacy as one's belief in one's ability to succeed in specific situations or to accomplish a task. Individual self-efficacy plays a major role in how the person sets goals and approaches tasks and challenges.[102]

Healthy Self-esteem

An employee with healthy self-esteem has a positive overall opinion of self and believes they deserve the respect of others. Low self-esteem leads to negative self-evaluations and negatively biased expectations of one's potential.

Who we perceive ourself to be is part of our self-concept (core self-evaluations). If we see ourselves as someone who messes up, it leads to more mistakes. If we see ourself as capable, we will display greater levels of confidence.

There are some core beliefs that lead to healthy self-esteem:

- At my core, the person I really am is good. This is true of others as well. Departures from my essential goodness are a form of illness. When I feel happy it is a sign that I am being more of my potential, good self. When I am not feeling happy, I have skills I can use to feel better before I take actions I may later regret.
- I can use my guidance to feel positive feedback when I think well about myself and others.
- Others' opinions represent their emotional state and not anything about my true value or worth.
- I, just like everyone else, provide value and worth to this world by my presence.
- I, and everyone else, does the best they can in any given moment. My best in the moment is not necessarily my potential best. My emotional state, sleep, nutrition, health, stress, meta-cognitive skills, and hydration can negatively or positively affect my best performance in any given moment.
- When I make a mistake I will learn from it and appreciate that I now know more than before and then I will move on.

It is useful to consider in this regard that high self-esteem has been included consistently among criteria used to define positive mental health. Yet an equally prominent theme in these conceptualizations is the interdependence of self-esteem with a range of other facets of positive mental health, such as a sense of mastery, autonomy, accurate perceptions of reality, a sense of optimism, interpersonal relatedness, and responsible behavior toward others. Only when self-esteem is pursued and attained in ways that promote these broad underpinnings of positive mental health does it seem reasonable to expect feelings of self-worth to be implicated consistently in overall health and well-being."[103]

> *The model assumes, in particular, that it is the patterning of both the level of self-esteem (and its various facets) in combination with the strategies relied on to acquire and sustain self-esteem that will be most influential in shaping outcomes. . . The combination of high self-esteem and adaptive processes for acquiring and sustaining self-esteem then would be assumed to promote overall health and well-being, with positive functioning in different areas (e.g., behavioral) having a reciprocal influence on self-esteem and other model components in desirable directions. . . The theory and research that we have reviewed indicate that both the level and pursuit of self-esteem can be influential in shaping overall health and well-being."[104]*

Applying *The Smart Way* with Emotional Guidance and metacognitive processes to self-esteem development and maintenance is easy and effective.

". . . boosting self-esteem temporarily increases positive affect [mood] and decreases negative affect including anxiety. . . pursuing self-esteem has fewer costs when one attempts to satisfy relatively internal contingencies of self-worth rather than external contingencies."[105]

There are millions of potential variations, but each has a path to thoughts that feel better, and all of them are in reach if the employee has been practicing *The Smart Way*.

I've found a way to have high self-esteem without it feeling egotistical to myself or others. I hold others in as high of regard as I do myself. Discomfort with my self-praise is always obvious.t when I tell my class, "I'm wonderful," followed by a long pause after which I say, "and so are you and you and you. Each and everyone one of you is wonderful in your beautifully unique way. Let yourself feel how wonderful you are."

It is as if our society has a mandate that makes it forbidden to think well of ourself. Yet, "high self-esteem is reported to be one of the strongest predictors of well-being . . . and it is so closely related to happiness that it could be considered a component of happiness."[106]

Self-esteem also effects people's decision about whether or not to pursue additional education, which is another pathway on which self-esteem can affect the ability to rise above poverty. Some say that self-esteem is the result of higher wages or higher educational attainment, but research shows my personal experience that higher self-esteem comes first is not an anomaly. Much the same way researchers know happiness increases success, self-esteem increases success. It makes sense that self-esteem would also come before the higher income because healthy self-esteem is a component of happiness.

Imagine someone with low self-esteem walking barefoot along a gravel path, being careful where he puts his feet so he does not bruise them on the small and sometimes sharp rocks on the path. Increasing self-esteem is equivalent to putting on a pair of shoes, and the more self-esteem one develops, the better the padding separating the man's feet from his rocky path. The same person walking on the same path after self-esteem increases walks with more confidence because he now has a pair of sturdy shoes or hiking boots between his feet and the gravel. It's a lot easier to move along when each step does not require caution.

Research conducted at Wake Forest University over twenty years ago highlighted some of the problems associated with low self-esteem, "Low self-esteem ranks among the strongest predictors of emotional and behavioral problems. Compared to people with high self-esteem, people with low self-esteem tend to be more anxious, depressed, lonely, jealous, shy, and generally unhappy. They are also less assertive, less likely to enjoy close friendships, and more likely to drop out of school. Furthermore, they are more inclined to behave in ways that pose a danger to themselves or others: low self-esteem is associated with unsafe sex, teenage pregnancy, aggression, criminal behavior, the abuse of alcohol and other drugs, and membership in deviant groups."[107] Shawn Achor said "One of the greatest buffers against picking up others' stress is stable and strong self-esteem."[108]

The pursuit of self-esteem can encourage a wide range of prosocial behaviors and creative accomplishments. However, because self-esteem is predicated on the beliefs and values of the meaning-providing worldview to which the individual subscribes, it can also contribute to horrible antisocial behavior, such as prejudice and aggression. The pursuit of self-esteem is thus neither a good thing nor a bad thing but rather, a part of the system that human beings use to both regulate their behavior and cope with their existential situation."[109]

Looking outside oneself for validation of what is personally right can cause negative outcomes. Whereas looking inside toward one's Emotional Guidance presents no such risks. Even if one's Emotional Guidance leads to perspectives that are significantly different than the norm of one's time, as experienced by Galileo, Semmelweis, Prince, Madonna, Lady Gaga, and countless others who were early adopters of new paradigms, reliance on Emotional Guidance as the basis of self-worth protects the avant-garde from experiencing damaging emotional blows to self-worth or self-esteem.

Crocker and Park said "The desire to believe that one is worthy or valuable drives behavior and shapes how people think about themselves, other people, and events in their lives."[110] Dr. Peter Kramer said, "Low self-worth and poor interpersonal skills—the usual causes of social awkwardness—are so deeply ingrained and difficult to influence that ordinarily change comes gradually, if ever."[111] This is one reason why learning about one's Emotional Guidance is so important. As soon as the guidance gains a person's trust, that person can begin using it to refute negative self-concepts and increase self-esteem. Trust in one's guidance can be built using subjects that do not have as much practiced resistance to better-feeling thoughts as self-concept sometimes carries.

It is important, maybe even critical, that self-esteem is built on a stable foundation. Crocker and Park noted:

"Success at this pursuit [of self-esteem] leads to positive emotions, reduced anxiety, and a sense of safety and control over events and can be highly motivating. On the other hand, failure at the pursuit of self-esteem can lead to feelings of worthlessness, shame, sadness, and anger, leaving people feeling vulnerable to mortality or social rejection or feeling unable to cope with life events . . . there is little evidence that pursuing self-esteem by attempting to satisfy standards of value and worth actually increases social inclusion, competence, efficacy, relatedness, or immortality or leads to improved objective outcomes . . . when relationships with significant others are perceived to be highly conditional or critical, thoughts about those significant others trigger concerns about self-esteem and self-worth. . . Consistent with self-determination theory, we assume that relatedness, competence, autonomy, and self-regulation are always needs (but are not always adopted as goals)."[112]

External contingencies of self-worth, which require validation from others, have greater costs . . . external contingencies of self-worth such as appearance, others' approval, competition, and academic competence are associated with more problems during the freshman year, whereas internal contingencies, such as virtue or religious faith, were associated with lower levels of these problems . . . Pursuing self-esteem by being virtuous, compassionate, generous, or altruistic would seem to have fewer costs, especially fewer costs for others."[113]

An even better source of consistent and stable self-esteem is created by using one's Emotional Guidance to affirm positive self-beliefs. While, for example, religious faith creates more stable self-esteem than appearance, it is still subject to potential questioning. Many people have *crises of faith* during the worst times of their lives when stable self-esteem would be of great benefit to them. Since Emotional Guidance provides consistent ongoing feedback to every individual in response to every thought, it is not likely to ever be questioned by anyone who has recognized its presence and understands its language.

Numerous researchers recommended that developing non-contingent self-esteem would be a path to achieving self-esteem goals without the potential costs of many common methods, but Crocker and Park were not sure anyone with truly non-contingent self-esteem exists. If non-contingent means not relying on one's Emotional Guidance, I would have to agree. However, it is possible to develop self-esteem using Emotional Guidance that is stable and secure and not reliant on external factors. The hypothesis that self-esteem was designed to be based on our properly interpreted emotional responses fits the evidence well because no other platform is as stable or reliable. Crocker and Park had more to say:

"Self-worth that is completely non-contingent is not vulnerable to threat and therefore does not need to be protected or defended from threat. When self-esteem is truly non-contingent, it is simply a given and therefore becomes unnecessary to pursue." [114]

When self-esteem is based on external validation, Crocker and Park's words are true:
"The pursuit of self-esteem interferes with relatedness, learning, autonomy self-regulation, and mental and physical health. Pursuing self-esteem can be motivating, but other sources of motivation, such as goals that are good for the self and others, can provide the same motivation without the costs. . . Although chasing after self-esteem can motivate excellent performance, performance itself is not a fundamental human need, and it can be achieved through other less destructive sources of motivation. Recognition and acknowledgement are not the same as love and acceptance, and they do not create the safety and security people desire." [115]

"Achieving a high level of self-esteem, or perhaps more important, avoiding low self-esteem, is important for health and well-being throughout the life span." [116]

People cannot protect themselves from dangers they experienced in childhood by proving that they are smart, strong, beautiful, rich, or admired or that they satisfy some other contingency of self-worth. In the words of Claire Nuer, a Holocaust survivor and leadership development trainer "The only way to create love, safety, and acceptance is by giving them." [117]

In Western societies, a backlash to high self-esteem sometimes occurs from multiple perspectives. High self-esteem can violate family or social group demands for being humble. High self-esteem can also be viewed as egotistical, or thinking you're better than others—especially when those around the employee have low self-esteem. A common saying is "You're getting too big for your britches" is not referring to weight, but to expansive and ambitious ideas. Individuals and society are not well-served when people discount their value and worth.

One of the most common frustrations my students express regarding family and friends is their negative beliefs about the students' goals and desires. Mostly, my student's aren't trying to be the next Michael Jordan or Steve Jobs—they're seeking a better life and being discouraged by the words and attitudes of their friends and family. Emotional Guidance gives them a reliable cheer leader in the form of positive emotional encouragement to pursue their dreams.

Core Self-Evaluations are another way to perceive human needs for thriving. Core self-evaluations including self-esteem, generalized self-efficacy, internal locus of control, and emotional stability which "independently and when combined into one higher order construct, have been shown to be significant positive predictors of goal setting, motivation, performance, job and life satisfaction, and other desirable outcomes." [118]

For example, a core self-belief that states, *I am good but not better than others*, or *I am wonderful but so is everyone else* holds a positive self-view without diminishing others in the process. By thinking a variety of statements pertaining to the situation and paying attention to how each one feels, one that serves one's interests can easily be identified. Using Emotional Guidance to find a statement that feels good leads to confidence that the stance one is taking is serving our highest good. When someone thinks about being wonderful and others not being as wonderful they'll feel negative emotion that indicates that perspective is not the best one they can hold. When they think about being personally wonderful and everyone else being wonderful as well a sense of calm contentment is felt, which is communicating a positive self-concept and a positive concept about others is moving them in the direction of self-actualization.

Looking to others to validate one's self-concept (self-esteem) puts an employee on an unstable platform because other's opinions of us vary as their emotional state changes. The emotional response one receives from Emotional Guidance validates positive self-images with positive emotion and refutes negative self-images with negative emotional feedback. Using Emotional Guidance to affirm self-esteem results in stable self-esteem because it does not depend on others validation or agreement. Holding oneself in high-regard is not the same as narcissism, which is as "preoccupation with one's status compared to, and in the eyes of others . . . [and] is associated with delinquency and aggression."[119]

Family resilience researcher Ann Masten said, "Interventions and policies that promote healthy development have the potential for spreading positive effects over levels and time. The observation that 'competence begets competence' in human development may well apply to family units as well as individuals."[120] My theory extends this concept into the workplace.

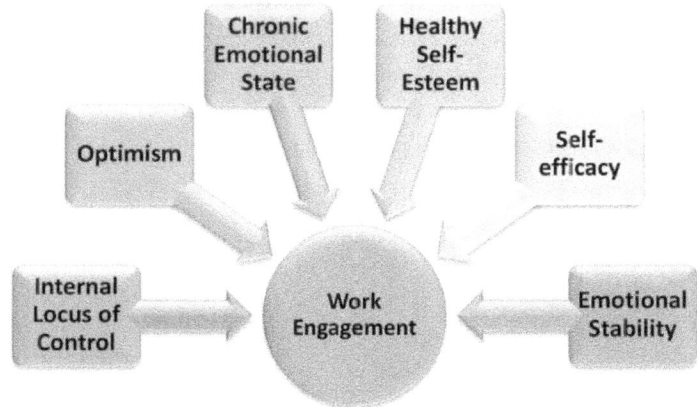

Diagram 2

Emotional Stability

"Individuals who score low on emotional stability (i.e. high on neuroticism) are more prone to feelings of insecurity, helplessness, and anxiety . . . and are likely to react adversely and show negative emotions towards undesired events, therefore, leading to lower job satisfaction."[121]

In Diagram 2, Chronic Emotional State is substituted for General Work and Life Satisfaction. This is to align the diagram with the terminology I use in my work. The meanings are virtually the same. Someone who evaluates their life as being good overall will be in a much better chronic emotional state than someone who evaluates their life as awful.

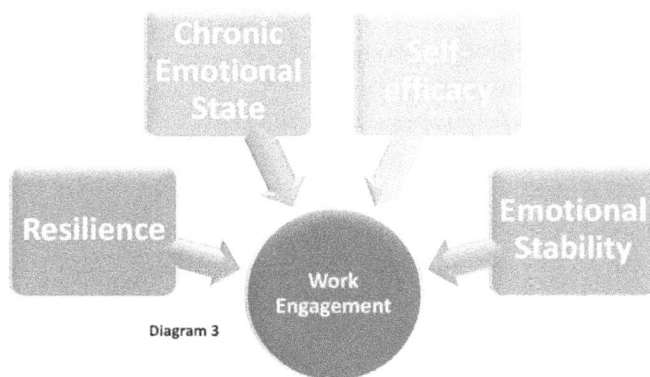

Diagram 3

A good-feeling chronic emotional state does not require a perfect life. It only requires positive future expectations about one's ability to achieve desired goals.

In Diagram 3, resilience is substituted for Internal Locus of Control, Optimism, and Healthy Self-esteem because the high order construct of Resilience is composed of those three factors.

In Diagram 4, Psychological Capital (PsyCap) is substituted for Resilience and Self-efficacy, further simplifying the diagram. The factors that are combined to create Resilience plus Self-efficacy are the factors that comprise Psychological Capital.

In Diagram 5, Happiness is substituted for Emotional stability, Psychological Capital, and Chronic Emotional State. Hope, an aspect of PsyCap, is always inherently present when one has attained True Happiness.

Diagram 5 is based on the following definition of **True Happiness**:

The State of True Happiness does not require a constant state of bliss. It is a deep sense of inner stability, peace, well-being, and vitality that is consistent and sustainable. Awareness that one possesses the knowledge and skills to return to a happy state, even when not in that state, is a critical component of sustainable happiness. True Happiness is sustainable because the individual deliberately and consciously chooses perspectives that create positive emotions and has cultivated this habit of thought until the natural and habitual response focuses on the positive aspects of the current situation.

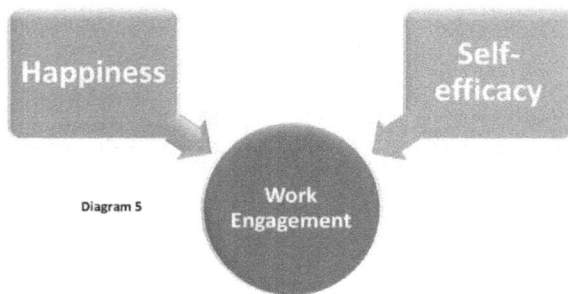

Diagram 4

True Happiness reflects positive life satisfaction and will also reflect Subjective Well-Being that is at the emotion of hope or above (see EGSc) because the thing that makes an individual feel hopeless is not knowing how they will ever be able to feel good again. Once an individual knows they have skills that will help them feel better, even if they aren't ready to use them yet, they at least have the hope of feeling better someday.

Diagram 5

In Diagram 6, self-efficacy is added to the definition of True Happiness because Self-efficacy exists even whilst learning new tasks because the belief (growth mindset) that one can accomplish established goals (including learning and mastery goals) is automatic when a positive perspective of the situation is cultivated. Optimism is holding a positive perspective and is an aspect of True Happiness.

An Internal Locus of Control can be created and reinforced by taking conscious control of one's mental response to situations and guiding oneself toard positive emotional states.

Healthy Self-esteem can be cultivated and reinforced using the same techniques that afford one the ability to achieve True Happiness. Emotional stability is a major factor of True Happiness. The reason some people *freak out* (become emotionally upset in difficult or stressful situations[122]) when they are faced with challenges to their esteem or autonomy is because they want to feel good and lack the skill to easily return to a positive (or comfortable) emotional state in the face of the current challenge. Skills-based Happiness, which True Happiness is, provides the assurance that regardless of circumstances one possesses the skills necessary to find the way back to better-feeling emotional states as discussed in the prior chapter.

Diagram 6

Now that we've boiled it down to the fact that happy people are engaged and people who aren't happy don't have the psychological make-up to be consistently engaged, it becomes obvious why traditional approaches that encourage management to behave differently and be accountable for employee engagement have led us to worldwide rates of 30% engagement.

Happiness is an inside job is a cliché but it is also true. On some level everyone knows this. Perhaps you were angry at someone who tried to cheer you up before you were ready to give up

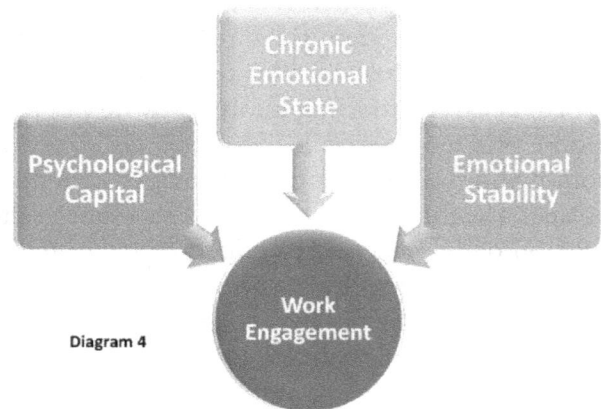

being angry. It didn't matter what the person did. They could do things that at other times (when you were in a better emotional state) would make you delieriously happy and you'd refuse to budge because you weren't done being angry.

Perhaps it was the opposite situation, where you tried to cheer someone up before they were ready. Their mood would only change when they were ready to change and not before.

Happiness is an inside job but it is also the result of habits of thought. The amount of our thoughts, words, and actions that are automatic throughout any given day is significant. That means habits of thought control what we think, say, and do. Habits of thought are heavily influenced by emotional states and the influence is bi-directional because habits of thought influence our emotional state.

Individuals tend to live in one primary emotional Zone (See Appendix I) most of the time. When really good things happen they'll move to a higher Zone temporarily. When bad things happen they'll move to a lower Zone for a while. But even the best and worst life has to offer does not usually lead to long-term changes in chronic emotional state. Getting married, having a baby or becoming a parapalegic change the chronic emotional state for about two years. That's it.

The only way I have found to permanently change one's chronic emotional state is by changing habitual thoughts. Since most thoughts are automatic responses, this requires changing the programming that elicits automatic thoughts. The good news is it is the easiest habit to change because positive emotions come with every change and there is no pain for gain. In fact, old pains (physical and mental) often disappear during the process.**

From a manager's perspective this is also great news because the research is clear that people want to feel good. Helping employees feel better by teaching them how to use their minds will quickly create employees who are both intrinsically motivated to feel better and have the skills to achieve and sustain better-feeling emotional states. As they feel better, their engagement will increase (right along with their energy levels, relationships, cognitive abilities, and health).

Mindset

Mindset can be separated into two major types of mindsets according to Carol Dweck's book, *Mindset* and her research. One is based on seeing oneself as a finished product with traits and abilities that are whatever they are, but with little ability of the individual to change them. That sort of belief is called a fixed mindset. An individual with a fixed mindset is at a decided disadvantage because there is no apparent reason to seek self-development and there is a high degree of motivation to prove the quality (or goodness) of what one is (because the idea of becoming more is not part of the person's worldview). Challenges to valued qualities can make a person with a fixed mindset feel vulnerable or anxious. They will focus on performance goals in an effort to prove their value and worth to others (and themselves).

On the other hand, an individual with a growth mindset perceives an ability to learn, grow, and adapt, and to become more along the way. The person with a growth mindset will seek new experiences for the knowledge to be gained from them. The growth mindset does not base self-esteem upon proving that he is smart enough, talented enough, pretty enough, or some other factor that is considered unchangeable. Individuals with a growth mindset are likely to enjoy studying and unlikely to experience test anxiety because the test is not determining the value of their personhood. Fortunately, like pessimism, a fixed mindset does not come with a life sentence. It can be changed to enhance the life experiences of the individual.

** There is a strong link between physical pain, chronic physical pain, and emotional state. Simply stated, pain decreases as mood increases. Citations and more information about this topic can be found in *Our Children Live in a War Zone: Use the Power of Resilience to Improve Their Lives, Applied Positive Psychology 2.1*

I'll look stupid if I fail.

Even if I fail, I'll learn a lot and be better next time.

Performance → Mastery

Goals → Stretch Goals

Beliefs

Fixed Mindset — Growth Mindset

Goal Achievement

Higher

Lower

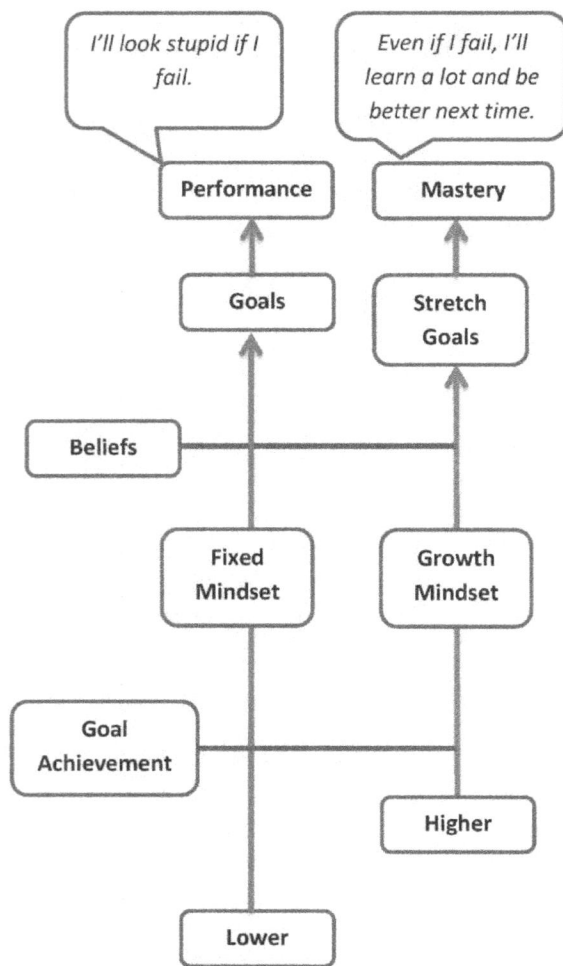

Someone who recognizes their personal power to create their own reality must have a growth mindset because our infinite abilities to fulfill an ever expanding personal and collective potential is recognized.

Internal Locus of Control

An internal locus of control is a universal requirement for high employee engagement. The human need for autonomy is so strong that no one can be truly happy unless they believe they have the ability to change their own life. Without an internal locus of control one feels disempowered and that makes the emotional state low on the EGSc. An internal locus of control is not defined as an aspect of Psychological Flexibility except for the fact that an employee has to believe their own thought processes will create changes before they will bother to use metacognitive processes to shift their emotional state. That belief is an internal locus of control. Teaching employees how to use metacognitive processes and demonstrating that they can change their emotional state can help employees shift from a fixed mindset to a growth mindset and help employees with a growth mindset who don't think about it consciously become more present and aware of their personal power to change their emotional state in healthy ways.

Job Satisfaction

Is how satisfied (or dissatisfied) one feels about their job

Respect

An article in the *Harvard Business Review* in late 2014, *Half of Employees Don't Feel Respected by their Bosses* mentioned many benefits that organizations receive when their employees feel respected including "56% better health and well-being, 1.72 times more trust and safety, and 89% greater enjoyment and satisfactions with their jobs, 55% more engaged, 92% greater focus and prioritization, and 1.26 times more meaning and significance."[123] Christine Porath, who authored the piece, stated "we watched performance plummet after incivility occurred."[124]

While the article mentioned the individual nature of respect, it also went on to say it is "tied to what a particular individual expects—and ***how the leader makes the person feel***." [Emphasis added]

The root of the problem is that no one can make us feel anything without our permission. We can give others the power to make us feel emotions based on responses to their words and actions, or we can understand that their behavior is reflecting their emotional state and has very little to do with us. The leader who barks orders at employees without bothering to say hello, how are you, or other civilities is demonstrating the leader's sense of urgency—not his or her feelings about the employee. In fact, in that moment the leader is not thinking about the employee other than as a means to an end.

Now, some may feel that is disrespectful. But if the employer did not respect the employees' ability to carry out the task the employee wouldn't be the one being called on when the manager feels a sense of urgency. The manager's behavior does not mean that, at other times, when the sense of urgency is lower, that the manager does not respect the employee. In many cases, the manager is on auto-pilot, lacking awareness (low Emotional Intelligence) about the impact of his words (or lack thereof) on the employee. But understanding what is going on in a manager's brain could help employees not feel disrespected.

Imagine a different scenario, one in which the manager and the employee are married with a child and the child has just broken his arm. The manager barks at the employee (in this imaginary scenario, the husband or wife) to call the doctor. Is that showing lack of respect, or trust? What is going on in many managers' minds is not too different from what is going on in the imagined parent's minds. There is a task that urgently requires attention and nothing else matters at that moment.

Managers often feel a greater sense of urgency than employees. They see the larger picture. Maybe getting the deal means the difference between meeting the division's numbers and a layoff. The manager may, in fact, be stressed because she is attempting to protect the employee's job. In an age when authenticity and transparency are valued, perhaps the employee should be told of the reasons the task is so urgent. But the downside of that is that if the manager believes the layoff can be averted he has conflicting loyalties. Being told that a layoff will occur if the numbers are not met; some staff will choose to leave the uncertainty for a new job where they feel their job security is better, which might be just the blow that leads to not meeting the numbers and others being laid off. Managers typically do the best they can in any given moment just like the rest of us do and they are often judged with hindsight and based on more information than they were aware of at the time.

There is another aspect to employees not feeling respected and that is the schema the employee has about whether or not he should be respected or is worthy of respect. This would be one aspect of the employee's self-esteem and core self-evaluation stemming from deep-seated beliefs established at a young age. If an employee does not feel they are worthy of respect, they will not see clues that they are respected, even obvious ones or vocalized ones. Remember, our minds interpret reality. One of the main factors that influence our personal interpretation of reality is our beliefs.

In *Learned Optimism*, Martin E. P. Seligman, the Father of Positive Psychology, talked about how we unconsciously create back stories to give our reality a sense of coherence and consistency. In *The Happiness Hypothesis*, Jonathan Haidt talked about research with individuals with brain damage where the two sides of their brain were no longer communicating with one another. You could show the eye on one side of the brain a picture of something, for example, a Coke and indicate the person should go to the Coke machine and get one. Then, when the individual got up and was crossing the room ask where they were going and why, they would make up a story (an unconscious back story) to explain where they were going and it would bear no relationship to reality as perceived by the researchers.

This is not the same as consciously making up a lie. It happens below conscious awareness and the individual typically believes the story is true. This happens with all of us, brain damaged or not. If you've ever had a disagreement about an event with someone else who was present but you perceive it and understand it very differently, it could be traced back to the different back stories each of you accepted as truth about the event.

If an employee does not feel they deserve respect, they will not feel respected. If the manager tells the employee who does not feel worthy of respect how valued and valuable the employee is to the organization, the employees mind will interpret the words differently than they were meant. The words do not match the core beliefs so they bounce off and end up being a back story that might go something like this, "My manager was buttering me up today because she wants me to work extra hours." The manager said the right words, but the employee's beliefs made it necessary to create a back story that retained the employees core beliefs.

In a scenario like this, the employee will not feel respected unless and until the core belief is changed. It does not matter how many times the manager tells the employee how valued he is—as long as the core belief contradicts the words, they will be interpreted in a way that supports the core belief. If the employee does the internal work to change the belief about deserving respect, the first time he is told how valued he is after the belief shifts will feel as if it is the first time it has ever been expressed to him. That is because it will be the first time he translated the respect accurately.

Too good to be true: The mind will create a back story to make it consistent with core beliefs

New input (event, conversation)

Core Beliefs

Accepted

Too awful to be true: The mind will create a back story to make it consistent with core beliefs

This same process happens with core beliefs in any area. The belief could just as easily be about intelligence, attractiveness, athletic ability, etc.

The good news is that employees want to feel better than they feel and when an employee learns how beliefs impact their ability to feel good and is given the tools that enables them to change beliefs that do not serve them well; they are intrinsically motivated to do so. We don't need to spend a lot of time figuring out where beliefs came from in order to understand their effect or to change them. One remark at a young age that the child often repeated in his mind can be the basis of a belief. It does not require repeated verbal abuse to create beliefs that do not serve a person well. In some cases, a misinterpretation of a situation can lead to a belief that does not serve the person well.

Beliefs are formed by thinking the same (or similar) thoughts repeatedly, creating a pathway in the neuro structure of the mind that is easier to follow than other paths. Creating beliefs that serve an individual better is as simple as consistently affirming a better-feeling thought that is believable over a period of about three months. It can happen faster, but one reason many people fail is that they expect immediate results. It's like trying to change the current of a river. It takes time to create the right environment that allows the water to flow in a new direction. It's a mind, you don't want to use a backhoe. A gentle process is much better and three months is a very short period of time compared to how long the old belief has been impacting one's perceptions.

Another example of this is when someone who was once trusted turns out to have been dishonest. Often the victim berates himself for not having seen the signs sooner. The determination that someone is trustworthy forms a belief and the mind interprets signs that the person should not be trusted with back stories that explain and excuse behaviors that would be obvious to someone who does not trust the person.

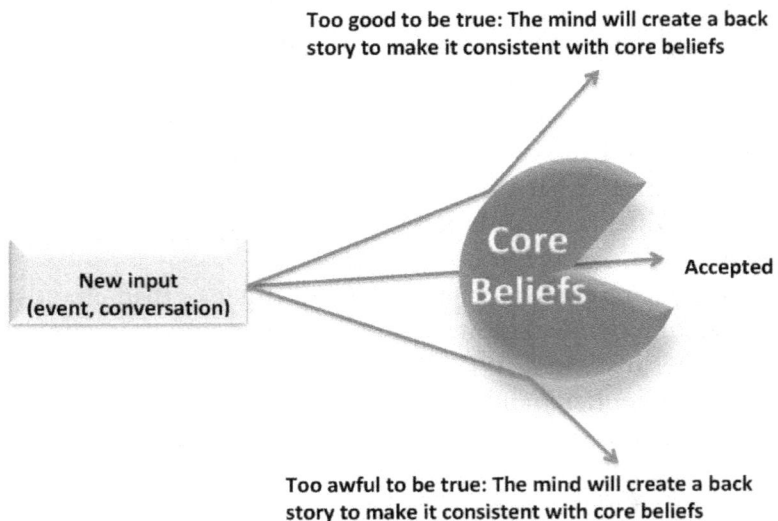

The solution is not to stop trusting people. It is to use another sense that science has shown provides critical information that is usually ignored or explained away because it is not given the priority it is meant to garner. Our Emotional Guidance has a lot of knowledge about the trustworthiness of every person we meet. All we have to do is interpret it accurately.

Co-workers (civility, bullying, etc.)

California mandates anti-bullying training for supervisors. Workplace bullying legislation backed by The Healthy Workplace Campaign has been introduced in 32 states and is currently pending in nine. The language of each bill varies somewhat but the core language is fairly consistent based on a model bill provided by healthyworkplacebill.org. Senate Bill 3863 in New York begins by stating some of the reasons the state feels the need to provide protection against workplace bullying to employees.

> *"The Legislature hereby finds that the social and economic well-being of the state is dependent upon healthy and productive employees. At least one-third of all employees directly experience health endangering workplace bullying, abuse, and harassment during their working lives. Such form of mistreatment is four times more prevalent than sexual harassment alone. Workplace bullying, mobbing, and harassment can inflict serious harm upon targeted employees including feelings of shame and humiliation, severe anxiety, depression, suicidal tendencies, impaired immune systems, hypertension, increased risk of cardiovascular disease, and symptoms consistent with post-traumatic stress disorder."*

After stating that existing laws do not provide adequate protection and recompense for employees who cannot prove that the abuse falls under a protected class, the language goes on to explain:

> *"The purpose of this article shall be to provide legal redress for employees who have been harmed psychologically, physically, or economically by deliberate exposure to abusive work environments and to provide legal incentives for employers to prevent and respond to abusive mistreatment of employees at work."*

Q – What is "abusive conduct"?

A – Acts, omissions, or both, that a reasonable person would find abusive, based on the severity, nature, and frequency of the conduct, including but not limited to:

Repeated verbal abuse such as:
- The use of derogatory remarks, insults, and epithets
- Verbal, Non-verbal, or physical conduct of a threatening, intimidating, or humiliating nature
- The sabotage or undermining of an employee's work performance
- If an employee's known psychological or physical illness or disability is exploited, it shall be considered an aggravating factor (read: stiffer potential legal liability). Risk Managers note: This increases risks from hiring individuals with known psychological or physical illnesses but other laws prohibit discrimination. The best strategy is to teach employees how to be happy where they are more likely to:
  1. Treat others well,
  2. Take other people's negativity in stride

- A single act will not normal constitute abusive conduct unless it is especially severe an egregious.

An **abusive work environment** is when an employer or one or more of its employees intends to cause pain or distress to an employee and subjects that employee to workplace bullying that causes harm. Bullied employees are granted protection against retaliation or "adverse employment action" under the proposed legislation. Employee's whose request for assistance with bullying behaviors in the workplace are not addressed will be considered constructively discharged if they have reported the conduct and appropriate actions were not taken.

The potential penalties to an employer are significant and depending on the unique circumstances may include any relief the court deems appropriate including, but not limited to, reinstatement, removal of the offending party from the work environment, reimbursement for lost wages, front pay, medical expenses, compensation for pain and suffering. It concludes by stating that remedies under this law would not preclude remedies available under other laws. So, for example, if someone is a member of a protected class, he or she might be able to seek damages under existing legislation and this new legislation, if it passes.

Although the proposed legislation has not yet been made into law, I believe it is one egregious and well publicized bullying situation away from being passed in a similar form in many states. The bill is being pushed by a grassroots effort that could quickly grow as the result of social media with the right stimulus.

The term, "going postal" originated when workplace bullying hit a crisis point. The documentary, *Murder by Proxy*, details what led to the Royal Oak Post Office murders in 1991. If a similar situation were to occur today, I believe the grassroots efforts would reach a crescendo and states would quickly pass legislation in response to the public outcries. If this were to occur when elections were on the horizon, employers could find themselves subject to anti-bullying legislation almost before they've had time to read the rules, much less take steps to ensure compliance and to mitigate their risks.

Murder is the number one cause of workplace deaths for women. But workplace bullying does not have to near the level of murder before the employer is liable for significant damages.

Today, Google returns eleven million results for the search term workplace bullying. The Huffington Post has run multiple articles on workplace bullying during the past few years. As awareness grows, the likelihood that an employee will complain about mistreatment increases. That is a good thing because that mistreatment has numerous negative effects on the organization including productivity, worker health, creativity, engagement, and turnover. Being aware of it is important to the health of the organization. But, you have to be prepared to act on what you know because the potential that an employee will file suit and win increases with your awareness and with the employee awareness that states are recognizing the negative impacts of workplace bullying on the employee.

We have moved to a culture that values collaboration and does not tolerate the mistreatment of employees in the ways that were once considered acceptable. If your organization's culture is not keeping pace with cultural change it is only a matter of time before it pays a price. That price may be loss of your best talent to a more advanced organization or a lawsuit that has devastating effects on your company's future.

The US Department of Labor's (DOL) Occupational Safety and Health Administration (OSHA) already provides a requirement that employers provide a safe work environment. OSHA provides a hotline and a form for employees to request assistance. Employees who observe harassment (but are not victims) should not stand by and do nothing. Standing by and allowing bullying could lead to the loss of your job--either because you did not act or communicate what you observed or because your company has to let people go or close its doors when it is hit with a valid complaint and resultant penalties.

Internationally, workplace bullying laws are already in place in some countries. Sweden passed the Victimisation at Work act in 1994 and Great Britain their Protection from Harassment Act in 2001. Canada, France, Australia, and Iceland also have legislation in place. Bullying does not have to cause physical damage to inflict harm. Psychological stress harms the mind and body.

Fairness

People feel upset when they perceive that a situation or decision is unfair but overlook that they don't know all the factors that went into the decision. That something is unfair is usually perceptional and can be changed using metacognitive reappraisal so that it feels better.

Stress

Soon after the link between stress and mental and physical health was first recognized, recommendations to monitor stress began back-firing because monitoring stress without the ability to change the situation (or perception of the situation) has the potential to increase stress. The awareness of high levels of stress, and the potential negative health effects of that stress without a release valve, increases stress by creating stress about being stressed.

Some individuals gave up activities they enjoyed because of time stress. Pleasurable pursuits contribute to our health and resilience by providing a stress relief valve that helped them maintain stasis.

The recommendations provided in the 1970's were about as helpful to the typical individual as telling a pessimist to *think positively*. Pessimism is a habit, not an inborn personality trait. However, it is an insidious habit that is difficult to break without the right knowledge and skills. With the right knowledge and skills, anyone determined to become more optimistic is able to do so. Without the knowledge and skills, it seems impossible.

Additional research has been done about stress relief and some of the recommendations being made today are more helpful. Some help reduce stress for brief periods and one (meditation) is effective both immediately and long-term (but long-term results occur **only** if the individual is persistent with their practice). Most of today's advice has still falls short of best practices. For the most part, today's common recommendations addresses symptoms rather than the root cause of stress.

The concept of positive thinking has become a common refrain. Sadly, the **how** is usually absent when the advice is given. Imagine giving someone who was raised by wolves a book and telling him to read it—without teaching him to read. Telling a pessimist to think positively is not much different. Teach the individual how—in either situation—and the goal becomes attainable.

Although some individuals evolve optimistically, or learn it from a positively focused parent or grandparent, once pessimistic habits are developed, the opportunity to be optimistic without conscious awareness and accurate interpretation of Emotional Guidance is greatly diminished. Even today, many teachers simply refer to the benefits of positivity and optimism and encourage people to think positively, but fail to provide knowledge and skills that help the person achieve success.

This often increases the level of stress because the person is now aware that being pessimistic is not in their best interest, but they do not have the skills and knowledge to change pessimistic habits of thought. No mention is usually made of the human ability to adjust ones mindset to reduce stress—the easiest response—also often the only one an individual has any control over.[125]

The absence of the answer to the **how** question is what motivated me to create Happiness 1st Institute—because life is better when you are happy first. The techniques commonly taught—from gratitude, affirmations, meditation, exercise, helping others, being in nature, etc.—all have some benefit. But real change, changes in default automatic responses requires a deeper level of knowledge—a level where the individual understands why these things work and facilitates shifts in mindset. Almost all the common techniques rely on changing focus to reduce stress which does not lead to permanent changes.

The Smart Way provides information about cutting edge science that demonstrates that each of us has Emotional Guidance that leads us away from harm and toward self-actualization. The first question most people ask when they hear we have guidance is why the world is not thriving if we have this guidance. The answer is that society habitually teaches us to misinterpret our guidance and to put other information ahead of our guidance.

Stress is much like the old analogy of the boiled frog. The metaphor that if you put a frog in a pot of water and heat it very gradually, the frog will not jump out and will remain until boiled to death. Whereas, a frog put in hot water will jump out immediately. Whether a frog will actually remain in the pot long enough to die is subject to debate. I am not going to try, so we'll leave it as an analogy—a very valid analogy about human behavior.

One of the most common situations where we see this play out is in the area of abusive relationships. This is true of both abused women and men. If the abuser began the relationship with abuse, the abused partner would have left immediately. The abuse would not have been tolerated beyond the first incidence. Abusers tend to introduce abuse gradually, increasing the reign of terror as their victims' tolerance increases. In many cases, those watching from the outside have difficulty understanding why the behavior is tolerated.

Abuse is a form of stress. The boiled frog analogy works with employees, too. If the employer had asked for what is demanded a few years into the arrangement on the first day of work, the employee would have immediately looked for a better job. Because demands increase gradually, we do not respond to the increasing levels of stress the same way. We are used to suffering with the level of stress and we continue to accept more until the proverbial straw that breaks the camel's back—which may be in the form of depression, heart disease, divorce (from taking the stress home), cancer[126] or other illness. This is bi-directional. Some employees' performance deteriorates over time until performance that would have led to termination the first week of employment is tolerated when it arises gradually. Kind-hearted people (including landlords) often harm themselves as tenant rent-paying performance declines.

It is not all the employer's fault. When an employee takes on too much the employee needs to communicate when the demands on them are stretching their ability to deliver. Bosses often forget all an employee's current tasks when more is requested. A long time ago, I worked for one of the big box banks. My schedule was four ten-hour days. One of my peers once remarked, "You don't work 4/10's. You work 7/14's." Unfortunately, she was right. However, the fault was not all on my management. I did not push back. I worked remotely and most of my interaction was across department lines with people around the country—not with my boss. My boss probably had no idea how many hours I was working.

It is easy for an employee to believe that pushing back will reflect poorly on their performance evaluation. The truth is, the reason they are overloaded is probably because they are reliable. The boss knows that work sent their way is done right the first time. The boss is not overloading them with work because he dislikes them, although they may perceive it that way. When I left my first management role, where I'd consistently worked 50 – 60 hours a week, they replaced me with three full-time people.

When I see someone having difficulty with stressful events in their life I feel compassion, knowing that not only are they in a difficult situation, they don't have the knowledge or tools they could have if knowledge of *The Smart Way* was widespread.

Learning to use our minds effectively is important. Worry is one of the mental processes that diminish well-being. I had a friend tell her daughter that as long as she lived she would worry "because she loved her daughter." She believes that if you love someone, you will worry about them. Worry makes now (the time) feel worse than it could out of fear that someday something bad will happen—something that usually never happens. She could just as easily practice seeing her daughter as competent and capable and enjoy now. But like anyone with an ingrained belief, if she is not asking for help with it, telling her that her belief is misguided just makes her defend her current stance. We can only help individuals who want help and wish the others well.

Continual worrying keeps the body in a state of stress that increases inflammation and reduces immune function. Stress increases the risk of chronic illnesses.

If you are a worrier, understand that the emotion of worry means, "There is a better-feeling thought you could be having about this exact same subject right now." Worry does not mean your worrisome thoughts are being validated as something you should spend your time worrying about.

Worry
Warts

That is not to say you should not look at and evaluate problems—but perceive them as solvable—not as insurmountable. Just believing there is a solution, even before you know the solution, eases worries. "I will find a way to solve this problem" is a far healthier outlook than, "I'm not capable of solving this problem." Even if you need help, gathering the resources you need to solve it is a form of problem-solving.

Burnout

Burnout is a significant problem in numerous fields. It is a significant contributor to the growing nursing and teacher shortages because nurses and teachers are departing their fields for less emotionally taxing occupations. The level of Emotional Intelligence an employee possesses is a significant determinant on the individual level of whether an employee stays in the profession. Low Emotional Intelligence leads some nurses and teachers to leave even before they've worked long enough to pay off the loans incurred to obtain their education. It can also lead to disability claims for severe depression associated with burnout.

Researchers describe burnout as "a psychological syndrome of emotional exhaustion, depersonalization, and reduced personal accomplishment that can occur among individuals who work with other people in some capacity. A key aspect of the burnout syndrome is increased feelings of emotional exhaustion; as emotional resources are depleted, workers feel they are no longer able to give of themselves at a psychological level. Another aspect of the burnout syndrome is the development of depersonalization (i.e. negative, cynical attitudes and feelings) . . . A third aspect of the burnout syndrome, reduced personal accomplishment, refers to the tendency to evaluate oneself negatively, particularly with regard to one's work with clients . . . Our findings suggested that burnout can lead to a deterioration in the quality of care or service provided by the staff. It appears to be a factor in job turnover, absenteeism, and low morale . . . burnout seems to be correlated with various self—reported indexes of personal dysfunction, including physical exhaustion, insomnia, increased use of alcohol and drugs, and marital and family problems."[127] Using metacognitive processes and Emotional Guidance to make in-the-moment adjustments would reduce burnout by reducing the daily stress load.

Turnover

Turnover is very expensive. The factors to be considered include, but are not limited to, the cost of lost productivity (including sales activity), impacts on customer service and company reputation, the effect on morale of remaining employees, lost institutional knowledge, direct and indirect costs of hiring a replacement, and more. The root cause of **motivation** to do a good job and motivation to stay with a specific employer is related at the root cause. Employees are very unlikely to leave if they are happy because the desire to feel better motivates human behavior.

Emotional Exhaustion

We really must move past the idea that energy is a fixed resource—especially as it relates to the energy available to our minds and bodies. We can easily prove to ourselves that we have the ability, the power, to change the amount of energy available to us.

The simple thought or spoken statement "I am tired" can deplete one's remaining energy. Rewording it with "I am exhausted" can be even more energy depleting.

But the statement "I feel good" can rejuvenate one's energy levels. It is even more powerful if they hear James Brown's version of *I feel good* in their mind when they say it.

A few minutes contemplating the positive attributes of a much-desired upcoming experience can invigorate us and restore our energy levels.

Believing, thinking, or speaking about how hard (or impossible) a task will be depletes our energy. Thinking about meeting a challenge as an opportunity to learn, or grow, increases the available energy. We have control of the flow of energy into our experience, but most people do not consciously realize how much control they could exert. It is common for many people, at the first hint of fatigue, to begin voicing how tired they are and making plans to go home immediately after work and *vegetate*.

There are other factors that impact our energy level including whether we are healthy, eating well, and well-rested. Our interest in the work can increase our energy level and we can often find a way to use our thoughts to make work more interesting. If we repeatedly tell ourselves it is boring, our energy level will decrease. Even piece work can be more interesting by making a game of it. Early in my career there were times when I had to spend hours folding letters and stuffing envelopes. By seeing how fast I could go through a stack and then challenging myself to do the next one faster the work became more interesting. Maintaining the quality of your output while you increase your speed can be part of your challenge.

It doesn't take that much to entertain and amuse our minds. How many people spend their weekends watching cars drive in circles or balls being hit across vast green lawns? By injecting small games or even exercises into routine work becomes more challenging and more interesting.

Our energy is not limitless and we should respect our body's needs, but in many instances it is habits of thought that deplete our energy. Also see the information on willpower. Employees who proactively manage their energy are less likely to have endless days that feel tiring and meaningless, which lowers their risk of emotional exhaustion. Consciously play with how what you think and say affects your energy level. You may find untapped resources.

Absenteeism/Presenteeism

In 2012 the estimated cost of employee absenteeism to US businesses was 15%.[128]

Increasing Emotional Intelligence

Studies show that it is possible to increase a person's emotional intelligence by increasing their knowledge and understanding in this area.[129] Experiential learning models that provide mastery experiences give employees an opportunity to internalize the information on a deeper level. Understanding information intellectually is not as productive as being able to use the information in one's day-to-day experiences. This book provides both knowledge about the basis—the why it works, and methods the reader can use to practice skills that increase Emotional Intelligence.

Core Self-evaluations

Judge found "that core self-evaluations influence the way in which the job is evaluated . . . an individual who is given a pay raise or promotion with low core self-evaluation may feel that their accomplishment as not deserved, whereas a person with a high core self-evaluation would feel that the reward was warranted."[130] Stories of people who secretly fear others will realize that they are imposters and that they aren't good enough to have the position they have are common even among highly successful CEOs. It is their core self-evaluations, not their talent and worth that is not up to the level they have achieved that creates this persistent fear.

The fear of discovery is very real to such individuals and can eventually become a self-fulfilling prophecy because fear diminishes cognitive abilities and indicates heightened levels of stress, which will impair their ability to function. It does not matter how good they are. Beliefs are stronger than reality because the mind filters reality using beliefs. Information that is inconsistent with one's belief about self (core self-evaluation) will be filtered out or interpreted in a way that preserves the belief.

How successful will an employee be throughout their working years? Their core self-evaluations determine between 27- 40% of job satisfaction which then determines earnings and success. Even someone who comes from privilege or someone who did well in school does not do well during their career if their core self-evaluations aren't positive. Low core self-evaluations limit success. Judge found that "self-esteem plays an important role in whether individuals capitalize on their socioeconomic status and academic achievement . . . even with the advantage of high socioeconomic family background these resources barely seemed to make a difference for individuals with low core self-evaluations."[131]

A meta-analysis that looked at 32 studies encompassing 16,670 participants found "the relationship between the core self-evaluations construct and job satisfaction is not only worthy of academic mention but also of practical application."[132] The good news is that core self-evaluations can be changed. They are usually stable, but that is because they are beliefs (habits of thought), but like any habit, they can be changed.

Misguided solutions:

Grant and Sonnetag tell us employees with low core self-evaluations are "more likely to experience work events negatively, thus feel emotionally exhausted . . . For employees with low core self-evaluations, perceived prosocial impact will provide a positive experience that counters their negative self-concepts, reducing emotional exhaustion."[133]

This approach fails to consider that employees' negative self-concepts adversely affect all areas of their lives. Low core self-evaluations impact the quality of personal relationships, parenting styles, goal setting, and co-worker relationships as well as productivity and other work related outcomes. The combination of negative experiences leads to an increased likelihood of alcohol or drug use, depression, divorce, and even suicide.

Helping employees feel more connected with work when core self-evaluations are low could lead to less focus in other areas where competence is not affirmed with a prosocial focus. If work feels better than other activities, the employee may begin ignoring social connections in favor of the better-feeling work—to the detriment of familial duties, thus leaving the next generation with issues. It is like covering a hole in the wall with a piece of art. The hole is still there. In the past, outside of expensive counseling to address low core self-evaluations, employers had few options with which to assist employees. That is no longer true. Now that science has formulated an accurate understanding of the purpose and use of emotions, employees with a little bit of training can begin auto-correcting low core self-evaluations using accurately interpreted emotional feedback.

Researchers who ask if focusing on prosocial aspects of the work offset emotional exhaustion are essentially asking if the artwork hung over the hole in the wall covers up the hole. This approach also leaves the employee especially vulnerable, for example, if the employee bases positive emotions on the prosocial nature of the work and learns the employer was acting in ways that were unethical.

Psychological Capital (PsyCap)

Psychological Capitol is a high-order factor, which essentially means that as a construct it provides more reliable information than the sum of its parts. PsyCap is essentially resilience plus hope and self-efficacy, or, broken down further, hope, optimism, self-efficacy, healthy self-esteem, and an internal locus of control. PsyCap has been defined as:

1. Having confidence (self-efficacy) to take on and put in the necessary effort to succeed at challenging tasks;
2. Making a positive reference (optimism) about succeeding now and in the future;
3. Persevering towards goals, and when necessary, redirecting paths to goals (hope) in order to succeed; and
4. When beset by problems and adversity, sustaining and bouncing back and even beyond (resilience) to attain success." [134]

Resilience is, itself, a high-order construct consisting of healthy self-esteem, an internal locus of control and optimism. I don't know why the PsyCap literature separates optimism from resilience. PsyCap is "a better predictor of" performance and job satisfaction "than the individual components." [135] It is important to note that PsyCap can be developed and increased through training and experience.

Collective Psychological Capital (Teams)

Collective Psychological Capital is the combined bandwidth of the team but if the team is well led, the bandwidth is more than the sum of each members psychological capital. The interactions and ability to coordinate in a flow-like manner determine the multiplier. One bad apple can be like a playing card attached to a bicycle wheel and slow the progress of the entire team by creating friction that provides no benefit—just noise. The criteria that contribute to collective psychological capital are "open to development and have performance impact." [136]

Employee Fit (Teams)

Milan Larson and a team of researchers looked at PsyCap as it relates to an employee's fit with leaders in the organization and reported the following:

Decades of theoretical and empirical research building and extending the theories of person-organization fit have ultimately led to at least two primary conclusions: fit matters, and more fit is usually better for the firm. The same conclusion can be drawn from nearly 50 years of research on job satisfaction with higher job satisfaction being more optimal for both organizations and employees. Finally, with less history, the management research on employee engagement reveals more engaged employees to usually be associated with higher performing employees. In sum, each of the proximal outcomes examined here are desirable by organizations . . . Overall, results of this study indicate that the level of PsyCap similarity between leaders and followers may be influential in how workers perceive their fit with the organization . . . In a similar manner, results of this study suggest that employees whose PsyCap is more similar to their leaders have a higher level of engagement with their organization . . . as well as a higher perceived value of job satisfaction . . . the importance of congruence can extend beyond simple demographic variables such as values, goals, and personality. [137]

The researchers indicated that hiring employees whose PsyCap was aligned with the managers would enhance engagement, other research indicates that PsyCap levels often vary with income and minority status, making the use of even validated questionnaires in the hiring process illegal in most countries due to anti-discrimination legislation. They suggested that when "employees are high in PsyCap and leaders are low, there can be dysfunctions at the individual level and the employee may have more negative evaluations of both their work environment and the likelihood of future success. This finding also underscores the importance of leader selection with higher PsyCap where possible, as well as support for PsyCap development programs aimed at enhancing overall PsyCap levels of both employees and leaders . . . enhancing PsyCap levels of all employees can create significant organizational benefit." [138]

Since you can't hire for PsyCap, training is better than doing without it.

Metacognitive abilities

In 2015, Mason reported that emotion regulation strategies that increase emotion regulation skills can be taught. [139] Because society is not yet universally teaching children these skills, despite the proven benefits, many employees lack them. Employers who want the best from their employees will have to provide training to close the gap between their existing skills and the knowledge and skills that empower employees to fulfill more of their potential.

"Deficits in emotion-regulation skills lead to difficulties in 'monitoring, evaluating, and modifying emotional reactions, especially their intensive and temporal features, to accomplish one's goals . . . studies suggest that the ability to cope effectively with negative emotions may mediate the association between stress and the development of psychopathological symptoms." [140]

Work and Working Conditions

There are many jobs where the work is boring and others where working conditions are abhorrent. It is not the nature of the work, but how the work is perceived that determines whether it is seen in a positive light. There are some exceptions in that in some cases the demands of the job are beyond human endurance. There are increasing reports of employees who push themselves too far and actually die from overwork. In Japan they've even created a name for this, karoshi, which means death by overwork. Our bodies give us a great deal of warning when we are going beyond what is healthy and damaging them. We have to be self-aware enough to recognize the signs and change our behavior to protect our body's health.

Employees shouldn't tolerate intolerable working conditions. They should be resilient enough to handle normal working conditions and self-reliant enough to leave untenable circumstances.

Purpose and Meaning

Work can relate to a purpose that is bigger than we are—even if we are in roles that seem routine.

Although the common thoughts on human competence at work focus on knowledge and skills, Sandberg's alternate viewpoint focuses on the "meaning work takes on for workers in their experience of it, rather than a specific set of attributes, constitutes competence." [141] Our thoughts, words, and actions are impacted by our emotional state.

It isn't a specific job that carries meaning; it is the interpretation an employee gives to the job. One does not have to be a doctor, nurse, clergy, soldier, or teacher to feel one's work has a deep and meaningful purpose—something larger than us. We are frequently told that are three ways to view one's role, a job, a career, or a calling. There is another way. All of us have thoughts that energize us. Some common ones are:

- Being helpful to others
- Improving the future
- Taking care of the home, which can be interpreted as one's home or the entire planet
- Preventing problems

There is no right or wrong about which one appeals to an employee. By paying attention to what energizes us, we can find ways to connect a greater purpose to our work, regardless of our specific role or tasks. The parent who changes a dirty diaper is doing a menial task but naturally connects the task to the greater purpose of a healthy and clean baby. No one has to wait until they are *changing the world* to feel their work is meaningful or fulfilling. In fact, when they connect something that is deeply meaningful to them to their work, they do change their world.

Researchers have reported that trash collectors can see their work as deeply meaningful by connecting it to the goal of keeping the world beautiful and healthy. Someone who flips burgers can see their role as helping families reduce stress by providing nourishment when they need it. Doing so doesn't mean that you're called to flip burgers for the rest of your life—just that while you're engaged in that activity you're feeling a greater sense of purpose.

Research shows that employees who feel their work is meaningful are healthier and they are more productive. It is a win-win for both the employee and the employer.

Stigma (i.e. low respect occupations)

Some people feel stigma because of the perceived lowly nature of their jobs. This makes it difficult to feel good about their work. Helping employees connect their tasks with the larger picture can help offset negative feelings about their role.

Connection to others

Some researchers point to the connection one develops with others as a core basis of employee engagement. There is significant evidence supporting the fact that happy people have better relationships of all types to conclude that increasing happiness will naturally result in stronger relationships at work.

Authenticity

Walumbwa, Luthans, Avey and Oke tell us "the key characteristics of authentic leaders are that they exhibit a pattern of openness and clarity in their behavior toward others by sharing the information needed to make decisions, accept others' inputs, and provide constructive feedback to their followers. As a result, followers tend to be more efficacious, hopeful, optimistic, and resilience (i.e. have higher PsyCap) and are more trusting, consequently facilitating high levels of effective behaviors."[142] High, stable self-esteem facilitates greater authenticity because the individual does not feel the need to protect ego. Also see my remarks in Chapter 1 about authenticity and transparency.

Transformational Leadership

Transformational leaders "motivate, inspire, and "transform" followers needs, values, and motives towards a collective, higher-order goal." Transformational leaders "communicate an attractive vision and ideological goals and express confidence in followers' actions."[143] They stimulate creativity and careful problem solving by encouraging followers to challenge existing assumptions and to view situations from different perspectives.

> *"Transformational leaders enhance followers' self-esteem and self-efficacy and, as a consequence, their motivation to perform well by setting high performance goals while showing confidence and faith in followers' competencies. Through this, followers come to believe that they can accomplish the task so that they persist in their efforts and overcome significant obstacles. Further, transformational leaders increase followers' intrinsic motivation by emphasizing higher ideological values and elevating the significance of the task. As a consequence, followers view their jobs as more meaningful and significant and are more motivated to perform well."[144]*

The question remains, how do transformational leaders do this? Beyond finding a perspective about the work that appeals to high ideological values that resonate with a lot of people, on the surface it is not obvious.

- How do you trust others to have the ability to accomplish stretch goals in a way that demonstrates you actually believe they can do what must be done?
- How do you increase self-esteem? Psychologists say it is one of the most difficult things to do.
- How do you increase self-efficacy?
- How do you get employees to rise above the fear of ridicule and come up with innovative ideas and solutions?

When you begin comparing the specifics of what transformational leaders do to PsyCap and Happiness, transformational leaders are essentially increasing numerous factors that increase PsyCap and Happiness and adding a high ideological value.

Since both PsyCap and Happiness are learnable skills, a leader can learn to be a Transformational Leader and use training that increases PsyCap and happiness to do so.

In fact, in one study that looked at the effect of Transformational Leadership and measured the core self-evaluations of the employees, the effect of Transformational Leadership on employees with low core self-evaluations was effective, but not on employees whose core self-evaluations were already high. They theorized that "there is no need for transformational leadership in order for followers to be motivated and perform well" when their core self-evaluations are already high.[145]

There is some evidence that transformational leadership may lead to higher presenteeism, which increases absenteeism of healthy workers over time due to exposure to workers who come to work while ill.[146] To counter this potential I recommend that leaders encourage good self-care, both to prevent illness and while ill. In the US, many employees were raised with vestiges of the Protestant Work Ethic that may lead them to come to work when ill unless and until they are clearly and strongly shown that it is acceptable in the work culture to take time to tend to the needs of their body.

I know this firsthand because I would go to work if I was physically able to get there and it wasn't until my last boss sent me home more than once with no negative repercussions from a performance perspective that I finally accepted the fact that I could take a break to care for myself when I was ill. I even remember going in early and closing my office door to prevent against infecting others by not interacting with them. He still sent me home when he heard my racking coughs.

Looking back it seems silly that I would push myself that hard, but going back to the schema's that lead us to create back stories to support our beliefs, I had a schema that mandated going to work if I was physically able. If memory serves, after my children were old enough to drive, there was even one instance when I did not feel well enough to drive safely so I had my daughter drop me off at work.

See the Potential in Others and in Self

This is not the same as seeing the good in others. While that is a good practice, seeing the potential looks deeper. Seeing the good usually refers to seeing good that is manifesting in their experience. An example would be to see the kind heart of the failing employee.

Seeing the potential in others, while not overlooking the kind heart of the aforementioned employee, would also see within the employee the potential to thrive instead of fail. I recommend this process for everyone to use to the best of their abilities.

Seeing the potential in others begins with an understanding that our best behavior in any moment is impacted by our emotional state in that moment. The current emotional state has significant impacts on all of the following:

Behavior	Intelligence	Relationships
Resilience	Well-Being	Emotional Intelligence (EQ)
Ability to think clearly	Health	

In addition, emotional state directly impacts decisions including those involving diet, exercise, alcohol, drugs, and risky behavior. Our society has a tendency to judge employees based on their current behavior. I will continue with the example of the employee who is failing.

When an employee is failing, there is a tendency to assume she cannot succeed; that in fact, she is not capable of being successful. If we look below the surface it is likely we will find that the employee is dealing with circumstances that would bring many people to their knees. She may have been abused as a child or she may be being abused now. We will realize that she is lower on the EGSc than she could be. Understanding that, we can see that given a better situation and knowledge of how to move to higher levels on the EGSc, she might become a valued employee. We could then choose to give her a hand up and earn significant loyalty as a result.

> *I know in my heart that man is good. That what is right will always eventually triumph. And there's purpose and worth to each and every life.*
> Ronald Reagan

This practice is important for both the person making the judgment and the employee. For the person making the judgment, understand that our stress level rises and our emotional stance decreases when we judge another negatively.

When mirror neurons are considered it becomes clear that whoever has the more dominant belief about the employee's potential for success will influence the other—without words having to be spoken. Researchers at USC and NYU have studied the consequences of affirming one's values and

> *Technology is nothing. What's important is that you have a faith in people, that they're basically good and smart, and if you give them tools, they'll do wonderful things with them.*
> Steve Jobs

found that doing so creates cognitive structure that results in an increased ability to see the big picture.[147] Students primed with a written self-affirming exercise before exams had lower stress on the day of their most stressful exam as measured by epinephrine and norepinephrine.[148]

In general, you can assume that someone behaving in undesirable ways has negative emotions that have not been responded to in of the three constructive methods. The best response to most negative emotion in modern society involves Right Responses (RRs).[149] If we judge ourselves based on our past actions without taking into consideration our emotional state when we made the choices we are judging, we significantly underestimate our potential.

Developing a habit of seeing others for their potential, rather than who they are being in the moment, makes us inspiring to them. By seeing what they cannot see in themselves, we help show them the way to become more of the dormant potential within them.

Humanity has been operating in a way that hinders its ability to thrive. Much like attempting to run a marathon with a weight strapped to one leg would hinder progress, misinterpretation of our Emotional Guidance has been impairing our ability to thrive. We now know enough to unlock the chains that have been holding us back.

Exercises:

Use your intention setting skills to set an intention to see the potential in yourself and others. I encourage you to reinforce this on a daily basis. You will love who you become.

Magnificence resides within all of us, and we need but tap into it and bring it forth.
Alan Cohen

The next time you think a negative thought about someone ask yourself if you are perceiving *who they are being* or *who they could be*. Then ask yourself, what is their potential? Who could this person become if she believed in herself? Who could he become if others believed in him? Who could she become if she understood how to be happier?

Pay attention to the difference in how you perceive the person after asking these questions. Take that new mental snapshot of the person and add detail to it, help to solidify that image as the person's potential in your own mind.

When you are going to interact with the person, imagine the person being their potential self. What does that look like? What does that feel like?

Do not use this potential self as a comparison to find fault with where the person is right now. Instead, use that image to encourage and uplift (even if just in the privacy of your own mind).

People will generally rise to your expectations. They'll also live down to your expectations if your expectations are low. If you doubt this, interact with someone you've decided is not trustworthy and see how the person treats you.

Wait. Oh, you don't think anyone is trustworthy. How does the world treat you? They are reflecting your opinion of them back to you. Try trusting someone for no reason whatsoever and see how they rise to your expectation as long as you trust them. Even someone who is generally not trustworthy behaves in a more trustworthy fashion when someone trusts them for no reason. Someone who is already trustworthy will become even more so when they are trusted for no apparent reason.

6: Unhealthy Cognitive Processes

Your business is never really good or bad "out there" your business is either good or bad right between your own two ears.
Zig Ziglar

As far as I can tell, everything moves along a continuum. On one end of the continuum are characteristics or traits that support employee engagement and on the opposite end are the ones that interfere with employee engagement. The same traits that interfere with employee engagement decrease the individual's ability to be happy and increase the risk of depression and anxiety.

I'm not a strong proponent of labels—they often do more harm than good, but in this case they may be helpful in identifying habits that are counterproductive for both the individual and the employer.

Surface Thinking

Surface thinking is reactionary thinking. Surface thinking doesn't think about why someone might be saying, or doing, what they've said or done. There is also no thought about what sort of outcome or interaction the employee wants from the encounter. Surface thinking involves merely reacting to what occurs. Surface thinking does not consider what underlying beliefs might be impacting interpretations of others words or actions.

Most disagreements are because the people involved are using surface thinking.

If only one person is using deeper thinking, the likelihood of the situation escalating into an argument or violence decreases tremendously. When one person is being aggressive and the other is thinking more deeply, it is easier to understand how to diffuse the situation. Two surface thinkers will just feed into one another, adding negative energy to their respective sides.

Surface thinking is the manager who jumps on the employee who has been late twice this week even though he is usually punctual and does not inquire (or care about why the behavior has changed). He doesn't learn that the employee's sister is in the hospital and the employee is attempting to care for his sister's newborn daughter while continuing to fulfill his responsibilities at work.

Surface thinking is the manager who jumps on the employee because they made a mistake even though the employee has always been accurate in the past because the manager interprets mistakes in one way—a lack of caring about one's work and a sign of lessening engagement. He doesn't bother to learn that her father is in hospice.

Surface thinking is the employee who thinks the boss thinks he is too good to speak to him when they pass in the hallway and doesn't consider that the boss doesn't speak because he's holding in his emotions until he can get to his office to process the fact that he's just been told he has to lay off 10% of his staff and doesn't want to lose it in public.

Surface thinking is when the employee berates his co-worker during a meeting because she forgot to bring a report and fails to dig deeper and learn that she just learned her husband is having an affair.

Surface thinking is assuming the guy who cut you off in traffic is an asshole, not that his child's school just called told him a bully had beat his child in the bathroom at school and he doesn't know how badly his son is hurt.

Surface thinking is reacting to the co-worker who smiled at you many times during the meeting you were both at by believing she was coming on to you, instead of learning that she just learned she and her husband are expecting and she is simply feeling joyful.

Even when the information is available, surface thinking leads to missed cues. The co-worker who asks another employee if she will go with him to hear a new DJ and receives a negative response delivered in a negative tone assumes the co-worker is irritated because he asked her to go when the truth is that she has too many responsibilities she has to deal with and is irritated because she wants to go but doesn't believe she has the time. He knows how much work she needs to complete, but doesn't make the connection because his insecurity about being accepted is a more dominant thought.

The cure to surface thinking is easy.
1. Decide to give other people the benefit of the doubt,
2. Use Emotional Guidance to notice negative emotion, and
3. Use metacognitive processes to help you identify alternative perspectives that feel better

In all the above examples, the person using surface thinking felt negative emotion that, if Emotional Guidance was understood, would have been a clue that the way they were perceiving the situation was not the best possible way to perceive the situation. It's amazing how much difference giving others the benefit of the doubt can make in how life feels on a daily basis. Try it—you'll like it.

It helps to understand that our thoughts are not rational. They are interpretations of a reality that has been condensed by filters that were programmed without conscious thought. The amount of information our subconscious mind processes is far greater than our conscious mind ever becomes aware of. It is estimated that ten million bits of information is processed in any given moment and only fifty bits reaches our conscious awareness. That is a lot of data that is missing from our conscious interpretations of others' words and actions.

In the examples one could argue that the employee should inform the boss about what is going on. I don't disagree but I also see many reasons why an employee would not share such information with management. All those reasons are based on fears. Fear of being perceived as having too much drama in one's life. Fear that if others know how much emotional pain you're in they'll say things that take you right over the edge you're clinging to with everything you've got left.

For example, when my first husband decided he wanted a girlfriend and a wife I did tell my boss. I was too distraught to go to work that day and she met me at a location away from work. But I didn't tell my employees for about nine months. I was in such a fragile emotional state that I knew I'd be reduced to tears if any of them said anything even if what they said was intended to be encouraging. The devastation began in September, we separated in November, and it was the following summer before I told my employees.

One thing that made the situation especially difficult was beliefs I'd been taught about divorced people. I had a lot of negative and limiting beliefs that made the situation much more difficult. Once I discarded those beliefs moving on became easier. If I had known about Emotional Guidance I would have been able to identify and refute many of the beliefs that kept me in emotional pain.

Catastrophizing or Awfulizing
Albert Ellis referred to thinking about situations (or life) in terms that reflect permanent and pervasive tendencies, such as "Nothing ever goes right for me" as *awfulizing* when he was

developing Cognitive Behavioral Therapy. Later, Martin E. P. Seligman used *catastrophizing* to describe one type of thinking that is associated with the development of depression. Both refer to taking something undesired and expanding it to other areas where it is not applicable (pervasive) and to the future (permanent).

These generalizations are not true—they are exaggerations. Refuting them helps employees see that they are not true, which helps them feel better. Emotional Guidance provides positive reinforcement when refuting permanent and pervasive thoughts.

Shoulding

I'm seeing a lot of push back against what some are calling the Happiness Movement. When I read the details, it always seems to be someone who has come to believe they should be happy because they have a good life, but they aren't happy. They are *should-ing* themselves to lower emotional states. There is no *should* about how you feel. You could be married to a very attractive person who is very good to you, live in a house many dream about, have 2.5 perfect children, the exact pet you always wanted, perfect health, a great career or a fat bank account, and an attractive physic and be legitimately unhappy. If you're focused on something you don't have, or on those who do not yet have what you have, if you believe you have too much, or you believe the other shoe will drop any day, or you are focused on a tragedy that has happened to others you consider your in-group, or something that is happening to animals, or on someone who left you or died, or you did something you are beating yourself up over, or you feel guilty about something from your past, or you feel like you don't deserve what you have or that they'll figure out you're an imposter and not the person who they thought you were and on and on and on, you'll be unhappy. You're not focused on something that feels good. Of course you're unhappy. You could be happy. But you get to choose. Frequently, you're violating what Dr. Robert Holden calls your personal Happiness Contract. I refer to is as believing a false premise. Just believing you *should* be happy is a false premise. You could be happy—that's true. But don't *should* all over yourself.

There is not really a "should have" that is accurate. Every employee, no matter how awful they have done in a given situation, did the best they could at that specific point in time given what they knew and the resources (internal and external) that they perceived were available to them.

This statement will, I know, receive a great deal of pushback. But when you remember that negative emotion restricts our cognitive abilities, what someone who is happy knows and is capable of doing is not the same as that person can do when they feel threatened. Nor is someone's best when well rested the same as their best when sleep deprived. Illness, nourishment, thirst, emotional state, time restrictions, and other factors change a person's in-the-moment best. One's best potential, or best ever is not the same as their best in a given moment. We can't use willpower to improve cognitions when our level of stress is high. Stress depletes our ability to use willpower. The best way to ensure we are at our best possible in any given moment is to learn ways to reduce stress and free our full cognitive powers so they are available to help us deal with any situation we encounter. We also need to give our bodies the care and respect they need to provide a highly functioning environment while seeing them as strong and possessing their own sort of wisdom.

Rumination

Humans have the ability to think about past, present, and future. Worry is thinking about the future with a negative slant. Rumination is thinking about the past with a negative focus. Thinking about the past is not the problem. It is thinking about the past and fretting about what wasn't as you wanted it to be. *Shoulding* and *could having* all over yourself is not productive. It's fine to take the lessons learned but doing that feels good.

The thought, "Now I understand that when I feel that way I might want to make a different decision than I did in the past" is helpful. You're smart enough to take the lesson and move on. You do not have to repeatedly rub your nose in it before you'll learn. And an attitude of *I did the best I could at that moment under the circumstances and with the knowledge I had at the time* will serve you well.

The most productive focus is one that is either in the flow on a task you're working on or looking ahead to something you want in the future. Rumination makes today worse and does not improve tomorrow.

Self-criticism

Self-criticism is often learned in our childhood home. Parents often spend more time pointing out perceived flaws or shortcomings in their children and little time reinforcing their strengths. They may be repeating a pattern from the way they were raised or they may be hoping to avoid raising someone who violates their beliefs about humility. The reason doesn't matter. The outcome does matter—a lot.

Low self-esteem is reinforced with self-criticism. The inner dialogue many people live with includes saying to themselves things they would not say to someone they don't like. Self-criticism can involve self-referent internal dialogue that reinforces ideas such as "I'm too stupid" or "I'm too dumb to learn" or "I'm too old to learn" or name-calling such as pathetic, useless, worthless, ugly, and worse.

Some people believe that self-criticism is necessary for motivation and to keep them from seeing themselves as too good. There is nothing wrong with having high self-worth. The problem comes when that high self-worth depends on negative comparisons to others. I'm good because I'm better than some other person demeans another. That is not the healthy way to develop or maintain healthy self-worth. The better way is to see that humans, all humans, have significant value and worth.

There are two easy ways to do this. One is to base the value of every human on the value of their unique perspectives. We all have different perspectives and the more perspectives we have available the more potential solutions we have to problems and the more interesting life can be. It also does not matter if someone is highly educated and has multiple Ph.D.'s—they could still learn something from the least educated persons. Everyone knows things that others do not know and no one knows everything.

There is a lot of research that supports the value diversity brings to teams and to Boards. By basing the foundation of each human's value on their unique perspectives, value judgments are unnecessary. Actually, they're impossible. One human cannot learn all that someone else might offer in terms of unique perspectives even if they spend their entire life attempting to learn just one person's ideas because our perspectives expand all the time. I teach a weekly class at a behavioral health center that serves primarily low-income and minority populations who are recovering from addictions. Many of the students are illiterate yet they have great wisdom that comes from hard-lived lives—wisdom that could benefit employees who think a bad commute means their day is ruined.

In a recent study[150] of individuals experiencing divorce, self-compassion, which would translate into less negative self-talk—was cited as ***the factor*** that uniquely predicts good outcomes. "Negative self-statements, also known as negative self-referent cognitions, have been linked with levels of social anxiety."[151]

End Self-criticism

Man often becomes what he believes himself to be. If I keep on saying to myself that I cannot do a certain thing, it is possible that I may end by really becoming incapable of doing it. On the contrary, if I have the belief that I can do it, I shall surely acquire the capacity to do it even if I may not have it at the beginning.
Mahatma Gandhi

The first step to ending self-criticism is to give yourself permission and then set your intentions. Many people have lived with a negative voice in their heads so long they mistake it for who they are. It isn't. It might be your mother, but it isn't your mother when she was in the Sweet Zone. (And yes, it is possible your mother was never in the Sweet Zone—the possibility of this is a common question in my programs.)

Think about what motivates you to exercise. If you exercise regularly, how do you explain your reason when asked? If you don't exercise regularly, do you tell yourself you should? Do you mentally beat yourself up for not exercising? Why do you tell yourself you should exercise more? If you are repeatedly telling yourself something like, "You don't exercise enough," or, "You're going to gain weight because you don't exercise enough," or, "If you don't start exercising you're going to die young," you are affirming the undesired. Affirming what you do not want leads to long term self-fulfilling prophesies.

The mechanics of negative self-talk are complex. First, self-criticism increases your level of stress. That causes biochemical changes in your body—including depressing your immune system, reducing your energy, and other stress responses. None of this is healthy for your body. Then, the mind, which is very malleable and obedient to repeated affirmations, forms beliefs that lead to the exact outcomes you are telling yourself you will experience by giving yourself the negative affirmations.

"Self-criticism is a form of negative self-judgement and self-evaluating, which can be directed to various aspects of the self, such as one's physical appearance, behaviour, inner thoughts and emotions, personality and intellectual attributes . . . and is associated with the development or a range of psychopathologies. In contrast, abilities to be self-reassuring and self-compassionate are negatively linked to psychopathology."[152] Training that increases the ability to support one's self-affirming abilities and decreases self-criticism can improve mental health.

If you are in the habit of negative self-criticism, do everything you can to stop it. Refuting it is a good tool. You can begin by shifting a little bit. For example, "I am learning to reduce my stress level. When my level of stress is lower, I will naturally feel like exercising more. My body enjoys moving and soon I will move it more." This refuting statement may be more than you can believe right now. If that is so, find something you do believe that feels better than the negative self-talk. Take baby steps.

As you learn stress-decreasing skills and your energy level rises, kick it up a little: "I feel more energetic than I used to. I am enjoying adding exercise to my day. My body really enjoys moving. Now I enjoy it, too." Find affirmations that you can believe and that support what you want. If you can't believe anything close to what you want yet, just move in that direction a step at a time. With an unhealthy mindset about ourselves, or aspects of physical activity, we can harm our health by increasing stress.

For example, people who beat themselves up about exercising harm themselves in these ways:

1. Self-induced stress caused by making exercise about preventing illness.
2. Self-induced stress from negative self-criticism related to not exercising or not doing it well enough or often enough.
3. Stress from peer and parental pressure to act grown-up and forgo fun childish physical activities.

If you do not make much progress eliminating the critic at first, put this intention aside and focus on building your trust in your guidance. Once you have experimented with your guidance and built trust in the answers you received from your guidance this task becomes easier. You can use your guidance to ask if what your critic is saying is true, if the self-criticism is beneficial, and other questions you may have about the inner critic.

When you are ready, refute the comments the inner critic is sharing. If the critic told me I couldn't do something, my response was "Watch me." If the critic told me I wasn't good enough, my response was to find evidence in the world that contradicted the critic. For example, if the critic told me I was unattractive, I would remember times when real people told me the opposite. If the critic told me I wasn't smart enough, I remembered how I have used my brain to solve problems.

If you feel ready to challenge your inner critic, try setting a timer on your phone to go off randomly several times a day during times when you may have a moment to think about what your inner voice is saying. When the alarm goes off, notice what your inner voice was saying and if it was negative use techniques in this book to challenge the premises of the negative words. You can refute it. You can go more general in what you're thinking about or you can look for facts that show the voice is wrong.

You can decide to change something about yourself without declaring your current state of being as bad or unworthy. You are like your life, a journey, not a destination. You are constantly changing and improvements can be part of that journey. There is not a requirement to declare that who you are is bad or wrong in order to grow. Does the crawling infant declare itself bad for not yet walking? No. The same holds true throughout life. You are where you are. Wherever that is can be improved.

The person in life that you will always be with the most, is yourself. Because even when you are with others, you are still with yourself, too! When you wake up in the morning, you are with yourself, lying in bed at night you are with yourself, walking down the street in the sunlight you are with yourself. What kind of person do you want to walk down the street with? What kind of person do you want to wake up in the morning with? What kind of person do you want to see at the end of the day before you fall asleep? Because that person is yourself, and it's your responsibility to be that person you want to be. I know I want to spend my life with a person who knows how to let things go, who's not full of hate, who's able to smile and be carefree. So that's who I have to be.
C. Joy Bell

Low self-esteem usually has one of two roots. One is a habit of comparing oneself to others and looking for flaws. Remember, you are comparing your bloopers to someone else's highlight reel. Don't do that. It is not helpful to you. It does not make you more motivated.

If you're comparing your income to what someone else makes and finding fault with your results, you may also be hastening ill health and an early demise on yourself. There is significant research indicating it is the comparison you make and not the lower income that causes less desirable health outcomes.[153] You can adopt a different perspective. How about, "I'm smarter than he is. If he can make that much, so can I." Accepting responsibility for where you are is more empowering than blaming others for your situation.

The other common root cause of low self-esteem is a parent or other significant influencer (sometimes a spouse) who repeatedly does and says things to make you feel less than you are. Remember what you have learned about the impact of emotional state on behavior. No one who was tearing you down was in a good emotional state. Someone in a good emotional state can find something to praise and love about anyone. Their comments, as hurtful as they felt at the time, only contain the power you gave them to hurt you. If you recognize that the comment reflects the person's emotional state at the time rather than a valid judgment of your worth, the pain lessens.

While teaching human thriving in high schools, I have had children ask me if it is possible their mom or dad has been angry their whole life. The relief on their face when I said yes let me know I mattered. I would also go on to explain that most people stay in their dominant emotional state for long periods—often for life—because society has not taught them how to change their emotional state. Even with the Think Positive movement, the concept was pushed but the **how** has been largely ignored.

Reframing prior experiences through a new lens that understands adverse behavior from others was evidence of their low Emotional State, and not of your worth, can be very healing. It also increases compassion.

Imagine a rebellious teenage girl who has been frequently unkind to her chronically angry, or chronically frustrated, Mother, the epitome of a relationship on a downward spiral without a good ending. The angry Mom is literally training those around her to treat her in ways that make her angry. The daughter has learned this well. Even though she is a good person, without a deliberate intention to be otherwise, she is sucked into the Mom's angry energy. But now, armed with the information that her Mom's behavior is the result of not feeling emotionally good, she can set a new intention. She can decide who she is. For example, she can decide, "I am a kind person. I will do my best to be a positive force in this world." It will take practice because by this time the daughter has developed some neurological pathways that will work against her in the beginning. Later the new neurological pathways she deliberately cultivates will help her maintain who she has decided to be.

She can be conscious during her interactions with her mom and when her mom is not being supportive, rather than becoming defensive, she can recognize that her mom is feeling emotionally bad. Armed with that knowledge, she can look for ways to uplift mom—which is the only thing that is going to improve the behavior. In saying this, recognize it is not the teenager's job to uplift her mom. It is not her responsibility. But, unless her mom understands the EGS, the other choices are not good ones. We can ignore mom; however, this could lead to worsening behavior for a teenager living in her mom's home.

Without an understanding of the EGSc, the teenager typically allows an inner critic to move into her mind and suffers low self-esteem that limits her life. With an understanding of the EGS, a much better outcome is possible.

My inner critic moved away a few years ago. You can encourage yours to move, too. Humor can help with the persistent inner critic. You can begin telling the critic how nice it is in some place far way, maybe Tahiti, and encouraging it to relocate and that you'll accept four critical postcards a year. Have fun with it. You give the critic its power by believing it. At any time, you have the ability to overthrow its reign.

Oh, and if it is your mom? Don't tell her. It won't help your relationship. It also does not mean she was a bad Mom. We live in an era when we have been trained to criticize those we love the most of all. The intention was good. Appreciate that you are learning a better way. Children tend to identify with their parents and therefore tend to internalize and self-inflict verbally abusive statements against themselves throughout their lives.[154] The life sentence is optional. The skills in this book can provide release from the self-critical thought patterns.

Being kind to yourself matters. Do it.

Exercise

Pay attention to negative thoughts you think about yourself and make a note of them in a notebook. Spend some time each day, preferably when you're feeling hopeful or above but if you're seldom in hopeful, just try to catch yourself when you're feeling your best, and work on shifting the thought patterns.

Pull out the negative thought and find ways to lessen its hold.

Let's use age as an example.

Original thought: *I'm too old to get a good job. No one wants to hire someone in their 50's.*

Contrary thoughts:

50 isn't that old. 50 is the new 30. I'm still vibrant and alive. I just picked up some bogus beliefs about age during my life but now that I'm here I see they were really off the mark. I'm experienced and gaining some wisdom, but I'm nowhere near old. Employers would be lucky to hire me. I'm responsible. I am at a point in my life where I can really focus on my career without a lot of distractions. I'm mature and responsible. I don't look old. I don't feel old. All I have to do is go in there feeling energetic and bright and they'll be delighted to hire me. I'll make them believe they're having a lucky day.

Negative self-talk often lacks a basis in reality. It is most often a bogus belief you picked up somewhere that just isn't serving you. Refuting it and substituting a belief that serves you better enables you to form new beliefs. Remember, beliefs are just thoughts you've thought repeatedly until they became beliefs. Think new thoughts repeatedly for a while and you'll establish new beliefs.

Refute

Refuting is an especially powerful process for anyone who has never questioned his thoughts before. Thoughts do not equate to truth. It is common for someone to have a mistaken impression about someone—leaning too good or too bad.

When we realize that we can decide whether we want to go along with a thought or not, it is empowering. When combined with the feedback our EGS provides, we can determine whether a thought is leaning toward truth or not. When the thought feels bad, it is not our truth. When it feels good, it is our truth.

Use your EGS to identify thoughts that are not serving you. When you find one, refute it. Look for evidence of reasons it is wrong.

For example, many people have a belief that goes like this, "Life is hard." If you look at the lives of people with that belief, life is hard for them—but there are many people whose lives are not hard. The belief, "Life is hard" is refutable. Because life is not hard for everyone you know it is a belief and not destiny. Well, it is destiny (for you) if you keep the belief. Refuting it is one way to loosen the belief—sort of like wiggling a loose tooth. The best way to replace beliefs that do not serve you is to overwrite them with beliefs that do.

If I had this belief (I don't because my life is not hard), I would begin by shifting to a belief along the lines of "Life is hard for some people but I'm learning new skills and it isn't going to be hard for me anymore." I would use this to refute the belief and reinforce the new, more desirable belief.

This would not be my final stop. After shifting from a belief that "Life is hard" to "Life is hard for some people but I'm learning new skills and it isn't going to be hard for me anymore." I would use this to refute the belief and reinforce the new, more desirable belief.

Eventually, I would move to the belief: "Life is easy and fun. I live a blessed life."

Remember, the negative emotion you feel when you think a thought that does not serve you means that thought is not the best perspective you can have on that subject. I like to call my thoughts like that "Bogus." It just feels good and lessens the power of those leftover beliefs that are not serving my highest good.

Exercise

What is true about your life that is not true of everyone else?

Think about things you feel jealous or envious about.

Jealousy and/or envy reflect that the person is seeing someone with something they want that they do not believe they can have.

Jealousy and envy are evidence that they do not believe they can have something. The negative emotion is their guidance telling them that they're not finding a good perspective on that topic.

Take one subject at a time and find a thought that feels better about the topic. During the first step, just weaken the original thought. In subsequent steps, find a thought that feels a little better that you can believe. Keep moving toward thoughts that feel better. You can do this over a period of months, days, hours, or minutes. The more you practice, the faster you can shift your perspective and feel better.

Or, just call the original thought bogus. Sometimes you already know it is bogus on some level and it is just a habit of thought that is not serving you. If calling it bogus feels great, you know you were primed for changing it.

7: Goals/Setting Intentions

Open-ended goals are not measurable and do not have specific time frames within which they can be reached. The pursuer cannot know when the objective has been reached, nor can he or she experience the positive emotions associated with successful goal attainment.[155] Goals should be:

1. Measurable,
2. Have specific time frames,
3. Described in a singular fashion,
4. Consistent with long-term goals,
5. Cause no harm to self or others and (ideally) uplift self and others

The first goal should be to feel as good as one can feel under the circumstances, day-in and day-out. This breaks down into being psychologically flexible in perception about one's situation and using skills to shift perspectives to ones that feel better as needed. As chronic emotional state improves, cognitive abilities will improve, bringing to mind solutions to current challenges.

Setting intentions is a form of goal setting. When you set intentions to do certain things, it sensitizes the filters that decide which information will be sent to your conscious mind, highlighting information in alignment with your intentions. Identify the most personally meaningful values to guide your decisions and actions.

I used to work with a very quick-witted COO from New York who frequently responded while I was still formulating my response in our executive meetings. Often, this took the conversation in a new direction and the opportunity for me to add value passed without my input. I began setting the intention "The best answers I can think of will come to me quickly" as I walked to the boardroom for our meetings. My responses became faster. The COO was no longer always ahead of me in his responses. I still remember his face the first time I answered ahead of him—he was truly surprised that I spoke before he did.

Intentions can be set for one's life—much like a mission statement. They can be set for a year, a month, a day, a relationship, a journey, a conversation. Setting intentions is a very versatile form of goal setting.

Intentions can be general or specific. You can set a goal that your decisions will always lean toward your highest good. You can set an intention to be aware of situations where you can be of benefit to others.

What would you like to have more of in your life? What would you like to do better in your life?

I like goal setting. I had a 1, 2, 5, and 20-year plan when I was 21. I am convinced that many of my successes were the result of setting specific goals.

I like setting intentions because they do not require a lot of preparation or thought. They help one be in the flow more often when the intention is to be the best you can in the moment. Research shows that setting intentions reduces the energy required to complete the action[156] because it lowers the self-control required because it aligns what you want to do with what you need to do.

Setting intentions is good for any level on the EGSc. Much like with the Positive Affirmation process, the key is to set intentions you believe you can achieve. The difference between Setting Intentions and Positive Affirmations is that Setting Intentions is about something you are going to do and the outcome you desire from the activity.

Exercise:

Do you have an area of your life where you often feel just a little less than you want to be? Try setting an intention for what you would like better in those situations and see what happens. Make a decision to focus on setting intentions throughout a single day to set intentions for your activities and pay attention to how the day works out.

When you awaken, set an intention:
I will have the best day possible today.

When you go to have breakfast, set an intention that you will choose healthy food:
The healthiest foods will appeal to me the most.

Before you head out for the day set an intention:
My day will be productive and work out the best for me.

When you answer the phone:
I will have the right words to have the best outcome from this conversation.

When you travel:
My journey will be fun. [††]

Goal setting

"Studies have found that priming general goals could influence behavior and cognitive processing."[157]

Long-term vs. Short-term Goals

Whether we're looking long-term or short-term when we make decisions about what will feel best depends on a variety of factors, but mostly on which ones we've focused on more. If long-term goals aren't given a lot of airtime in our mind, short-term goals will steer our decision-making because we have not created **thought-paths** about the potential consequences of our actions as they related to our long-term goals.

Focusing on long-term goals increases the consideration we give the consequences of our words and actions. However, it is important that the goals be our own--not goals others attempt to impose upon us.

Self-Management

Marilyn Gist compared self-management to goal-setting training and found self-management training superior to goal-setting training for improving maintenance of learned interpersonal skills and both were superior to didactic programs that highlight the risks of adverse behaviors. The Chapter Summary in the 27th chapter of *Applied Behavior Analysis* defines self-management as follows: [158]

[††] I do not recommend reaching for a safe journey because it often contains the fear that it will not be safe. Fun inherently implies safe and enjoyable.

"Self-management is defined as the personal application of behavior change tactics that produces a desired change in behavior. The term self-control is also used to refer to this type of behavior change program. However, self-control as a term implies several additional constructs beyond the reference of a person acting in some way in order to change subsequent behavior.

Self-management is a relative concept—a behavior change program may necessitate a small level of self-management or a wide-spanned scale of self-management. Self-management can be used to live a more effective and efficient daily life, break bad habits and acquire new ones, accomplish difficult tasks, and achieve personal goals. Learning and teaching self-management skills have many advantages and benefits to the individual actually learning or implementing the skills, those teaching it, and others who may benefit from the individual's use of the skills.

Self-monitoring is often a component of a self-management program and is the procedure by which a person observes and responds to the behavior she is trying to change. Self-monitoring was originally developed as a method of clinical assessment for behaviors that were thought to be observable only by the client herself. Self-monitoring is frequently combined with additional strategies such as goal setting, self-evaluation, and reinforcement delivered for meeting predetermined criteria."

Many prevention programs, from corporate wellness programs to anti-drug programs rely heavily on less effective didactic programs that emphasize potential adverse consequences of doing certain behaviors (drinking, drugs, unsafe sex, and smoking) and not doing certain behaviors (exercise, healthy diet, adequate sleep). Emotional Guidance training is a more powerful way to increase desired behaviors and prevent drug and alcohol abuse.

Research has repeatedly linked stress to lower pro-health behaviors and to increases in risky behaviors and drug and alcohol abuse. Skills that reduce stress make it easier to make good decisions.

The following chart contains beliefs that support thriving and beliefs that hinder thriving. You can use it to help you shift your beliefs. Don't try to jump all the way from one side to the other in a single exercise. Use the beliefs that feel like ease as the final destination. Every move toward those beliefs will provide a sense of relief.

	Beliefs that feel like Struggle	Self-Control Beliefs that feel like Ease
School	I hate school	I am a good student
	School is hard for me	I can have fun while learning
	I don't like school.	I am good at learning
Work	My job sucks	I like _____ about my job
	My work is meaningless	My work is important
	My boss doesn't value me	My contributions have value to my boss
	I'm undervalued at work	I am respected at work
	I'm a F. U.	I am good at my job
	I don't understand how to get ahead	I learn more every day
	I'm in a no-where job	I make the most of myself
	I live for weekends	I can enjoy myself every day
Popular	No one wants to spend time with me	I am easy to get along with
	I'm afraid of what people think of me	Most people like me
	I don't want to show my true self	People are interesting
	Will they like me?	I like people
	The world has a lot of bad people	I have friends I can trust
Being Nice	No one can make me be nice	I am a nice person
	My teacher is mean	My teacher cares about me
	I won't do nothing for nobody	I feel good when I do nice things
	They'll let me down if I trust them	People will live up to my expectations
Drugs/Alcohol	Drugs make me feel better	I value my brain
	Alcohol makes me feel more social	I'm happy
	I don't know how to feel better	I can change my focus and feel better
	I can't stand this emotional pain	I can love and let go
	Drinking gets me through the day	I'm strong, I can make it
	Everyone I know does drugs	I can be whoever I want to be
Eating	Food comforts me	Food fuels my body
	I binge on junk food when I'm sad	I can eat what I want in moderation
	I'm eat when I'm lonely	I enjoy my own company
Crime	I can get away with this	I am a law abiding person
	I only care about myself	I'm an ethical person
	I deserve this –they owe me	My life has lots of potential

8: Resilience

There is no problem that doesn't have some underlying need for more optimism, stamina, resilience and collaboration.
Jane McGonigal

What is resilience?

Resilience is the ability to bounce back following adversity or stress and return to one's prior state or better. By definition, resilience involves flexibility because adverse situations humans encounter vary in great degree. Sometimes there is a single event and at other times employees experience a series of adverse events. Some employees can be resilient enough to handle a single adverse event but crumble under a series of misfortunes while others seem to take them all in stride. Resilience is "not related merely to the availability of resources in the social environment, but also to the agency shown by young people as they identify these resources, recognize them as opportunities and mobilize or activate them towards helpful engagement."[159]

van der Werff et al. tell us resilience is "Reflective of the capacity of an individual to avoid negative social, psychological and biological consequences, and cognitive impacts of extreme stress that would otherwise compromise their psychological or physical well-being." [160] I would add avoiding damage to one's relationships. Stress can be damaging to one's relationships and marriages frequently end because of heightened stress caused by a variety of factors including the loss of a child or building a new home.

Six years before the twin towers fell; van der Werff et al. conducted a review of the lifetime prevalence of exposure to severe traumatic events in the United States which indicated ranges between 51.2 to 60.7% of the population experienced such an event during their lifetime. Events being reported in the news media, from school shootings, the war, and terrorist attacks on American soil indicate the number may be higher today. Exposure to traumatic events leads some people to develop mental illnesses such as anxiety, PTSD, and depression while others experience posttraumatic growth, becoming more than they might have become if they had not had the traumatic experience.

When stressful events happen, resilience makes a tremendous difference in how an employee responds. Even the most vulnerable members of our society, children from economically disadvantaged environments, are able to avoid the poor outcomes so many of their less resilient neighbor's experience. Simmons and Yoder found that the "Consequences of having high resilience include positive factors such as decreased mental health symptoms and career and personal success, especially when placed in stressful situations . . . Conversely, consequences of having low resilience include increased risk for mental illness, such as anxiety, depression, PTSD, and suicidal ideations."[161] Wingo et al. concluded that over the course of one's life, resilient characteristics are like a steady friend who protects against illicit drug use across the lifetime, mitigate risks of PTSD, major depression, and suicidality.[162]

Individual resilience plays out on a large scale following adverse events such as prolonged war. "Public resilience seems to be linked with more beneficial postwar responses, which contribute toward returning to normal life after experiencing the distress of war."[163] Public resilience increases "belief in a better future, and belief in its ability to overcome hardship and to strive for improvement despite current anxiety and distressing conditions."[164] Worldwide this has very relevant impacts. While many would say that this is not true in the United States, I would argue that for many people living in urban poverty, the circumstances of their surroundings are no better than those people living in war torn countries and in some cases their circumstances are worse.

Lyubomirsky & Porta report in *Boosting Happiness and Buttressing Resilience: Results from Cognitive and Behavioral Interventions* that psychological interventions that increase positive emotions can increase resilience. [165] Southwick et al., a panel of resilience experts at International Society for Traumatic Stress Studies, concluded that although "interventions to enhance resilience can be administered before, during or after stressful/traumatic situations . . . Ideally, interventions/training will occur prior to stressful events so that the employee is better prepared to deal with adversity." [166] I completely concur because when resilience is high, the amount of time someone spends suffering in negative emotional states following a stressful or traumatic event is minimized. One study that looked at 230 outpatients suffering from depression and anxiety disorders found "cognitive emotion regulation strategies of refocus on planning, positive reappraisal, and less rumination contribute to resilience in patients with depression and anxiety disorders." [167]

Endurance can be increased by changing how we look at what we have to endure. Smaller increments of time can make the unbearable, bearable. I only have to stay here five more minutes is easier to endure mentally than thinking you have to be there ten hours. Calculating the days until you can leave a bad situation on your terms can make it easier to endure.

Wingo, Ressler, and Bradley, "theorize that resilience characteristics mitigate risks for substance use disorders in individuals exposed to childhood abuse or other traumatic experiences via a combination of factors including emotional and cognitive control under pressure, tolerance of negative affect, utilization of cognitive reappraisal, goal orientation, spiritual coping, nurturing role models, or strong social support." [168] There is broad agreement that a lack of resilience leads to a wide variety of problems. Khanlou and Wray attribute low resilience to "unsafe sex, poor educational performance and completion, bullying, crime, employment, job productivity and the likelihood of poverty." [169]

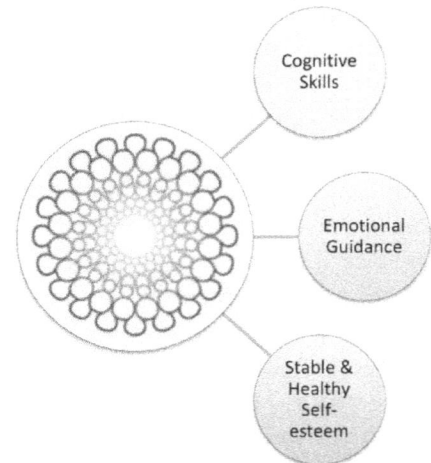

Cognitive Skills

Emotional Guidance

Stable & Healthy Self-esteem

Resilience is derived from a combination of internal and external resources although some of the external resources are perceptually based (i.e. support from friends), which I would argue is internal because one might have highly supportive friends but not perceive them as supportive so their willingness to offer support is ignored. In other situations, employees might perceive their friends as supportive and as providing a back-up plan to fall back on when their friends would not actually be willing to provide the support. As long as the back-up plan is not needed, the employee will benefit from perceiving that it is available.

An article in the *International Journal of Hospitality Management* reads as if it comes from a mechanistic viewpoint, as if we are mechanistic beings, where when a button or switch is pushed or pulled the reaction of the organism will be based on the physical apparatus in terms of its genetic make-up and neurological construction. [170] This sort of approach leaves no space for the very real potential for coping methods to be learned and incorporated in one's psychological responses. Since we know the quality of one's coping skills affect whether stressful life events lead to "anxiety, depression, psychological distress, and somatic complaints" it makes sense to teach the best possible coping skills to everyone.

Their mechanistic assumptions could not be further from the truth. Neurology is created by the thoughts that a person thinks which then affects the chemical composition of the body. We have free will to choose our thoughts. Many people feel their thoughts choose them, but that is only because they have not yet learned how to use their minds. Our education system currently teaches children to memorize, not to think in ways that support our highest good.

Humans possess the ability to think about what they are thinking about. This is called metacognition. An employee who has experienced a traumatic event can find herself repeatedly re-playing the event in her own mind, which neurologically, is like repeating the actual event. An employee experiencing this can react emotionally and physically to the re-play or she can take a step back and observe herself replaying the event in her mind and deliberately intervene to stop the re-play. In such a situation, the best way for someone who has not practiced metacognitive skills to stop the re-play is to deliberately re-focus. Even if all she does the first time she uses metacognition is decide she will come up with a focus-shifting strategy for the next time, significant progress has been made.

Then, when she is not in the middle of a re-play she can come up with a strategy about something to focus on instead of the re-play. The first time she implements the strategy she may be five minutes into the re-play before she remembers she has a plan and implements it. But in the moment she does it, she will feel more empowered than she has in a while. Taking control of one's own thought processes and deliberately shifting focus to something that feels better is a liberating experience. The next time she finds herself in the re-play, she will remember she has a strategy sooner, so she'll experience less of the re-play than she did the time before. Each time recognition that she can use a strategy to stop the re-play will come faster and the time between re-plays will be longer until the re-plays become rare. Eventually she will realize it has been years since she thought about something that used to bother her frequently.

An employee who has learned to use metacognitive practices and practices them to reduce stress in their daily life before a traumatic event can use metacognition during the actual event. It can be used to help escape the reality of what is happening or to increase one's chances of escape by reducing fear, which improves one's ability to think clearly and identify opportunities for escape. It can even change one's perception of an event from traumatic to a simple bump in the road. What is considered traumatic varies significantly from person to person. It's one reason one of the Zones on the EGSc is referred to as the Drama Zone.

> *Nothing can stop the man with the right mental attitude from achieving his goal; nothing on earth can help the man with the wrong mental attitude.*
> *Thomas Jefferson*

Scientists who have begun looking at habits of thought to evaluate individual differences in outcomes are discovering that a positive mental attitude greatly increases the chance of Posttraumatic Growth—the best possible outcome following an adverse life event. They are also discovering that a negative mindset is common among those who suffer the worst outcomes including PTSD, psychosis, and suicide. Research published in 2015 is beginning to reflect this, "These findings suggest that difficulties with using cognitive reappraisal, specifically to decrease negative affect, might be linked to suicide risk."[171]

Negative Life Events defined:

The death of a parent, life-threatening illness in a parent or child, parental psychological disorders, economic patterns necessitating parents working long hours and thereby being less available and/or less responsive, divorce, war, military deployment of a parent, eviction.

Negative life events do not automatically translate into bad outcomes. The reasons attributed to the negative event have a significant impact on long-term outcomes. Individuals who blame themselves or who believe that things happened because they *were bad* or *not good enough* have worse outcomes.

Emotional Guidance is helpful in refuting negative cognitions about responsibility, blame, and guilt. Carol Dweck found that children who have similar negative life events who do not use negative self-attributions to explain the event fare better. [172] Individuals can be taught to use their Emotional Guidance to identify better-feeling perspectives about any life event. Once they have some experience finding new perspectives, they can use Emotional Guidance to reverse emotional pain from past events. The better-feeling the perspective they can find about any subject, the better their outcomes will be.

Fredrickson and Branigan found that disempowered perspectives create negative emotional states, which exacerbate situations by constricting cognitive processes while positive emotional states broaden and build thought-action repertoires. [173] Okon-Singer et al. found "that stress, anxiety, and other kinds of emotion can profoundly influence key elements of cognition, including selective attention, working memory, and cognitive control." [174] Pietrzak and Southwick found that individuals who are more resilient going into combat have fewer problems following traumatic experiences and are more likely to experience posttraumatic growth. [175]

Individuals have far more control over how they perceive any given situation than most realize. They could feel fearful about a situation, which would result in a pessimistic outlook and a more disempowered perspective than other possible perspectives. Lerner and Keltner reported that if a person felt angry about the same situation, they would feel more optimistic and empowered than someone who is fearful. [176] Voss found that perspectives about any given situation is usually based upon habits of thought rather than thoughtful consideration of the current situation. [177]

In Zimmer-Gembeck and Skinner's 2014 research, *The Development of Coping: Implications for Psychopathology and Resilience*, the prevalence of "major life stressors, including the death of a loved one, witnessing a traumatic event or experiencing abuse by family members or others, are common experiences among children and adolescents, occurring for about 25%." [178] By the time they've lived as adults for a while, the prevalence of exposure to traumatic events soared to 89.7% and exposure to multiple traumatic events was more common than a single exposure. [179]

> A negative mental attitude is a self-imposed handicap. It makes a person more susceptible to adverse outcomes from traumatic events.

Roughly half the participants in the study had experienced a disaster, accident, fire, physical or sexual assault, or the death of family or a close friend due to violence, accident or disaster and only 7.8% was combat exposure. Out of this group of 2,953 individuals, Kilpatrick et al. found 9.4% had experienced PTSD as defined by DSM-V during their lifetime and 5.3% had experienced PTSD during the past year. [180]

Clearly, there is a high likelihood that an employee will experience a traumatic event during his or her lifetime. Developing a resilient mindset that will lead to the best possible outcome before the event is much like wearing a seatbelt in a car or an airplane. It's a preventative measure. The risk of exposure to a traumatic event is greater than the risk of being in a plane crash.

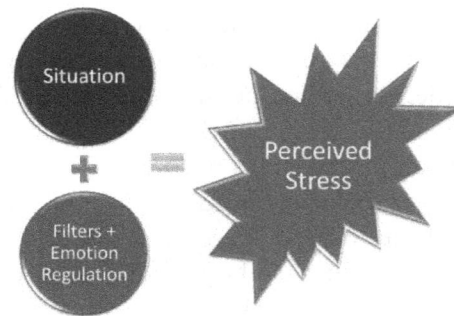

Developing a resilient mindset, unlike wearing a seatbelt, comes with many other advantages. A resilient mindset is a positive mental attitude, which improves physical and mental health (even if a traumatic event doesn't occur), because less stress is experienced in everyday situations with a positive mental attitude. Success in all areas of life and relationship health is also better with a resilient mindset.

No one can accurately predict what adversities life might bring to an employee or business. Preparation creates stability and lessens the impact of undesired situations. Potentially traumatic events are events that can lead to the dysfunction the media so often reports, such as PTSD. But Bonanno and Diminich found that the same type of situation can have a minimal impact or even lead to posttraumatic growth in others.[181]

Special consideration should be given to an employee's level of resilience when they are assigned roles relating to a business continuity plan. Business continuity plans must consider the potential that an employee does not survive the initial disaster or is too injured to assume the assigned responsibilities. By knowing whether the employee is resilient before a disaster, the chances that the employee will fulfill the assigned duties can be determined with greater accuracy. Also, resilience can be increased so employees whose resilience levels are low can be given training to increase their resilience.

In her research and in *Positivity*, Barbara L. Fredrickson shares three factors that are critical to resilience:

1) Internal locus of control
2) Optimism
3) Healthy self-esteem[182]

What is an internal locus of control? It is the belief that your words and actions matter—that what you do can change the outcome of your life. The thought, "If I go to college and get a degree, I'll be able to make more money" represents an internal locus of control. An external locus of control, often associated with a victim mentality that blames others for what happens, believes someone or something outside of oneself determines the outcome. The thought, "Even if I go to college and get a degree, no one will pay me well because _____" is indicative of an external locus of control. A severe form of external locus of control is *Learned Helplessness*, where an animal or individual won't take an action that others can clearly see would be beneficial and possible. In a *Learned Helplessness* state, the person does not believe his or her actions will matter.

Shifrer and Langenkamp found that people who believe life events are a product of their own effort, rather than fate, experience better outcomes in multiple domains."[183] In *Resilience as a Positive Youth Development Construct: A Conceptual Review*, Lee, Cheung, and Kwong noted that:

"Studies have shown that the main difference between individuals who adapt very well despite facing risks and individuals who end up in maladaptation is the existence of protective factors. Thus, enhancing both internal and external protective factors of adolescents may help them adapt to stressful and risky life situations. For internal protective factors . . . optimism, perceptions of control, self-efficacy, and active coping are associated with better health."[184]

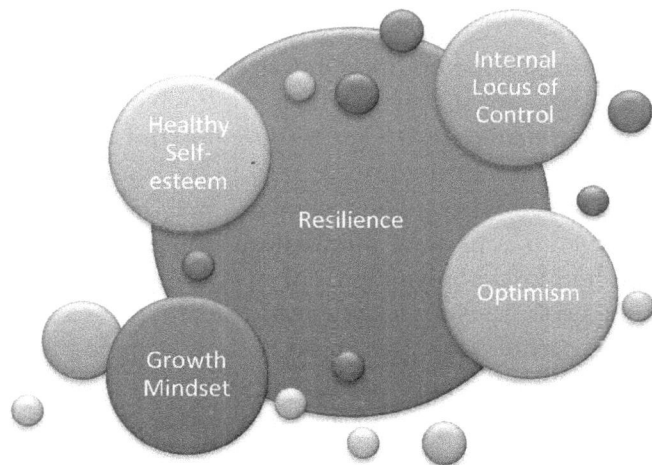

Understanding and following our Emotional Guidance increases all three of the factors that are critical to resilience. Lee, Cheung, and Kwong also noted that:

Additional factors including psychological/emotional flexibility, social problem solving skills, and cognitive skills were cited as elements that contribute to individual resilience by van der Werff, van den Berg, Pannekoek, Elzinga, and van der Wee.

Although conscious awareness of our Emotional Guidance is not required to develop resilience, conscious awareness strengthens the benefits of our Emotional Guidance because the employee becomes more attuned to the subtle energies of Emotional Guidance and is able to resolve negative emotion much more quickly. When it is interpreted accurately, Emotional Guidance continually reinforces the three critical elements of resilience (internal locus of control, optimism, and healthy self-esteem).

Hope

"Hope as we define it[185] is a future-oriented pattern of thinking that involves the abilities to:
1. Set clear and challenging 'stretch goals,'
2. Develop the strategies or pathways to those goals, and
3. Muster the necessary motivation to use those pathways to pursue objectives.

All three hope components are necessary in order to successfully attain goals. Success in this context does not simply mean "getting what one wants," but rather **getting what one wants in such a way that mental health benefits are maximized** [emphasis added].

When each of the hope components is present in sufficient magnitude, people will **expect** to succeed. Even when they do not succeed, however, high- as compared to low-hope people are better able to cope with their failure experiences.

When low-hope people fail to achieve goals, they typically cannot create alternate pathways to go around obstacles. Accordingly, these individuals with low hope are prone to:

- Give up,
- To criticize their own abilities,
- And to experience strong negative emotions.

Optimism + > Internal Locus of Control > Hope

On the other hand, when individuals with high hope fail to attain goals, they:
- Simply acknowledge that they did not try hard enough,
- Or that they did not have access to the most useful pathways.

Instead of becoming stuck in criticizing themselves, the high hopers get busy in finding solutions. As a result, any negative emotions experienced by high-hope people are not likely to incapacitate them. On this point, we have found that high- relative to low-hope people **try harder and persevere longer after failure experiences precisely because of their abilities to retain their positive emotions.**"[186]

When individuals know they have guidance, and have practiced using it, they also know that no matter how bad their current circumstances may seem, they can find ways to feel better. Hope, a belief that a positive or desired outcome is possible, is a key emotional state for resilience. Just knowing that guidance exists builds a firm foundation for hopefulness.[187] Without this knowledge, it is easier to feel hopeless, which can lead to inertia or giving up.[188]

A report from the Regional Research Institute for Human Services at Portland State University found that the ability to maintain hope is an indicator of what outcome will be achieved. According to that paper published in *Research, Policy, and Practice in Children's Mental Health,*

"When low-hope people fail to achieve goals, they typically cannot create alternate pathways to go around obstacles. Accordingly, these individuals with low hope are prone to give up, to criticize their own abilities, and to experience strong negative emotions. On the other hand, when individuals with high hope fail to attain goals, they simply acknowledge that they did not try hard enough or that they did not have access to the more useful pathways. Instead of becoming stuck in criticizing themselves, the high hopers get busy in finding solutions. As a result, any negative emotions experienced by high-hope people are not likely to incapacitate them. On this point, we have found that high- relative to low-hope people try harder and persevere longer after failure experiences precisely because of their abilities to retain their positive emotions."[189]

What the researchers describe as high-hopers could easily be described as optimists although there is a difference. Hope is the belief that the future will be better than the present and that the person has some power to make it so.

Harvey and Delfabbro add clarification to the definition of resilience by pointing out that "Merely avoiding a stressful situation or negative event does not constitute resilience because no active process is involved."[190] Resilience is encountering a problem and returning to a psycho-socio-emotional state that is the same as or better than the state one was in before the situation is encountered.

The Regional Research Institute for Human Services at Portland State University suggests "that having hope is vital for the successful transition from adolescence to satisfying adult roles . . . and [they] proposed that ***intentionally instilling hope in young people should be a societal priority.***"[191] Since society isn't doing this, employers who make the effort can achieve a competitive advantage by training their employees to use stress relieving metacognitive processes and Emotional Guidance.

Resilience is sometimes recommended as a way to cope with the ravages of chronic diseases and while it is useful in that way, the greatest power of resilience is in reducing chronic stress, which reduces the risk of developing the chronic disease that one would then have to deal with.

Stress Inoculation

Researchers are leaning toward a stance that, "resilience develops in response to challenges, not in their absence, and the person (or system) can become stronger than before."[192] I disagree. My stance is that resilience is *displayed* following adversity, when it is present. But it is the way a person thinks and how she approaches problems (or avoids them) that leads to resilience. If the thinking patterns do not support thriving, repeated adversity will simply wear a person down, and for many, lead to addictions and in extreme cases, psychosis. I do agree that adversity helps build confidence, but the adversities can be slight. A child being picked last for the team, not making the team, rejection by a desired person, a college rejection letter, and other common events can help a young person realize that they can be fine following something undesired. Those experiences will help them when they are faced with more severe adversities, but only if they find a way to think about small adversities that allow them to move on.

If the person who is not picked for the team makes it into a personal and global rejection of self, which would stem from dysfunctional habits of thought (catastrophizing), no resilience would be built. If the person who is rejected by a desired other decides that means no one will ever love him, he will not build resilience as the result of the experience. Healthy thinking must come first and that is what *The Smart Way* is designed to provide.

A theory exists for resilience that is supported by "research in rodents" that suggests the protection "may be due to neuroplasticity induced by stress inoculation."[193] There may be some neural basis for higher levels of resilience, but I think it can be described more simply. When you experience adversity, recover, and find the silver lining in the experience you're more likely to do so the next time because humans are creatures of habit and repeat our patterns. When something works well for us, habitual patterns are very good for us. When things don't work out, the habits do not serve us and we would be better off disrupting the pattern.

Monkeys that experienced brief separations from their mothers periodically over ten weeks "were less anxious and . . . showed higher cognitive control, higher curiosity when they were older."[194] That sounds like self-confidence. I don't think we need to create artificial stressors to inoculate our children but neither do we need to artificially remove stressors. We need to provide them support and guidance about how to deal with stressors, provide a firm platform of healthy self-esteem, an internal locus of control, and optimism.

We've done generations of children a disservice by not allowing them to lose when they were children and had the emotional support of parents to help them recover from the pain of a loss. The degradation to resilience between today's young adults and what is often referred to as The Greatest Generation is startling. We see it in demands for trigger warnings and complaints of microaggressions. This week several schools have voted to do away with Valedictorians citing unhealthy competition.

Teaching children resilience would be a better approach that would help prepare them for success and emotional stability throughout life.

9: Motivation, Maslow's Errors, and Autonomy

A creative man is motivated by the desire to achieve, not by the desire to beat others.
Ayn Rand

Autonomy

Multiple scientific theories attempt to conceptualize human needs. Self-Determination Theory (SDT) by Deci and Ryan posits that there are three basic needs:

- Autonomy
- Competence
- Relatedness (social connection)

When human needs are not met, the outcomes are less than ideal. Non-Suicidal Self-Injury (NSSI) is a growing problem among adolescents and young adults. In 2015, Emery, Heath and Mills found individuals who have lower levels of personal satisfaction with the core human needs identified in Self-Determination Theory experience "more difficulties with all aspects of emotion regulation."[195] Compared to students who had never engaged in self-injury, Emery, Heath, and Mills found that, "University students who had engaged in self-injury:

- Did not accept their own emotional responses
- Experienced difficulty engaging in goal directed behavior
- Experienced impulse control problems
- Lacked emotional awareness
- Lacked knowledge about healthy emotion regulation strategies"

A strong human need is for autonomy, the sense that one is in charge of one's own life and decisions. Edward Deci and Richard Ryan have done extensive research on the self-determination theory of motivation. When an individual autonomously makes decisions about goals, they are intrinsically motivated to self-actualize toward those goals. "Several studies have shown that when intrinsic motivation is lacking, employees are more likely to be emotionally exhausted."[196] When goals are externally imposed motivation is not as strong. Self-determination theory attempts to explain the "needs necessary for psychological growth, integrity, and well-being."[197] In their paper, they explain that "Social contexts and individual differences that support satisfaction of the basic needs facilitate natural growth processes including intrinsically motivated behavior and integration of extrinsic motivations, whereas those that forestall autonomy, competence or relatedness are associated with poorer motivation, performance, and well-being." Emotional Guidance supports autonomy while society often does not.

Autonomy is also important for pro-health behaviors and good health outcomes. Attempting to control the pro-health behaviors of our partner can backfire.[198]

"To have the freedom to decide how you will carry out a task is a basic human need. As the psychologist Ron Friedman has noted, 'Grow people's experience of competence and you'll inevitably grow their engagement.' You have to have small wins to feel confident that you could be successful in larger endeavours."[199]

Autonomy is perceptual. Even an inmate in prison can find a perspective that affords autonomy by focusing on what he is allowed to control—his thoughts, the time he focuses on in his thoughts (past, present, future), and he can even control mood by choosing thoughts for the way they will make him feel. It takes practice to perceive freedom when most would not and it is equally difficult to perceive freedom when what was once allowed is forbidden. Smokers who remember being able to smoke at their desk and on airplanes will remember how the loss of their freedom to smoke when and where they wanted to smoke felt as each new law encroached on prior freedoms.

Motivation

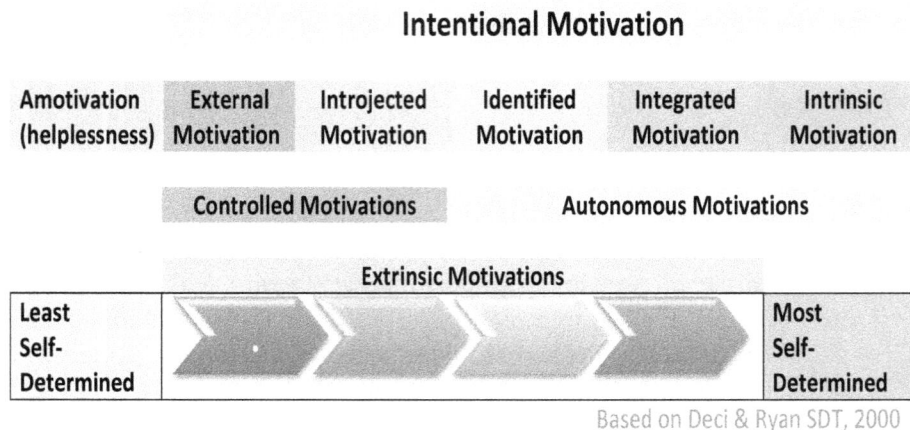

Based on Deci & Ryan SDT, 2000

According to Deci and Ryan,

Intrinsic Motivation is:
- More autonomous
- More Stable
- Done with greater care and quality
- Accompanied by more positive experiences

Intrinsic Motivation Leads to:
- Higher persistence
- Lower anxiety
- Higher adherence

Example: Because I want to vs. because the boss told me I have to.

Emotional Guidance responds to the freedom one feels when following intrinsically motivated goals by reinforcing it with positive emotions.

Integrated Regulation occurs when the person identifies with regulation and has coordinated that identification with other core values and beliefs

Integrated Regulation is:
- Stable and persistent
- Fully self-endorsed basis for action
- Behavior is willing with no sense of coercion
- Fully self-determined

Integrated Regulation Leads to:
- Compliance with requirements is higher
- Work outcomes are better
- Employee is engaged

Example: Self-identity might be "I help people" and lead to an attitude of "I will do this task in a timely manner because that helps the customer." Emotional Guidance will provide positive feedback in response to the example.

Identified Regulation involves the conscious acceptance of behavior as important to achieve personally valued outcomes. Strong incentives can overcome difficulties in maintaining behavior.

Identified Regulation leads to:
- Stable and Persistent effort
- Commitment
- Positive experiences

For example, doing this moves me toward accomplishment of my personal goals. Emotional Guidance would provide positive feedback for actions that support

Introjected Regulation, one's self-esteem is at risk. Tasks are considered self-esteem contingent. There is pressure on the self, which may lead to self-disparagement or shame at failure. Pride and self-approval may occur with success
- Individual may feel ambivalent
- Unstable maintenance
- Can include negative emotion
- Tension
- Inner conflict

For example, I have to finish this task on time or Harry will think Bob is better than me. Emotional Guidance will provide negative feedback to thoughts about someone else being better, causing stress that decreases the employee's ability to accomplish the task.

External Motivation involves externally regulated behaviors, rewards, punishments, and mandates that exude pressure to comply on the individual
- Regulatory efforts are temporary (only when controls are in place)
- Only when rewards are meaningful
- Compliance only when controls are operating
- Minimal effort
- Poor quality
- Individual is not invested and does not care

For example, I can take it easy today because the boss is on vacation. Emotional Guidance will not support the accomplishment of these goals with positive emotion.

When a person aligns externally created goals with self-determined goals, life feels easier. Progress seems like less work and more like doing what you want to do. Stress levels are lower, even when the same actions are taken. There is a greater sense of freedom (autonomy and/or empowerment), which equates to a higher level of happiness.

Given the importance of autonomy to intrinsic motivation, Deci, Koestner, and Ryan's "meta-analysis of 128 laboratory experiments confirmed that, whereas positive feedback enhances intrinsic motivation, tangible rewards significantly undermine it."[200] Gagné and Deci reported that decreasing one's perceived competence undermined motivation.[201]

An article in the *Academy of Management Journal* recently reported that lunch break autonomy "plays a complex and pivotal role in conferring the potential energetic benefits of lunch break activities."[202] In other words, employees who are free to choose their lunch break activities find the breaks more restorative than those whose breaks are restricted, such as employees who are required to remain on the premises or whose breaks are so short that leaving the premises is not practical.

Research by Lloyd, Smith and Winger demonstrated that stress that reduces one's sense of autonomy (i.e. work stress caused by low decision latitude) significantly increased the risk for Type II diabetes.[203] Even when someone does not have the ability to make decisions at work, they can reframe their position by focusing on the fact that they could change jobs, thus increasing the personal sense of autonomy. Even if the person is incarcerated and does not have the ability to change jobs, they can focus on their ability to focus on different aspects of the job and the fact that they have control over what they think about.

Buzinski and Price found that highly restrictive goals are likely to create a sense of "restricted personal freedom."[204] Restrictive goals feel disempowering, which activates the natural desire to feel empowered leading to resistance. In teenagers, this resistance is seen as rebellion. Highly restrictive goals also make it more difficult to integrate the goals with personal motivators because once the urge to resist is born, the individual is not looking for ways to cooperate and comply— she's looking for ways to resist. Someone who has developed metacognitive skills by paying attention to her own thoughts, emotions, and motivations for those thoughts could recognize what is happening and decide to consciously look for ways to align with highly restrictive goals. If finding a way to align with the restrictive requirements is not the choice, Emotional Guidance will encourage the individual to leave the situation, if possible.

For example, someone who has been diagnosed with diabetes who is told he can no longer indulge in some of his favorite sweets, not even chocolate peppermint cake, may feel rebellious despite the fact that he does not want his illness to worsen. The restrictions activate rebellion because freedoms are being threatened. If he decides to consciously align with the restrictions, he might think of his 4-year-old granddaughter and how he enjoys dancing with her. She puts her tiny little feet on top of his shoes and leans back, allowing him to hold her weight up as they move to the music. He dreams of dancing with her at her wedding. He could decide that he wants to comply with the dietary restrictions because he wants to dance at her wedding many years in the future. By focusing on his personal desire, he can align with the required behaviors and become a cooperative patient who does not feel the desire to rebel.

Before he goes to the grocery store or to a party where he might feel tempted, he can prime his mind by imagining dancing with his granddaughter at her wedding. By keeping that desire active in his mind, his compliance with the restricted diet becomes something he does to achieve a self-inspired goal—not one that is being forced upon him by his doctor or circumstances.

It is not the difficulty of the goals that make them authoritarian. It is the lack of flexibility in how the goal is achieved that makes them feel as if they are limiting one's freedom. In 2015, Buzinski and Price reported there is significant research demonstrating that "highly difficult goals increase performance on more than 100 different experimental tasks, including behavioral measures of self-control, like persistence."[205] Their research points to the fact that commitment is as important, and possibly more important, than one's abilities in relationship to success on difficult goals. This points to how important employee engagement is to the accomplishment of an organization's goals.

Buzinski and Price's paper also discussed ego-depletion that occurs from complying with highly restrictive goals and how the need to comply can deplete the ability to exert self-control on subsequent tasks.

Observing behavior while considering the continuum associated with the Emotional Guidance Scale, it is easy to see that the restrictive environment is not just a process of learning, but also one of disempowerment that is associated with many undesirable outcomes. Extensive research on employee health shows that lack of control leads to worse health outcomes. The diagram below illustrates the relationship between emotional states, immune function, and motivation.

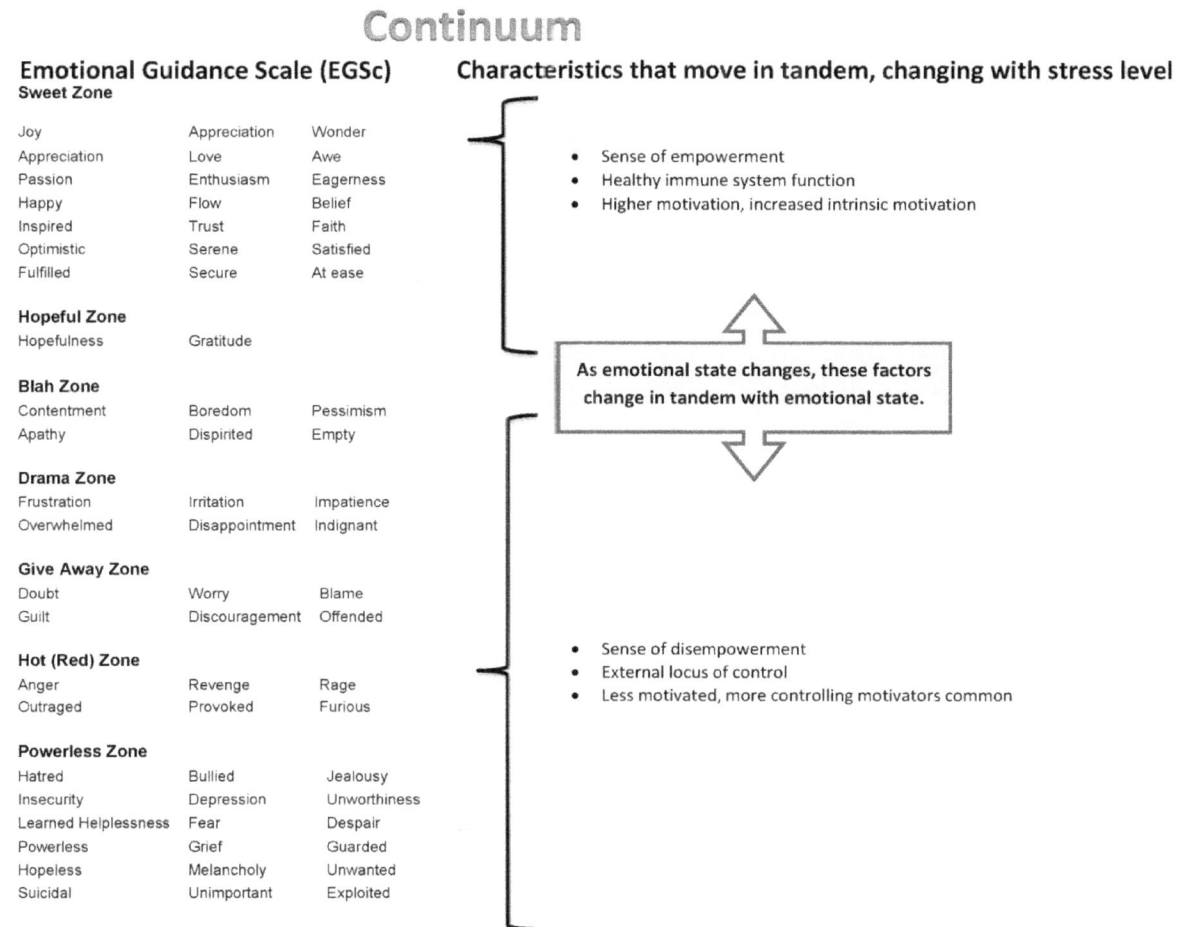

Continuum

Emotional Guidance Scale (EGSc)

Sweet Zone

Joy	Appreciation	Wonder
Appreciation	Love	Awe
Passion	Enthusiasm	Eagerness
Happy	Flow	Belief
Inspired	Trust	Faith
Optimistic	Serene	Satisfied
Fulfilled	Secure	At ease

Hopeful Zone

Hopefulness	Gratitude

Blah Zone

Contentment	Boredom	Pessimism
Apathy	Dispirited	Empty

Drama Zone

Frustration	Irritation	Impatience
Overwhelmed	Disappointment	Indignant

Give Away Zone

Doubt	Worry	Blame
Guilt	Discouragement	Offended

Hot (Red) Zone

Anger	Revenge	Rage
Outraged	Provoked	Furious

Powerless Zone

Hatred	Bullied	Jealousy
Insecurity	Depression	Unworthiness
Learned Helplessness	Fear	Despair
Powerless	Grief	Guarded
Hopeless	Melancholy	Unwanted
Suicidal	Unimportant	Exploited

Characteristics that move in tandem, changing with stress level

- Sense of empowerment
- Healthy immune system function
- Higher motivation, increased intrinsic motivation

As emotional state changes, these factors change in tandem with emotional state.

- Sense of disempowerment
- External locus of control
- Less motivated, more controlling motivators common

Employers should provide latitude for autonomy whenever possible. When it is not possible, employees with psychological flexibility can adjust their perceptions. The integration of external motivations is a key concept for socially desirable behaviors in the home, at work, and in the community. The idea culture would encourage sharing helpful perspectives. For example, one of my dear friends is visiting me for a few weeks from the UK. This afternoon as we sat on the deck enjoying the end of the day she said, "I want to tell you something. I hope I don't offend you, but if I do, 'It's your problem.'"

We both laughed because we both understand the truth of her statement. She proceeded to tell me something that might have offended me in the distance past but today I recognize it as a friend being helpful and offering her unique and valuable perspective. I felt no offense and am contemplating her words. Whether I decide that her words reflect something I will take action on or not, I appreciate her willingness to share her perspective. Her perspective has value and her willingness to share it with me is a gift. With awareness that perspectives have value, even when they are not the same as our own, the risk of offending someone declines enough to allow the open exchange of information.

The ability to take external goals and perceive them in alignment with intrinsic goals is a key factor in success in every area of life. The worker whose employer has high demands may resist those demands or slack off if the only motivating force is coming from external demands. If that same worker perceives successful fulfillment of the employer's demands as supporting self-determined intrinsic goals, the worker will be self-motivated to complete them. Emotional Guidance helps identify thoughts that align with job goals.

The employee that perceives the purpose of a work assignment as *making the boss happy* or *following dumb rules* will not be motivated to complete the work. If the employee sets his own goals about attaining accomplishments and can perceive the work assignments as one aspect of successful completion of self-determined goals, the employee will be motivated to complete the work. *The Oxford Handbook of Happiness* "outlines the function of positive emotions as broadening attention, cognition, and social cognition, all of which contribute to building well-being and resilience."[206]

Numerous esteemed researchers including Ed Diener, Robert Biswas-Diener, Shawn Achor, Sonja Lyubomirsky, King, and Barbara Fredrickson have concluded that individuals who are positively focused (optimistic) are more successful. How does understanding and using Emotional Guidance create greater success? It naturally makes the employee more optimistic, which is a key component of success in every area of life. Some of the common roadblocks to success are:

- Feelings of unworthiness
- Lack of self-confidence
- Negative thoughts
- Worrying

- Fear
- Lack of forgiveness (of self and others)
- Negative beliefs (especially about money)
- Self-criticism

Emotional Guidance can be used to successfully refute thoughts that reflect each of the above roadblocks to success.

Fear is at the root of much of the employee engagement problem. Fear someone else will get what the employee wants and deprive them of it. Fear that the employee will not be successful. Fear that the employee will lose his job. Fear that someone else is better than the employee and fear that the employee is not good enough can cause misguided thinking and sabotage the employee's efforts to be successful.

When we're feeling anxious and overwhelmed, we're different people than when we're calm and secure.
In the later state, our prefrontal cortex runs the show, and we're capable of making informed choices.
When fear intrudes, our amygdala and the lower regions of our brain take over, and we can't think straight.
Tony Schwartz, The New York Times, December 5, 2014

Success requires the right attitude, a positive mindset, about:

- Happiness
- Open mindedness
- One's reason why
- One's potential
- Growth and Learning

- Failure (it's a stepping stone)
- Sense of control (autonomy)
- Faith/Trust
- The small voice within
- The goodness of self and others

When the work is rewarding it is not work and the employee enjoys going to work—those are signs an employee is matched well with his role. If it's not, the employee has two choices. One is to move elsewhere but he will be wherever he goes, which means habits of thought that cause self-sabotage will continue diminishing the success he experiences. The other is using his Emotional Guidance to find his purpose and deliberately align his current role with his purpose in order to find more meaning in what he is doing by changing his perception about it. When an employee thinks about something related to his purpose, he will feel eager excitement and can follow the thread of good-feeling emotional responses.

Once an employee sees their current role as aligned with her desires, she feels better. When she feels better, she gains all the benefits of positive emotions. It may eventually lead to a different job or career, but the self the employee takes to that new role will be a more evolved version of who she was. Using Emotional Guidance reinforces an internal locus of control and will aid in the alignment process by helping the employee find thoughts about work that feel best. An employee who is consciously aware that emotions are guiding him toward self-actualization can quickly find mental stances that feel the best under a wide variety of circumstances.

An employee's emotional state is not dependent upon life circumstances and is especially not dependent upon a comparison of the employee's life and other's lives. Emotional Guidance will help the employee feel good about what the employee is doing, even when it is not the same as what others are doing. The employee who understands how emotions are formed will understand that others may not want what she wants.

Mindset is a significant contributor to success. Mindset is the habitual pattern of thoughts that an individual usually has. Because they are habits, they are the default mode of that individual. Like all habits, they can be changed. Habits of thought include many things, but one that is important to this topic is whether a person tends to react to situations with appreciation, irritation, frustration, anger, envy, despair, etc. Chronic emotional state is the product of our habits of thought.

Two people can have the exact same meal with the exact same waiter at the same table and one can thoroughly enjoy it while the other is frustrated because he finds it lacking in many ways. Both are right, from their personal perspective. Individuals can choose the perspective from which they view any situation. Consciously making those choices is a function of psychological flexibility and a key element of resilience, both of which strongly support good mental health (even following trauma), good relationships, and greater success in all areas of life.

The more an employee is guided to the choice the employer wants her to make, the more she may resist if it violates her sense of autonomy. Researchers looking into motivation discovered how powerful the desire for autonomy is. Even when someone has decided he wants to achieve a specific goal, encouragement to achieve the goal from outsiders given in several ways, decreases intrinsic motivation of self-determined goals.[207]

It's easy to be happy while pursuing goals that are personally important to us if our habits of thought aren't sabotaging us.

The chart on the following pages will be useful when I discuss oversights in Maslow's Hierarchy of Needs theory.

Emotional State

Emotional Guidance Scale (EGSc)

Sweet Zone

Joy	Appreciation	Wonder
Appreciation	Love	Awe
Passion	Enthusiasm	Eagerness
Happy	Flow	Belief
Inspired	Trust	Faith
Optimistic	Serene	Satisfied
Fulfilled	Secure	At ease

Hopeful Zone

Hopefulness	Gratitude

Blah Zone

Contentment	Boredom	Pessimism
Apathy	Dispirited	Empty

Drama Zone

Frustration	Irritation	Impatience
Overwhelmed	Disappointment	Indignant

Give Away Zone

Doubt	Worry	Blame
Guilt	Discouragement	Offended

Hot (Red) Zone

Anger	Revenge	Rage
Outraged	Provoked	Furious

Powerless Zone

Hatred	Bullied	Jealousy
Insecurity	Depression	Unworthiness
Learned Helplessness	Fear	Despair
Powerless	Grief	Guarded
Hopeless	Melancholy	Unwanted
Suicidal	Unimportant	Exploited

Engagement and Behavior

- More time 'In Flow'; higher engagement levels
- Higher employee engagement & alignment with corporate mission
- Associated with better corporate citizenship
- Associated with better customer service
- Associated with pro-health behaviors
- Associated with pro-social behaviors
- Associated with better relationships, less discord at work & fewer divorces
- Associated with problem-solving
- Rarely associated with crime; Low association with alcohol and drug abuse

Associated with decreasing engagement and other undesirable outcomes

- Higher levels of dissatisfaction with job and organization, lower engagement
- Increasing intrusion of non-work problems into work time
- Increasing discord with co-workers and managers; lower pro-social behaviors
- Potential for alcohol and drug abuse increases
- Less regard for established rules and procedures
- Less likely to accept responsibility for errors and missed goals
- Crimes of opportunity become more likely
- Crimes of retaliation for perceived wrongs
- Increasing crimes due to financial needs and fear
- Increasing depression, risk of suicide
- Increasing absenteeism
- Increate turnover
- Increasingly poor health and chronic illnesses; fewer pro-health behaviors
- As emotional state declines, clarity of thinking declines
- The phrase "Going Postal" is usually the result of someone who has been in the Powerless Zone for a long time and it's a last ditch effort to regain a sense of power

Re-visit Maslow

Maslow's Hierarchy of Needs Theory was introduced without supporting empirical evidence and quickly became accepted as truth. Catherine McGonagle's doctoral thesis, *Happiness in the Workplace: An Appreciative Inquiry,* reported, "While Maslow's work is widely cited . . . it has also received criticism both related to the theory itself and in relation to a lack of empirical evidence."[208] Soper, Milford, and Rosenthal concluded "Maslow's Hierarchy of Needs theory is frequently uncritically cited in texts, even though most evidence has failed to support its validity."[209] Neher's review of Maslow's Hierarchy of Needs theory found "many deficiencies in Maslow's theory" despite its wide acceptance.[210] Even though there have been successful empirical challenges, Maslow's Hierarchy of Needs has remained popular with businesses and educators.

Where Maslow's theory makes its first mistake is isolating self-actualization from other needs. In truth, our entire life is the pursuit of self-actualizing experiences. When you're young and learning to support yourself, your self-actualized self is that of someone who can provide adequate food, water, transportation, and shelter. The potential person the typical young adult imagines becoming is nothing compared to who the person can (and often will) become. But the shift from depending on others to satisfy basic needs and becoming independent and capable of providing those needs for oneself is self-actualization.

There are always four of versions of a person:
- Who they are
- Who they used to be
- Who they believe they can become
- Their fully self-actualized self (their spiritual, quantum, or higher self)

Kivetz and Tyler remind us that:

> *"The realization that the self-system is dynamic and consists of multiple self-conceptions has led researchers to abandon the goal of exploring the self as a unitary and stable construct. Instead, current research focuses on identifying different self-concepts and the circumstances under which they are activated."*[211]

Within the "who they were" self-concept a multitude of people they were at one time or another in their lives exist (i.e. infant, toddler, preschooler, 1st grader, someone who is learning the alphabet, someone who has learned to read, someone who has their first crush, someone who experiences their first major loss, who they were yesterday, etc.). In each self-concept, they were expressing as someone different than they are at this very moment. They cannot go back and be who they were; they can only be who they are now and move toward who they are becoming.

If you look at any of the charts in this book that link emotional Zones to behaviors it becomes easy to see that we are not the same person and would not make the same decisions when our emotional state is different.

Individual priorities tend to focus on immediate needs, but self-realization is a continuous process. If a person is hungry, they usually focus on satisfying their hunger before they worry about other needs. But they can continue working even when they're hungry if they've made achieving a work-related goal a higher priority. They can remain at the bedside of a loved one who is ill even when they are hungry or have other urgent biological needs.

I also hypothesize that safety needs are misunderstood. It is the expected level of safety compared to existing safety levels that matters the most. For example, an office worker does not expect to be exposed to hazardous working conditions and will not react well to safety threats at work. A soldier, on the other hand, expects danger at work and has a very different reaction to safety threats. Part of that is the result of training, but a bigger part is expectation vs. actuality. Someone who served as a soldier but is now an office worker will respond differently to unexpected violence than someone who has never had training, but their reaction (emotionally/psychologically) will be different than it would be if the violence had occurred in an environment where it was expected.

If safety was all-compelling, people would not become comfortable in uncomfortable **comfort zones**.

Observers who are not directly at risk also respond differently. When a person watches a movie where someone is living a life they expect to be safe and the person meets a tragic end it affects the watcher more than it does when they watch a war movie and a soldier dies. The outrage is greater when a civilian life is lost than when it is a military or law enforcement life. It is not that they value military or law enforcement lives less—they don't. It's that they don't see civilian lives as at risk. They simply don't expect civilian lives to be lost as the result of violence. When a soldier or law enforcement officer dies when he is not on active duty, the sense of injustice about the loss is greater than if the same loss had occurred while on duty.

It is difficult to imagine how people live through awful times—wars, plagues, etc.—and retain their sanity. If they adjust their expectations of possible norms the difference between expectations and reality will be closer and thus less disturbing. There are men and woman who put their lives on the line every day for decades to serve and protect others. Maslow's safety first concept does not explain that type of behavior. For these employees, self-actualization requires risking life and limb in service to others.

The third level of Maslow's Hierarchy of Needs is social needs. This, too, varies by individual. Some people enjoy their own company and have solo pursuits they find very satisfying. They don't pursue socialization and are happy in their solitary existence. Others have solo existences because they don't know how to develop the type of relationships required to satisfy their social desires. In 2012, Sani et al. found that our sense of belonging is more important than social time. Many people report feeling intense loneliness while surrounded by other people.

Esteem needs, self-respect, and the approval of others are another need where Maslow's Theory was misguided. If one possesses true confidence in oneself the approval of others is not a necessity. It is only when a person doubts their own value or worth, or feels unstable in their belief about their value, that others' opinions become important. I'm not referring to someone who is egotistical. Braggadocio is usually hiding insecurities. The truly confident person can move through life quietly sure that they, like everyone else, have value. Emotional Guidance provides positive emotions that affirm one's value without requiring negative judgments of others.

Excellence is a moving target

10: Psychological Flexibility and Career Adaptability

Individuals, too, who cultivate a variety of skills seem brighter, more energetic and more adaptable than those who know how to do one thing only.
Robert Shea

Kashdan and Rotterburg "define **psychological flexibility** as the measure of how a person:
(1) adapts to fluctuating situational demands,
(2) reconfigures mental resources,
(3) shifts perspective, and
(4) balances competing desires, needs, and life domains."[212]

"Over the past decade, experimental and longitudinal research has shown that psychological flexibility is an important determinant of mental health and behavioral effectiveness in the workplace . . . interventions can also enhance it, and, as a result, improve mental health and behavioral effectiveness in the workplace."[213]

A study involving 1723 employees found that "overall career adaptability positively predicted both career satisfaction and self-rated career performance . . . suggesting that overall career adaptability is a transactions, self-regulatory resource that enables employees to achieve subjective career success independent of more stable dispositions."[214]

Because of the way our brains interpret reality humans tend to respond to new situations in the same way they responded in the past—even when the old response is not productive. "If the context has changed and requires new strategies, the problem solver must notice the shift in context. In addition, the problem solver must have the cognitive resources to inhibit the previous response and develop a new response . . . people are generally prone to inflexibility. For example, we apply non-relevant past experiences to present situations, we try to confirm pre-existing hypotheses, and we persist in mental sets."[215]

Two new labels have been created to describe the less structured career paths that are gaining prominence. Both protean and boundaryless attitudes may indeed help employees develop career skills and ultimately cope with uncertain career environments"[216] Interestingly, "Research has shown that in terms of the self-directed and boundaryless mindset attitudes . . . there is not an inherently decreased chance of organizational commitment . . . Thus encouraging a full range of internally and externally focused career orientations may be a prudent if unintuitive course for organizations to pursue. Because these protean and boundaryless orientations are considered attitudinal, they can be taught and learned, which has great implications for career development."[217]

Protean career attitudes
Protean career attitudes involve the ability to change frequently or easily. For example, after my first experience with a layoff I developed a couple of attitudes that served me well during the next decade.

1. My job security is my knowledge and abilities—not my employer. This led to continuing self-development and improvement because every new credential I earned and everything I learned contributed to my sense of job security.

2. Job security was not tied to my employer's decisions or fate so when times were tough I simply affirmed my positive work related qualities, knowledge, and experience as a marketable commodity in any economic environment and my fear dissipated.
3. I deliberately built relationships at work and continued them even when co-workers left for other environments.

"Self-directed protean are more internally focused, facilitating self-exploration that enables individuals to attend to identity issues."[218]

Boundaryless careers
A boundaryless career involves:
- "movement across the boundaries of separate employers;
- drawing validation from outside the present employer;
- sustained by networks or information that are external to the current employer;
- breaking traditional organizational career boundaries;
- rejection of traditional career opportunities for personal or family reasons;
- perceiving a boundaryless future regardless of structural constraints.

In terms of potential and often actual employee mobility it is *extra*-organizational and *inter*-organizational. People in boundaryless careers have career goals, expertise, and networks that go beyond their current employer, so that their careers are 'sequences of opportunities that go beyond the boundaries of single employment settings'"[219] "Boundaryless attitudes are more externally focused, thus allowing individuals to cross boundaries of the organization in seeking support and opportunities."[220]

Having lived through both the downturn following the terrorist attacks on 9/11 and the economic downturn of the 2007-11 era with primarily a protean career attitude with elements of the boundaryless attitude it seemed that co-workers with a more structured career attitude experienced more fear and were quicker to jump at opportunities that appeared to provide greater assurance that their job would continue. Even highly skilled, marketable employees voiced much greater fear about the economic downturn than I felt. That fear fueled the prevalent anger we're seeing in the 2016 Presidential election cycle. The employees who were fearful developed habits of thought that created a chronic emotional state that is lower than it was before the downturn.

Even earlier, after Transamerica was purchased by Aegon in 1999 and employees were given a six-month severance if they stayed until their uncertain "job end date" which might be as much as two years in the future, employees frequently left despite the promise of six-months' severance pay if they stayed. I stayed for what turned out to be 18-months and focused on earning new industry credentials (protean behavior) and starting a new organization for professionals in my field (boundaryless behavior). Once my job end date was determined, I began looking and was immediately hired. My new employer initially wanted me to begin before my job end date and just pay me out of the severance until they learned it was six months' pay. At that point they waited nearly two months for me to become available.

Being able to align external motivators with intrinsic motivators is important because it reduces the stress of achieving the external goals and increases the likelihood of success. Zacher's recent research shows that "Career adaptability predicts subjective career success above and beyond personality traits and core self-evaluations."[221]

Career adaptability is "a psychosocial construct that reflects' employees resources for managing present and impending work and career challenges that may affect their integration in their social environment." [222] Career adaptability is the result of self-regulatory capacities (i.e. metacognitive processes) that can change over time.[223] In other words, the self-regulatory capacities can be learned and developed.

In Zacher's article about career adaptability, he cited numerous "benefits of career adaptability including:[224]

- Positively predicted teamwork skills
- Job search self-efficacy
- Tenacious goal pursuit
- Flexible goal adjustment
- Increase promotability and career satisfaction
- Predicted employees breadth of interests
- Predicted employee orientation to happiness
- Predicted general and professional well-being
- Predicted employee quality of life
- Predicted lower work stress
- Employee perceives fewer career barriers
- Predicted career commitment
- Predicted career identification
- Predicted career exploration
- Positively related to self-esteem
- Positively related to promotion focus
- Predicted engagement beyond the Big Five Traits
- Negatively related to general anxiety
- Negatively related to fear of failure"

One factor critical to long-term career success is being able to use the training one has spent time and money attaining. Some occupations, like nursing, require extensive schooling but have a high burnout rate—which means nurses are sometimes not using their education long enough to obtain the maximum benefits from it. When an employee from a lower socioeconomic background makes it through college to become an RN, they often have student loans. If they don't stay in the profession long enough to repay their loans, they would probably have been better off in another profession. There is no shortage of nursing jobs; in fact, we're seeing more frequent articles about nursing shortages. Job burnout is contributing to nursing and teacher shortages.

Burnout is an outcome of low resilience and usually preceded by low levels of engagement. Nursing can be emotional labor—work that takes a toll on one's psychological health. It can also be a physically demanding job, requiring long hours on one's feet. Even before a nurse graduates from college, some drop out of their course of study. In one study, 57% of Native American nurses dropped out before they completed their nursing training. This type of outcome means that the nurses paid for an education (or part of one) that they won't be able to use. It also means that there are not enough nurses who are Native American. There is a high demand for nurses who are the same ethnicity as the patients they serve. In some populations, the patient is more comfortable with someone from the same race.

Patchell tells us The HeartMath method of increasing heart coherence was introduced in the nursing program and subsequent years had much lower drop-out rates for Native Americans, down to 37% from 57% and test scores on standardized tests increased by an average of 17 points. Numerous research reports from The HeartMath Institute report that improved mood is associated with increased heart coherence.

Scientists have shown us that career adaptability has a significant influence on career success. Psychological skills contribute to career adaptability. Everyone has the necessary elements to use their Emotional Guidance System to improve their life, understand their own mind, and their emotions. Using Emotional Guidance increases Emotional Intelligence (EI) significantly. Coetzee & Harry documented that EI strengthens career adaptability.

"In today's global economy, coping with the stress associated with career uncertainty and the unpredictability of ongoing changes requires frequent emotional and cognitive adjustments. To respond effective to career transitions, individuals must display both emotional intelligence and career adaptability" [225]

Zacher tells us two factors that contribute to career adaptability are a *concern* for the future that intrinsically motivates employees to prepare for upcoming tasks and challenges and *confidence*, the belief that they can achieve their career goals and solve problems that arise. [226] In *Be Your Own Mentor*, female CEO's provide career-related encouragement. From Zoë Baird:

"From my own experience and from observing and working with other women, particularly younger women developing their careers, being confident comes through and creates comfort in others. If you're going to be a leader, you need to understand who you are yourself and then lead through strength and confidence." [227]

and Judy Sprieser encourages us to:

"Trust your gut and take chances. You may have marvelous intuition and if you have the confidence to trust it, it's a powerful asset." [228]

Understanding one's Emotional Guidance is the best way to develop confidence in yourself and in your intuition. In some cases, intuition and Emotional Guidance may be the same subject. Emotional Guidance will encourage self-development that prepares an employee for greater challenges in the future.

In James Farr's book, *Supra-Conscious Leadership*, Ed Crutchfield said, "Most of all, we had to build a culture that welcomed—even embraced—change as the only way to endure as a lasting, flexible, adaptable enterprise." [229]

James Farr said,

"The culture creates beliefs, and then the beliefs create the culture. This interaction helps create a stable society—and also makes it difficult to solve some of the culture's problems that afflict the minority. It also means that when the slow evolutionary rate of social change gives way to a rapid, transformational rate of change, as has occurred in recent years, we have a problem. Because minds work to sustain their programs and to resist change, we end up with leaders applying old programs to new problems." [230]

James Farr, on keeping an open channel between our higher self and our conscious mind, "Training that would teach us all to keep that channel open would infuse our world with a great deal more of the inventiveness and compassion of the higher self." [231]

Compassion
"Training in psychological flexibility should be considered as one element of programs designed to increase organizational compassion." [232] "Over the past decade, experimental and

longitudinal research has shown that psychological flexibility is an important determinant of mental health and behavioral effectiveness in the workplace.

Practitioner points

- Experimental and longitudinal research has shown that psychological flexibility is an individual characteristic that is an important determinant of mental health and behavioural effectiveness in the workplace, and"[233]
- Psychological flexibility can be enhanced with interventions and "improve mental health and behavioural effectiveness in the workplace."[234]

A positive work culture goes a long way toward improving personal and business outcomes. Positive and negative influences can come from within and from without. Positivity in the subconscious mind can be increased using a variety of techniques including affirmations and self-hypnosis. The conscious mind can direct itself using metacognitive strategies and reappraisal to be more positively focused. The actual work environment (positive or negative) can have a significant influence on how much work is involved in maintaining a positive mental attitude.

Develop Psychological Flexibility

Go General

Anytime someone is in a low emotional state, he is focused on specifics. For example, if a health problem has him upset, he is focused on the specific aspect of his body that is not functioning the way he wants it to. As long as we are alive, more of our body is functioning well than not. He could have a kidney that is bad, but his mind, heart, lungs, arms, legs, eyes, nose, tongue, skin, and so much more are functioning perfectly. The narrow focus on the specific feels bad. As we deliberately think more generally about our entire body, we feel better.

When you have some quiet time, play with the concept of going general to feel better. If you are upset about a situation at work, mentally take a step back and identify how specifically you are focused. Are you focused on something that happened for only a few minutes out of an entire week? Are you focused on something one person out of 100 did? Are you focused on one day out of an entire year? If you feel strong negative emotion about it, you are focused specifically.

This is true even if you are looking at something you perceive as a global problem. If you focus on world hunger, you can bring yourself to your knees with the hit of negative emotion. From that position, you cannot be effective in resolving the problem. In that negative state, your cognitive abilities are severely restricted.

If you step back and think about how many people have adequate food, your emotional stance will improve. You may immediately think again of those who do not—it is your habit of thought if this issue is on your mind frequently. Deliberately think again of those who have enough to eat. While you are in that higher emotional state, ask yourself, "How can more people have enough to eat?" Give time a chance to bring solutions. When you find yourself thinking about the problem, begin telling yourself things like, "We'll figure it out soon" or "We're making technological advances all the time, a solution could be found any time now" or "There are a lot of smart people in the world who would like to solve this problem. I am not the only one who is concerned. The right idea will come to one of us."

Remember, it does not matter what the problem is, your ability to solve it is diminished when you feel negative emotion. That means the most you can do from that negative state is make yourself feel better. From that better-feeling state, you have more resources to help you find a solution.

Gabel and Harmon-Jones's research supports this process by demonstrating that high intensity emotion (positive and negative) narrow attention while low-intensity emotions broaden attention.

When you're being very specific (about something that feels bad or something that feels good), you can lessen the intensity by going more general, which will broaden your thought-action repertoire.[235]

This process is recommended for all Zones below the Hopeful Zone. Increase your happiness first, then solve problems.

Exercise:

Let's try it now. Get a blank piece of paper. It can have lines or be completely blank. Write a sentence to describe something that has been bothering you. Think about the issue by asking yourself questions, such as "What is the opposite of this?" and "What does the big picture look like?" as well as "Will this matter tomorrow (or in 5 years)?"

Put the issue that is bothering you in a broader context. Then feel how your emotion about the topic shifts.

If your emotions become worse, you are going more specific, not more general. Be patient with yourself and try again. If you have been practicing negative thoughts for a long time it can be a little bit like starting the lawn mower the first time in the spring, which means it requires a little more effort to get going but once you start, it is easier the next time.

Specifically Negative to Generally Negative Shift

When you are in low emotional states (See the EGSc in Appendix I), you are being specific about something that does not feel good when you think about it. Shift your focus to more general thoughts and you will feel better. This example below explains the process.

Specifically negative > generally negative

Thought: *David does not like me.*

More general thought: *David does not like a lot of people, including me.*

Even more general thought: *Unhappy people are more likely to find reasons to not like someone. Unhappy people may not like me.*

Generally negative > Generally Positive

Not everyone in the world is unhappy. Happy people are more likely to like me.

More specific generally positive: *The happier I become the more other happy people will like me.*

Generally Positive > Specifically Positive

I am developing some skills and thought processes that will help me be happier in a sustainable way.

As I become happier those people who were annoyingly happy are no longer annoying.

I can see how my emotional state impacts my perception of others.

I can find more to appreciate about everyone in my life from my new, happier state.

It's fun to deliberately feel better.

Now that I know how to feel better on purpose, I won't freak out so much when I feel bad because I know how to get back to feeling-better.

I don't think I'll ever go back to feeling as bad as I once did because part of the reason I felt so bad was I did not know how to feel better and that was scary. It was like being lost but now I can find my way. I can feel happier anytime I want. It is up to me. I am in control. I like this. It feels really good. I am so glad that I can decide to be happier and then find mindsets that allow me to feel better.

If you just remember that when you feel bad go more general and when you feel good if you want to feel even better you can get more specific.

When going specific, sometimes you can try to go more specific than what will feel good so just back up and be more general.

For example, if you have decided that you are going to college the thought of going to college can feel really good.

But if you don't yet know where you are going and someone is pushing you for answers about that it can feel bad not to know the answer yet. Just stay general. Say things like, "It is not yet time for me to make that decision. I will know when the time to decide is right. There is plenty of time. I don't have to decide today."

Likewise, if you know you are going it is fine to take a stance that you don't know how you'll pay for it, but just relish the belief that you are going. Your faith that it will work out serves you well. It allows the filters in your mind to remain open to ideas. If someone begins pressuring you about that, just stay general and not so specific that it begins feeling bad. "I don't know but that is OK. There are many people who went to college and finished college who did not know how they would do it when they were where I am. There are many ways to pay and I am open to all possibilities. I am not ready to close the doors on other possibilities by deciding on just one. There is plenty of time. I don't have to figure this out today. I am going and I know I will figure it out."

> *When you have tools that help you feel better, it is not necessary to backslide.*

It is important that you decide how specific or general you can be on a subject in that moment. You are not required to go more specific than feels good. You could even say, "One thing I've learned is that things go better for me when I feel good and on this subject a general stance of faith serves me best right now. I understand your concern but trying to get more specific than I am ready for will not serve me well. It won't help me achieve this so I am going to stay general until something more specific feels as good. I'll be sure to let you know when I know more but for now maybe you can decide to feel good just knowing that I have confidence I will figure it out. I do. I am confident about that."

This same conversation can be modified to deal with those pesky people (especially prevalent at reunions) who want to know things you don't yet know. You can modify these answers for questions about when you're going to get married, buy a home, have children, decide on a career, retire, or any number of other questions that inquiring minds seem to want to know about.

Then, there is always my favorite, "Why would you ask me that?" It is great way to diffuse a question (especially inappropriate ones) you do not want to address.

Let's bring this back around to drugs and alcohol for a moment. If those are paths you've been using to feel better, I encourage you to try the Emotional Guidance system. Once you master the Emotional Guidance system you'll be able to feel better without those risky and expensive crutches. If your body has become addicted, it only takes about three days to end the physical/chemical addiction. The reason so many backslide after going through withdrawal is not the chemical addiction—It is the untended desire to feel better.

Programs that convince you that you are bad for having wanted to feel better and using the only thing you knew that worked don't tend to the root cause—the desire to feel better. If that desire is not addressed and alternate solutions found, it is not likely that overcoming the physical addiction will lead to a permanent solution. Once the root cause—the desire to feel better—is addressed, any method of overcoming the chemical dependence has a far greater chance of long-term success.

No one can be shamed into a happier life.

No one can be showered with guilt (for an addiction) and find a happier life.

Myths about Stable Human Factors

Myth # 1: Personality is who we are.

Our personality is far more an indicator of our chronic emotional state and far less an indicator of who we are than is commonly believed.

Emotional state and behavior are tightly linked. A tremendous amount of organizational and motivational research has been published assuming personality is fixed. The research remains valid insofar as it describes individuals who are in an emotional state where their personality comes forth according to the description. But the label cannot be permanently tied to an employee who has learned how to change emotional state because that employee will naturally strive to achieve better-feeling emotional states and will often be successful in those efforts.

The change of chronic emotional state will cause changes in personality. Those changes will feel pleasing. It is not uncommon to hear comments such as, "I did not know I was missing out on the best of life." Or, "It feels like I was living with my eyes closed before I learned how to adjust my filters."

Most people will like the personality changes. New friends will like the new version far better than they would have liked the old one.

Our personalities, including our shyness or boisterousness, is the result of the filters that shape our reality more than any other factor. My personality changed considerably when I began using my Emotional Guidance. Researchers are just now beginning to acknowledge that long-held beliefs about the stability of personality were misleading and longitudinal studies are reporting significant changes in personality over the lifespan.

Myth # 2: Personalities don't change.

The reason personality seems to be unchanging is our habits of thoughts are HABITS.

Like any habit, conscious effort is required to change habitual thoughts. Until now, few people have known how to change their habits of thought. While working on this book, I read a great synopsis of many of the personality models by Carver.[236] What was most obvious to me, however, was the lack of consideration given to emotional state and chronic emotional state. Note: Carver's more recent work is recognizing the impact of emotional state on personality.

Researchers describe personality as if it is fixed and unchangeable without regard to the emotional state of the individual. But we all know that is ridiculous. Our behavior changes with our mood. In better-feeling moods, we are nicer, kinder and even more likely to help strangers. In bad moods, we are not as nice, even to those we love. Sustained low emotional states can lead to the most egregious behaviors. Better accuracy and completeness of personality models can be obtained by including mood/emotional state in the data collected when research is done. Existing personality models seem to explain behavior because most individuals maintain a relatively consistent chronic emotional state throughout life.

Emotional State (ES) is a way of referring to the emotion someone is feeling in-the-moment. (i.e. happy, sad, depressed, hopeful, hopeless, frustrated, angry, anxious, eager, etc.) Chronic Emotional State (CES) is the set point, or emotional state a specific individual tends to return to repeatedly in the absence a significant reason to feel otherwise.

The behavior individuals exhibits is tied most closely with the current Emotional State. Personality model research looks at behavior, but not emotional state at the time the behavior is observed. Self-reports of behavior also do not gather data on emotional state at the time of the behavior. Note the exception of Carver's new work published after this chapter was first written.

An employee whose Chronic Emotional State is happy exhibits behaviors consistent with that Emotional State. There will be variances due to occasional lower Emotional States and during times of resource depletion (i.e. illness and sleep deprivation). High stress will cause temporary changes in Emotional State.

The consistency of Emotional State is well documented in the scientific literature. Lottery winners, newlyweds, and newly disabled individuals typically return to their Chronic Emotional State within two years after these significant life changes. The reason for the stability of Chronic Emotional States is not because it is genetic or a fixed human trait.

Chronic Emotional State is the result of habits of thought.

Why isn't this commonly recognized? The first reason is because researchers do not tend to explore individual difference at the level of thought. The work would be extremely time-consuming and would lack consistency because at the level of thought the uniqueness of each one of us becomes very apparent. Even two people who make identical choices can follow very different thought processes to reach the decision.

Secondly, because habits of thought are habits--but not recognized as such and we are taught our personalities are who we are, few people change their thought patterns. Many people have a fear that if they change their personality they will no longer be the same person. Some fear they will no longer know their self. The truth is, those who deliberately change their habits of thought know their self better than they ever did before they experienced the liberating power of changing habits of thought that weren't serving them well. They also like themselves more.

Like any habit, changing habits of thought takes commitment and does not happen overnight. Patience with oneself is required, but the knowledge and establishment of realistic expectations about how long it takes to create new habits of thought is not readily available. We can think, and can even believe, new thoughts immediately. But even when we believe something that opposes our former habits of thought, the old habitual thoughts (beliefs) will continue coming to mind until the thought-paths (neurological connections) that supported the beliefs are allowed to diminish and new thought-paths that support the new belief are developed. Until this process is completed, you may find yourself thinking (and in the early stages) even speaking things you no longer believe. It's just old programming that is still stronger than the new programming you're creating. It's natural and it does not mean you can't change the habit of thought, just that the process is not yet complete.

What we do and why

We do what we believe will feel better, vis-a-vis approach or avoidance.

We know optimism can be learned. Researchers have shown the old myths about personality being fixed traits were wrong. Personality traits are not fixed,[237, 238, 239, 240] "much of personality is a flexible and dynamic thing . . . it also includes the way one perceives self, others, and events."[241] Changes toward increasing negativity increases mortality in older men. A study of 1663 men showed that neuroticism (fear, anxiety, moodiness, worry, envy, frustration, loneliness, and jealousy) that increased with age significantly increased the risk of mortality (40% over a decade).[242] Recent research by Paulus, Vanwoerden, Norton and Sharp found that neuroticism was associated with psychological inflexibility, lack of emotion regulation strategies, and shame.[243] Participants in the same study that had goal-directed behavior, psychological flexibility, and emotion regulation strategies were able to reduce or avoid neuroticism tendencies.

11: Important Relationships: Emotions and Behavior

The 'self-image' is the key to human personality and human behavior. Change the self-image and you change the personality and the behavior.
Maxwell Maltz

Twenty-five years after Positive Psychology was born, the evidence that humans function better in every area of life when they feel positive emotions is conclusive. The only rational step is widely implementing programs that increase positive affect and reap the benefits for individuals, families, communities, and organizations.

Our emotional state reflects the quality of our thinking (measured in terms of our ability to thrive). The same person will think different thoughts about the same situation when they are in different emotional Zones. When your emotional state is higher, your mind will have thoughts that provide solutions. When you are in a lower emotional state, the thoughts you think will be focused on the problem and you may not be able to perceive a solution.

Training and experience can help you find solutions to problems but the confidence the training and/or experience provides increases your emotional state. If you have a history of successfully solving problems, you're more likely to be in the Hopeful Zone or higher when you become aware of a new problem.

One example that has helped many people realize the truth of this relationship between emotional state and problems is when they recognize that it was when they took a break—whether it was a vacation, a walk, a nap, or a shower that the solution suddenly occurred to them.

"In a meta-analysis of 27 studies of affect and job satisfaction, Connolly and Viswesvaran concluded that 10%–25% of the variance in job satisfaction was accounted for by measures of **dispositional affect**."[244]

"Once a happy person obtains a job, he or she is more likely to succeed. Employees high in dispositional positive affect receive relatively more favorable evaluations from supervisors and others . . . happy people receive higher ratings from supervisors, work performance may be more strongly predicted by well-being than by job satisfaction . . . job performance, as judged by supervisors, was significantly correlated with well-being but uncorrelated with measures of job satisfaction . . . as rated by objective observers, those high in dispositional positive affect performed objectively better on a manager assessment task (including leadership and mastery of information) . . . individuals high in dispositional positive affect are more likely to be in the supervisory in-group, Dormitory resident advisors were rated by residents as being more effective if they were high on trait positive affect, and happier cricket players had higher batting averages . . . service departments with happy leaders were more likely to receive high ratings from customers, and that the positive affective tone of the sales force was an independent predictor of customer satisfaction . . . CEOs of manufacturing companies with high positive affect were relatively more likely to have employees who rated themselves as happy and healthy, and who reported a positive, warm climate for performance. In turn, organizational climate was correlated with productivity and profitability . . . optimistic life insurance agents appear to sell more insurance and optimistic CEOs receive higher performance ratings from the chairpersons of their boards and head companies with greater returns on investment . . . the causal relation between pleasant affect and strong performance is bidirectional. Undoubtedly, one of the reasons that happy, satisfied workers are more likely to be high performers on the job is that they are less likely to show "job withdrawal"—namely, absenteeism, turnover, job burnout, and retaliatory behaviors . . . positive moods at work predicted lower withdrawal and organizational retaliation and higher organizational citizenship behavior, as well as lower job burnout. Positive affect at work has also found to be directly associated with reduced absenteeism . . . those who experience low arousal positive affect on the job are less likely to want to quit and to be in conflict with other workers."[245]

The most important contribution I can make is helping individuals understand the connection between Happiness, Stress, Health, and Behavior and how to achieve optimal outcomes. All of the following move in tandem along a continuum. If it helps, picture line dancers moving across the a dance floor, each one moving together back and forth and side to side. In much the same way the following aspects of our lives move in the same direction as one another.

- Stress
- Behavior
- Mental Health
- Relationship quality
- Intelligence
- Employee Engagement
- Immune system function
- Digestive Function
- Pain (Physical and Emotional)

- Emotional State (i.e. happy, sad, frustrated, fear)
- Physical Health
- Success
- Crime (both as victim and committing crime)
- Drug and alcohol abuse
- Racism
- Central Nervous System Function
- Cognitive Function

All of these things move in tandem along a continuum. Increase stress and mood declines. Lower mood and the risk of the person committing a crime increases. There are other factors that affect the outcomes, such as moral values, which might lead one person to commit suicide and another to commit murder/suicide. Factors such as self-esteem are accounted for because someone who has low self-esteem is generally not happy and when someone with low self-esteem is happy, it seldom lasts very long.

Understanding the purpose or meaning of your emotions is critical if one is to thrive in any area of life—much less all areas of life. Charts on the following pages reflect the continuum along which the above factors move. When you reduce stress, happiness increases. When you increase happiness, stress declines.

When you attempt to reduce crime, alcohol abuse, drug use, physical, mental, or behavioral health without addressing stress, you're focused on a symptom and not the root cause. It's an uphill battle when you work on symptoms. When you work on the root cause, problems are solvable. This book shows you how to shift your perceptions about existing and past problems in order to develop metacognitive processes that, when used in conjunction with Emotional Guidance, reduce the amount of stress experienced. It is not intended as an intellectual exercise. You have to actually begin paying attention to how you feel and looking for alternate perspectives with the intention of finding other perspectives that feel better to you. When you begin actually using the techniques, the processes will make sense to you and you will soon feel better and be able to help others do the same.

Emotional State

Emotional Guidance Scale (EGSc)

Sweet Zone

Joy	Appreciation	Wonder
Appreciation	Love	Awe
Passion	Enthusiasm	Eagerness
Happy	Flow	Belief
Inspired	Trust	Faith
Optimistic	Serene	Satisfied
Fulfilled	Secure	At ease

Hopeful Zone

Hopefulness	Gratitude	

Blah Zone

Contentment	Boredom	Pessimism
Apathy	Dispirited	Empty

Drama Zone

Frustration	Irritation	Impatience
Overwhelmed	Disappointment	Indignant

Give Away Zone

Doubt	Worry	Blame
Guilt	Discouragement	Offended

Hot (Red) Zone

Anger	Revenge	Rage
Outraged	Provoked	Furious

Powerless Zone

Hatred	Bullied	Jealousy
Insecurity	Depression	Unworthiness
Learned Helplessness	Fear	Despair
Powerless	Grief	Guarded
Hopeless	Melancholy	Unwanted
Suicidal	Unimportant	Exploited

Engagement and Behavior

Empowered

- More time 'In Flow'
- Higher productivity
- Higher employee engagement & alignment with corporate mission
- Associated with better corporate citizenship
- Associated with better customer service
- Associated with pro-health behaviors and pro-social behaviors
- Associated with resilience (optimism, internal locus of control, healthy self-esteem)
- Associated with better relationships, less discord at work & fewer divorces
- Associated with problem-solving
- Rarely associated with crime; Low association with alcohol and drug abuse
- Increased cognitive abilities

Disempowered

Associated with decreasing engagement and other undesirable outcomes

- Higher levels of dissatisfaction with job and organization, lower engagement
- Increasing intrusion of non-work problems into work time
- Increasing discord with co-workers and managers; lower pro-social behaviors
- Lower Core Self-evaluations
- Potential for alcohol and drug abuse increases
- Less regard for established rules and procedures
- Less likely to accept responsibility for errors and missed goals
- Crimes of opportunity become more likely
- Crimes of retaliation for perceived wrongs
- Increasing crimes due to financial needs and fear
- Increasing depression, anxiety, risk of suicide
- Increasing absenteeism
- Increasing turnover
- Increasingly poor health and chronic illnesses; fewer pro-health behaviors
- As emotional state declines, clarity of thinking declines
- The phrase *Going Postal* is usually the result of someone who has been in the Powerless Zone for a long time and it's a last ditch effort to regain a sense of power

Emotional State

Emotional Guidance Scale (EGSc)

Sweet Zone

Joy	Appreciation	Wonder
Appreciation	Love	Awe
Passion	Enthusiasm	Eagerness
Happy	Flow	Belief
Inspired	Trust	Faith
Optimistic	Serene	Satisfied
Fulfilled	Secure	At ease

Hopeful Zone

Hopefulness	Gratitude

Blah Zone

Contentment	Boredom	Pessimism
Apathy	Dispirited	Empty

Drama Zone

Frustration	Irritation	Impatience
Overwhelmed	Disappointment	Indignant

Give Away Zone

Doubt	Worry	Blame
Guilt	Discouragement	Offended

Hot (Red) Zone

Anger	Revenge	Rage
Outraged	Provoked	Furious

Powerless Zone

Hatred	Bullied	Jealousy
Insecurity	Depression	Unworthiness
Learned Helplessness	Fear	Despair
Powerless	Grief	Guarded
Hopeless	Melancholy	Unwanted
Suicidal	Unimportant	Exploited

Behavior

- Associated with increased kindness
- Associated with better corporate citizenship
- Associated with pro-health behaviors
- Associated with pro-social behaviors
- Associated with better relationships, fewer divorces
- Associated with problem-solving
- Rarely associated with crime
- Low association with alcohol and drug abuse

Associated with increasing levels of crime

- Early signs = crimes of boredom
- Increasing levels of disruption (fighting, arguing, discord) in relationships
- Potential for alcohol and drugs
- Mid-level increasing violence, physical fights
- Crimes of opportunity
- Crimes of retaliation for perceived wrongs
- Increasing crimes due to financial needs and fear
- Increasing disregard for others life, limb, property
- Murders, rapes, cover-ups that escalate
- Horrific crimes that are perceived as ways to regain power or as retribution for withholding of power
- As emotional state declines, clarity of thinking declines
- In the Powerless Zone individuals may become more complacent, but they continue to want to move up and the longer they are held in the Powerless Zone the higher likelihood they will use violence against self or others

12: Happiness

Happiness is the meaning and the purpose of life, the whole aim and end of human existence.
Aristotle

What is Happiness?

"…happy individuals—that is, those who experience frequent positive emotions, such as joy interest, and pride, and infrequent (though not absent) negative emotions, such as sadness, anxiety, and anger." [246]

". . . happy people—those who experience a preponderance of positive emotions—tend to be successful and accomplished across multiple life domains." [247]

The difference between happiness that depends on something we cannot control and happiness we can achieve because we want to is the difference between sustainable and momentary happiness. There are two main philosophical definitions of happiness with **hedonic** referring to feeling good and **eudaimonic** refers to self-actualization and being authentic (true to one's nature). *The Smart Way* Metacognitive Processes used in conjunction with Emotional Guidance combines both philosophies. Emotional Guidance provides information that lets us know the best thoughts, words, and actions for us to use in order to move toward self-actualization by providing positive emotion when our motion is toward fulfilling our potential. Emotional Guidance provides a stable relationship that is always there for you, always supportive, and always reliable when interpreted correctly. Appropriate use of Emotional Guidance allows employees to develop stable Self-Esteem so relationships with others can be entered into without fear because your self-esteem is not dependent upon the success of the relationship. Relationships can be deeper when you're fearless. Emotional Guidance always leans toward love and forgiveness and away from hate and other negative emotions. *The Smart Way* makes it easy to find the healthiest perspective about the situations life brings to you.

"The State of True Happiness does not require a constant state of bliss. It is a deep sense of inner stability, peace, well-being, and vitality that is consistent and sustainable. Awareness that one possesses the knowledge and skills to return to a happy state, even when not in that state, is a critical component of sustainable happiness. True Happiness is sustainable because the individual deliberately and consciously chooses perspectives that create positive emotions and has cultivated this habit of thought until the natural and habitual response focuses on the positive aspects of the current situation."

Sonja Lyubomirsky and Matthew D. Della Porta provide a good summary of known benefits of happiness in *Boosting Happiness and Buttressing Resilience: Results from Cognitive and Behavioral Intervention,* which included:

- Superior work outcomes
- More activity, energy, and flow
- To live longer
- Higher levels of resilience

- More likely to show good coping abilities
- To have bolstered immune systems
- Less likely to display symptoms of psychopathology
- More likely to act cooperatively and pro-socially
- Associated with relatively stronger social relationships
- Other researchers have identified:
- Better digestive system function
- Lower stress

Boehm's work adds:
- Lower risk of heart disease
- More pro-health behaviors

McCarthy's work adds:
- Less likely to commit crimes
- Lower risk of obesity and diabetes
- Lower risk of depression & anxiety

Why Happiness is Important

The Smart Way empowers employees to more directly achieve the benefits positive emotions confer. Much of positive psychology still behaves as if we are subjects that respond to buttons being pushed and if you push a particular button on a subject that has certain past experiences, the response of one speaks about the response of another. It comes from the concept of **Anthropic mechanism,** as if humans are machines.

Garland explains,

"Positive emotions are not mere epiphenomena. They broaden thought and action repertoires, increase mental flexibility, augment meaning-based coping, and motivate engagement in novel activities and social relationships. Importantly, positive emotions . . . have lasting consequences; they build durable personal resources whose accrual triggers further positive emotions, leading to self-sustaining upward spirals of well-being. Conversely, when negative emotions accrete into downward spirals of defensive behavior, focus on threat, and feelings of inefficacy, these self-destructive, vicious cycles can lead to impoverished life experiences, and potentially, devastating psychopathology." 248

Emotional Guidance provides a connection between emotional state and behavior. This position is supported by Shahba and Allahvirdiyani, who reported that increasing emotional intelligence, resilience, and coping skills reduces aggression. Increased resilience equates to lower stress, which equates to a better-feeling emotional state. Research clearly demonstrates that behavioral outcomes can be improved via "…efficient self-regulation, active coping styles, optimism, and secure attachment. . ."[249]

Jeanne Segal tells us that:

"Many organizations are severely crippled by people devoting more time to protecting themselves from real and imagined threats than to working. When fear rules, productive hours are lost in attempts to

keep the upper hand, dodge the boss's wrath, or jockey for position. The undeniable fact that some people have more power than others in any organization does not have to overwhelm you with fear in the workplace."[250]

When employees understand the connection between emotional state and behavior, uncomfortable behavior from others begins to make sense. The co-worker who is rude may be worried about her job or about relationship problems outside the office. Reacting with compassion and not taking negative emotions personally may win a strong ally and even if it doesn't, the level of job strain the employee feels as a result will be far lower than if he took it personally.

Happiness at Work

A meta-analyses that looked at the relationship between job satisfaction and subjective well-being found that the relationship was bi-directional. In other words, one feeds the other. However, the effect of subjective well-being on job satisfaction was stronger than the effect of job satisfaction on subjective well-being.[251] In other words, being happy first is more likely to lead to job satisfaction than job satisfaction is to lead to happiness. This is supported in a growing and already considerable volume of other work and is the reason my company is named Happiness 1st Institute, because when you get happy first, everything else is better.

For many the hardest part of learning to follow the Emotional Guidance feedback system is overcoming conflicting instructions they received throughout life to use the opinions, expectations, and desires of others as guidance. The personal guidance provided by the Emotional Guidance sensory feedback system includes our goals in the order of importance the employee has assigned to them. On the surface, it sounds very selfish, but an employee whose goals include being loving or respectful to others will be guided in a way that takes goals about good relationships with others into consideration and will incorporate work goals.

A person who puts her interests lower than those of others becomes sacrificial and may become apathetic toward life because she won't be experiencing the joy of moving toward becoming who she wants to become. When she does for others because it fulfills her personal goals (i.e. I take good care of my child because I want a good relationship with her, or I am pleasant to my co-workers because it feels better to be nice than to be unkind) there is no sense of giving up what is wanted in order to please another so resentment does not build and keeping score about who has done more for the other makes no sense because nothing was done for someone else—the actions were done to support the accomplishment of personal goals, and those actions just happened to benefit more than just the person taking the action so the person is being good or doing good because it is what she wants to do.

Being good and doing good can lead to resentment when the employee feels forced, coerced, manipulated into, or encouraged using extrinsic motivations. Think about a time when you were forced to apologize to someone when you did not feel it. How would that have felt different if you had apologized simply because you want to live in peace and harmony with others? Research calls this *emotional labor* in the workplace, and it depletes personal resources and can lead to burnout. Being forced to display inauthentic emotions is not healthy.

You have to understand that being good and doing good feel really good when you are being good or doing good because it is what you want to do. There also seems to be something at work that I cannot explain fully, and although research supports my observations, it does provide an explanation. I have seen many people use these techniques to improve their chronic emotional set point and their desire for others to be happy always seems to increase in tandem with their increases in happiness. Schnall et al. were able to show that happier people are kinder to others.[252] Ito and Urland found happy people display less racism.[253] Isen and Schnall both independently found that happy employees are better corporate citizens.[254] In general, happy people have better relationships with others. Anyone who is concerned about how pursuing personal happiness seems to have a selfish focus should become familiar with how emotional state affects behavior.

Trusting the process and paying attention to how your own behavior shifts as your chronic emotional state improves is the best way to develop confidence in the process. Remember, as Adam Smith said centuries ago, "It is not from the benevolence of the butcher, the brewer, or the baker that we expect our dinner, but from their regard to their own interest." The commonly used Biblical saying is not "Love thy neighbor," it is "Love thy neighbor as thyself." People do better when they are good to themselves.

Many people have self-imposed limits on their ability to be happy. The limits may be conscious or unconsciously imposed. Use your Emotional Guidance to test the validity of any condition that puts your happiness off until another day or after a goal is reached. By shifting beliefs, its adverse effect on happiness can be stopped.

Each individual has developed beliefs about happiness. In *Be Happy*, Dr. Robert Holden wrote "Your Happiness Contract asserts every condition, rule, and law that you absolutely must abide by in order to be eligible for any amount of happiness. Any happiness that you experience without first fulfilling these conditions is strictly 'illegal' and may result in personal penalties of guilty feelings, inner discomfort, and moral foreboding."[255] A personal happiness contract is the result of the way the person perceives the life experiences she has lived. If she had to be good for Santa Claus to bring her a much desired toy, she probably has a requirement to *be good* in her happiness contract.

When I trained with Dr. Holden, he asserted that happiness is our right. Happiness is free. There are no dues, no conditions, and no way to earn happiness. If others seem able to be happy under conditions where you are not able to be happy changing you belief would increase your ability to be happy.

Employee Happiness isn't Your Responsibility, But It Should Be Your Goal

You may see employee happiness as a personal problem and not really a business issue. The truth is, every business goal will come faster and easier if you and your employees are happy. It is not an employer's job to make employee's happy. In fact, employers can't make an employee happy. Happiness is an inside job. If an employee is chronically less than happy, it does not really matter how much an employer tries to make him or her happy, the beneficial results will be temporary at best. At worse, the attempts will be viewed in a negative light.

Employees all want to feel happier. The desire to feel better is universal and it is the reason we do the things we do. We go to work because being employed feels better than not having income. If we're lucky, we may go to work because we love our job but even then, doing something you love feels better than not doing it. If we don't do something we might want to do, maybe have a piece of chocolate cake, we don't do it because we believe we will feel better not having it than the benefit from having it. But if we're in a low mood we may opt for the cake because the desire to feel better now is more important than a goal we will be more equipped to handle when we feel better. If we perceive we would feel guilty if we did not visit our parents on Sunday, we will visit our parents on Sunday even when we would prefer to do something else. The personal benefit of not feeling guilty feels better than the pleasure of the preferred activity.

Employee mood affects the decisions they make. Research has shown that employees who are in good moods demonstrate better corporate citizenship than employees in low moods.

So, if you can't make them happy, what can you do?

You can take advantage of the natural desire to feel better and give them skills they can use to better manage their emotions. Stress reducing, happiness increasing skills provide their own intrinsic motivation because the result of using them is feeling emotionally better.

The benefits of providing skills to increase employee happiness serve a great many corporate goals that I've already detailed in these pages. From all perspectives, teaching employees skills that increase their resilience, emotional state, and emotional intelligence are beneficial to the employer.

Why skill-based techniques instead of just providing a wonderful environment like Zappos?

A nice environment contributes toward mood, it does not cause it. Someone whose focus is habitually negative will not become positive just because the environment is wonderful. If you've ever been on a cruise, you may have noticed that even with one's every need catered to, some people remained unhappy and even miserable. Both unhappiness and misery are habits of thought more than anything else. Researchers have found many people living in poverty who were happy—happier than others who were living in luxury.

If you've not been on a cruise, read through the reviews on Cruise Critic. You'll see that some people had a great time when others found all sorts of reasons to maintain their habitual low mood.

Skills that help employees change habits of thought that usually keep employees in lower moods are intrinsically motivated by the positive emotions the employees feel when they use the skills. Even a brief increase in mood can benefit employers. Increased mood expands cognitive abilities, which could result in the employee solving a work-related problem that he'd been working on for months in a matter of minutes. Insights, intuition, and epiphanies increase as mood increases.

Even though immediate rewards are possible, the long term rewards are even better. Skill-based happiness provides immediate positive feedback in the form of improved mood so employees continue using the techniques causing mood to continue improving over time, increasing the chronic emotional state. Like any skill, as expertise develops, the outcome continues to improve with practice.

Make Happiness a Priority

Everyone has acceptable levels of positive emotion that they will strive to manage their emotional state into, regardless of whether they have the skills to do so or not. Many people with low emotion regulation skills become comfortable in an uncomfortable comfort Zone on the EGSc. If your comfort zone is not really comfortable, making happiness a priority will help you stay focused on learning and using the emotion regulation strategies to achieve a more comfortable comfort zone.

Pay attention to how you feel. "People with different emotionality standards had equally intense emotions when self-focus was low, yet they differed significantly when self-awareness was high . . . People have intricate sets of standards concerning emotion. Like other standards, they only participate in self-regulation to the extent that attention is oriented internally."[256]

When you make happiness a priority, pay attention to your Emotional Guidance, and use metacognitive skills to find the best-feeling emotional state you can find, your life will feel better. However, be sure to apply the skills because making happiness a priority without skills has been linked to bi-polar disorder.

Stress

Happiness

> *It is not possible to look at the negative aspects of a situation and be happy. A positive mindset can look at the same situation and feel happy because the positive mind focuses on the positive aspects of the situation.*

Happiness

Stress

A negative mindset is not happy because it looks at the negative aspects of what it is focused on. For example, a few years ago my husband and I took a Mediterranean cruise. The second day of the cruise my husband was under the weather and wanted to stay in our cabin all day. If I was negatively focused I could have railed against the fates for making him sick when we were on a cruise, which would have made the situation even worse. Instead, I had some work on a chapter for a peer reviewed textbook that I had not finished before we left for our trip. I considered the quiet day a boon that would allow me to finish the edits while my husband rested and recovered.

I would not have wished for him to be ill during our cruise, but it was easy to see the positive aspects of the situation because I have trained my mind to look for the positive in every situation. It has not always been an automatic process, but life is far better now that it is. Someone who has a negative mindset would have a difficult time perceiving anything good about becoming ill while on vacation.

In fact, it would not be unusual for a negatively focused individual to find a lot of negativity in such a situation. The actual mild illness could be seen as a pattern, "Nothing ever goes right for me." The negatively focused individual might lament, "Why does this always happen to me?" The situation could become a tragedy in the negatively focused individual's mind, "Why do I bother trying to have fun. Something always goes wrong." I've even seen individuals take a single day illness during vacation like this and use it to define the vacation. For the rest of the vacation they talk about how it was ruined by the day of illness. After they return home they continue telling the story about how the vacation was ruined by a day of illness. The other 20 days of the trip are barely remembered because the one day that did not go as planned is the primary focus.

Mindset matters more than most recognize.

Another point of clarification is that many individuals have been taught that optimism and pessimism are personality traits that cannot be changed. New research demonstrates that personality, including optimistic and pessimistic traits, is far more malleable than we have ever believed possible. I've seen many people make these changes in their lives and the happiness they've attained as a result.

Believing you must pursue happiness or that you should be happy because the circumstances of your life are considered desirable by many others stem from believing false premise. Happiness is based on individual factors that are unique to each individual. The definition of sustainable (True) happiness includes feeling negative emotions on occasion. It is the way those emotions are perceived as temporary that leaves the door open for a quick return to better-feeling emotional states. Remember not to should all over yourself if you aren't happy.

Positivity

Researchers are using numerous terms to describe happiness including positivity, optimism, General Well-Being (GWB), and Subjective Well-Being (SWB). In some instances, happiness is measured by a small action that creates a better emotion temporarily. This research demonstrates that the more positive emotion is good for the individual feeling it and also for those she interacts with, including strangers.

It does feel great to experience something that causes a temporary lifting of one's mood. The difference between a mood temporarily uplifted by something outside of ourselves over which we have no real control, and deliberately adjusting our perspective to feel better is like the difference between a baby who has learned to crawl and a world-class Olympic decathlon gold medalist.

The recent focus on happiness has received some backlash from some researchers. One common criticism of positivity is the belief that negative emotions are being repressed. This is not based on empirical evidence. In fact, in *Positivity*, Barbara L. Fredrickson, Ph. D. states, "On the contrary, resilience is marked by exquisite emotional agility."[257]

There have been publications arguing that anxiety is good for us. They are right that we should feel anxiety—anxiety, like any other emotion—is communication. We should feel anxiety for 60 seconds or less, just long enough to assure ourselves that a solution is possible. We don't have to solve the problem to reduce or eliminate anxiety—just the knowledge (which our EGS will affirm) that the problem is solvable—reduces anxiety. Reducing anxiety increases our cognitive abilities. Believing a solution is available primes our mind to be ready when information leading to a solution comes into our awareness. I'm serious about the sixty seconds. In fact, for someone who has been utilizing her guidance consistently for a few years, sixty seconds may be longer than necessary. Solutions and the belief that solutions exist creates intrinsic motivation. You cannot believe a solution is possible and remain anxious (unless you doubt you'll be able to accomplish the solution). In anxiety, you do not have cognitive access to the best path to the solution.

Someone who has established (practiced) thoughts that lead to anxiety will have to build new neuro-connections, but it is a very achievable goal requiring nothing more than practice thinking thoughts that create less anxiety. Body chemistry changes with each thought we think and imbalances will improve as thoughts that elicit better-feeling emotions are thought more often.

Some arguments have been put forth that positive emotions are not always good because anxiety can be a call to action. The goal is not to remain always joyful and carefree. The goal is to know that no matter what happens an individual knows how to return to being joyful. The accomplishment of a goal is not necessary to feel happy. Just progress toward the goal will bring emotional relief. When we feel anxiety, we should recognize it for what it is, Emotional Guidance, and then take appropriate action. Once appropriate actions begin, we can feel immeasurably better knowing that we are moving in the right direction. Emotional Guidance provides this feedback.

The "call to action" resulting from anxiety pales in comparison to the "call to action" from passionate interest. The anxious individual does not dream the big dream. The anxious call is protective, not expansive. Typically, anxiety involves moving away from something undesired. Essentially, retreat. Passionate interest, on the other hand, is a movement toward something bigger than oneself that increases energy and motivation.

Optimists and pessimists are often adamant about the correctness of their stance. Looking deeper, we find that they are both right because of the impact of expectation on outcome. Examined more deeply, it becomes clear that positive expectation results in more desirable outcomes.

Bandura told us "People who regard themselves as highly **efficacious act**, think, and feel differently from those who perceive themselves as inefficacious. They produce their own future, rather than simple foretell it."[258]

Sustainable Happiness

When an individual learns how to follow their Emotional Guidance, they can reach sustainable happiness without learning any other processes. The other processes are tools that assist in finding the better-feeling perspectives guidance points to, but they are not necessary when someone simply learn to understand and follow their guidance. The skills just make it easier for people who have been trained away from their Emotional Guidance to identify better-feeling perspectives.

That being said, do not beat yourself up for not being in a high emotional state. The path to feeling better does not include self-criticism or beating oneself about the head and shoulders with negativity. The path that supports you in becoming all you can become never requires condemnation of where you are, even if in your current emotional state there are awful behaviors. The focus is always on continuous improvement.

Step #1 only requires recognition that you have guidance.

It helps if you accept that you have a desire to feel better.

It is also common for people to ask me, "How can I be happy when X is happening?" in reference to a tragedy somewhere in the world. First, using that analogy, no one ever could have been happy because our world has never had a time when there weren't awful things happening somewhere. Even if all the countries were at peace, how could we know whether the atrocities that occur in homes had stopped?

But an even more important point to consider is the research that demonstrates our cognitive abilities are better when we're in a better emotional state. So, if you really want to do something about bad things happening in the world, you'll get happy first so that you'll bring your best cognitive power to the table. The point that being happy first causes success[259] is so important.

Step # 2 is knowing you can move to perspectives that feel better. You can't jump from awful to terrific in one fell swoop. It requires baby steps. But it does not take

> *How you feel will improve with every step along the way.*

long between first baby steps and running. A baby step, followed by a baby step, followed by a baby step, with your EGS supporting you every step of the way, saying, "Yes, come this way. That's right. Good." via emotional responses that feel better as you take those steps will help you build confidence.

When you have developed confidence, you can begin moving faster. You begin trusting that changing perspective has rewards—sometimes great rewards. You begin accepting the new perspectives faster because you no longer doubt the process. Once that happens you're off and running. You're still not leaping tall buildings—you're still going one step at a time, but the time between steps can be so short that on a single subject you can move from very disempowered to empowered in under an hour. Don't beat yourself up if you're not at this speed yet. If you have trouble with this, compare yourself to your prior self, comparing how it used to take months to move as far as you can now shift in a day.

Even if you forget for a while and wallow in negativity, you still know the process. At any time you can decide to begin the process on a sore subject. It is not about beating yourself up if you do not immediately apply the process to every area of your life. In fact, don't start with your biggest issue. Start with small things and build your confidence. Then, when you tackle the bigger areas they will be far easier than you expected. What sort of big things can seem easy? With practice, the list is endless. It definitely includes facing an abuser and finding inner peace about the past, divorces that were devastating at the time, the loss of a child, unexpected heartbreak, loss of a job, overcoming long-term PTSD, child abuse, beating chronic depression, reducing/eliminating fears that limit your life, and more.

You will also find that when you fix a problem in one area, it often helps in many other areas. A frustrating focus manifests in myriad ways throughout your day. It can include inept store clerks or waitresses, or inept driver's in front of you who fail to move when the light is green, it can involve teachers who seem to do things the hard way—whether it is letting you know the day before your child has to have something that you have to go to the store to buy or who mandate a field trip you have to take that conflicts with a business trip. It can include a manager at work who schedules you three weeks in advance on an important day you want off, but the policy does not allow you to request time-off more than two weeks in advance. It can involve someone putting the spaghetti back in the cupboard so when you pick it up, it all spills on the floor—the last box, now spread all over the floor instead of in the boiling pot on the stovetop—ten minutes before company is due to arrive.

When you move to a less frustrating Zone, you will feel inspired actions that let you know the spaghetti is not in the cupboard correctly before it spills, you'll feel instincts to change lanes and not be behind the frustrating driver, you'll have a casual conversation with your manager where you mention the important date and she makes a note not to schedule you that day or allows you to go ahead and put in for more time off more than two weeks in advance. When you begin doing this deliberate work to shift your emotional state, it almost feels magical. I can talk about it for days—you will not really understand until you do the work yourself. When you experience the difference it makes, you'll feel more empowered.

Remember, the filters in our brain are designed as if we understand how they work. They literally hide information that is inconsistent with how they are programmed—whether it is in our best interest or not. They are not malicious or vindictive or determining our deservability (worthiness)—we do that. The filters only carry out their programming. Conscious programming is of enormous value.

Your Emotional Guidance provides reliable guidance and is appropriate when you are in any emotional state.

Step #3 is simple. As stated earlier, Emotional Guidance works just like the child's game, *Hot* or *Cold*. While it does feel different to move from rage to blame than from frustration to hopefulness, or from hope to enthusiasm, each of these steps is a step in the right direction; each is *getting warmer*. Remember, any mental change in the right direction provides a feeling of relief (a releasing of tension or stress). The emotion that is in the *warmer* direction always feels better than emotions that are *getting colder*.

Emotions are responses to thoughts. Thinking about something pleasing (past, present, or future) will create *getting warmer* Emotional Guidance. Thinking about something unpleasant (past, present, or future) will create *getting colder* Emotional Guidance. Everyone has the ability to make the choice to think about someone or something and focus on an aspect that feels good or an aspect that feels bad. The Emotional Guidance system provides feedback to each thought.

Emotional Guidance leads to better feeling emotions, whether it is away from fear in a harmful environment or toward becoming the most we can imagine being.[260] Emotional Guidance is able to guide you to situations that satisfy two views that seem opposing and irreconcilable when viewed rationally.

> *Adjusting your thoughts toward better-feeling perspectives will provide the most benefit to you.*

Your guidance can be like that, inclinations and urges that don't seem to make sense have led me to some of the best experiences of my life. They have also saved me from harm on more than one occasion. It has guided some of the best decisions I've ever made.

Many teachers throughout the ages have encouraged us to love and respect our self because most people will treat us no better than we treat ourselves. I have seen this in my own life. The more I respect myself the more I am respected. The more I treat myself kindly, the more others treat me kindly. This is true when you love yourself and it is true when you don't. Others treat you much the way you treat yourself.

The rational mind is not just filtered by beliefs. Expectations, emotional stance, and focus have a tremendous impact. That is one reason it is so hard for someone who has been in a chronic unhappy state to move to a better-feeling state using the rational mind. Habits of thought, like other habits, take time to change. Using the EGS as a guide to better-feeling thoughts, the rational mind is able to be reconditioned to support better-feeling emotional stances.

Our upbringing can have a significant effect on our ability to feel what emotion we are feeling. Some people were trained from young ages that being emotional was bad behavior. In many cases, emotions have been suppressed and these employees may have a more difficult time labeling their emotions. However, this person will feel relief when a better-feeling thought is felt. Reaching for a feeling of relief will enable an employee with difficulty figuring out which Zone he is in on the EGSc to use his guidance.

Both affirmations and setting intentions can help the employee who has subdued emotions to become more aware of them. Even individuals who have not been conditioned to suppress their emotions become more aware of subtle differences as they gain experience using their EGS.

Some affirmations that could be helpful:

I will recognize my emotional response to my thoughts.

I will be aware as soon as my thoughts take my emotional state to a less comfortable one so that I can make adjustments early.

I am safe feeling my emotions because I have tools to help me find thoughts that will allow me to feel good.

My emotions affect my behavior. My job is to feel good so I'll be good.

I am strong. I am invincible. I am (fill in the blank with something that resonates with you)

It is important to only use affirmations that you believe are achievable. If you find your inner critic arguing with an affirmation, it will not help you. Try to affirm something that is less different from what you are already doing while you work on evicting the inner critic.

Your current perspective is valid and right, from how you are perceiving the situation in this moment. That does not mean it is the only valid perspective about the topic. It does not mean it is the only perspective you can have about the topic. It does not mean the perspective is true or right. It

> *When you find yourself feeling negative emotion about somebody else, recognize it as a situation where a Right Response would serve you well.*

certainly does not mean it is the perspective that is best for your health, relationships, career, or overall well-being. In fact, if you feel anything less than excited expectation, joy, love, or appreciation, there is a perspective that is more supportive of your highest good.

One of Einstein's well-known quotes is:
We cannot solve our problems with the same thinking we used when we created them.

Hopefully, any fears you may have developed about being positively focused have been soothed. Employees will still see problems and will still take the necessary steps to resolve them. What they won't do is catastrophize the problem, or allow it to derail their life. They won't ruminate about it and will be far less likely to lose sleep over it, which increases their ability to solve problems because their brain is well-rested. The following processes directly address the root cause of stress, providing each employee who practices them a level of emotional agility that will make them more resilient, increase their emotional intelligence, and provide the other benefits listed above.

The Smart Way changes filters the brain uses to process information before an individual is consciously aware of it. But each individual decides how to adjust their filters. Also remember, the filters are already programmed. For almost everyone, this means that your current default settings are based on their early life experiences. That is great news because it typically means deliberately shifting the filters will provide significant life enhancing results.

> *One important aspect not usually considered by most teachers is that the specific process that will be most effective varies due to the current emotional state. There are other variables, but this one always matters.*

The purpose of the processes provided throughout this book is to help employees move up the EGSc and achieve the health, well-being, relationship, and success benefits that naturally occur in higher Zones.

Subtle Differences

The way every moment of life is experienced is the result of many factors. One of the factors you have the potential to control is your emotional state. To demonstrate the subtle differences the same experience is presented twice, side-by-side. In one, emotional state is the result of observations about the situation and the emotional reaction to those perceptions about the situation. In the second experience, the individual takes a few moments here and there to soothe yourself about disliked elements of your current situation. You've purchased new software for your computer and it's time to install it.

You're feeling a bit frustrated. You'd rather buy a new computer than upgrade this one but you don't feel you can justify a new computer right now.

You're feeling a bit frustrated. You'd rather buy a new computer than upgrade this one but you don't feel you can justify a new computer right now. *You tell yourself this is just a temporary situation and soon you'll be able to have a new computer. In the overall scheme of things, life is good. Your family is healthy and you have a lot of hopes and dreams you're looking forward to.*

You insert the CD into the drive to do the upgrade. You should be done in about five minutes and you're looking forward to using this new photo editing software.

You insert the CD into the drive to do the upgrade. You should be done in about five minutes and you're looking forward to using this new photo editing software.

The little bar appears that indicates the software is loading but then it seems to stop, stuck about ¼ of the way. The computer hums for a while, with no progress showing then a pop-up appears that says, "This software is not compatible with your operating system."

The little bar appears that indicates the software is loading but then it seems to stop, stuck about ¼ of the way. The computer hums for a while, with no progress showing then a pop-up appears that says, "This software is not compatible with your operating system."

Your frustration spikes and you do that thing you do when you're beginning to feel a little anger. *Your emotional state is not pleasant but you don't do anything specific to change it. If your spouse or child shows up during this time the interaction will be less than you want it to be. You may say something that is unpleasant or give them less time than you want to. You may even be ugly to yourself in your own mind, "How could I not notice this software would not work with my operating system? I'm so dumb." If your relationship with your spouse is not supportive, your spouse may say this to you.*

Your frustration and low level anger have already caused your cognitive processes to constrict. Your thinking is not as clear as you would like them to be. You decide to go back to the computer store and see if you can get photo editing software that will work with your operating system. *You forget that you had plans to go to a new restaurant your spouse wanted to try for lunch.*

Your frustration spikes and you do that thing you do when you're beginning to feel a little anger. *You quickly recognize that you're not feeling how you want to feel and deliberately soothe yourself, "I'll figure this out." Or "I've solved other problems with my computer before. This is just going to take a little longer than I wanted it to." After you've soothed yourself, your interactions with family are pleasant because you're not blaming them or yourself for your frustration— it's just something you have to do in order to get what you want—photo editing software you are excited about.*

Your emotional state is fluctuating between a little frustration and a feeling of confidence that you'll figure this out. While not where they would be if you were feeling passionate enthusiasm, your cognitive processes are not significantly constricted. You decide to go back to the computer store and see if you can get photo editing software that will work with your operating system. *You remember your plans to have lunch with your spouse and ask if you can go a little early so you can stop at the computer store before lunch. While your spouse gets ready to go, you use a search engine to find several software options that would work with your operating system. You look at the features and identify two that seem as good as the one that you're returning and one that is even better. The even better one is just a few dollars more than you paid for the one that does not work and you begin feeling this situation is not a problem, but a lucky accident.*

You and your spouse get in the car and begin driving to the computer store. You don't notice the traffic. You're enjoying telling your spouse about the better software you found and being happy that things always seem to work out well for you. When the big truck pulls in front of you without using his blinker you notice a bumper sticker on it that makes you laugh out loud and share an inside joke with your spouse. You arrive at the computer store safely *in an optimistic mood.*

You get in the car and begin driving to the computer store. You're still feeling very frustrated. Traffic seems terrible and that makes you even more frustrated. When the big truck pulls in front of you without using his blinker, you feel a little angry. You arrive at the computer store safely but not in a good emotional state.

The computer store employee who helps you knows how to solve your problem, but he has also been having a frustrating morning, which has caused his cognitive processes to constrict and the information he needs to properly advise you is not available to him while he is focused on problems, which is all he can do in his current emotional state.

The sales clerk doesn't remember what product will solve your problem. He walks out onto the floor with you but every box he picks up is for a newer operating system than you have. He's getting frustrated and begins trying to get you to buy a new computer, which is not in your budget right now and you're already frustrated about that. The two of you walk around, both frustrated and neither accomplishing anything when you hear a text come into your phone. You check your phone and it's your spouse, asking if you forgot your plans to go to lunch together at a restaurant just a few minutes away from the computer store.

You know that if you don't have lunch at the agreed upon time it won't be a pleasant lunch so you tell the sales clerk you have to go and leave for home so you can have lunch with your spouse. Your trip was a waste of time. You still don't have working photo editing software.

You arrive at the restaurant with your spouse, who is not pleased you did not think about going to the computer store together. Your spouse is irritated that you're frustrated because lunch won't be much fun with you in your current mood. Your

The computer store employee who helps you knows how to solve your problem, but he has also been having a frustrating morning, which has caused his cognitive processes to constrict and the information he needs to properly advise you is not available to him while he is focused on problems, which is all he can do in his current emotional state.

Because your mood is significantly better, you recognize an opportunity to make him laugh, which improves his mood. The constriction of his cognitive processes eases and he suddenly remembers seeing that the exact product you're asking for, which usually has to be ordered because they don't carry it in the store, in the return area. He checks and someone had ordered it but returned it unopened because their hard drive crashed before it arrived and they bought a new computer instead.

This sales clerk is feeling friendly to you. He was feeling frustrated before you came in but you got him laughing and the two of you are having a good time. He decides to ask his manager if you can have a discount because it is already in the store and if you buy it, they don't have to return it. The manager agrees to give you a 20% discount on the price.

You leave the store with software you're pretty sure will work and you're excited about the additional features and feeling lucky about getting the good deal. With the 20% off the new software was actually less than the one that did not work.

You arrive at the restaurant with your spouse, who is pleased with the deal you got on the software. You're both ready to relax and enjoy a nice lunch together. You're focused on one another, catching up after a busy week. Because you're not in a hurry for lunch to be over and want to focus spouse does nothing to try to uplift you. Instead your spouse piles more reasons to feel bad on your already low emotional state.

Because you just want lunch to be over, you're hyper aware of how attentive the waitress is and she seems slow. The food does not taste as good as you both thought it would. (Food tastes better when you're in a good mood.)

Because neither of you enjoyed lunch very much, you leave a miserly tip and on your way out, complain to one another about how disappointed you are with the new restaurant you had been excited to try. You don't recognize you brought your own bad mood to lunch and if you'd changed your mood your lunch would have been much better.

When you get home you decide to give up for now and plop down in front of the TV for the rest of the afternoon.

on your spouse, the waitress seems attentive enough. The food is even better than you both thought it would be. (Food tastes better when you're in a good mood.)

After lunch you leave an extra nice tip for the waitress because you're feeling flush from saving money on the software. Your spouse likes it when you're nice to waitresses and squeezes your arm in appreciation of your generosity.

When you get home you install the software and begin learning to use the photo editing software.

This example was very detailed to demonstrate that just a little bit of deliberate tuning of perspective can make a tremendous difference in one's experiences. There was no long drawn out use of processes that took time. There were just deliberate shifts, mostly going more general about the subject.

The left column is a typical early 21st century experience where mood is derived by the current circumstances. When something that is not that big of a deal goes wrong, it adversely affects other things such as restricting cognitive processes. What was not evident in this example, but very important in the overall scheme of things is that immune function also decreased when frustration increased. Over time this has a significant bearing on quality of life. Also, it is not just that food does not taste as good when your mood is lower; the entire digestive function is at less than ideal levels when your mood is lower. Over time this increases the risk of both obesity and diabetes.

The individual on the right is not someone who was introduced to happiness increasing skills today. But within three months of remembering to use the skills by paying attention to how you feel and responding to discord with the process that feels best to you in your current circumstances, the column on the right could be representative of your experience. Most people have been living life much like the individual in Column 1 does for a long time. Three months is not a long time to wait for significant improvements.

In fact, you don't really have to wait three months. Three months is for the automated responses to begin feeling natural to you. You can have the emotional relief now by using the processes.

Happiness is a thing to be practiced...
...like the Violin.
John Lubbock

Don't be discouraged if the things Column 2 used to soothe frustration are not currently true for you. Life generally reflects the results of your chronic emotional states. As you feel increasingly better, other areas of life will improve, too.

You cannot STOP thinking about something by trying to stop thinking about it because when you try to stop thinking about the thing you don't want to think about, you are thinking about it. You can, however, decide to think about something else and every time you begin thinking about the topic you don't want to think about have something more pleasant to think about already planned as a diversion.

KNOW that you can change your thoughts, even habitual thoughts. You have control. *You think them; they do not think you.* I would not label repetitive thoughts with a label that gives them more power than they deserve. With consistent effort, everyone can change their thought paths. The more power given to labels, the harder it is to believe in your ability to change and to find the hope that you can do it. Labels have power. Only use the ones you want to keep.

What you affirm is not as important as how it feels. If it feels better it is helping. Once you believe the affirmation fully, which means you've thought about it long enough that it has become a belief; you're ready to take another step.

There are many uses for positive affirmations. You can use them to protect against the Pygmalion Effect and to be the more dominant belief when mirror neurons sync. You can use them to increase self-esteem. You can use them to improve competency at tasks or to make the group you identify with feel better, which leads to less negative feelings about groups you do not belong to.[261]

I have used them to affirm that the group I belong to is the human race. This has led to numerous changes in the way I think about myself and my relationship with the world. By making my dominant view about the group I belong to be human, national borders became less important and other man made labels (religion, race, national origin, etc.) became unimportant because everyone is part of the group I belong to. The broader you define the group you belong to, the more comfortable you become in different experiences.

The different ways in which we dim our light of happiness seem endless. Once a person has developed skill in reducing stress, the journey continues as their Emotional Guidance continues to highlight thoughts they can adjust in order to feel even better. Emotional states that were once uncomfortable comfort zones become too uncomfortable which increases intrinsic motivation to use the skills to feel better. When an employee learns how good he can feel without a great deal of effort his willingness to remain unhappy decreases. Since the skills work, the result is an individual who is chronically in a better mood and whose mind and body are functioning better as a result.

There is really no end to how happy a person can feel—the only limitation I've identified is the lack of words the English language has for describing joy, ecstasy, enthusiasm and the bliss of unconditional love. Our current vocabulary doesn't come close to describing the feelings.

13: Business Case

Success is not the key to happiness. Happiness is the key to success. If you love what you are doing, you will be successful.
Albert Schweitzer

Widely available research shows that employee engagement has a significant effect on every area of your business, from customer satisfaction to employee theft, safety, absenteeism, and turnover. Employee engagement impacts both quality and productivity. All of these factors have the ability to impact profitability and even the viability of a business.

Business Benefits of Happiness

Some people object to an optimistic outlook or a Pollyannaish perspective. The research is clear that less stress is better for us in every area of life. It is helpful to realize that stress and happiness are essentially opposite ends of the same continuum.

Mental access to Solutions	• Sweet Zone • Hopeful Zone
Mental access to Problems	• Blah Zone • Drama Zone • Give Away Zone • Hot (Red) Zone • Powerless Zone

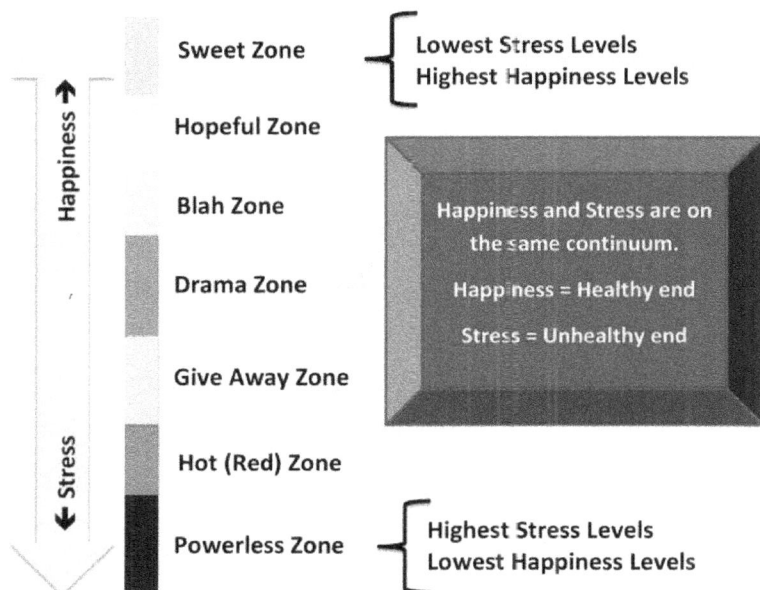

This translates into real benefits. The happy person lives in a different world than the stressed person. The way the brain of the same person interprets reality when the person is happy is different from the way the person interprets reality when he is stressed. The happier the person is, the more her interpretation of reality differs from her interpretations when she is stressed.

When thinking about problems, it is not that the person with a positive mindset ignores the problem so much as it is that the positive mind has access to the solutions. A positively focused person may not see the problem—not because they don't understand the situation—but because they see it as an opportunity, not a problem. When something goes wrong, they'll see the silver-lining faster. They'll be more resilient.

Annually more than 10% of the world's population experience episodes of depression according to the CDC and the University of California, Davis reports that 20% of the population has trouble with anger issues. These people are often also employees.

Remember: Research demonstrates lower stress levels benefit you and everyone you interact with in many ways, including benefits that increase the potential for thriving and decrease

Happiness ↑
↓ Stress

Sweet Zone — Lowest Stress Levels / Highest Happiness Levels

Hopeful Zone

Blah Zone

Happiness and Stress are on the same continuum.

Happiness = Healthy end

Drama Zone

Stress = Unhealthy end

Give Away Zone

Hot (Red) Zone

Powerless Zone — Highest Stress Levels / Lowest Happiness Levels the risk of unhealthy choices and negative life events. Lower employee stress and increased employee happiness provide significant benefits to businesses including, but not limited to:

Better:

Increased productivity[262]

Higher employee engagement[263]

Better alignment with corporate mission[264]

Associated with better corporate citizenship[265]

Associated with better customer service[266]

Associated with pro-health behaviors[267]

Associated with pro-social behaviors[268]

Rarely associated with crime[269]

Low association with alcohol and drug abuse[270]

Less likely to experience non-work problems that affect performance at work (i.e. divorce)[271]

Better cognitive abilities[272]

Improved Immune function (less absenteeism)[273]

Fewer chronic diseases[274]

More Resilient[275]

- (Resilience includes optimism, internal locus of control, and healthy self-esteem)

Higher PsyCap (Psychological Capital)[276]

- (PsyCap includes confidence (self-efficacy), optimism, hope, and resiliency)

Relationships

Endocrine system function in your body

Digestive function in your body

Energy level

Sleep habits

Lifestyle habits

Long-term career success

Resilience

Self-efficacy

Healthier Self-esteem

Intrinsic motivation

Creativity

Less likely to:

Abuse drugs

Abuse alcohol

Commit a crime

Commit suicide

Bully others

Be bullied

Develop eating disorders

Smoke

Develop chronic health issues

Divorce

Become depressed

Develop heart disease

Have a pre-term delivery

Have a child who has asthma

Other factors

"It has been suggested on several occasions that assessing a person's core self-evaluations before hire can be useful in predicting important work outcomes, such as job satisfaction . . . job performance . . . and employee turnover. However, the interaction obtained in the study with demographic characteristics represents potentially undesirable outcomes of using the construct for such a purpose . . . Relationships of core self-evaluations with job satisfaction varied based on both gender and race, indicating that this would not be a reasonable measure to use for hiring decisions . . . although appealing for such a use, it should not be considered for such purposes" at this time.[277]

There is a viable and brilliant alternative. Most companies today, have at least some desire for their organization to contribute to the betterment of humanity. Low core self-evaluations are a factor that contributes to the continuing disparities women, minorities, and the poor encounter on a daily basis. Instead of hiring employees based on core self-evaluations, employees can be trained to increase their core self-evaluations and therefore improve the trajectory of their career. There is significant research to support the idea that doing so would afford long-term benefits to individuals, organizations, and communities.‡‡

Training should stretch across 12-weeks because the goal is to re-wire neuro connections in the brain and that takes time and repetition. Because the techniques provide positive emotional feedback, they are intrinsically motivated and improvements will continue after the completion of the program.

One way companies can address the time-consuming nature of the program is to offer it to both employees and their families during non-work hours. This has a social good element, but it can also be of significant benefit to the company. One outcome of learning metacognitive processes that create True Happiness is improved relationships of all types. Improved relationships at work have obvious benefits, but so do improved relationships at home. Relationship discord in one's home life adversely impacts work performance and can lead to increased absenteeism (due to divorces and subsequent single parenthood childcare needs). Including teenagers (mature ones from age 13 or 14 up) can greatly reduce the potential they will create turmoil in the home. In my work with teenagers I've seen sullen attitudes disappear and suicide averted.

Judge tells us "it is not enough to change people's behaviors and life circumstances only without changing self-views."[278]

The Smart Way metacognitive processes and Emotional Guidance support all the factors commonly associated with high employee engagement including healthy self-esteem, optimism, and an internal locus of control. Learning to be conscious about reappraising one's emotional state lowers negative rumination.

The reduction of stress provides benefits across the board:
1. Science routinely reports that stress is the root cause of up to 95% of all illnesses. I agree. The research links everything from heart disease, cancer, Alzheimer's, and even the flu and common cold to stress.
2. Stress is strongly linked to mental health diagnoses from depression, anxiety, OCD, all the way up to psychosis.[279]
3. Behavior that is less than the best it could be, whether we are speaking of a preschooler, a spouse, a CEO, or a murderer is always rooted in stress.
4. Stress diminishes our ability to think, which compromises our ability to make the best decisions.
5. Relationships are negatively impacted by both the diminished mental capacity and the diminished pro-social behavior caused by stress.
6. Stress affects digestive function in a way that increases the risk of both obesity and diabetes—calories in and calories out does not tell the full story.

---

‡‡ My book, *Our Children Live in a War Zone: Use the Power of Resilience to Improve Their Lives, Applied Positive Psychology 2.1,* detailed numerous studies including longitudinal studies demonstrating improved outcomes across the lifespan when low-income and minority individuals were provided with resilience increasing training.

7. Stress and happiness have an inverse relationship. When you reduce stress, happiness increases. When you increase stress, happiness declines.
8. Addiction to both drugs and alcohol begin with a stressed individual seeks relief from the negative emotion and does not have the knowledge or skills to feel better in a way that exacts a lower price.
9. Behavior is decided by what will feel best. Even someone in a violent criminal situation who chooses to sacrifice his life to save another does so because he believes it will feel better to save the person than to let the other person (perhaps a woman or child) die and live with the guilt.
10. Turnover is often because of uncomfortable levels of stress
11. It isn't the difficulty of a job, it is the perception of one's capacity compared to the requirements that causes stress. Challenges can be energizing when viewed from some vantage points.

Metacognitive Processes and emotional guidance help employees connect with the purpose of their company's mission in a way that is personally meaningful above and beyond the value of the paycheck and facilitates the development of social connections with their co-workers.

Employees create their own meaning from the way they interpret their reality. How an employee perceives management, co-workers, peers, the corporate mission, and job assignments is far more about the employee's emotional state and core self-evaluations than about an actual reality. Their words and actions reflect their personal perception of reality.

When employees are unhappy or have low core self-evaluations, it is unlikely they will be fully engaged. Their full potential cannot be realized unless and until they understand their Emotional Guidance and develop habits of thought that support self-actualization.

Movement toward ever-expanding goals significantly contributes to life satisfaction, which contributes to improved health and behavior across the lifespan. Individuals, who lack the characteristics that improve outcomes struggle more, experience higher levels of chronic psychosocial stress, and poorer health and behavior outcomes. An individual with higher self-efficacy will set higher goals and then manage to those goals.

Beliefs have a significant effect on behavior. The subconscious mind creates back stories to explain experiences and observations that are consistent with an individual's beliefs. If a person believes they cannot do something, or that they aren't good at something, the back story their mind creates supports their belief. If they succeed at something that they don't think they can do or be good at, their back story will reflect that—perhaps crediting luck for the success. Because most beliefs are established by age 6, most employees have not evaluated their beliefs to determine if they support their goals or detract from their ability to achieve them. Because Emotional Guidance bypasses the filtering process that the mind uses to create back stories, it can help employees and management overcome limiting beliefs that hinder achievement of their full potential.

The ability to integrate external motivators with intrinsic motivators is a metacognitive process that can be learned. Although some seem to accomplish this merging intuitively, once the skill is learned, there should be no difference between those who intuitively do it and those who learn how to do it. In fact, those who learn how to do it as a skill may be better off than those who intuitively merge the two motivators because in situations where it is more difficult to do, the one with the skills will be more aware and will more consciously pursue finding alignment between the two. The one who intuitively found this balance may not consciously realize what led to earlier successes.

Teaching employees how to feel better using Emotional Guidance and metacognitive processes (primarily reappraisal in conjunction with Emotional Guidance) will improve their perceptions about self and others, which will increase engagement.

Many factors that are important to employers are linked to emotional state, as shown in the charts on the following pages.

The diagrams illustrate many of the benefits a positive mindset provides. When research from positive psychology, social psychology, public health and other disciplines is combined the power of a positive mind becomes very clear. When you look at the detrimental effect of a negative mindset it tells the opposite side of the story. A mirror image of the positive effects is revealed in the literature that looked at the effects of chronic stress. An evil twin analogy fits the circumstances.

One of the most notable aspects is the effect of a positive mindset on lifespan in longitudinal studies. The net result is about 18 years of healthier life because debilitating illnesses arrive closer to death in the positively focused individuals, who live an average of 10.7 years longer and remain healthy until the last two years of life. People with a pessimistic outlook tend to begin suffering from chronic illnesses about seven years prior to death. That's a difference worth talking about. If we could teach people how to reduce the number of years they spend chronically ill prior to death from seven to two, health care expenses would plummet. This is something we could do—we know how to develop more positive mindsets.

Chronic stress is a significant contributor to serious physical, mental and behavioral health problems. A review of the scientific literature on the relationship between emotion regulation and depression shows that applying cognitive reappraisal reduces "stress-elicited emotions leading to physical disorders."[280] Unproductive thought patters such as "rumination and emotion suppression" lead to depression and physiological disease."[281] Teaching individuals to use positive emotional regulation techniques would prevent many instances of depression.

While therapy combined with learning these techniques is what I would encourage for individuals with diagnosed mental illnesses, everyone, especially individuals who are stressed but not yet severe enough to rate a diagnosis can benefit enormously from learning these skills, which may prevent them from ever reaching the diagnosis stage.

The flip side of the picture shows the debilitating impact of a negative mindset. A life lived with a negative mindset is frequently assaulted by bad luck on all fronts—health, relationships, and career. Individuals seem to no sooner survive one crisis and another one arrives. A negative mindset leads to poor outcomes. Even among the most advantaged, a negative mindset results in more divorces, alcoholism, business failures, bankruptcies, and suicides.[282]

The detriments of a negative mindset extend beyond undesired physical health outcomes. Mental and behavioral health suffers as well, often creating multigenerational problems. Two individuals in the same circumstances have decidedly different outcomes when one is optimistic and the other is pessimistic. It can lead to the difference between divorce and developing a deeper, more meaningful relationship. At its worse, it is the difference between life and death.

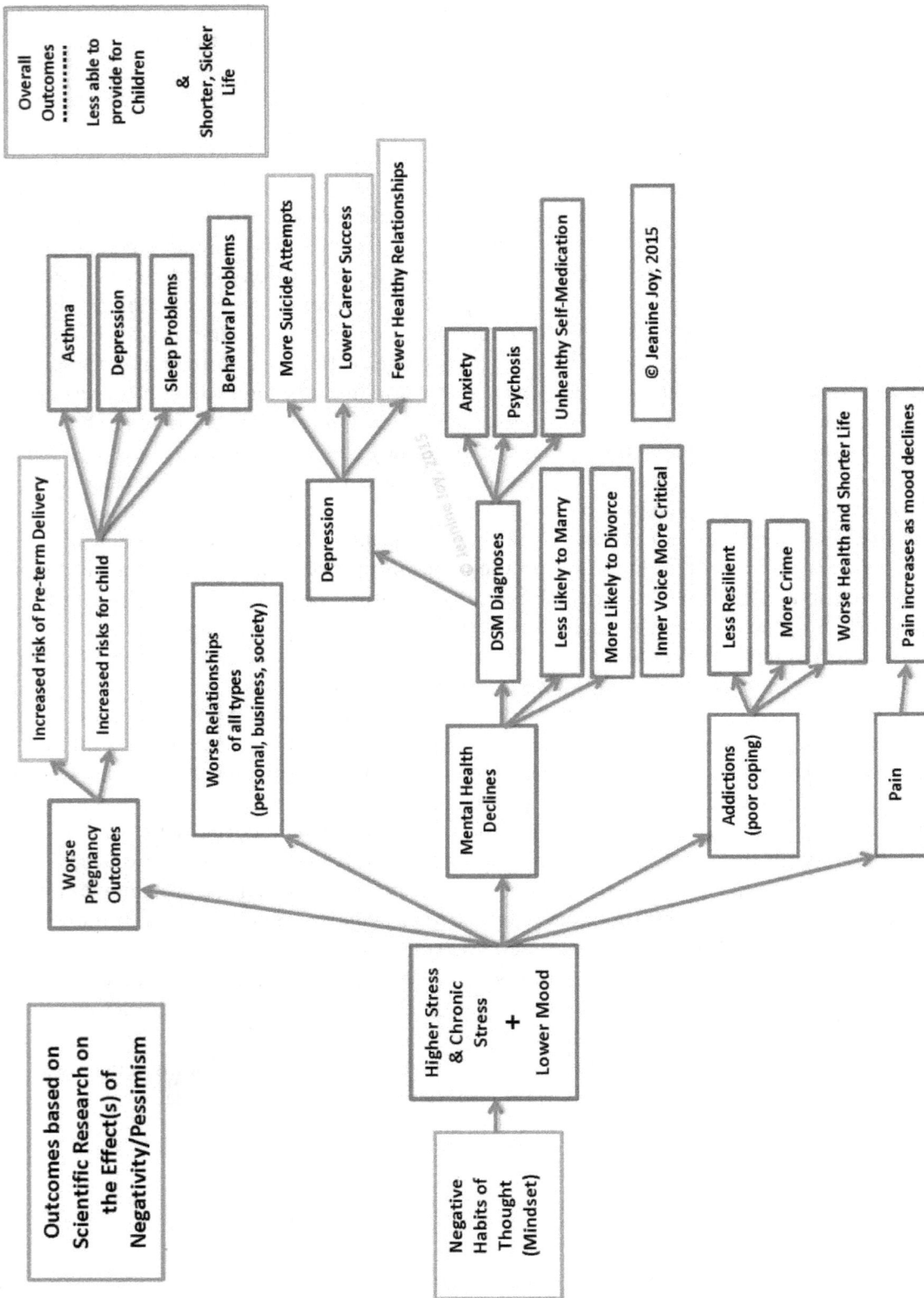

Outcomes based on Scientific Research on the Effect(s) of Negativity/Pessimism

Overall Outcomes
·········
Less able to provide for Children

&

Shorter, Sicker Life

Negative Habits of Thought (Mindset) → Higher Stress & Chronic Stress + Lower Mood

Higher Stress & Chronic Stress + Lower Mood → Worse Pregnancy Outcomes

Worse Pregnancy Outcomes → Increased risk of Pre-term Delivery

Worse Pregnancy Outcomes → Increased risks for child

Increased risks for child → Asthma

Increased risks for child → Depression

Increased risks for child → Sleep Problems

Increased risks for child → Behavioral Problems

Higher Stress & Chronic Stress + Lower Mood → Worse Relationships of all types (personal, business, society)

Depression → More Suicide Attempts

Depression → Lower Career Success

Depression → Fewer Healthy Relationships

Higher Stress & Chronic Stress + Lower Mood → Mental Health Declines

Mental Health Declines → Depression

Mental Health Declines → DSM Diagnoses

DSM Diagnoses → Anxiety

DSM Diagnoses → Psychosis

DSM Diagnoses → Unhealthy Self-Medication

Mental Health Declines → Less Likely to Marry

Mental Health Declines → More Likely to Divorce

Inner Voice More Critical

Higher Stress & Chronic Stress + Lower Mood → Addictions (poor coping)

Addictions (poor coping) → Less Resilient

Addictions (poor coping) → More Crime

Addictions (poor coping) → Worse Health and Shorter Life

Higher Stress & Chronic Stress + Lower Mood → Pain

Pain → Pain increases as mood declines

© Jeanine Joy, 2015

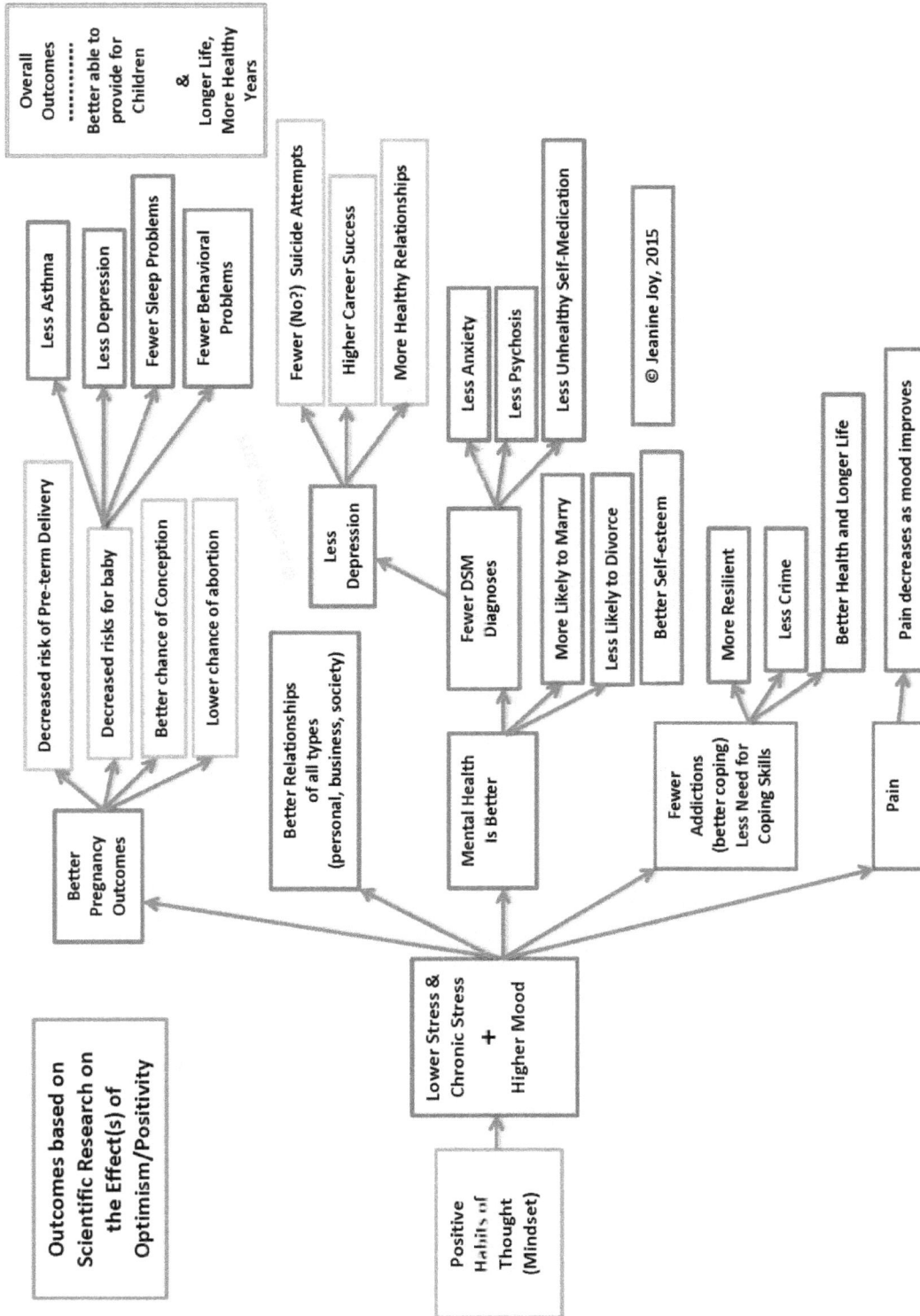

Outcomes based on Scientific Research on the Effect(s) of Optimism/Positivity

Overall Outcomes
....
Better able to provide for Children
&
Longer Life, More Healthy Years

Positive Habits of Thought (Mindset)

Lower Stress & Chronic Stress
+
Higher Mood

Better Pregnancy Outcomes

Decreased risk of Pre-term Delivery

Decreased risks for baby

Better chance of Conception

Lower chance of abortion

Less Asthma

Less Depression

Fewer Sleep Problems

Fewer Behavioral Problems

Better Relationships of all types (personal, business, society)

Mental Health Is Better

Fewer DSM Diagnoses

Less Depression

Fewer (No?) Suicide Attempts

Higher Career Success

More Healthy Relationships

Less Anxiety

Less Psychosis

Less Unhealthy Self-Medication

More Likely to Marry

Less Likely to Divorce

Better Self-esteem

Fewer Addictions (better coping) Less Need for Coping Skills

More Resilient

Less Crime

Better Health and Longer Life

Pain

Pain decreases as mood improves

© Jeanine Joy, 2015

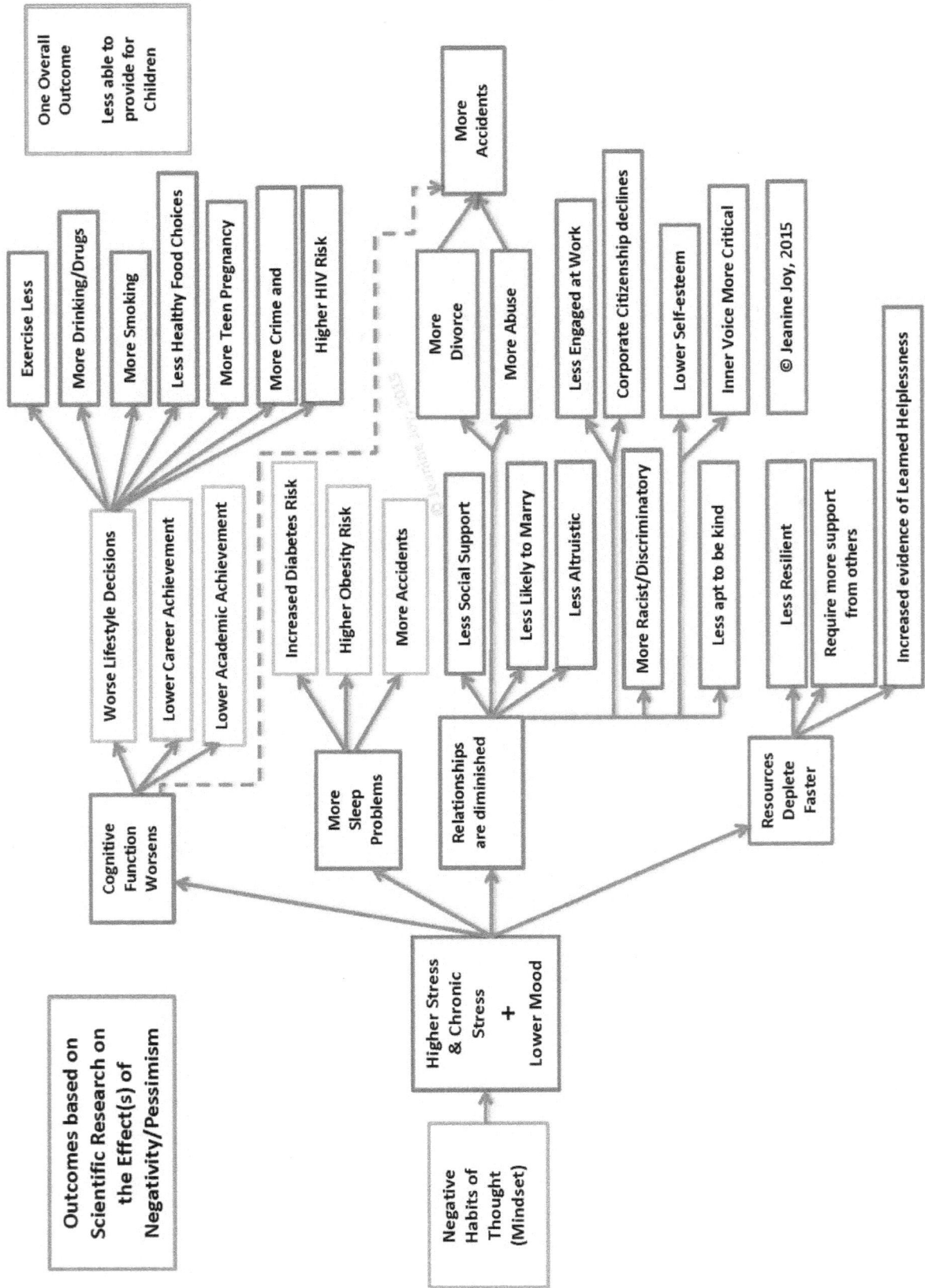

Outcomes based on the Effect(s) of Negativity/Pessimism

One Overall Outcome

Less able to provide for Children

Negative Habits of Thought (Mindset)

Higher Stress & Chronic Stress + Lower Mood

Cognitive Function Worsens

Worse Lifestyle Decisions

Lower Career Achievement

Lower Academic Achievement

Exercise Less

More Drinking/Drugs

More Smoking

Less Healthy Food Choices

More Teen Pregnancy

More Crime and

Higher HIV Risk

Increased Diabetes Risk

Higher Obesity Risk

More Accidents

More Sleep Problems

Relationships are diminished

Less Social Support

Less Likely to Marry

Less Altruistic

More Racist/Discriminatory

Less apt to be kind

More Divorce

More Abuse

More Accidents

Less Engaged at Work

Corporate Citizenship declines

Lower Self-esteem

Inner Voice More Critical

Resources Deplete Faster

Less Resilient

Require more support from others

Increased evidence of Learned Helplessness

© Jeanine Joy, 2015

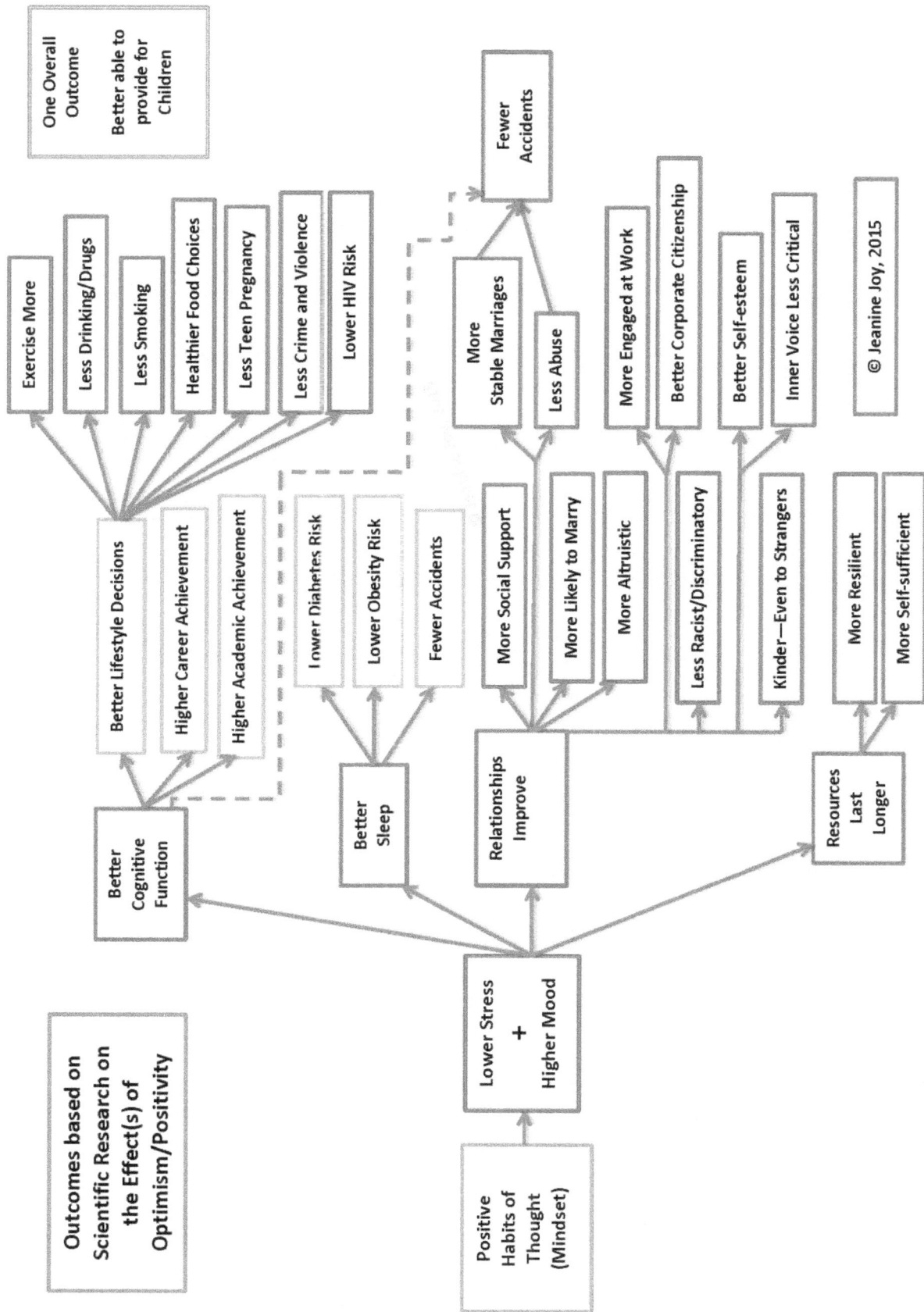

One Overall Outcome

Better able to provide for Children

Exercise More

Less Drinking/Drugs

Less Smoking

Healthier Food Choices

Less Teen Pregnancy

Less Crime and Violence

Lower HIV Risk

Fewer Accidents

More Stable Marriages

Less Abuse

More Engaged at Work

Better Corporate Citizenship

Better Self-esteem

Inner Voice Less Critical

© Jeanine Joy, 2015

Better Lifestyle Decisions

Higher Career Achievement

Higher Academic Achievement

Lower Diabetes Risk

Lower Obesity Risk

Fewer Accidents

More Social Support

More Likely to Marry

More Altruistic

Less Racist/Discriminatory

Kinder—Even to Strangers

More Resilient

More Self-sufficient

Better Cognitive Function

Better Sleep

Relationships Improve

Resources Last Longer

Outcomes based on Scientific Research on the Effect(s) of Optimism/Positivity

Lower Stress + Higher Mood

Positive Habits of Thought (Mindset)

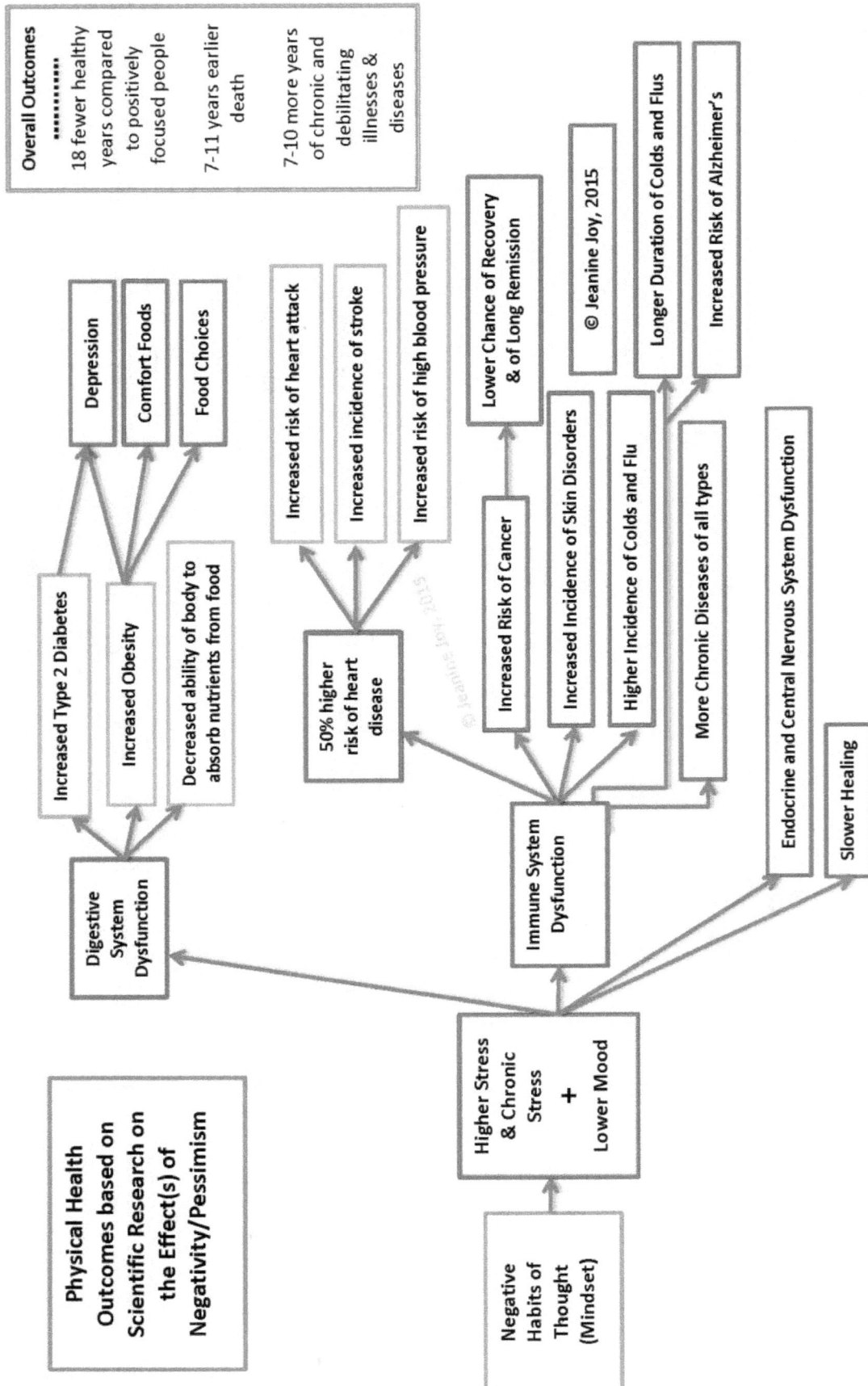

Physical Health Outcomes based on Scientific Research on the Effect(s) of Negativity/Pessimism

Negative Habits of Thought (Mindset)

Higher Stress & Chronic Stress + Lower Mood

Digestive System Dysfunction

Increased Type 2 Diabetes

Increased Obesity

Decreased ability of body to absorb nutrients from food

Depression

Comfort Foods

Food Choices

50% higher risk of heart disease

Increased risk of heart attack

Increased incidence of stroke

Increased risk of high blood pressure

Immune System Dysfunction

Increased Risk of Cancer

Increased Incidence of Skin Disorders

Higher Incidence of Colds and Flu

More Chronic Diseases of all types

Lower Chance of Recovery & of Long Remission

Longer Duration of Colds and Flus

Increased Risk of Alzheimer's

Endocrine and Central Nervous System Dysfunction

Slower Healing

© Jeanine Joy, 2015

Overall Outcomes

18 fewer healthy years compared to positively focused people

7-11 years earlier death

7-10 more years of chronic and debilitating illnesses & diseases

Your Body on Stress

Thoughts are more negative
Worrisome and fearful thoughts are more likely

Words are less likely to be kind
Verbal responses match lower emotional state; relationships suffer

Muscle Tension & Pain Increase
More likely to be injured and more likely to be in an accident

Heart Disease (CVD) increases > 50%
Stroke, high blood pressure, and heart attack risk increase

Skin Problems Increase
Acne, aging, dermatitis and psoriasis

Addictions Increase
Alcohol, smoking, and drug use increase. Other addictions (shopping, sex, excessive television, etc.) increase

Reproductive Problems
Pre-term birth, infertility and impotence risk increases. Offspring more likely to have sleep and behavior problems

Behavior Worsens
More likely to commit crimes, lie, and divorce

Less Likely to Succeed
Increased failures, bankruptcies, lower income, less career success

Cognitive function decreases
Solutions become more difficult to identify

Attention to undesired things increases
More likely to view situations as problems than opportunities

Immune Function Declines Immediately
Illnesses from cancer to the common cold to infections are more likely to occur and to have less positive outcomes

Asthma Risk for You & Your Children Increases
Children of stressed Mom's ae more likely to develop asthma

Stomach Upset More Likely
Indigestion, diarrhea, gas

Digestive function decreases
Risk of obesity, poor food choices, diabetes increase

Pro-health Behaviors decline
Even individuals who understand healthy behavior and the stress reduction benefits of some activities are less likely to exercise, eat healthy, and meditate when they are highly stressed.

Insomnia Increases
Lack of sleep creates dangerous cycles and can lead to downward spirals

Mental Health Declines
Increased problems, from depression to psychosis to suicide

© Jeanine Joy, 2015

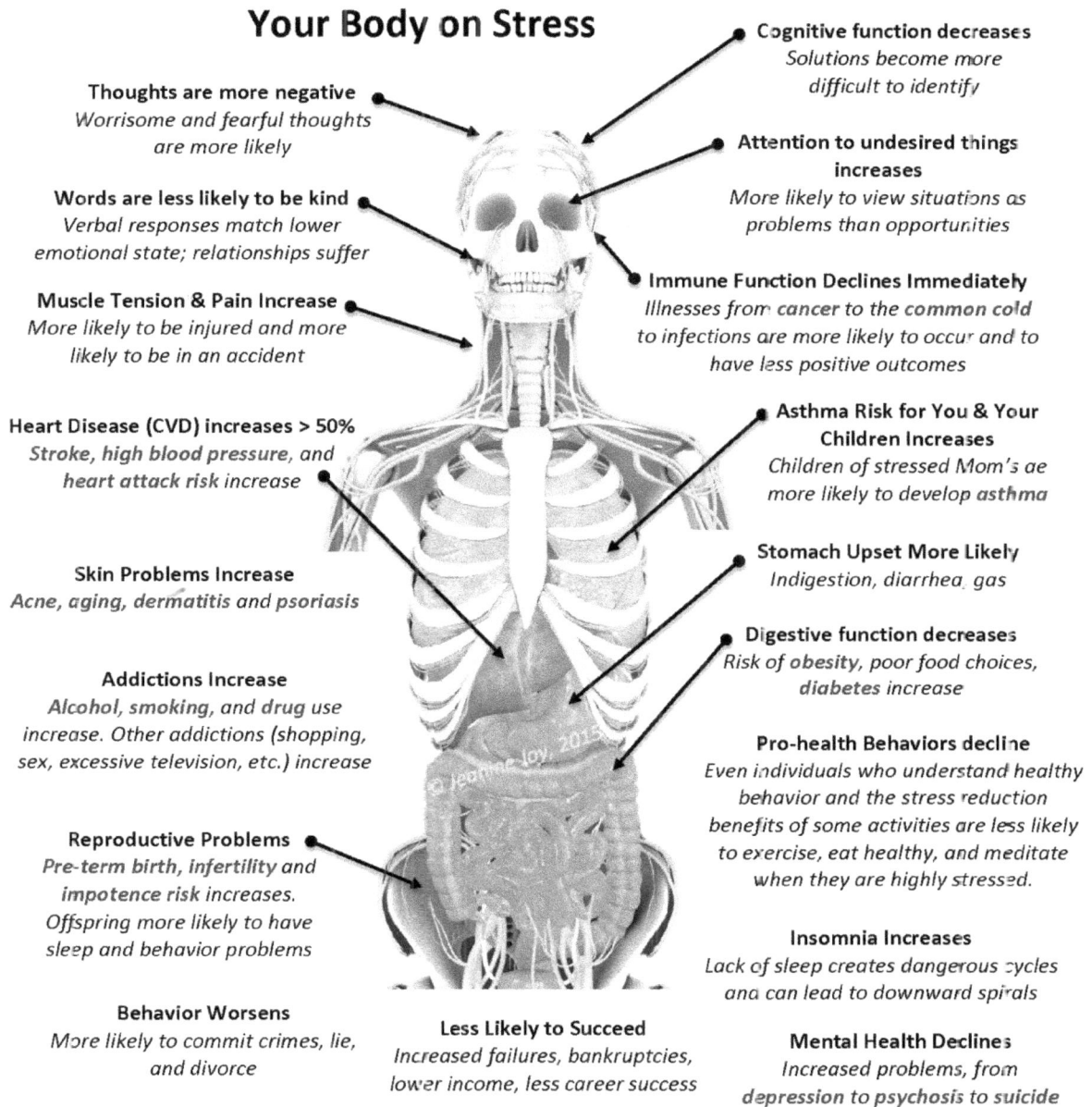

Most Americans are chronically stressed. We have become so accustomed to being stressed that it feels normal to us. But normal does not mean healthy. Many of us brag about how much stress we can experience and keep going as if it is a badge of honor. Stress management does not work. Doctors treat stress symptoms but are helpless against the root cause because the root is in the mind. Corporate wellness programs are designed to address symptoms, not the root cause. It's time for change. Many people believe they can ignore mild signs of stress such as headaches and stomach acid, but it's easier to fix before it becomes hypertension, obesity, diabetes, or heart disease.

> *It is important to note that the absence of negative emotions is not the same as the presence of positive emotions. The significant benefits are caused by positive emotions, not the absence of negative emotions.*

14: The Smart Way

In order to improve the mind, we ought less to learn, than to contemplate.
René Descartes

The combination of Emotional Guidance and metacognitive processes is called *The Smart Way* because as an approach to life it is smarter to be happy first. *The Smart Way* optimizes the way the mind is used. Metacognitive simply means thinking about thinking. You're not thinking on auto-pilot. You think about what you're thinking and how it feels when you think what you think. It is actually natural. Like any skill, skills get better with practice. Like any new skill, no one is an expert the first time. But they can learn how to do it and the best part about it is that doing it feels good. Once they feel the empowerment the first time they are successful, they will want to do it again—because it feels good. The effort they exert toward self-empowerment today provides a stepping stool that provides empowerment for higher steps they'll climb tomorrow.

"One particularly adaptive type of emotion regulation is reappraisal, which refers to changing how individuals appraise the situation they are in to alter its emotional significance."[283] Individuals who engage in reappraisal tend to:[284]

- Feel a higher sense of purpose in life
- Feel less depressed
- Have strengthened social bonds
- Higher well-being
- Greater social adjustment

In a sample of 222 individuals that recently faced stressful life events, those who habitually used cognitive reappraisal were experiencing higher levels of well-being, better social adjustment, and fewer depressive symptoms.[285] Several aspects of *The Smart Way*, which pre-dates the study, are designed to increase individual's motivation to use cognitive reappraisal techniques, both by overcoming common limiting beliefs and by educating participants about the benefit of maintaining better-feeling emotions. A meta-analysis of 51 independent studies with a total of 21,150 participants confirmed that cognitive reappraisal (a skill taught as part of *The Smart Way*) significantly contributes to positive mental health and protects against indicators of poor mental health.[286] Imagine how much more powerful cognitive reappraisal is when you add Emotional Guidance to the tool kit.

When you "accept thoughts and feelings without judgment and focus on the present moment,"[287] depression and anxiety decline. If therapies effectively treat mood and anxiety disorders because of individuals using cognitive reappraisal, wouldn't directly teaching individuals how to use Cognitive Reappraisal be more powerful because it would increase the conscious directing of the mind to use the technique. Wouldn't doing it before a diagnosis have the ability to prevent the illness from manifesting? Or the big question, is it really an illness or is it simply dysfunction thinking that we've labeled as a larger problem?

When depression and anxiety happens, it causes significant problems in people's lives. I'm not diminishing the realness of the illness when it is occurring. I'm diminishing the difficulty of the cure (or, preferably, prevention) when the right tools are used.

The way we think is connected to everything else—mental and physical health issues as well as behavior and relationships.

Another area of research that points to the benefit of using *The Smart Way* in conjunction with Emotional Guidance demonstrates that self-compassion is important in recovery from stressful life events and can reduce or eliminate PTSD symptoms following "severe and repeated interpersonal trauma."[288] A study of women going through divorce found that women recovered faster when they were compassionate toward themselves.[289] Give yourself permission to be self-compassionate.

There is not just one of you. You are multiple people and you do not act the same way all the time nor do you think of yourself the same way all the time. We all have multiple selves that emerge in different situations.[290]

As a son or daughter, you have a certain perspective of yourself. You may view yourself as a good son or daughter, or you may view yourself as a disappointing son or daughter. You may view yourself as a duty-bound son or daughter. The number of ways you can view who you are as a son or daughter is endless.

> *The findings suggest that interventions may be beneficial that enhance positive implicit valuing of emotion regulation. Techniques that allow individuals to experience successful emotion regulation may positively influence the value they give such regulation. Training procedures that specifically enhance cognitive reappraisal would be promising as cognitive reappraisal abilities play a distinct and important role in successful psychotherapy. (Hopp et al., 2011)*

As an employee or student, you have another view of yourself. It may be more or less positive than your view of yourself as a son or daughter. You may be both a student and an employee. When I was in high school, the school treated us as if we were children, my parents treated me as if I was semi-adult and my employer treated me as a full blown adult. The more free I felt in the environment, the better I felt, so I liked work better than home or school.

We also have ideas about who we are right now and who we will be in the future. For example, the last few years I've been very focused on my research and writing which has led to a more sedentary lifestyle than I prefer. In my mind I am where I am, but I am also the person I'll be when the next two books are done and I can allow myself more time to care for my body. My future self is in better physical condition than my current self.

Who are you today?
Who do you see yourself being tomorrow?

I also see myself as reaching out to more people and doing more training than writing in the future so my future self will seldom stay home all day reviewing research and writing. My future self will spend a lot of time traveling to teach and speak. Who are you? Now? Who will you be tomorrow?

The Smart Way provides a stable foundation for success throughout life. It includes evidence-based techniques that develop core skills that make the difference between choosing a path toward self-actualization and success or a less enjoyable one.

The objectives of the curricula are:

- Foster skills and social competence through training that increases core self-evaluations.
- Provide goal setting training that reinforces inherent desires for autonomy and competence.
- Reduce susceptibility to negative external pressures and stress.
- Increase growth mindset and intrinsic desire for continuous self-development.
- Develop skills that increase both happiness and resilience, which reduces stress.
- Develop a thorough understanding of how to accurately interpret emotions and respond to their signals in pro-health and pro-social ways (Emotional Intelligence Plus).
- Recognize the connection between emotional state and behaviors.
- Teach skills that lead to the development of habitual bias that allocates attention during new situations in ways that elicit positive emotions more often, essentially resulting in healthy implicit emotion regulation.[291]
- Increase the sense of Internal Locus of Control (empowerment).
- Increase optimism and hope.
- Reinforce a growth mindset.
- Increase emotion regulation skills and psychological flexibility which leads to greater career flexibility and success.

Skills that empower an employee to regulate their emotional response to the events occurring in their life (self-regulation) significantly reduce the risk of mental illnesses including depression, anxiety, panic disorders, bi-polar disorder and even psychosis. Individuals with the ability to self-induce desired emotional states "are happier in both positive and negative circumstances."[292] Regulating negative emotions downward reduces stress, which leads to improved physical health. "The existence of automatic, unconscious processes influencing human emotion, cognition, and behavior is widely accepted and confirmed by numerous studies."[293]

Although the processes provide regulation below conscious awareness, the actual way they regulate emotion and whether those ways support greater health, varies by individual. Some individuals have automatic emotion regulation that operate in ways that diminishes their ability to achieve and maintain health. Their automatic responses can be adjusted to improve outcomes. When they are adjusted and begin automatically supporting healthy emotional states they are not dose-dependent. In other words, frequent use of *The Smart Way* techniques for just a few months can improve the automatic stress and happiness regulation done by the brain. And, unlike most self-improvement techniques, *The Smart Way* feels good every step of the way so its use is intrinsically rewarded. All other techniques and processes that are currently used (pharmacological, mindfulness, meditation, exercise, yoga, gratitude, helping others, journaling, and more) are dose-dependent. Research clearly shows that individuals do not give themselves the dose they need to maintain optimal emotional states when their stress levels rise.[294]

The Smart Way was designed by combining characteristics of individuals who thrive against the odds with the latest research in positive psychology, resilience, psychoneuroimmunology, psychological flexibility, self-determination theory, and other research that reveals the basis of human thriving.

Happiness and stress have an inverse relationship. Research on the presence of happiness and the presence of stress reveal the following benefits of higher levels of happiness and lower levels of stress:

Increased pro-social behaviors
- Reduced anti-social behavior
- Better corporate citizenship
- Increased kindness (even to strangers)
- Intrinsically motivated diversity appreciation (a significant step-up from tolerance)
- Reduced (or no) criminal behavior
- Increased positive goal setting

Increased pro-health behaviors
- Reduced likelihood of alcohol, drug, and cigarette use
- Increased physical activity
- Better dietary choices
- Improved sleep habits and quality of sleep

Physical and Mental Benefits
- Improved immune function
- Improved cognitive function
- Improved digestive function
- Improved Central Nervous System Functioning
- Reduced risk of mental illness (including depression/anxiety)[295] and suicide,[296] which are all are strongly correlated to stress and poor emotion regulation skills

The Smart Way program is designed to build strengths associated with positive outcomes including:

- Autonomous Intrinsic Motivation
- Positivity/optimism
- Growth Mindset
- Emotional Intelligence
- Psychological Capital & Flexibility
- Authenticity
- Positive goal-setting
- Happiness
- Resilience

- Internal Locus of Control
- Healthy self-esteem
- Metacognitive Skills
- Physical, Mental, Emotional, and Behavioral Health
- Positive self-image
- Acceptance of responsibility for actions and results
- Core self-evaluations

The Smart Way has been compared to Cognitive Behavioral Therapy in the following way:
Cognitive Behavioral Therapy (CBT) is done one-on-one and resembles having an expert marksman stand next to an amateur who is blindfolded while attempting to hit a target by following instructions from the expert, who is the only one who knows the location of the target.

The Smart Way can be delivered in large group settings where large groups can be taught at the same time because it removes the blindfold and makes the target fully visible to each individual, who is given skills that empower them to identify the right target and continually improve their aim. Intrinsic motivation occurs naturally because each step results in positive emotional feedback. Even when the overall emotional state is still negative, the employee feels the relief of feeling better and the hope that comes from knowing one has the skills to shift to increasingly better feeling emotional states.

Cognitive Behavioral Therapy is further hampered by:

- ❖ Stigma associated with mental illness
- ❖ High cost of one-on-one therapy
- ❖ Recurrent need because CBT resolves current issues without necessarily developing skills to address future issues
- ❖ Cognitive Behavioral and other types of therapies are reactive

Therapists have typically been trained to move people from a minus state to zero on the following scale:

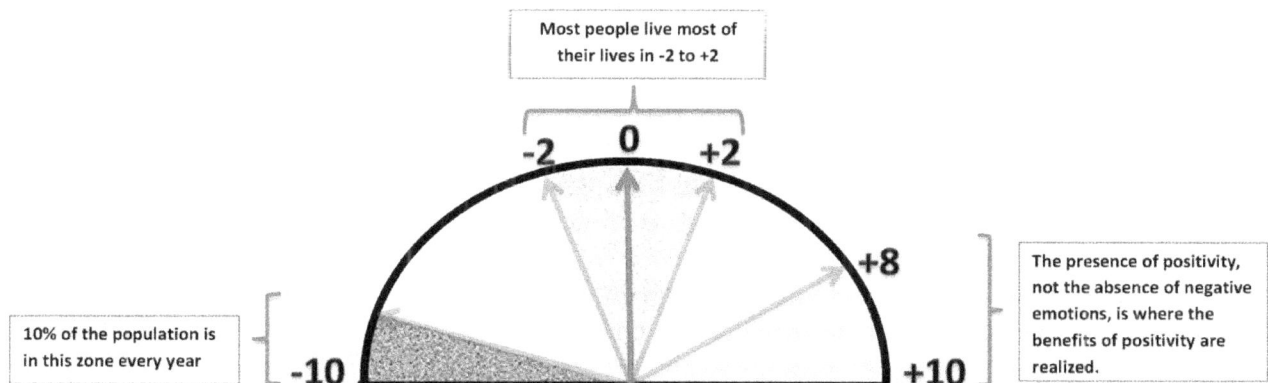

Most people live most of their lives in -2 to +2

-2   0   +2

+8

10% of the population is in this zone every year

-10   +10

The presence of positivity, not the absence of negative emotions, is where the benefits of positivity are realized.

The Smart Way is proactive, low-cost, develops skills that improve results throughout life, and is designed to help individuals achieve and sustain emotions in the +8 range (from hope to joy). Because it is educational and structured to correct prevalent misconceptions, some due to prior errors in scientific hypotheses, there is no stigma. It is an evidence-based form of Primary Prevention. Training comes with added benefits, including improving morale and employee engagement, reducing burnout, enhancement of any existing wellness programs and reduction in any existing prejudices or biases.

"Cognitive behavioral therapies can be defined as those interventions with the core assumptions that what individuals think directly impacts how they feel and what they do."[297] Despite the fact that Cognitive Behavioral Therapy is used as a curative rather than a preventative method of improving mental (and in some cases, physical), health, "it is clear that the evidence-base of CBT is enormous." Hoffman, et al. conducted a review of meta-analyses of the use of CBT to address a wide variety of issues and concluded by recommending that countries adopt it as a first-line defense against mental disorders. I go a step further in my hypothesis.

My Hypothesis is that anything Cognitive Behavioral Therapy is effective at treating, The Smart Way can prevent from happening in the first place.

The Smart Way is not synonymous with Cognitive Behavioral Therapy provided before an individual develops a mental or physical health problem. It is **CBT Plus** delivered primarily to groups or provided in as self-help using videos and books. It is significantly more cost effective because it does not require one-on-one therapy and because it prevents the problems before they happen, thus avoiding the costs associated with problems that have manifested. Also, it is more difficult to permanently cure a condition than to prevent its occurrence in the first place and there is no relapse risk because the illness did not manifest in the first place. Another major difference is that Cognitive Behavioral Therapy does not include Emotional Guidance. *The Smart Way* also disabuses negative beliefs about the subconscious portions of personality that often include beliefs that the subconscious is secret, dark, and frightening as well as unreliable and dangerous to explore.

Cognitive Behavioral Therapy works by helping patients change the way they think to healthier thought patterns which significantly reduces the likelihood a person will relapse after treatment. Instead of waiting for someone to develop a mental health disorder, which may or may not receive treatment at some point, *The Smart Way* provides information and skills that empower employees to develop healthy habits of thought before problems develop.

Understanding that mental illness exists along a continuum and only man-made labels create the difference between mental health and mental illness is important. The Smart Way increases employee engagement because low employee engagement is a symptom of low emotional state. Low emotional state is a symptom of where someone is on the Mental Health/Mental Illness continuum.

Deci and Ryan point to another aspect of therapy that is designed to correct a manifested problem that makes waiting until the problem arises to adjust dysfunctional thinking a less beneficial alternative. Apparently, the current treatment paradigm puts so much pressure on therapists to achieve results that therapists end up "being controlling rather than autonomy supportive is often a function of the pressures they experience in the treatment . . . external pressures from clinic directors or insurers or internally controlling introjection and ego-involvements can lead therapists to make clients change."[298]

When the therapist is in charge and the patient is essentially blind (blindfolded) to the target, a controlling therapist is a problem. When the patient knows the target and is merely being advised of processes that can be used to get to the target the opportunity to be controlling is reduced.

While there is a strong emphasis on prevention with *The Smart Way*, I have case studies demonstrating that *The Smart Way* is effective in restoring mental health to individuals who were suffering from severe long-term PTSD, severe chronic depression, and that is has been effective in preventing imminent suicides. It was those successes combined with the increased experience of positive emotions in those I taught that convinced me of the power *The Smart Way* has to help people even though the techniques are delivered to groups.

After Butler, Chapman, Forman, and Beck, conducted a meta-analysis to review the existing research relating to Cognitive Behavioral Therapy in 2006, they concluded, "The meta-analyses reviewed strongly suggest that across many disorders the effects of CBT are maintained for substantial periods beyond the cessation of treatment. More specifically, significant evidence for long-term effectiveness was found for depression, generalized anxiety, panic, social phobia, OCD, sexual offending, schizophrenia, and childhood internalizing disorders. In the cases of depression and panic, there appears to be robust and convergent meta-analytic evidence that CBT produces vastly superior long-term persistence of effects, with relapse rates half those of pharmacotherapy."[299]

> *Cognitive Behavior Therapy techniques produces vastly superior long-term improvements, with relapse rates half those of pharmacotherapy.*

The robust support for persistence of Cognitive Behavioral Therapy suggests that learning metacognitive processes protects against the occurrence of many chronic problems our society would like to eliminate. The persistence of the results suggests (strongly, in my opinion) that prevention is possible.

There is evidence-based support that Cognitive Behavioral Therapy (CBT) is effective in reducing and/or healing many problems. Providing knowledge and skills that prevent the maladaptive cognitions Cognitive Behavioral Therapy is designed to correct will prevent the problems from manifesting in the first place, thus preventing a significant portion of the suffering that currently affects people around the world. Here is a long, but not exhaustive, list of issues CBT can improve or heal (and thus, I believe, prevent):

Anxiety[300, 301, 302]

Depression[304 , 305]

Panic Disorders[307]

Bi-polar disorders[310, 311]

Crime Reduction[313, 314, 315]

Improved High School Graduation Rates[317, 318]

Treatment of and Reduction in Physical Pain[321, 322, 323]

Educational Success[326]

Phobias[328]

Posttraumatic Stress Disorder (PTSD)

Hypochondria[331]

Insomnia[334]

Coronary Heart Disease (CHD)[336, also see 337]

Anger and Aggression[339, 340]

Teacher (Trainee) Stress Levels[343]

Type II Diabetes[345]

Distress Due to General Medical Conditions[347]

Chronic Fatigue Syndrome[349]☒

Bullying (Recovery from)[303]

Bullying Prevention[306]

Violence Reduction[308, 309]

Prevent relapse of Mood Disorders[312]

Substance Use Disorders[316]

Smoking Cessation[319, 320]

Problematic Gambling[324, 325]

Schizophrenia & Other Psychotic Disorders[327]

Obsessive Compulsive Disorder (OCD)[329]

Body dysmorphic disorder (BDD)[330]

Eating Disorders[332, 333]

Hypertension[335]

Personality Disorders[338]

General Stress[341, 342]

Early Stage Breast Cancer[344]

Disease Management[346]

Irritable Bowel Syndrome[348]

Rheumatoid Arthritis[350]

Premenstrual Syndrome[351]

> And via general stress reduction:
> *Prevent pre-term births*
> *Prevent adverse epigenetic changes*

As you can see, the list of physical, mental, and behavioral health issues that Cognitive Behavioral Therapy techniques are effective at treating is lengthy. Since CBT is essentially teaching people to think in healthy ways, it makes sense that teaching them to do that before a problem manifests would effectively prevent many issues from ever arising. It is not about what to think per se. It is about whether one focuses on the positive or the negative, ruminates or moves on, or catastrophizes. The benefits to employees, employers, schools, and society of reducing the incidences of the problems in the above list should be obvious. We live in a time where families are struggling and enduring many hardships, from job volatility and loss, foreclosures, to deployments, divorces, and random violence that strikes more frequently than ever at shopping malls, movie theaters, and other venues.

If we have skills and habits of thought that make us resilient, we fare much better than those who are not resilient when we survive a traumatic event. Random violence is not necessary to trigger PTSD in individuals who aren't resilient. Child birth and traffic accidents can cause PTSD. Resilient individuals also do not experience the high level of chronic daily stress that leads to diminished physical and mental health.

Add the improvements in employee engagement and happiness that result from learning *The Smart Way* and it begins to look like a miracle drug, except it's not a drug. I believe it is so effective because it corrects thinking that exists only because many common beliefs in our society are slightly off base. Metacognitive processes and Emotional Guidance correct those issues, helping people who learn them live up to their potential. One of the reasons so many suffer is because they know intuitively that life should be better for them, but without understanding their Emotional Guidance or the false premises that are negatively affecting their life experience, they don't know why it isn't working out the way they feel it should. *The Smart Way* makes all the difference.

There is no need for a diagnosis before teaching *The Smart Way* because it is simply teaching individuals about how their brain works and how to think in ways that optimize outcomes. While learning *The Smart Way* may lead to recovery or better outcomes from manifested chronic illnesses, the main purpose is:

> *Just the thought of thinking about our innermost feelings can be enough to cause fear. But when one begins considering that Cognitive Behavioral Therapy is essentially about helping someone change the way they think to healthier thought patterns, doesn't it make sense to teach people what healthy thought patterns are in the first place?*

1. To prevent new manifestations of physical, mental, and behavioral problems that can be prevented by using a skilled level of cognition,
2. To improve chronic moods, which facilitate the development and maintenance of strong social connections,
3. To promote wellbeing,
4. To assist individuals in developing habits of thought that support their efforts to become more of their best potential self (self-actualized).

Cognitive Behavioral Therapy teaches people how thoughts influence feelings and behaviors.[352] That is something everyone needs to know. To the average person, mental health care is shrouded in mystery, stigma, and secrecy. Just the thought of thinking about our innermost feelings can be enough to cause fear. But when one begins considering that Cognitive Behavioral Therapy is essentially about helping someone change the way they think to healthier thought patterns doesn't it make sense to teach people what healthy thought patterns are in the first place? When you delve more deeply and see how many mental health problems can be healed or at least improved with CBT, does it not point to the fact that information about how the mind works would be highly valuable to everyone?

The litany of mental, physical and behavioral health issues that CBT helps is not exhaustive. How an employee uses her mind determines how much stress is felt in a given situation. Everyone who receives a lay-off notice does not feel the same degree of stress. Not even everyone with two children and a mortgage and no spouse feels the same degree of stress when a lay-off is announced. The amount of stress felt depends on the perspective the employee takes about the situation. When the employee understands *The Smart Way*, she has control over the level of stress. Low stress doesn't mean she won't take action. It means smarter actions will be taken.

How our brains, emotions, and thoughts are connected should not be information reserved for the elite. "CBT is a psychotherapeutic approach that focuses on the way in which people's thoughts influence their feelings and behaviors. CBT includes a number of different approaches that share the belief that it is not the event that causes our feelings and behaviors, but rather how we perceive or think about what happened . . . Socratic reasoning is a central technique."[353] The only aspects that really make CBT therapeutic is that it is done after-the-fact (once someone is already suffering from a diagnosis) and CBT includes assessment procedures to measure progress toward healing. If done before an illness manifests there is no need for assessments to be done to determine when health is restored to a level where insurance will no longer pay and no need for a diagnosis because the point is to avoid developing a diagnosable illness.

Albert Ellis developed a form of therapy in the 1940's that was much like CBT because the wisdom from philosophers such as Bertrand Russell, Marcus Aurelius, and Epictetus helped him with his own problems. His path is eerily similar to my own. I was teaching people to use early versions of *The Smart Way* techniques for years before my knowledge of CBT expanded and I realized that the techniques I'd developed independently were essentially a preventive form of CBT. Dr. Ellis and I even benefited from the wisdom of the same philosophers.

> *People are not disturbed by things, but by the view they take of them.*
> *Epictetus*

At about the same time Ellis developed his version, Aaron T. Beck was starting to lean toward a cognitive form of treatment. Both are considered founders of CBT although when Ellis's associates came to him upset that Beck was calling himself the Father of CBT, Ellis was undisturbed and simply referred to himself as the Grandfather of CBT. Now, that sounds like the way someone who has learned *The Smart Way* would respond to a situation many people would find highly distressing. It is a real reaction, not suppression of rage. The mind that uses skilled metacognition finds perspectives that feel good under almost any circumstances.

Ellis believed that "dysfunctional thinking came from cognitive errors including but not limited to overgeneralizations, un-validated assumptions, rigid or absolutistic ideas, and exaggeration "including:[354]

- Awfulizing that includes exaggerating negative consequences of what is happening
    Later, Seligman would refer to this tendency as catastrophizing—a thought pattern associated with depression.
- Should, musts, or ought's which are connected to unrealistic demands on the world, self, or others
- Evaluating human worth, which includes self-worth and worth of others
- Need statements which express requirements that have to be met for the individual to survive or be happy
- In 1991, Ellis added "goals to his model, hypothesizing that we are goal seeking and that goals are to:
    - To survive
    - Be relatively pain free
    - Be satisfied with our lives

Later, Ellis stated his use of rational referred to cognitions that "are effective and self-helping, not merely cognitions that are empirically and logically valid."[355] This is an important distinction and one I also make. As long as you understand on the meta-cognitive level that you're fantasizing even when you create something that feels real on the basic cognitive level, if it feels good when you do it, it's helpful. You can't spend all your time in a fantasy world, but you can do it often enough to improve your emotional state.

"Beck's system included different classifications of thoughts. Automatic thoughts are quick, evaluative thoughts that seem to come to mind immediately, without the person being aware of them and therefore without deliberation. People tend to accept their automatic thoughts as truths. Individuals use their core beliefs as a lens through which they interpret life situations."[356] That is what I refer to as *surface thinking*. Beck seemed to think that people consciously accept core beliefs as true. I disagree. Many core beliefs are not consciously understood—that is one of the reasons for dysfunctional thinking—accepted but erroneous core beliefs.

The difference between of Beck's "consciously accept core beliefs as true" and my hypothesis "the brain filters information using accepted core beliefs" is that Beck assumes the thinker is aware they have internalized the core beliefs and consciously and deliberately decided to view the world that way. Researchers have repeatedly found that many core beliefs are established by age 6. I don't think 6-year-olds are consciously and deliberately evaluating whether they should see the world as a good place or an evil one, or whether they should see the world as a competitive kill or be killed environment vs. one of mutual cooperation and co-existence with the potential for peace.

My hypothesis is that the core beliefs develop based on the back stories our subconscious mind creates about our experiences. We could live in a mansion situated in a peaceful island paradise and have an older brother who resents us and physically harms (trips, punches, pushes, etc.) us every chance he gets and we could decide the world is a mean and violent place.

We could live in a slum where the sounds of knife and gun-fights ring out at all hours of the day and night, navigating past drug dealers and women reduced to selling their bodies to survive, to get to the bus stop but have an older sibling who is protective and always there for us and feel protected and safe.

It is not our circumstances that lead to what we internalize about the world. It is what we are taught and the back stories we create about our experiences. The good thing is that our worldviews are not chiseled in marble. We can change them with a little bit of concentrated effort.

"Beck's theory also examines intermediate beliefs that the client may hold about self or others. Intermediate beliefs include rules, attitudes, and assumptions . . . the therapist who works with this model attends to relevant childhood information that may contribute to the client developing and maintaining the unworkable core belief."[357]

In Cognitive Behavioral Therapy: [358]	In The Smart Way:
Finding the client's irrational beliefs	Feeling the emotional discord and using meta-cognition to find thoughts that feel better
Automatic thoughts	When automatic thoughts don't feel good, question them and use metacognition to find better feeling thoughts
Assisting the client in changing them	Individual directs his or her own change. If a therapist is needed, Emotional Guidance will encourage assistance and help client overcome concerns about stigma
Verbally disputed by client and therapist	Mentally disputed by client. Individual may also verbalize (i.e. See Bogus Process)
Pragmatic: How is it working for you in your life?	Same: This question is used in *The Smart Way*
Empirical dispute: Prove to me that this belief is accurate by just giving me the facts	Individual uses emotions to gain greater clarity about the potential perspectives of a distressing situation, leading to a less emotional and more fact-based evaluation
Elegant dispute: Generate a new more effective belief to replace the old one for client to test in homework assignments to see how the new belief works in his actual life	Individual understands beliefs are thoughts they've thought repeatedly until easy to follow neuropathways are created and that changing neuropathways simply requires thinking new, better-feeling thoughts repeatedly until those neuropathways are easier to travel. Moment-to-moment adjustments in the new beliefs can be evaluated by how they feel—there is no need for the trial and error process to be applied in real life without knowing in advance (by how the idea feels) that it will bring improvements.
Shame-attacking	*The Smart Way* sees shame as an inescapable double-negative and refutes it directly. Sustained negative emotional states are inherently harmful to both body and mind, so shame is refuted as something based in unhealthy beliefs about self or others.

In the above chart CBT is compared and contrasted with *The Smart Way* to demonstrate how much more efficient it is to give people information they can use to effectively use Emotional Guidance and metacognition to adjust their thoughts in-the-moment. For example, the client can reappraise the thought now instead of waiting until the next session to discuss it. If the thought causes emotional pain or positions regarding a relationship that are detrimental to the relationship, decisions that may not be the best choice can be avoided. The time they would spend recording the frequency and events that co-occur with specific beliefs and how frequently those undesired behaviors occur so they can share the information with a therapist could be spent applying the processes and making progress toward adopting better-feeling perspectives.[359]

Often, traditional methods address symptoms of the root cause, such as assertiveness training, anger management and social skills training.[360] The problem is that these programs do not address the root cause of the problem. They help, but not as much as using the same time spent improving the root cause would help.

When it comes to ethnic minority populations, there are a number of problems: [361]

1. They are largely underserved by the mental health services community.
2. They tend not to seek mental health care (stigma is an issue with every population, but on average, ethnic minorities tend to perceive mental health care as even more stigmatized.
3. When they do enter psychotherapy, minorities often leave treatment after a single session.
    a. Taking culture into consideration during therapy can be important because what would seem to be the dominant culture's prerogative might be seen as disrespectful of core beliefs held by other cultures, such as obeying one's parents about decisions the dominant culture would consider personal and not an area where the parent's preferences should be given much, if any, weight

This not just a minority or cultural issue. There are wide individual variances. *The Smart Way* provides a decided advantage for a number of reasons:

1. It can be delivered cost effectively to large groups.
2. It is prevention, not mental health treatment for a manifested illness so there is no stigma. The focus is on increasing happiness and resilience, which requires healthy cognition and self-esteem.
3. Because it is not a one-on-one therapeutic relationship, cultural differences are not a significant element. The employee can use Emotional Guidance to decide what is personally meaningful and best. Classes should always include the instruction to follow one's own Emotional Guidance over and above the instructor's viewpoint. Instructors will disclose that they have their own core beliefs and that having different core beliefs is acceptable, and adds to the value and worth of each individual. Diversity is recognized as a form of collective strength that is to be appreciated.
4. It empowers the employee with skills and knowledge that leads to more functional thinking capabilities.

CBT focuses on client empowerment, positing that the client is capable of change by controlling her/his thoughts and emotions, conveying respect for the client's abilities and understanding. [362] *The Smart Way* does the same but reinforces it by putting the knowledge and power in the client's hands, helping to develop and reinforce a healthy internal locus of control. Despite its limitations, Cognitive Behavioral Therapy is highly effective, but I believe *The Smart Way* has greater potential because it can be delivered as a preventative measure and it overcomes some of the objections that our most vulnerable populations have about mental health services.

The Smart Way is **Cognitive Behavioral Therapy Plus** because it adds Emotional Guidance and a direct understanding of how the mind works, not just insights garnered by a guided tour led by a therapist.

I'm not suggesting mind-control—at least not by anyone other than the individual controlling his or her own mind. In fact, when individuals do not understand how the mind works or how what they expose themselves to affects their outcomes and the thoughts they think, they make decisions that harm themselves without any awareness of what they are doing. We're careful about exposing ourselves to toxic chemicals, but most people do not realize that over a period of time, negative habits of thought are just as toxic as the chemicals they try so hard to avoid. Not understanding how the mind works is no different than giving someone the keys to a car without a map when some paths take them through hostile and even deadly territories.

Each technique describes which emotional states they are most effective in and provides flexibility so employees can choose techniques that feel comfortable to them. Even some of the most common techniques, such as positive affirmations, can have negative impacts when used by individuals in certain emotional states. Metacognitive processes are capable of effecting permanent improvements in emotional state on any subject.

We encourage providing *The Smart Way* training classes and materials to both employees and their families because it will provide consistent reinforcement and the techniques help families manage personal stressors, contributing to a more supportive and harmonious home environment. Improving the emotional state of any member of the family benefits every family member and the evidence suggests it can reduce family problems that eventually affect the quality of work and absenteeism.

The Smart Way is the only training program we are aware of that incorporates current scientific findings about the purpose and meaning of emotions and overturns common false premises about the purpose of emotions that contribute to adverse outcomes.[363, 364, 365, 366, 367, 368, 369] The chart on the next page demonstrates some of the advantages.

Hinders Thriving	*Helps Thriving*
Thinking on auto-pilot Exception: when you've rehearsed§§	Metacognitive thinking
Misinterpreting meaning of emotions	Understand emotions are guidance, correct interpretations, and pro-thriving responses
Rigid psychological processes	Psychological Flexibility
Negative mindset	Positive mindset
High stress, especially chronic high stress	Low stress and positive stress
External locus of control	Internal locus of control
Fixed Mindset	Growth Mindset
Not resilient	Resilient
Beliefs and desires are not coherent	Beliefs and desires are coherent
Limiting beliefs	Supportive, expansive beliefs
Struggle with relationships	Healthy relationships
Struggle with health	Good health
Negative or Neutral self-regard	Positive self-regard
Problem focused	Solution focused
Competition	Cooperation (Competition is prior self)
Complete (finished product)	Ever-evolving
Look for faults in others	Look for best in others
Surround self with people who are there by happenstance or detractors	Surround self with positive influencers

Your brain has many abilities or functions including:

Cognitive Abilities and Functions:

Awareness	Perception	Reasoning
Judgment	Intuition	Attention
Memory	Motor	Language processing
Auditory processing	Smell processing	Visual and Spatial processing

Executive Functions include: [370]

- Meta-cognition
- Setting and Focusing on goals
- Insight
- Pattern recognition
- Decision-making
- Emotional self-regulation
- Perception of our emotions
- Behavior Self-Regulation
- Planning
- Flexibility
- Anticipation
- Problem-solving
- Working memory
- Perception of other's emotions
- Breaking tasks into parts

---

§§ i.e. tactical training for dangerous occupations

Most of our activities require multiple functions. For example, when someone knocks on your door you have to perceive the knock, decide to respond or not, take physical action to respond (walk, turn handle), and you must use language skills including talking and understanding what is said. The decision to answer may be made multiple times. You may automatically go to the door but when you see strangers at the door, you may decide not to open the door—after evaluating whether or not you should—using both your emotional and rational response to their appearance. Then come social skills (interpreting tone of voice, responding properly, using the right language if you are multi-lingual, using the right language (age-level) for example if a child is selling cookies vs. a neighbor who has arrived to join you to watch rival football teams.

It is a commonly believed myth, that you can't teach an old dog new tricks. This has been considered true of humans for a long time but new research has shown that it is not true.[371] Our brains can change throughout life. New neuron connections form when we learn new information. New neuron connections also form when we re-write the back story that explains events in our life. A painful memory can be transformed into a less painful (or even a good) memory by changing our back story. It does not matter how old the story is—changing the back story can remove the pain.

I'll give you an example. One of my clients always felt a degree of pain inside because his father was seldom there during his childhood. His father never went to any of his games or school events and was usually not home for dinner. When I met him many years later he still felt resentment against his father for not having been there for him when he was growing up. At a deep level, he equated being loved and lovable with whether his father paid attention to him.

When his father died he went to the funeral and learned a lot about the work his father was doing during his childhood that he had not known until then. It became obvious that his father's absence from the home on so many evenings was because he was actively working to make the world a better place—a better place for his son to live. The father was in Detroit, Michigan in the 1960's. When he passed away more than 50 years later, the work he did during those tumultuous times was still remembered and viewed as far ahead of its time.

With the new information the man was able to reframe his memories, giving them the back story that his father was so intent on helping to create a better world for him to live in that he sacrificed time with his family for the greater good. His memories are less painful today. He feels less abandoned. He can see that his father knew he had married a woman who was a wonderful mom, who could be there for his son while he worked to make the world a better place. Eventually, his automatic response when he thinks of his father will be pride about what his Dad accomplished, work that was decades ahead of its time in race relations.

How fast the change takes place is completely up to him. In the beginning, the old neural connections took him to the same emotional state but as he repeatedly redirects his thoughts to his new back story, the new neural connections become the easier path for his thoughts to follow. Based on my experience with motivated clients, the painful perspective about past memories that have been thought about often can be fully replaced in just three months. The more an individual goes through this process for different memories, and the more deliberately new back stories are chosen for current events, the faster the reframing of old memories becomes the person's new normal.

Einstein said, "I have no special talent. I am only passionately curious."

New science adds truth to this statement. When we learn about a subject, the part of our brain that deals with the subject grows. Research on the brains of London taxi cab drivers was instrumental in revealing how our brains grow as we learn.[372]

The ability of something to be shaped or molded is called plasticity. It is where plastic got its name. Brains have **plasticity**. I believe the root of the myth that old dogs cannot learn new tricks stems not from an inability, but from a lack of knowledge that we create our back stories. When we perceive reality with the same back stories for too long, we believe our back story is the only accurate back story. This can manifest in stubbornly clinging to ideas and concepts even when there is more than enough evidence to overturn the old belief.

Our perception of reality is about whom we are, not what reality is. When we believe something is possible, our brain will show us information that helps us achieve our goal. If we believe the goal is impossible, our brain will not pass information that would be helpful to our conscious mind and will create assertions that explain why we are right about the impossibility of the goal.

Our brains interpret reality in ways that support our beliefs. Our brains continually change as we experience life.

People often claim their pessimism is realistic or objective. Those claims demonstrate that they do not understand how the brain works. No one can come to purely objective observations. Objectivity requires us not to be influenced by personal opinions or desires. We interpret reality through filters that show us information that supports our beliefs and do not show us information that contradicts our beliefs. Our perception of reality is about whom we are, not what reality is. When we believe something is possible, our brain will show us information that helps us achieve our goal. If we believe the goal is impossible, our brain will not pass information to our conscious mind that would be helpful and will create assertions (back stories) that explain why we are right about the impossibility of the goal, even if we want to achieve it. This is one reason why negative self-talk and pessimism have such a detrimental impact on the outcome of lives.

For example, when I first began talking to a wider audience about how understanding the brain's filtering system and Emotional Guidance could solve many of the world's social problems it was common for people to tell me that you could not teach happiness to people with significant problems, such as homeless people and drug addicts. They used many arguments including that such people had bigger problems than being unhappy. I always maintained that anyone could be learn how to use this information in their life and that anyone who had the opportunity to learn would welcome it.

They called me naïve and an idealist. They told me I was living in la-la land and that I did not understand reality. They didn't hurt my feelings. I knew I could help such people learn to be happier and to understand that their past did not have to dictate their future. The fact that they did not know what I knew did not have the power to hurt my feelings.

For the past eight months I've had the privilege of teaching a group of adults that include a large percentage of recovering addicts, some who are still using, many who were once homeless and some who are still homeless, and some with significant health challenges. While I knew I could help them and that I had higher expectations of their potential than the general public has, even I severely underestimated the wisdom and talent I would discover in their ranks.

Life has taught them wisdom in many areas. Many are talented artists. All are capable of love and all want to love more and to feel peaceful in their hearts. Are they happier because of what they're learning? Yes. They're also more hopeful and hope is very near happiness on the Emotional Guidance Scale and hope is a long way from despair. Hopeful represents a state of empowerment from which someone can get anywhere. Increasing happiness improves cognitive abilities which will aids decision-making.

Many of them lack basic skills in reading and writing, but I don't despair. I remember stories of people who were completely illiterate who were able to be successful. I believe this group can begin where they are and go anywhere they chose to go. The lives they've led have taught them a great deal that is valuable to the rest of humanity.

Ralph Waldo Emerson observed, "Nothing great has ever been achieved without enthusiasm." Enthusiasm is in the Sweet Zone. Learning to navigate emotional Zones empowers employees with the knowledge and skills they need to create and sustain enthusiasm for their roles.

15: Harmonious Co-worker Relationships

After searching in vain for a positive quote about co-worker relationships I decided I need to write an entire book on the subject. One chapter is not enough.
Jeanine Joy

After an hour reading through co-worker quotes and failing to find even one that could be considered positive I gave up because the negativity in the quotes was taking my mood lower. I want to be at my best when I write this chapter and that requires a good mood. Also, once a person has become accustomed to feeling good most of the time they become reluctant to adopt perspectives that lower their mood.

For example, I can lament the lack of examples of good co-worker relationships or I can see it as an opportunity to help change that dynamic. The former feels pretty awful and the later feels pretty good which makes the choice easy to make. Is it true that many co-worker relationships are painful to the people involved? Absolutely! Is it true that those bad relationships lower the contribution those individuals are able to make to their employer? Again, that is absolutely true. Is it true that those bad relationships have a negative impact on the personal lives of the employees who are involved? Again, yes. Can that negative impact be extrapolated into society as a whole as we consider the impact on children and spouses and their friends and co-workers? Again, yes.

The negative aspects of the situation can be documented ad infinitum. But what good does documenting the negative effects do? Some would say it points out the problem and motivates people to solve it. But if an individual understands her emotional guidance, the negative emotion provides all the motivation necessary to want to solve a problem and does not require spending a great deal of time feeling bad before the solving part of the equation begins.

Can the situation be resolved? Absolutely! Is it true that negative relationships originate in the perceptions of the people involved? Again, this is absolutely true. Is it true that those bad relationships are not what the person desires? Again, yes. Is it true that the individuals' involved have a great degree of control over whether the relationship is perceived as negative or positive? Again, the answer is yes.

I'll give you an example where a couple of co-workers were irritated by another co-worker over something she had absolutely no control over. Those co-workers attempted to make the co-worker they perceived as receiving an undue perk upset by taking it away from her but she was aware of her emotional guidance and aware that their behavior was negatively impacted by their low emotional state so she did not take their efforts personally and did not allow them to lower her emotional state.

It all began when she arrived at work and the best parking spot right next to the front doors was open even though she was arriving after most of the office began working for the day. At first she was delighted that her timing was so perfect especially because she often worked late and left the office after dark when the parking lot was nearly empty. It felt safer to be parked near the front doors because her office was one of the first buildings in a new office park so the area was deserted in the evenings.

Then she looked up and saw that a new sign was in front of the parking spot she was in. She had her hand on the gear shift, already expecting she would have to move before she read "Hybrid Vehicle Parking." As she read the words, a grin spread across her face. She was driving a hybrid Escape. She was immediately ecstatic because it looked like she hadn't just scored a great parking space one day. It looked like she was going to be lucky every day. No one else in the four story building was driving a hybrid.

She gathered her things and walked in to her office with her usual jaunty grin and greeted the Office Manager with a bright "Good morning." Later in the day she heard the Office Manager, the COO, and some of the other employees complaining about the hybrid parking spaces. She ignored their conversation. They tended to find things that made them feel bad and focus on them when they could just as easily find and focus on something that made them feel good. She didn't attempt to change their attitudes. They probably wouldn't have listened anyway and that would have made her feel worse.

The next morning she arrived to find the Office Manager's Bronco with its bright orange Clemson paw on the rear window parked in the hybrid parking spot. She immediately recognized that the Office Manager was acting out because she was upset about her co-worker getting a special parking spot just because she drove a hybrid. She swung around the building and parked near to the side door which was her usual choice. When she got to the office she deliberately walked in with her usual jaunty grin and greeted the Office Manager with a bright "Good morning" and did not mention that her Bronco was parked in the hybrid spot. It was difficult not to mention it but not because she was upset about the Bronco being in the spot. She knew the Office Manager was saving for a down payment on a house and she didn't know if parking a non-hybrid in a hybrid spot was a ticketable offense. It was hard for her not to caution the employee about the possibility.

Later she heard her co-workers talking about the fact that she hadn't said a word about the Bronco being in the hybrid spot. The next morning the COO's high-performance sports car was in the hybrid spot. Once again, she ignored it and behaved in her usual cheerful demeanor all day. She was far more motivated to feel good than she was to argue over the temporary loss of a perk she appreciated receiving but had not anticipated. After two days with no apparent ability to disrupt her equanimity, her co-workers ceased their efforts.

I tell this story to demonstrate that one person who is intent on feeling good can feel good even when others attempt to disrupt the good emotional state. It's not even difficult to do once the person has some practice. I know it wasn't difficult because it was my hybrid. I also know there were no feelings of wanting to get back at the co-workers who were attempting to make me feel badly. More than anything, I felt compassion for them because they didn't realize how easily they could have felt better nor did they realize how much harm they were doing to themselves by attempting to make someone else feel bad.

When their attempts failed they felt worse, not better. They didn't ask how I managed to feel good when they were attempting to make me feel bad. They probably thought I was faking it. The truth was that their shenanigans weren't worth the loss of my positive emotional state. For someone who understands the actual price they pay to remain in a low emotional state . . . in terms of immune, cognitive, digestive, and central nervous system function, relationship health, and long-term success the price will nearly always be too high. It is simply too easy to find perspectives to feel good to pay the price of feeling badly.

Awareness that other people's emotional states have more to do with how they speak and behave toward you than anything personal really helps keep interactions in perspective. Chapter 1 provides some examples of how emotional state affects an employee's interpretation of new situations. The same is true of how an employee responds to co-workers. This is especially true of co-workers who are in different emotional states. Someone who is often angry may find a comrade in another employee who is angry if they see the world in similar ways. Someone who is often frustrated may find a friend in another employee who is also often frustrated if they share similar views.

The co-worker friends who are often frustrated may find the co-worker who is often in a state of appreciation frustrating and may also find the co-workers who are often angry frustrating. The saying, "Birds of a feather flock together" is very true about emotional states.

Researchers found that team members whose PsyCap was close were more successful than teams where the members PsyCap was more diverse.[373] This indicates that team PsyCap should be matched. When research that considers whether high or low PsyCap contributes more to success it becomes clear that the ideal situation is a team where the members all have high levels of PsyCap. Given the components of PsyCap (Hope, Optimism, Internal Locus of Control, Healthy Self-esteem, and Self-efficacy) are also critical components of happiness, it would be almost impossible for a team to have high levels of PsyCap and not be in the higher emotional Zones.

Since testing for high levels of PsyCap for employment selection violates anti-discrimination statutes in most countries, an employer's best option is a training program for all employees. As the company's reputation as a positively focused employer grows they will attract like-minded talent.

I first began having the opportunity to be in large groups of positively focused individuals about a decade ago. It was the first time I saw highly diverse individuals having fun together without judging others choices. The groups I've participated in have contained individuals with many different worldviews including religions, nationality, race, gender, gender identity, sexual orientation, age, marital status, socioeconomic status and more and all of them got along very well.

Compared to situations in which people aren't focused on feeling good where even people who have highly similar backgrounds and worldviews often fuss and feud with one another, the ease of focusing on and taking responsibility for one's own emotional state was astonishing. It gave me insights into the power of positivity that I would not have imagined possible.

Once an employee understands how to feel good the natural instinct to feel good takes over and encourages the use of the skills. The difference is that someone with a skill-based ability to feel good doesn't see the need to diminish someone else in order to feel better. Emotional Guidance provides the validation that most people seek from others. I've become convinced that the need for others' to make decisions that are similar to our decisions is driven by the desire for validation because we intuitively know our choices should be validated but having been steered away from our Emotional Guidance we look for validation in all the wrong places.

When we find the stable validation from our Emotional Guidance we no longer seek it from others. We have all lived long enough to know that people can be fickle and that depending on someone else to validate our value and worth is a risky proposition. It is far better to base our core self-evaluations on our Emotional Guidance because it is always available to us and it is never distracted. We can relax and be comfortable with diverse choices because we don't feel insecure about our personal choices.

Harmonious co-worker relationships have the same root cause as employee engagement. The mindset of the employee and his or her skill at managing their emotional state to good-feeling levels is the factor that determines whether they have good relationships. Now, you can go back to the hybrid vehicle incident and find that the relationship I had with my co-workers was not as good as it might have been but that was because of their focus on the negative aspects of someone else getting a perk. They even had conversations about whether the company could or would buy them parking space to even things out despite the fact that the company was not profitable at the time.

That is not surprising because individuals in lower emotional states who do not possess skills that empower them to feel good will still attempt to feel better in whatever ways they believe will work. These decisions may not be entirely conscious in that they don't necessarily recognize that the reason they park in the hybrid parking space in a high-powered sports car is that it makes them feel better about something they feel badly about. They don't consciously recognize that the hybrid parking space is just an excuse to continue feeling how they were predominantly feeling even before the hybrid car parking space signs were erected.

Metacognition must become a habit before such decisions are made with conscious intentions. In many ways, individuals who don't use metacognition fumble through life somewhat blindly often not seeing their own underlying motivations clearly. Once metacognition is conscious the employee will perceive and choose words and actions that have better long-term consequences. The employee will recognize that what they really want is to feel good.

Eventually, every individual who discovers their Emotional Guidance realizes that it is not possible to see others in a negative light and feel good at the same time. This doesn't mean that the person condones bad behaviors, but they do feel compassion and may understand how the person arrived at the point where they made poor decisions. They will also see ways of preventing others from following in the person's footsteps.

This aspect is especially important when it comes to any type of diversity. It is not possible to find fault with a group of people for characteristics about them that are different from our own characteristics and feel good. The choice becomes one between feeling good or finding fault and our nature if to feel as good as we can. At that point, the individual who has felt negative emotion about a group of people in the past begins looking for personal perspectives they can take that will feel better. Those perspectives are always found in the direction of greater acceptance and inclusion.

Going back to the high human need for autonomy it becomes easy to see that when an employer or society demands someone change their views or behavior toward groups of individuals the person may currently see in a negative light that demand can feel as if it is infringing on one's autonomy. Approaching it from the perspective of wanting to feel better and figuring out that it is not possible to find fault with groups of people and feel good makes the decision to see diverse groups in a more favorable light feel like an autonomous decision. Emotional Guidance reinforces such decisions continuously.

Exceptions can occur when the individual has low self-esteem and bases his or her self-worth on being better than some group of others. In such cases it is important to increase self-esteem using Emotional Guidance to create a firm platform for higher self-worth before the individual will let go of negative stereotypes about others that provided self-worth in the past. The employer doesn't have to figure this out. Once the employee understands Emotional Guidance and some metacognitive processes, the natural progression will eventually take care of the rest—especially if the employee is in an environment that supports finding positive perspectives.

Everyone does not progress at the same pace. This is not something to be measured using external tools. Often the better-feeling emotional states release employees from pretending to feel better than they felt during the initial stages. The internal changes in emotional state and confidence occur first. Questions that are general such as, "Are you feeling better than you did before you learned about Emotional Guidance?" are more valuable than questions that attempt to score the current emotional state.

Many employees are fantastic actors who have lived most of their lives hiding emotional pain. In the early stages you may notice that someone is more likely to laugh with more abandon than they once did or more likely to shrug off things that used to bother them. You may notice the employee is making fewer errors or is more likely to lend a hand to a co-worker than he once did. Support systems that aid in understanding and share success stories can be very valuable. Judging how well someone else is doing is not helpful.

The biggest key to harmonious co-worker relationships is taking responsibility for how you feel. Blaming others for how you feel gives your power away. When you take responsibility for how you feel you have the power to change how you feel. Just having the power feels better. Look at the chart that reflects where empowered and disempowered are in relationship to the EGSc and it quickly becomes clear that taking responsibility for how you feel is a good decision.

Behaviors towards others changes with emotional state with better behaviors associated with better emotional states. If you want employees who treat one another well the easiest way is to empower them with skills that allow them to be happier.

Appendix I
Appendix I – Emotional Guidance Scale (EGSc)

In general, emotional states can be defined (broadly) with the following feelings:

Sweet Zone

- Joy
- Empowered
- Passion
- Happy
- Inspired
- Optimism
- Fulfilled

- Appreciation
- Love
- Enthusiasm
- Positive Expectation
- Trust
- Serene
- Secure

- Freedom
- Awe
- Eagerness
- Belief
- Faith
- Satisfied
- At ease

Hopeful Zone

- Hopefulness

- Gratitude

- Upbeat

Blah Zone

- Contentment
- Apathy

- Boredom
- Dispirited

- Pessimism
- Empty

Drama Zone

- Frustration
- Overwhelmed

- Irritation
- Disappointment

- Impatience
- Indignant

Give Away Zone

- Doubt
- Guilt

- Worry
- Discouragement

- Blame
- Offended

Hot (Red) Zone

- Anger
- Outraged

- Revenge
- Provoked

- Rage
- Furious

Powerless Zone

- Hatred
- Insecurity
- Grief
- Powerless
- Hopeless
- Suicidal

- Bullied
- Fear
- Depression
- Learned Helplessness
- Melancholy
- Unimportant

- Jealousy
- Unworthiness
- Despair
- Guarded
- Unwanted
- Exploited

The EGSc is a compilation of scales used by a variety of teachers including David Hawkins, L. Ron Hubbard, and Abraham-Hicks. The Zones are my addition. The science supporting the Emotional Guidance Scale, or that emotions provide guidance, did not exist when the earlier scales were created. All emotions could be placed on the scale. It is simplified to reflect emotions that are similar in degrees of empowerment in each Zone. The higher the Zone, the greater the sense of empowerment the person feels.

Appendix II

Future research should consider individual thought processes (i.e. coping skills, cognitive reappraisal, etc.) when determining long-term health outcomes of adverse events. Unless and until research is done on actual thought processes, the strong link between reappraisals that lower stress levels and positive outcomes will not have the empirical documentation that will allow them to be widely implemented and supported with the funding they deserve.

Appendix III – Self-Test[374]

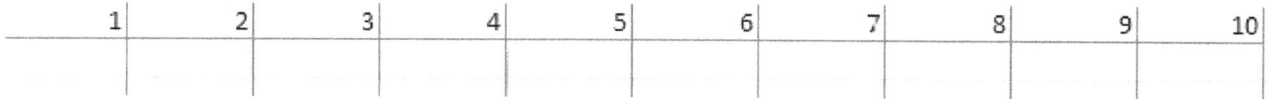

	1	2	3	4	5	6	7	8	9	10

Mark the line below to indicate where you are now.

Example: Use a "E" to mark how you feel now (at the end of the book)

Tired frequently_____E ____Well-rested

The location of this E indicates you feel rested more than you feel too tired

Sad frequently_____Rarely sad

Fuzzy thinking_____Clear headed

Not sleeping well_____Sleeping well

Hopeless_____ __Hopeful

Exhausted_____ __Energized

Scattered_____ ____Focused

Overwhelmed_____ __ _Capable

Stuck_____Letting go

Resentful_____ __Forgiving

Close-hearted_____ _Open-hearted

Frustrated_____ __ Appreciative

Broken_____ _Whole

Depressed_____ _Happy

Anxious_____ ___Calm

Unbalanced_____ _Balanced

Uncomfortable_____ __Comfortable

Defined by my illness/problem/or past_____Self-defined

Low self-esteem_____High self-esteem

Complete_____Evolving

No energy_____Vital and alive

Angry_____Accepting

Vengeful_____Understanding

Old_____Wise

My body does not recover quickly_____My body is strong

Isolated_____Connected

Bored_____Interested

Boring_____Fun

Life is hard_____Life is easy

Appendix IV

These are the citations for the High-Level Factor Chart.

[1] (Nubold, Muck, & Maier, 2013)
[2] (Fredrickson B. L., 2010)
[3] (Larson, Norman, Hughes, & Avey, 2013)
[4] (Dweck, 2008)
[5] (Bryan, 1991)
[6] (Estrada, 1997)
[7] (Fredrickson B. L., 2005)
[8] (Ashby, 1999)
[9] (Johnson, 2010)
[10] (Zimmer-Gembeck & Skinner, 2014)
[11] (Nubold, Muck, & Maier, 2013)
[12] (Larson, Norman, Hughes, & Avey, 2013)
[13] (Dweck, 2008)
[14] (Vaillant, 2012)
[15] (Lyubomirsky, King, & Diener, The Benefits of Frequent Positive Affect: Does Happiness Lead to Success?, 2005)
[16] (Nubold, Muck, & Maier, 2013)
[17] (Larson, Norman, Hughes, & Avey, 2013)
[18] (Larson, Norman, Hughes, & Avey, 2013)
[19] (Nubold, Muck, & Maier, 2013)
[20] (Larson, Norman, Hughes, & Avey, 2013)
[21] (Larson, Norman, Hughes, & Avey, 2013)

[22] (Larson, Norman, Hughes, & Avey, 2013)
[23] (Larson, Norman, Hughes, & Avey, 2013)
[24] (Larson, Norman, Hughes, & Avey, 2013)
[25] (Larson, Norman, Hughes, & Avey, 2013)
[26] (Larson, Norman, Hughes, & Avey, 2013)
[27] (Larson, Norman, Hughes, & Avey, 2013)
[28] (Christian, 2012)
[29] (Voellmin, Entringer, Moog, Wadhwa, & Buss, 2013)
[30] (Liberman, Anderson, & Ross, 2010)
[31] (McCarthy & Casey, 2011)
[32] (Peterson & DeHart, 2013)
[33] (Wong, Tschan, Messerli, & Semmer, 2013)
[34] (Boehm, 2012)
[35] (Danner, 2001)
[36] (Dockray & Steptoe, 2010)
[37] (Khansar, Murgo, & Faith, 1990)
[38] (Lai JC, 2005)
[39] (Ong, Mroczek, & Riffin, 2011)
[40] (Robertson, Stanley, Cully, & Naik, 2012)
[41] (Steptoe, 2005)
[42] (Bhatia & Tandon, 2005)
[43] (Armstrong, Galligan, & Critchley, 2011)
[44] (Baratta, Rozeske, & Maier, 2013)
[45] (Bonanno, 2004)
[46] (Bond & Shapiro, 2014)
[47] (Cohn, 2009)
[48] (Infurna & Luthar, 2016)
[49] (Lyubomirsky & Porta, Boosting Happiness and Buttressing Resilience: Results from Cognitive and Behavioral Interventions, (in press))
[50] (Catalino & Fredrickson, 2011)
[51] (Boehm, 2012)
[52] (Wingo, Ressler, & Bradley, 2014)
[53] (Boehm, 2012)
[54] (APA, 2013)
[55] (Creswell, et al., 2005)
[56] (Martin & Dahlen, 2005)
[57] (Ong, Bergeman, Bisconti, & Wallace, 2006)
[58] (Steptoe, 2005)

Bibliography for the High-Level Factor Chart

Bibliography

APA. (2013). *Stress in America: Missing the Health Care Connection* .

Armstrong, A. R., Galligan, R. F., & Critchley, C. R. (2011). Emotional Intelligence and psychological resilience to negative life events. *Personality and Individual Differences*, 331-336.

Ashby, F. G. (1999). A neuropsychological theory of positive affect and its influence on cognition. *Psychological Review*, 106, No. 3, 529-50.

Baratta, M. V., Rozeske, R. R., & Maier, S. F. (2013). Understanding Stress Resilience. *Frontiers in Behavioral Neuroscience*, 1-112.

Bhatia, V., & Tandon, R. K. (2005, March). Stress and the gastrointestinal tract. *Journal of Gastroenterology and Hepatology, 20*(3), 332-339.

Boehm, J. K. (2012, July). The heart's content: The association between positive psychological well-being and cardiovascular health. *Psychological Bulletin, Epub April 2012,* 138(4):655-91 .

Bonanno, G. (2004). Loss, trauma, and human resilience: Have we underestimated the human capacity to thrive after extremely aversive events? *American Psychologist,* 59: 20-28.

Bond, S., & Shapiro, D. (2014). *Tough AT The Top? New Rules of ResilieNce foR womeN's leAdeRship success.* Research report.

Bryan, T. a. (1991). Positive mood and math performance. *Journal of Learning Disabilities,* 24:490-94.

Catalino, L. I., & Fredrickson, B. L. (2011). A Tuesday in the Life of a Flourisher: The Role of Positive Emotional Reactivity in Optimal Mental Health. *Emotion, 11*(4), 938-950.

Christian, L. M. (2012). Psychoneuroimmunology in pregnancy: Immune pathways linking stress with maternal health, adverse birth outcomes, and fetal development. *Neuroscience and Biobehavioral Reviews, 36*, 350-361.

Cohn, M. A. (2009). Happiness unpacked: Positive emotions increase life satisfaction by building resilience. *Emotion,* 9: 361-368.

Creswell, J. D., Welch, W. T., Taylor, S. E., Sherman, D. K., Gruenewax, T. L., Gruenewald, T. L., et al. (2005). Affirmation of Personal Values Buffers Neuroendocrine and Psychological Stress Responses. *Psychological Science, 16*(11), 847-851.

Danner, D. D. (2001). "Positive Emotions in Early Life and Longevity: Findings from the Nun Study." . *Journal of Personality and Social Psychology.*, 804-13.

Dockray, S., & Steptoe, A. (2010). Positive Affect and psychobiological processes. *Neuroscience and Biobehavioral Reviews*, 69-75.

Dweck, C. S. (2008). *Mindset: The New Psychology of Success*. New York: Ballantine Books.

Estrada, C. I. (1997). Positive affect facilitates integration of information and decreases anchoring in reasoning among physicians. *Organizational Behavior and Human Decision Processes*, 72: 117-135.

Fredrickson, B. L. (2005). Positive Emotions broaden the scope of attention and though-action repertoires. *Cognition and Emotion*, 19: 313-332.

Fredrickson, B. L. (2010). *Positivity.* Three Rivers Press.

Infurna, F. J., & Luthar, S. S. (2016, March). Resilience to Major Life Stressors Is Not as Common as Thought. *Perspectives in Psychological Science, 11*, 175-194.

Johnson, K. J. (2010). Smile to see the forest: Facially expressed positive emotions broaden cognition. *COGNITION AND EMOTION*, 24(2): 299-321.

Khansar, D. N., Murgo, A. J., & Faith, R. E. (1990). Effects of Stress on the Immune System. *Immunology Today, 11*, 170-176.

Lai JC, E. P. (2005). Optimism, positive affectivity, and salivary cortisol. *British Journal of Health Psychology*, 4:467-84.

Larson, M. D., Norman, S. M., Hughes, L. W., & Avey, J. B. (2013). Psychological Capital: A Ne Lens for Understanding Employee Fit and Attitudes. *Internal Journal of Leadership Studies, 8*(1), 28-43.

Liberman, V., Anderson, N. R., & Ross, L. (2010). Achieving difficult agreements: Effects of Positive Expectations on negotiation processes and outcomes. *Journal of Experimental Social Psychology, 46*, 494-504.

Lyubomirsky, S., & Porta, M. D. ((in press)). Boosting Happiness and Buttressing Resilience: Results from Cognitive and Behavioral Interventions. In J. W. Reich, A. J. Zautra, & J. Hall (Eds.), *Handbook of adult resilience: Concepts, methods, and application.* New York, NY, USA: Guilford Press.

Lyubomirsky, S., King, L., & Diener, E. (2005). The Benefits of Frequent Positive Affect: Does Happiness Lead to Success? *Psychological Bulletin, 131*(6), 803-855.

Martin, R. C., & Dahlen, E. R. (2005). Cognitive emotion regulation in the prediction of depression, anxiety, stress, and anger. *Personality and Individual Differences*, 1249-1260.

McCarthy, B., & Casey, T. (2011). Get Happy! Positive Emotion, Depression and Juvenile Crime. *American Sociological Associaion Annual Meeting.* Las Vegas: UC Davis.

Nubold, A., Muck, P. M., & Maier, G. W. (2013). A new substitute for leadership? Followers state core self-evaluations. *The Leadership Quarterly, 24,* 29-44.

Ong, A. D., Bergeman, C. S., Bisconti, T. L., & Wallace, K. A. (2006). Psychological Resilience, Postve Emotions, and Successful Adaptation to Stress in Later Life. *Journal of Personaltiy and Social Psychology 91,* 730-49.

Ong, A. D., Mroczek, D. K., & Riffin, C. (2011, August 1). The Health Significance of Positive Emotions in Adulthood and Later Life. *Social and Personality Psychology Compass, 5*(8), 538-551.

Peterson, J. L., & DeHart, T. (2013). Regulating connection: Implicit self-esteem predicts positive non-verbal behavior. *Journal of Experimental Social Psychology,* 99-105.

Robertson, S. M., Stanley, M. A., Cully, J. A., & Naik, A. D. (2012). Positive Emotional Health and Diabetes Care: Concepts, Measurement, and Clinical Implications. *Psychosomatics, 53,* 1-12.

Steptoe, A. W. (2005). Positive affect and health-related neuroendocrine, cardiovascular, and inflammatory responses. *Proceedings of the National Academy of Sciences.*

Vaillant, G. E. (2012). *Triumphs of Experience: The Men of the Harvard Grant Study.*

Voellmin, A., Entringer, S., Moog, N., Wadhwa, P. D., & Buss, C. (2013). Maternal positive affect over the course of pregnancy is associated with the length of gestation and reduced risk of preterm delivery. *Journal of Psychosomatic Research, 75,* 336-340.

Wingo, A. P., Ressler, K. J., & Bradley, B. (2014). Resilience characteristics mitigate tendency for harmful alcohol and illicit drug use in adults wiht a history of childhood abuse: A Cross-sectional study of 2024 inner-city men and women. *Journal of Psychiatric Research.*

Wong, E., Tschan, F., Messerli, L., & Semmer, N. K. (2013). Expressing and Amplifying Positive Emotions Facilitate Goal Attainment in Workplace Interactions. *Frontiers in Psychology,* 188.

Wu, G., Feder, A., Cohen, H., Kim, J. J., Calderon, S., Chamey, D. S., et al. (2013). Understanding Resilience. *Frontiers in Behavioral Neuroscience,* 10.

Zimmer-Gembeck, M. J., & Skinner, E. A. (2014). The Development of Coping: Implications for Psychopathology and Resilience. In D. Cicchetti (Ed.), *Developmental Psychopathology* (Vol. Resubmission #2, pp. 1-117). Oxford, England: Wiley & Sons.

Sources of More Information

I have several websites with information that will be helpful.
www.Happiness1st.com
www.ThriveMoreNow.US
www.AchieveAffinity.org

I am available to teach *The Smart Way Program* and for motivational or educational speeches.

The focus of each is on increasing Human Thriving.

- Happiness 1st Institute offers classes to individuals and companies that teach skills that increase resilience, happiness, employee engagement, lower stress, and provide other significant benefits.
- Achieve Affinity is a non-profit organization I co-founded with my husband to bring the information provided by Happiness 1st Institute to schools and others who cannot afford the services of Happiness 1st Institute

I blog on all my websites, on LinkedIn, and BizCatalyst360°.
You can follow me on Twitter: @JeanineJoyJOY
You can also follow me on Goodreads.com
Radio shows I've been on are archived on Happiness1st and I will soon be broadcasting a weekly radio showl
Facebook: https://www.facebook.com/Happiness1st

There are some situations where more detailed instructions would be helpful. More detailed information about dealing with problem issues such as being unable to forgive past transgressions or a specific situation are covered in more depth in *Our Children Live in a War Zone*. It is possible to literally change the past by changing the perspective from which it is viewed. Emotional pain can be greatly reduced or even eliminated. It's 514 pages so there was room for a lot more information.

Please remember to review the book on Amazon and Goodreads to let me know how it helped you. Thank you!

Special Offer

I hold Introductory Sessions to introduce individuals, businesses, physicians and clergy *The Smart Way*. Please come to one of the sessions as my guest. If the Introductory Session is not serving a meal, you may attend as my guest free of charge. If a meal is being served, I ask that you cover the cost of your meal.

If you are interested in a program for your school, business or other organization, please contact me at Thrive More Now Publishing, P.O. Box 6888, Concord NC 28078 (704) 251-5150.

If you are interested in having me speak at your event, please contact me via LinkedIn (preferred), Twitter (JeanineJoyJOY), my publisher, or my website, Happiness1st.com

Glossary

Note: I am so involved in this work that it is difficult for me to determine what managers know and don't know about the concepts outlined here. Based on some of my speaking engagements where concepts I thought would be well-known were foreign to many members of the audience, I am erring on the side of caution and explaining terms if I think they might not be known by most of my readers. If I have not included a term that is unfamiliar I'd be happy to hear from you so I can update future versions.

Abusive Work Environment is where 1) enduring the offensive conduct becomes a condition of continued employment, or 2) the conduct is severe or pervasive enough to create a work environment that a reasonable person would consider intimidating, hostile, or abusive. (EEOC)

Actively Disengaged refers to an employee who is actively sabotaging the organization. The sabotage can come in many forms including being disruptive to co-workers or undermining the company's reputation on social media.

Appreciative Inquiry (AI) is a change management approach that focuses on identifying what is working well, analyzing why it is working well and then doing more of it. The basic tenet of AI is that an organization will grow in whichever direction that people in the organization focus their attention. (Whatis.com)

Autonomy is exercising independence in one's thoughts, actions, and decisions without coercion or undue influence from others.

Autopilot Life is the opposite of being mindful. It involves moving through life and not really thinking about why you do what you do (from what you think, say, and do). A person living on autopilot goes through the motions but doesn't consider alternative perspectives, ways of communicating, or actions.

Back story is a term the Father of Positive Psychology uses to refer to stories our subconscious mind makes up so our conscious experience of the world makes sense. You could say a psychic break occurs when the subconscious is not able to create a back story to explain a shift in one's reality.

Biofield covers a lot of territory. Wiki states that biofield can refer to:
- Energy medicine - Alternate, complementary or integrative medicine
- Electrophysiology - Scientific study of electrical properties of cells and tissues
- Electroreception - sensory of electric fields by organisms
- Magnetoception - sensory of magnetic fields by organisms
- Bioelectromagnetics - scientific study of electric biofields of organisms
- Scientific magnetic or electrical biofield imaging
- Magnetoencephalography - Brain imaging by magnetic field sensing
- Electroencephalography - Brain imaging by electric field sensing
- Magnetocardiography - Heart imaging by sensing its magnetic field

- Magnetogastrography - Stomach imaging by sensing magnetic fields
- Magnetomyography - Muscle imaging by sensing magnetic fields, produced by electrical impulses

Bio-information is biological information (pertaining to the body)

Biophotons are photons of light in the ultraviolet and low visible light range produced by a biological system.

Classic Physics is a physical system can be described by classical physics when it satisfies conditions such that the laws of classical physics are approximately valid (i.e. Newtonian). In practice, physical objects ranging from those larger than atoms and molecules, to objects in the macroscopic and astronomical realm, can be well-described (understood) with classical mechanics. Beginning at the atomic level and lower, the laws of classical physics break down and generally do not provide a correct description of nature. (Wiki)

Comfort Zone is a comfort zone refers to an individual's usual habitat, which can refer to non-physical characteristics such as emotional state. The term Comfort Zone refers to the fact that the person is accustomed to the state and not that the Comfort Zone is comfortable for any other reason than familiarity. For example, long-term prisoners are sometimes more comfortable while incarcerated than when they are out of jail. Also, someone who is sad or depressed may be afraid to attempt to change their emotional state because they have decided they can stand being where they are even if it is not comfortable. Individuals can be in their personal Comfort Zone anywhere on the EGSc.

Constructive Interference magnifies the power of a desire on the quantum level. It multiplies the power of the desire.

Core Self-Evaluations (CSE) are an individual's opinion about themselves formed by subconscious (usually) fundamental evaluations of their abilities and self-control. High core self-evaluations result in a positive outlook about oneself and one's abilities. People with low core self-evaluations will think negatively of themselves and be insecure about their own abilities. People believe their core self-evaluations about themselves are true and interpret the world as if they are true.

Destructive Interference diminishes the power of a desire on the quantum level. The power of a desire is divided or multiplied by a fraction.

Dispositional Affect is similar to mood, is a personality trait or overall tendency to respond to situations in stable, predictable ways. This trait is expressed by the tendency to see things in a positive or negative way. (Wiki)

Downward Spiral is a series of thoughts or actions which feeds back into itself, causing a situation to become progressively worse. It is worse than a vicious circle, which is self-sustaining in its current state. (Yourdictionary.com)

Efficacious Act is an act that produces or has the potential to produce the desired outcome.

Eudaimonic refers to self-actualization and being authentic (true to one's nature)

Equanimity refers to the maintenance of one's composure, mental calmness, and evenness of temper especially in a difficult situation.

Emotional Intelligence (EQ/EI) has four parts:
1. Identify one's own emotional state
2. Respond to emotions with maturity and awareness of its implications
3. Recognize other people's emotions
4. Use emotional information to manage relationships with a win-win focus

While IQ helps an ambitious individual reach high positions, a lack of EQ/EI often makes their tenure short-lived. EQ/EI can be developed.

Employee Engagement is the emotional connection or commitment an employee feels toward the employer and the goals of the organization. At high levels an employee is passionate about their work and may act as an ambassador for the company. High engagement increases the effort an employee willingly puts forth.

Evidence-Based Method refers to decisions that consider unique characteristics of the situation and that are informed by scientific research.

Heart Coherence is a healthy state of the heart that could be described as the state of the heart when an individual's thoughts are creating Constructive Interference on the quantum level. It could also be said to occur when someone is in the Sweet Zone.

Hedonic refers to the fact that it feels good.

Homogenous incomes refers to people having the same incomes.

Intrinsic motivation see chapter 9.

Metacognition is thinking about thinking including what is being thought, why it is being thought and alternative thoughts one could think.

Mood-congruent refers to memories that are consistent with a patient's mood or mental disorder.

Mood-incongruent refers to emotions that seem to be out of sync with the current situation. For example, laughing when you're fired.

Physiological regulation refers to the regulation of a biological system (such as body temperature).

Plasticity is the ability to be molded or altered.

Psychosocial genomics focuses on the how the highly personal and subjective states of human consciousness can modulate gene expression in the brain and body for illness or health. (Rossi, 2002)

Positivity is the tendency to focus on the positive aspects of a situation even if many people would choose to focus on the negative aspects of the same situation. For example, while being informed they are being laid off, the positively focused individual might consider their tendency to stay in a role longer than they should when their long-term career goals are considered and see the forced departure as an opportunity to move up to the next level, perhaps recognizing that they had once again stayed longer than necessary in a role they had outgrown.

Psychoneuroimmunology is a branch of medicine that deals with the influence of emotional states (as stress) and nervous system activities on immune function especially in relation to the onset and progression of disease.

Psychological Flexibility is defined by Kashdan and Rotterburg[375] as the measure of how a person:
1. Adapts to fluctuating situational demands,
2. Reconfigures mental resources,
3. Shifts perspective, and
4. Balances competing desires, needs, and life domains.

Quantum Coherence See Constructive and Destructive Interference.

Resilience is the ability to bounce back to one's prior level of function (or better) following a set-back.

Root Cause refers to the original cause of a problem that is solvable. For example, someone may have low self-esteem which makes them interpret management's compliments as attempts to coerce them into doing things they do not want to do instead of authentic compliments. The low self-esteem is the root cause of the lack of engagement that results. There would be a deeper root, the one that led to the development of the low self-esteem in the first place, but root cause solutions focus on aspects we can change. Another example is poor health related decisions are also the result of stress. While poor dietary decisions contribute to the problem, stress is a deeper root and mindset is an even deeper root. Using root cause solutions means we would address the problem by empowering the employee with skills that allow him to adjust his mindset so that he feels better more often.

Salutogenesis describes an approach focusing on factors that support human health and well-being, rather than on factors that cause disease.

Self-Efficacy is an individual's belief in his or her capacity to execute behaviors necessary to produce specific performance attainments.[376] An individual who has self-efficacy has achieved a certain level of confidence in their ability be successful at a task or series of tasks.

Self-regulation researchers study the human ability to regulate their own behavior.

Subatomic particles are smaller than an atom.

Suppressive Emotion Regulation is the attempt to resist feelings evoked by one's experiences. Suppressive Emotion Regulation is associated with poor mental and physical health outcomes.

Thought-Paths (Neurological Connections) are neurological connections in the brain that are easy to follow than other thoughts due to their having been thought previously (and probably repeatedly).

Transduction is the action or process of converting something and especially energy or a message into another form.

Upward Spiral is a self-reinforcing process with increasingly good outcomes.

Willpower is an attempt to change behavior that is supported by personal beliefs that support the behavior one wishes to change.

Index

Bibliography

Achor, S. (2010). *The Happiness Advantage: Seven Principles of Positive Psychology That Fuel Success and Performance at Work.* Random House.

Achor, S., & Gielan, M. (2015, September 2). Make Yourself Immune to secondhand Stress. *Harvard Business Review*, p. Epub.

Allison, S. T., Uhles, A. N., Asuncion, A. G., Beggan, J. K., & Mackie, D. M. (2006, July 28). Self-serving outcome-biases in trait judgments about the self. *Current Research in Social Psychology*, 202-214.

American Academy of Pediatrics. (2012, October 22). *Children with Mental Health Disorders More Often Identified as Bullies.* Retrieved from aap.org: https://www.aap.org/en-us/about-the-aap/aap-press-room/pages/Children-with-Mental-Health-Disorders-More-Often-Identified-as-Bullies.aspx?nfstatus=401&nftoker=00000000-0000-0000-0000-000000000000&nfstatusdescription=ERROR%3a+No+local+token

American Psychological Association (APA). (2010). *Stress in America Findings: Mind/Body Health: For a Healthy Mind and Body, Talk to a Psychologist.* American Psychological Association (APA).

ANB. (2016, 5 31). 30-minute meetings with your boss. (J. Joy, Interviewer)

Anderson, J. G., & Taylor, A. G. (2011). The Metabolic Syndrome and Mind-Body Therapies: A Systematic Review. *Journal of Nutrition and Metabolism*, 8. doi:10.1155/2011/276419

APA. (2013). *Stress in America: Missing the Health Care Connection .*

APA. (2014). *Stress in America: Are Teens Adopting Adults' Stress Habits?* American Psychological Association. American Psychological Association. Retrieved from http://www.apa.org/news/press/releases/stress/2013/stress-report.pdf

Armstrong, A. R., Galligan, R. F., & Critchley, C. R. (2011). Emotional Intelligence and psychological resilience to negative life events. *Personalit and Individual Differences, 51*, 331-336.

Atkins, P., & Parker, S. (2011). Understanding individual compassion in organizations: the role of appraisals and psychological flexibility. *Academy of Management Review*, ePub.

Bandura, A. (1986). *Social Foundations of Thought and Action.* Prentice-Hall.

Barasch, M. I., & Hirshberg , C. (1995). *Remarkable Recovery: What Extraordinary Healings Tell Us About Getting Well and Staying Well.*

Barn, R., & Tan, J.-P. (2012). Foster youth and crime: Employing general strain theory to promote understanding. *Journal of Criminal Justice, 40*, 212-220.

Barnica, B. (2014, April 18). *How Biophotons Show that we are made of light.* Retrieved from thespiritscience.net: http://thespiritscience.net/2014/04/18/biophotons-demonstrate-were-al-made-of-light/

Barry, C. T., Grafeman, S. J., Adler, K. K., & Pickard, J. D. (2007). The relations among narcissism, self-esteem, and delinquency in a sample of at-risk adolescents. *Journal of Adolescence*, 933-942.

Baumeister, R. F. (2015). Self-Regulation and Conscientiousness. *NOBA Syllabus*.

Baumeister, R. F., Vohs, K. D., DeWall, C. N., & Zhang, L. (2007, May 16). How Emotion Shapes Behavior: Feedback, Anticipation, and Reflection, Rather Than Direct Causation. *Personality and Social Psychology Review, 11*(2), 167-203. Retrieved September 23, 2015, from <file:///C:/Users/Jeanine/Documents/baumeister%20how%20emotion%20shapes%20behavior.pdf>

Baumeister, R. F., Vohs, K. D., DeWall, N., & Zhang, L. (2007, May). How Emotion Shapes Behavior: Feedback, Anticipation, and Reflection, Rather Than Direct Causation. *Personality and Social Psychology Review, 11*(2), 167-203. doi:DOI: 10.1177/1088868307301033

Baumesiter, R. F., Vohs, K. D., & Tice, D. M. (2007). The Strength Model of Self-Control. *Current Directions in Psychological Science*, 351-355.

Beck, R., & Fernandez, E. (1998). Cognitive-Behavioral Therapy in the Treatment of Anger: A Meta-Analysis. *Cognitive Therapy and Research, 22*(1), 63-74.

Ben-Itzhak, S., Bluvstein, I., & Maor, M. (2014). The Psychological Flexibility Questionnaire (FPQ): Development, Reliability, and Validity. *WebmedCentral Psychology, 5*(4). Retrieved April 2016

Berking, M., Margraf, M., Ebert, D., Wupperman, P., Hofmann, S. G., & Junghanns, K. (2011, June). Deficits in Emotion-Regulation Skills Predict Alcohol Use During and After Cognitive Behavioral Therapy for Alcohol Dependence. *Journal of Consulting and Clinical Psychology, 79*(3), 307-318. doi:http://dx.doi.org/10.1037/a0023421

Berlew, D. E., & Hall, D. T. (1966). The Socialization of Managers: The Effects of Expectations on Performance. *Administrative Science Quarterly, 11*, 207-223.

Berry, M. E., Chapple, I. T., Ginsberg, J. P., Gleichauf, K. J., Meyer, J. A., & Nagpal, M. L. (2014, March). Non-pharmacological Interention for Chronic Pain in Veterans: A Pilot Study of Heart Rate Vriability Biofeedback. *Global Advances in Health and Medicine, 3*(2), 28-33.

Black, P. H. (2003). The inflammatory response is an integral part of the stress response:Implications for atherosclerosis, insulin resistance, type II diabetes and metabolic syndrome X . *Brain, Behavior, and Immunity*, 350-364.

Boehm, J. K. (2012, July). The heart's content: The association between positive psychological well-being and cardiovascular health. *Psychological Bulletin, Epub April 2012*, 138(4):655-91 . doi:DOI: 10.1037/a0027448.

Bonanno, G. A., & Diminich, E. D. (2013). Annual Research Review: Positive adjustment to adversity--trajectories of minimal-impact resilience and emergent resilience. *Journal of Child Psychology and Psychiatry, 54*(4), 378-401. doi:doi:10.1111/jcpp.12021

Bond, F. W., Lloyd, J., & Guenole, N. (2012). The work-related acceptance and action questionnaire: Initial psychometric findings and their implications for measuring psychological flexibility in specific contexts. *Journal of Occupational and Organizational Psychology, 86*(3), 331-347. doi:DOI: 10.1111/joop.12001

Boroujeni, I. N., Asadi, H., & Tabatable, M. S. (2012). Relationship between happiness and organizational commitment of the employees of Youth and Sports Department of Chahar Mahal and Bakhtiari province. *International Journal of Sports Studies, 2*(9), 427-431.

Bowling, N. A., Eschlerman, K. J., & Wang, Q. (2010). A meta-analyti examination of the relationship between job satisfaction and subjective well-being. *Journal of Occupational and Organizational Psychology, 83*, 915-934.

Boyce, C. J., Wood, A. M., Daly, M., & Sedikides, C. (2015, February 9). Personality Change Following Unemployment. *Journal of Applied Psychology*. doi:http://dx.doi.org/10.1037/a0038647

Briscoe, J. P., Henagan, S. C., Burton, J. P., & Murphy, W. M. (2012). Coping with an insecure employment environment: The differing roles of protean and boundaryless career orientations. *Journal of Vocational Behavior, 80*, 308-316.

Brissette, I., Scheier, M., & Carver, C. S. (2002). The Role of Optimism in Social Network Development, Coping, and Psychological Adjustment During a Life Transition. *Journal of Personality and Social Pscyhology, 82*(1), 102-111. doi:DOI: 10.1037//0022-3514.82.1.102

Broderick, J. (2013). Trusting One's Emotional Guidance Builds Resilience. In Venkat Pulla, Shane Warren and Andrew Shatte (Ed.), *Perspectives on Coping and Resilience* (pp. 254-279). Laxmi Nagar, Delhi: Authors Press.

Bujoreanu, PhD, S., Benhayon, M.D., PhD, D., & Szigethy, M.D., PhD, E. (2011 November). *Treatment of Depression in Children and Adolescents*. Retrieved from Pediatric Super Site: PediatricSuperSite.com

Business Collective. (2016). *12 Ideas to Improve Employee Engagement*. Retrieved from Business Collective: https://businesscollective.com/12-ideas-to-improve-employee-engagement/

Butler, A. C., Chapman, J. E., Forman, E. M., & Beck, A. T. (2006). The empirical status of cognitive-behavioral therapy: A review of meta-analyses. *Clinical Psyhology Review, 26*, 17-31. doi:doi:10.1016/j.cpr.2005.07.003

Buzinski, S. G., & Price, A. (2015, July - September). Don't Tell Me What to Do: Highly Restrictive Goals Promote Temptation Indulgence. *Sage OPEN*, 1-11.

Campbell, D. T. (1975). On the conflicts between biological and social evolution and between psychology and moral tradition. *American Psychologist, 30*, pp. 1103-1126.

Carey, Ph.D., M. P., & Forsyth, A. D. (2016). *Self-Efficacy*. Retrieved from American Psychological Association: http://www.apa.org/pi/aids/resources/education/self-efficacy.aspx

Carr, P. B., & Steele, C. M. (2009). Stereotype threat and inflexible perseverance in problem solving. *Journal of Experimental Social Psychology, 45*, 853-859.

Carver, C. S. (2015, July 9). Control Processes, Priority Management, and Affective Dynamics. *Emotion Review, 7*(4), 301-307.

Chang, J. (2011). A Case Study of the "Pygmalion Effect""Teacher Expectations and Student Achievement. *International Education Studies, 4*(1), 198-201. Retrieved 2015

Cheng, H., & Furnham, A. (2003). Personality, self-esteem, and demographic predictions of Happiness and Depression. *Personality and Individual Differences, 34*, 921-942.

Cisler, J. M., & Olatunji, B. O. (2012). Emotion Regulation and Anxiety Disorders. *Current Psychiatry Reports, 14*(3), 182-187.

Clark, P. (2010, April). Preventing Future Crime With Cognitive Behavioral Therapy. *National Institute of Justice Journal No. 265*, 22-24.

Clore, G. L., & Palmer, J. (2009). Affective guidance of intelligent agents: How emotion controls cognition. (J. Gratch, Ed.) *Cognitive Systems Research, 10*, pp. 21-30. doi:doi:10.1016/j.cogsys.2008.03.002

Coetzee, M., & Harry, N. (2014). Emotional intelligence as a predictor of employees' career adaptability. *Journal of Vacational Behavior, 84*, 90-97.

Cohn, M. A. (2009). Happiness unpacked: Positive emotions increase life satisfaction by building resilience. *Emotion*, 9: 361-368.

Compare, A., Zarbo, C., Shonin, E., Van Gordon, W., & Marconi, C. (2014). Emotional Regulation and Depression: A Potential Mediator between Heart and Mind. *Cardiovascular Psychiatry and Neurology*, 10. doi:http://dx.doi.org/10.1155/2014/324374

Cooper, J. O., Heron, T. E., & Heward, W. L. (2007). *Applied Behavior Analysis* (2nd ed.). Pearson. Retrieved 2016

Correll, J., Spencer, S. J., & Zanna, M. P. (2004). An affirmed self and an open mind: Self-affirmation and sensitivity to argument strength. *Journal of Experimental Social Psychology, 40*, 350-356. doi:doi:10.1016/j.jesp.2003.07.001

Costa, P. T., & McCrae, R. R. (1988). Personality in Adulthood: A Six-Year Longitudinal Study of Self-Reports and Spouse Ratings on the NEO Personality Inventory. *Journal of Personality and Social Psychology, 54*(5), 853-863.

Creswell, J. D., Welch, W. T., Taylor, S. E., Sherman, D. K., Gruenewax, T. L., Gruenewald, T. L., & Mann, T. (2005). Affirmation of Personal Values Buffers Neuroendocrine and Psychological Stress Responses. *Psychological Science, 16*(11), 847-851.

Crocker, J., & Park, L. E. (2004). Reaping the Benefits of Pursuing Self-Esteem Without the Costs? Reply to DuBois and Flay (2004), SHeldon (2004), and Pyszczynski and Cos (2004). *Psychological Bulletin*, 430-434. Retrieved 2016

Crocker, J., & Park, L. E. (2004). The Costly Pursuit of Self-Esteem. *Psychological Bulletin, 130*(3), 392-414. doi:DOI: 10.1037/0033-2909.130.3.392

Dan-Glauser, E. S., & Gross, J. J. (2013). Emotion Regulation and Emotion Coherence: Evidence for Strategy-Specific Effects. *Emotion*, 832-842.

Danner, D. D. (2001). Positive Emotions in Early Life and Longevity. Findings from the Nun Study. *Journal of Personality and Social Psychology, 80*, No. 5.804-813. doi:10.1039//0022-3514.80.5.804

De Neve, J.-E., Diener, E., Tay, L., & Xuereb, C. (2013). The Objective Benefits of Subjective Well-Being. In J. Helliwell, R. Layard, & J. Sachs (Ed.). (pp. 1-35). New York: United Nations. Retrieved 2015

De Vriendt, T., Moreno, L. A., & De Henauw, S. (2009). Chronic stress and obesity in adolescents: Scientific evidence and methodological issues for epidemiological research. *Nutrition, metabolism, & Cardiovascular Disease, 19*, 511-519.

Deci, E. L., & Ryan, R. M. (2000). The "What" and "Why" of Goal Pursuits: Human Needs and the Self-Determination of Behavior. *Psychological Inquiry, 11*(4), 227-268. doi:doi:10.1207/S15327965PLI1104_01

Deci, E. L., Koestner, R., & Ryan, R. M. (1999). A Meta-Analytic Review of Experiments Examining the Effect of Extrinsic Rewards on Intrinsic Motivation. *Psychological Bulletin, 125*(6), 627-668.

Deechakawan, PhD, RN, W., Cain PhD, K. C., Jarrett, PhD, RN, M. E., Burr, MSEE, PhD, R. L.. & Heitkemper, PhD, RN, FAAN, M. M. (2012, November 20). Effect of Self-Management Intervention on Cortisol and Daily Stress Levels in Irritable Bowel Syndrome. *Biological Research for Nursing*, 26-36. doi:10.1177/1099800411414047

Diener, E., & Chan, M. Y. (2011). Happy People Live Longer: Subjective Well-Being Contributes to Health and Longevity. *The International Association of Applied Psychology: Health and Well-Being*, 1-43. doi:10.1111/j.1758-0854.2010.01045.x

Diener, E., & Tay, L. (2012 (draft)). *A Scientific Review of the Remarkable Benefits of Happiness for Successful and Healthy Living*. United Nations, Report of the Well-Being Working Group, Royal Governmentof Bhutan Report to the united Nations General Assembly, Well-being and Happiness: A New Deveopment Paradigm. New York: UN. Retrieved 2012

Dissanayake, R. K., & Bertouch, J. V. (2010, October). Psychosocial interventions as adjunct therapy for patients with rheumatoid arthritis: a systematic review. *International Journal of Rheumatic Diseases, 13*(4), 324-334. doi:DOI: 10.1111/j.1756-185X.2010.01563.x

Dossey, M.D., L. (2013). Unbroken Wholeness. *Explore, 9*(1), 1 - 8.

Driessen, E., & Hollon, S. D. (2010). Cognitive Behavioral Therapy for Mood Disorders: Efficacy, Moderators, and Mediators. *Psychiatric Clinics of North America, 33*(3), 537-555. doi:10.1016/j.psc.2010.04.005

DuBois, D. L., & Flay, B. R. (2004). The Healthy Pursuit of Self-Esteem: Comment on and Alternative to the Crocker and Park (2004) Formulation. *Psychological Bulletin, 130*(3), 415-420. doi:DOI: 10.1037/0033-2909.130.3.415

Dudovitz, R. N., Li, N., & Chung, P. J. (2013). Behavioral Self-Concept as Predictor of Teen Drinking Behaviors. *Academic Pediatrics, 13*(4).

Duke, W. M. (2016, 2016). How Military Concepts Can Help You in the Corporate World . . . . *Richtopia.*

Dweck, C. S. (2008). Can Personality Be Changed? The Role of Beliefs in Personality and Change. *Current Directions in Psychological Science, 17*(6).

EDi. (2016, 5 30). Millennial in IT and public recognition. (J. Joy, Interviewer)

Eiser, J. R., & Pahl, S. (2001). Optimism, Pessimism, and the Direction of Self-Other Comparisons. *Journal of Experimental Social Psychology, 37*, 77-84. doi:doi:10.1006/jesp.2000.1438

Emery, A. A., Heath, N. L., & Mills, D. J. (2015, December 19). Basic Psychological Need Satisfaction, Emotion Dysregulation, and Non-suicidal Self-Injury Engagement in Young Adults: An Application of Self-Determination Theory. *Journal Youth Adolescents*, Epub.

Entrepreneur. (n.d.). Retrieved from <https://www.entrepreneur.com/article/244590>

Farr, J. N. (1998). *Supra-Conscious Leadership: New Thinking for a New World.* (J. P. Grace, Ed.) Huntington, WV: Grace Associates, Limited. Retrieved April 2016

Feldman, B. L., Tarr, M. J., & Lebrecht, S. (2012). 'Micro-Valences: Perceiving Affective Valence in Everyday Objects'. *Frontiers in Psychology.* doi:10.3389/fpsyg.2012.00107

Foss, B., & Dyrstad, S. M. (2011). Stress in obesity: Cause or consequence? *Medical Hypotheses, 77*, 7-10. doi:doi:10.1016/j.mehy.2011.03.011

Fredrickson, B. L. (2001). The role of positive emotions in positive psychology: The broaden-and-build theory. *American Psychologist*, 56: 218-26.

Fredrickson, B. L. (2003). What good are positive emotions in crises?: A Prospective study of resilience and emotions following the terrorist attacks on the United States on September 11, 2001. *Journal of Personality and Social Psychology*, 84: 365-76.

Fredrickson, B. L. (2005). Positive Emotions broaden the scope of attention and though-action repertoires. *Cognition and Emotion*, 19: 313-332.

Fredrickson, B. L. (2009, May). The Science of Happiness. (A. Winter, Interviewer) The Sun Magazine.

Fredrickson, B. L. (2010). *Positivity.* Three Rivers Press.

Fredrickson, B.L., et al. (2008).

Friborg, O., Hjemdal, O., Rosenvinge, J. H., Martinussen, M., Aslaksen, P. M., & Flaten, M. A. (2006). Resilience is a moderator of pain and stress. *Journal of Psychosomatic Research, 61*, 213-219. Retrieved 2015

Gable, P., & Harmon-Jones, E. (2010). The Blues Broaden, but the Nasty Narrows: Attentional Consequences of Negative Affects Low and High in Motivational Intensity. (A. f. Science, Ed.) *Psychological Science*, 211-215.

Gable, S. a. (2004). What do you do when things go right? The intrapersonal and interpresonal benefits of sharing positive events. *Journal of Personality and Social Psychology*, 87: 2: 228-45.

Gagné , M., & Deci, E. L. (2005). Self-determination theory and work motivation. *Journal of Organizational Behavior, 26*, 331-362.

Garland, E. L., Fredrickson, B., Kring, A. M., Johnson, D. P., Meyer, P. S., & Penn, D. L. (2010). Upward spirals of positive emotions counter downward spirals of negativity: Insights. *Clinical Psychology Review*, 849-864. doi:doi:10.1016/j.cpr.2010.03.002

Gist, M. (1997). Training Design and Pedagogy: Implications for Skill Acquisition, Maintenance, and Generalization. In M. Gist, M. A. Quiñones, & A. Ehrenstein (Eds.), *Training for a rapidly changing workplace: Applications of psychological research* (pp. 201-222). Washington DC, US: American Psychological Association.

Goldberg, B. (2002). *Bias: A CBS Insider Exposes How the Media Distort the News.* Washington DC: Regnery Publishing, Inc.

Gouin, J.-P., Hantsoo, L., & Kiecolt-Glaser, J. K. (2008). Immune Dysregulation and Chronic Stress Among Older Adults: A Review. *Neuroimmunomodulation, 15*, 251-259. doi:doi:10.1159/000156468

Grant, A. M., & Sonnentag, S. (2010). Doing good buffers against feeling bad: Prosocial impact compensates for negative task and self-evaluations. *Organizational Behavior and Human Decision Processes, 111,* 13-22. Retrieved 2016

Grant, B. F., Goldstein, R. B., Saha, T. D., Chou, P., Jung, J., Zhang, H., . . . Hasin, D. S. (2015). Epidemiology of DSM-5 Alcohol Use Disorder: Results from the National epidemiologic Survey on Alcohol and Related Conditions III. *JAMA Psychiatry, 72*(8), 757-766. doi:doi:10.1001/jamapsychiatry.2015.0584

Greenberg, M. H. (2007). Optimistic managers and their influence on productivity and employee engagement in a technology organization. *Gallup Management Journal, Vol. 2, No. 1.*

Haidt, J. (2006). *The Happiness Hypothesis: Finding Modern Truth in Ancient Wisdom. Why the Meaningful Life Is Closer Than You Think.* New York: Basic Books.

Harter, J. K., Schmidt, F. L., & Hayes, T. L. (2002). Business-Unit-Level Relationship Between Employee Satisfaction, Employee Engagement, and Business Outcomes: A Meta-Analysis. *Journal of Applied Psychology, 87,* 268-279. doi:DOI: 10.1037//0021-9010.87.2.268

Harvey, J., & Delfabbro, P. H. (2004). Psychological resilience in disadvantaged youth: A critical overview. *Australian Psychologist, 39*(1), 3-13.

Helson, R., & Kwan, V. S. (2002, September). Personality change over 40 years of adulthood: hierarchical linear modeling analyses of two longitudinal samples. *Journal of Personality and Social Psychology, 83*(3), 752-66.

Hoffman, B. (2010). "I think I can, but I'm afraid to try": The role of self-efficacy beliefs and mathematics anxiety in mathematics problem-solving efficiency. *Learning and Individual Differences, 20,* 276-283. doi:doi:10.1016/j.lindif.2010.02.001

Hofmann, S. G., Asnaani, A., Vonk, I. J., Sawyer, A. T., & Fang, A. (2012, October 1). The Efficacy of Cognitive Behavioral Therapy: A Review of Meta-analyses. *Cognitive Therapy and Research, 36*(5), 427-440. doi:10.1007/s10608-012-9476-1

Holden, R. (2009). *BE Happy: Release the Power of Happiness in you.* Carlsbad: Hay House.

Hopp, H., Troy, A. S., & Mauss, I. B. (2011). The unconscious pursuit of emotion regulation: Implications for psychological health. *Cognitive Emoiton,* 532-545.

Hryhorczuk, C., Sharma, S., & Fulton, S. E. (2013, October). metabolic disturbances connecting obesity and depression. *Frontiers in Neuroscience,* 177.

Hu, T., Zhang, D., Wang, J.-L., Mistry, R., Ran, G., & Wang, X. (2014, April). Relation between emotion regulation and mental health: A meta-analysis-review. *Psychological Reports, 114*(2), 341-362. doi: DOI: 10.2466/03.20.PR0.114k22w4

Infurna, F. J., & Gerstorf, D. (2014). Perceived Control Relates to Better Functional Health and Lower Cardiac-Metabolic Risk: The Mediating Role of Physical Activity. *Health Psychology, 33*(1). doi:DOI: 10.1037/a0030208

Inkson, K. (2008). The Boundaryless Career. In S. Cartwright, & C. L. Cooper (Eds.), *The Oxford Handbook of Personal Psychology* (pp. 545-560). Oxford, UK. doi:DOI: 10.1093/oxfordhb/9780199234758.003.0023

Isen, A. M. (1972). Effect of feeling good on helping: Cookies and kindness. *Journal of Personality and Social Psychology,* 21: 384-88.

Isen, A. M. (1976). Duration of the effect of good mood on helping: Footprints in the sands of time. *Journal of Personality and Social Psychology,* 34: 385-93.

Isen, A. M. (1991). The influence of positive affect on clinical problem solving. *Medical Decision Making,* 11:221-27.

Ito, T., & Urland, G. R. (2003). Race and gender on the brain: Electro-cortical measures of attention to the race and gender of multiple categorizable individuals. *Journal of Personality and Social Psychology,* 616-26.

Jauch-Chara, K., & Oltmanns, K. M. (2014). Obesity - A neuropsychological disease? Systematic review and neuropsychological model. *Progress in Neurobiology,* xxx-xxx (In Press).

Johnson, K. J. (2010). Smile to see the forest: Facially expressed positive emotions broaden cognition. *COGNITION AND EMOTION,* 24(2): 299-321.

Johnson, M. B., Bertrand, S. W., Fermon, B., & Foley, J. (2014). Pathways to Healing: Person-centered Responses to Complimentary Services. *Global Advances in Health and Medicine, 3*(1), 8-16.

Judge, T. A., & Bono, J. E. (2001). Relationship of Core Self-Evaluations Traits—Self-Esteem, Generalized Self-Efficacy, Locus of Control, and Emotional Stability—With Job Satisfaction and Job Performance: A Meta-Analysis. *Journal of Applied Psychology, 86*(1), 80-92. doi:DOI: 10.1037//0021-9010.86.1.80

Kashdan, T. B., & Jonathan, R. (2010). Psychological flexibility as a fundamental aspect of health. *Clinical Psychology Review,* xxx-xxx (In Press). doi:doi:10.1016/j.cpr.2010.03.001

Khanlou, N., & Wray, R. (2014). A Whole Community Approach toward Child and Youth Resilience Promotion: A Review of Resilience Literature. *International Journal of Mental Health Addiction, 12*, 64-79. doi:DOI 10.1007/s11469-013-9470-1

Khansar, D. N., Murgo, A. J., & Faith, R. E. (1990). Effects of Stress on the Immune System. *Immunology Today, 11*, 170-176. doi:DOI: 10.1016/0167-5699(90)90069-L

Kiecolt-Glaser. (1999). Stress, Personal Relationships, and Immune Function: Health Implications. *Brain, Behavior, and Immunity 13*, 61-72. Retrieved 10 8, 2014

Kilpatrick, D. G., Resnick, H. S., Milanak, M. E., Miller, M. W., Keyes, K. M., & Friedman, M. J. (2013, October). National Estimates of Exposure to Traumatic Events and PTSD Prevalence Using DSM-IV and DSM-5 Criteria. *Journal of Trauma and Stress, 26*(5), 537-547. doi:doi:10.1002/jts.21848

Kim, H. J., & Agrusa, J. (2011). Hospitality service employees' coping styles: The role of emotional intelligence, two basic personality traits, and socio-demographic factors. *International Journal of Hospitality Management, 30*, 588-598. doi:doi:10.1016/j.ijhm.2010.11.003

Kimhi, S., & Eshel, Y. (2009). Individual and Public Resilience and Coping with Long-Term Outcomes of War. *Journal of Applied Biobehavioral Research, 14*(2), 70-89.

King, R. B., McInerney, D. M., & Watkins, D. A. (2012). How you think about your intelligence determines how you feel in school: The role of theories of intelligence on academic emotions. *Learning and Individual Differences*(22), 814-819.

Kivetz, Y., & Tyler, T. R. (2006). Tomorrow I'll be me: The effect of time perspective on the activation of idealistic versus pragmatic selves. *Organizational Behavior and Human Decision Process*, 193-211. doi:doi:10.1016/j.obhdp.2006.07.002

Kobylinska, D., & Karwowska, D. (2015, October 27). How automatic activation of emotion regulation influences experiencing negative emotins. (P. Kusev, Ed.) *Frontiers in psychology*, 1-4.

Koerner, N., Antony, M. M., Young, L., & McCabe, R. E. (2013, April). Changes in Beliefs about the Social Competence of Self and Others Following Group Cognitive Behavioral Therapy. *Cognitive Therapy Research, 37*(2), 256-265.

Kok, B. E., Coffey, K. A., cohn, M. A., Catalino, L. I., Vacharkulksemsuk, T., Algoe, S. B., . . . Fredrickson, B. L. (2012). How Positive Emotions Build Physical Health: perceived Positive Social Connections Account for the Upward spiral Between Positive Emotions and Vagal Tone. *Psychological Science, 24*(7), 1123-1132. doi:DOI: 10.1177/0956797612470827

Kramer, P. D. (2012, June 20). *The Transformation of Personality*. Retrieved from psychologytoday.com: www.psychologytoday.com/articles

Kudinova, A. Y., Owens, M., Burkhouse, K. L., Barretto, K. M., Bonanno, G. A., & Gibb, B. E. (2015, May). Differences in emotion modulation using cognitive reappraisal in individuals with and without suicidal ideation: An ERP study. *Cognitive Emotion, 15*, 1-9.

Kwong, J. Y., Wong, K. F., & Tang, S. K. (2013). Comparing predicted and actual affective responses to process versus outcome: An Emotion-as-feedback perspective. *Cognition, 129*, 42-50. doi:http://dx.doi.org/10.1016/j.cognition.2013.05.012

Laloyaux, J., Dessart, G., Van der Linden, M., Lernaire, M., & Laroi, F. (2016, February 1). Maladaptive emotion regulation strageties and stress sensitivity mediate the relation between adverse life events and attenuated positive psychotic symptoms. *Cognitive Neuropsychiatry*, 1-14 (Epub).

Lansing, A. H., & Bert, C. A. (2014). Topical Review: Adolescent Self-Regulation as a Foundation for Chronic Illness Self-Management. *Journal of Pediatric Psychology, 39*(10), 1091-1096. Retrieved 2016

Larson, M. D., Norman, S. M., Hughes, L. W., & Avey, J. B. (2013). Psychological Capital: A New Lens for Understanding Employee Fit and Attitudes. *Internal Journal of Leadership Studies, 8*(1), 28-43.

Lazarus. (1991). *Cognition and Emotion*.

Leary, M. R., Schreindorfer, L. S., & Haupt, A. L. (1995, September). The Role of Low Self-Esteem in Emotional and Behavioral Problems: Why is Low Self-Esteem Dysfunctional? *Journal of Social and Clinical Psychology, 14*(3), 297-314.

Legal , J.-B., Chappe, J., Coiffard, V., & Villard-Forest, A. (2012). now that you want to trust me? Subliminal goal priming and persuasion. *Journal of Experimental Social Psychology, 48*, 359-360.

Leith, K., & Baumeister, R. F. (1996, December). Why do bad moods increase self-defeating behavior? Emotion, risk tasking, and self-regulation. *Journal of Personality and Social Psychology, 71*(6), 1250-1267.

Lemelle, C. J., & Seielzo, S. A. (2012). How You Feel About Yourself Can Affect How You Feel About Your Job: A Meta-Analysis Examing the Relationship of Core Self-Evaluations and Job Satisfaction. *Journal of Business Diversity, 12*(3), 116-133.

Lerner, J. S., & Keltner, D. (2000). Beyond valence: Toward a model of emotion-specific influences on judgement and choice. *Cognition and Emotion, 14*(4), 473-493. Retrieved 10 8, 2014, from http://www.tandf.co.uk/journals/pp/02699931.html

Limar, I. V. (2011). C.G. Jung's Schronicity and Quantum Enganglement: Schrodinger's Cat 'Wanders' Between Chromosomes. *NeuroQuantology*(9), 313-321.

Lindstrom, B., & Eriksson, M. (2006). Contextualizing salutogenesis and Antonovsky in public health development. *Public Health & Epidemiology, 21*(3), 238-244.

Livingston, J. S. (2003, January 1). Pygmalion in Management (HBR Classic). *Harvard Business Review*.

Lloyd, C., Smith, J., & Weinger, K. (2005). Stress and Diabetes: A Review of the Links. *Diabetes Spectrum, 18*(2).

Lloyd, S. J., Malek-Ahmadi, M., Barclay, K., Fernandez, M. R., & Chartrand, M. S. (2012). Emotional intelligence (EI) is a predictor of depression status in older adults. *Archives of Gerontology and Geriatrics, 55*, 570-573.

Lohmann, MS, LPC, R. C. (2013, June 27). *Teen Bullying: A CBT Approach to Addressing the Issue*. Retrieved from Psychology Today: https://www.psychologytoday.com/blog/teen-angst/201306/teen-bullying-cbt-approach-addressing-the-issue

Longe, O., Maratos, F. A., Gilbert, P., Evans, G., Volker, F., Rockliff, H., & Rippon, G. (2010). Having a word with yourself: Neural correlates of self-criticism and self-reassurance. *NeuroImage, 49*, 18-49.

Luthans, F., & Youssef, C. M. (2007). *Emerging Positive Organizational Behavior*. Leadership Institute. Leadership Institute Faculty Publications.

Luthans, F., Avolio, B. J., Avey, J. B., & Norman, S. M. (2007). Positive Psychological Capital: Measurement and Relationship with Performance and Satisfaction. *Personnel Psychology, 60*, 541-572.

Lyubomirsky, S. (2008). *The How of Happiness: A Scientific Approach to Getting the Life You Want*. New York: The Penguin Press.

Lyubomirsky, S., & Porta, M. D. ((in press)). Boosting Happiness and Buttressing Resilience: Results from Cognitive and Behavioral Interventions. In J. W. Reich, A. J. Zautra, & J. Hall (Eds.), *Handbook of adult resilience: Concepts, methods, and application*. New York, NY, USA: Guilford Press. Retrieved 2015

Lyubomirsky, S., King, L., & Diener, E. (2005). The benefits of frequent positive affect: Does happiness lead to success? *Psychological Bulletin, 131*(6), 803-55.

Lyubomirsky, S., King, L., & Diener, E. (2005). The Benefits of Frequent Positive Affect: Does Happiness Lead to Success? *Psychological Bulletin, 131*(6), 803-855. doi:DOI: 10.1037/0033-2909.131.6.803

Maguire, E. G. (2000). Navigation-related structural change in the hippocampi of taxi drivers. *Proceedings of the National Academy of Sciences, USA, 97*(8): 4398-4403.

Mansor, A., Kirmani, S., Tat, H. H., & Azzman, M. (2012). Harnessing Positivity at Workplace from Perception to Action. *Social and Behavioral Sciences, 40*, 557-564.

Maslach, C., Jackson, S. E., & Leiter, M. P. (n.d.). *Maslach Burnout Inventory Manual*.

Mason, D. (2011). *The H Factor: how Happiness Will Improve Your Bottom Line and Healp Your Organization Thrive*. Alpharetta: Dyer Publishing.

Mason, W. A., January, S. A., Fleming, C. B., Thompson, R. W., Parra, G. R., Haggerty, K. P., & Snyder, J. J. (2016, February). Parent Training to Reduce Problem Behaviors over the Transition to High School: Tests of Indirect Effects through Improved Emotion Regulation Skills. *Child Youth Services Review*, 176-183.

Masten, A. S., & Monn, A. R. (2015). Child and Family Resileince: A Call for Integrated Science, Practice, and Professional Training. *Family Rlations: Interdisciplinary Journal of Applied Family Studies, 64*, 5-21.

Maston, A. S. (2001). Ordinary magic: Resilience processes in development. *American Psychologist*, 56: 27-38.

McCarthy, B., & Casey, T. (2011). Get Happy! Positive Emotion, Depression and Juvenile Crime. *American Sociological Associaion Annual Meeting*. Las Vegas: UC Davis.

McGonagle, C. (2015, July). Happiness in the Workplace: An Appreciative Inquiry. *A thesis presented to Dublin City University*. Ireland: Dublin City University.

McGregor, B. A., Antoni, M. H., Boyers, A., Alfen, S. M., Blomberg, B. B., & Carver, C. S. (2004, January). Cognitive-Behavioral stress management increases benefit finding and immune function among women with early-stage breast cancer. *ournal of Psychosomatic Research, 56*(1), 1-8.

McGregor, I., Haji, R., & Kang, S.-J. (2008). Can ingroup affirmation relieve outgroup derogation? *Journal of Experimental Social Psychology, 44*, 1395-1401. doi:doi:10.1016/j.jesp.2008.06.001

McHugh, R. K., Hearon, B. A., & Otto, M. W. (2010, September). Cognitive-Behavioral Therapy for Substance Use Disorders. *Psychiatric Clinics of North America, 33*(3), 511-525. doi:10.1016/j.psc.2010.04.012

Min, J.-A., Lee, C.-U., & Lee, C. (2013). Mental Health Promotion and Illness Prevention: A Challenge for Psychiatrists. *Psychiatric Investigations*, Epub.

Mohd, R. S. (2008, October). Life Event, Stress and Illness. *The Malaysian Journal of Medical Sciences, 15*(4), 9-18.

Morley, S., Eccleston, C., & Williams, A. (1999). Systematic review and meta-analysis of randomized controlled trials of cognitive behaviour therapy and behaviour therapy for chronic pain in adults, excluding headache. (I. A. Pain, Ed.) *Pain, 80*, 1-13.

Mroczek, D. K., & Spiro III, A. (2007, May). Personality Change Influences Mortality in Older Men. *Association for Psychological Science, 18*(5), 371-376. doi:doi:10.1111/j.1467-9280.2007.01907.x.

Muehsam, D., & Ventura, C. (2014, March). Life Rhythm as a Symphony of Oscillatory Patterns: Electromagnetic Energy and Sound Vibration Modulaes Gene Expression for Biological Signaling and Healing. *Global Advances in Health and Medicine, 3*(2), 40-55.

Murphy, E. R., Barch, D. M., Pagliaccio, D., Luby, J. L., & Belden, A. C. (2015 (in press)). Functional connectivity of the amygdala and subgenual cingulate during cognitive reappraisal of emotions in children with MDD history is associated with rumination. *Developmental Cognitive Neuroscience*.

Murphy, R., Straebler, S., Cooper, Z., & Fairburn, C. G. (2010, September). Cognitive Behavioral Therapy for Eating Disorders. *The Psychiatric Clinics of North America*, 611-627. doi:10.1016/j.psc.2010.04.004

Neher, A. (1991). Maslow's Theory of Motivation A Critique. *Journal of Humanistic Psychology, 31*(3), 89-112. doi:doi: 10.1177/0022167891313010

Nelson, S. K., Fuller, J. A., Choi, I., & Lyubomirsky, S. (2014, April 29). Beyond Self-Protection: Self-Affirmation Benefits Hedonic and Eudaimonic Well-Being. *Personality and Social Psychology Bulletin, 40*(8), 998-1011.

Nettles, R., & Balter, R. (Eds.). (2011). *Multiple Minority Identities.* New York, NY, USA: Springer Publishing Company.

Nielsen, K., & Daniels, K. (2016). The relationship between transformational leadership and follower sickness absence: the fole of presenteeism. *Work and Stress, 30*(2), 193-208.

Nisbett, R. E. (2003). *The Geography of Thought: How Asians and Westerners Think Differently...and Why.* New York: The Free Press.

Nubold, A., Muck, P. M., & Maier, G. W. (2013). A new substitute for leadership? Followers state core self-evaluations. *The Leadership Quarterly, 24*, 29-44.

Okon-Singer, H., Hendler, T., Pessoa, L., & Shackman, A. J. (2015, February). The neurobiology of emotion-cognition interactions: fundamental questions and strategies for future research. *Frontiers in Human Neuroscience, 9*, 1-14. doi:doi: 10.3389/fnhum.2015.00058

Okunda, M., Balán , I., Petry, N. M., Oquendo, M., & Blanco, C. (2009, December). Cognitive Behavioral Therapy for Pathological Gambling: Cultural Considerations. *American Journal of Psychiatry, 166*(12), 1325-1330. doi:doi:10.1176/appi.ajp.2009.08081235.

Ong, A. D., Bergeman, C. S., Bisconti, T. L., & Wallace, K. A. (2006). Psychological Resilience, Postive Emotions, and Successful Adaptation to Stress in Later Life. *Journal of Personaltiy and Social Psychology 91*, 730-49.

Ornstein, R. E. (1977). *The Psychology of Consciousness.* Harcourt Brace Jovanovich, Inc.

Oswald, A. J., Proto, E., & Dgroi, D. (2009). Happiness and Productivity. *Institte for the Study of Labor*, 1-51.

Ozier, A. D., Kendrick, O. W., Leeper, J. D., Knol, L. L., Perko, M., & Burnham, J. (2008). Overweight and Obesity Are Associated with Emotion-and Stress-Related Eating as Measured by the Eating and Appraisal Due to Emotions and Stress Questionnaire. *Journal of the AMERICAN DIETETIC ASSOCIATION*. doi:doi: 10.1016/j.jada.2007.10.011

Padgett, D. A., & Glaser, R. (2003). How stress influences the immune response. *TRENDS in Immunology, 24*(8). doi:doi:10.1016/S1471-4906(03)00173-X

Parashar, F. (2015). *Optimism and Pessimism.* Retrieved from www.positivepsychology.org: www.positivepsychology.org

Parton, S. (2016, March 12). Complaining is Terrible for You, According to Science. (J. Stillman, Interviewer)

Paul, K. I., & Moser, K. (2009). Unemployment impairs mental health: Meta-Analysis. *Journal of Vocational Behavior, 74*, 264-282.

Paulus, D. J., Vanwoerden, S., Norton, P. J., & Sharp, C. (2016, January 15). Emotion dysregulation, psychological inflexibility, and shame as explanatory factors between neuroticism and depression. *Journal of Affective Disorders, 190*, 376-385. doi:http://dx.doi.org/10.1016/j.jad.2015.10.014

Peil, K. T. (2014). Emotion: A Self-regulatory Sense.

Perez-De-Albeniz, A., & Holmes, J. (2000). Meditation: concepts, effects and uses in therapy. *International Journal of Psychotherapy, 5,* 49-59.

Peterson, C. (2006). *A Primer in Positive Psychology.* Oxford, UK: Oxford University Press.

Peterson, S. J., Luthans, F., Avolio, B. J., Walumbwa, F. O., & Zhang, Z. (2011). Psychological capital and employee performance: A Latent Growth Modeling approach. *Personnel Psychology, 64,* 427-450.

Petit, G., Luminet, O., Maurage, F., Tecco, J., Lechantre, S., Ferauge, M., . . . de Timary, P. (2015, December). Emotion Regulation in Alcohol dependence. *ALCOHOLISM: CLINICAL AND EXPERIMENTAL RESEARCH, 39*(12). doi:10.1111/acer.12914

Pietrzak, R. H., & Southwick, S. M. (2011). Psychological resilience in OEF–OIF Veterans: Application of a novel classification approach and examination of demographic and psychosocial correlates. *Journal of Affective Disorders, 133,* 560-568.

Pool, G. J., Wood, W., & Leck, K. (1998). The Self-Esteem Motive in Social Influence: Agreement With Valued Majorities and Disagreement with Derogated Minorities. *Journal of Personality and Social Psychology, 75*(4), 967-975. doi:0022-3514/98/$3.00

Pool, L. D., & Qualter, P. (2012). Improving emotional intelligence and emotional self-efficacy through a teaching intervention for university students. *Learning and Individual Differences, 22,* 306-312.

Popp, F., Nagl, W., Wolf, R., Li, K. H., Scholz, W., & Weingartner, O. (1984). New evidence for Coherence and DNA as Source. *Cell Biophysics,* 33-52.

Porath, C. (2014, November 18). Half of Employees Don't Feel Respected by Their Bosses. *Harvard Business Review,* pp. e-pub.

Praveen, K. S., Dhamodharan, V., & Chandrasekar, M. (2015). Empirical study on employee engagement,increased productivity, happines and job satisfaction resulting through proper P-J fit and P-O fit among BPO professionals in Chennai, Indian Scenario. *International Journal of Physical and Social Sciences, 5*(10), 442-453.

Pyszczynski, T., Greenberg, J., Solomon, S., Arndt, J., & Schimel, J. (2004). Why Do People Need Self-Esteem? A Theoretical and Empirical Review. *Psychological Bulletin, 130,* 435-468. doi:DOI: 10.1037/0033-2909.130.3.435

Quigley, K. S., & Barrett, L. F. (2014 (in press)). Is there consistency and specificity of autonomic changes during emotional episodes? Guidance from the conceptual act theory and psychophysiology. *Biological Psychology,* xxx-xxx. Retrieved 2014

Regional Research Institute for Human Services. (2005, Summer). Building Hope for Adolescents: The Importance of A Secure Social Base. *FOCAL POINT Research, Policy, and Practice in Children's Mental Health,* p. 1.

Ricard, M. (2003). *Happiness: A Guide to Developing Life's Most Important Skill.* Little, Brown and Company.

Riccomini, P. J., Bost, L. W., Katsiyannis, A., & Zhang, D. (2005). *Cognitive Behavioral Interventions: An Effective Approach to Help Students wtih Disabilities Stay in School.* National Dropout Prevention Center for Students with Disabilities (NDPC-SD) , College of Health, Education, and Human Development - Clemson University. Clemson: Office of Special Education Programs of the U.S. Department of Education. Retrieved from http://www.ndpc-sd.org/documents/Practice_Guides/CBI_Practice_Brief.pdf

Rollin, M., Bradley, R. T., & Atkinson, M. (2004). Electropsyciological Evidence of Intuition. Part 1: The Surprising Role of the Heart. *Journal of alternative and Complementary Medicine,* 10(1) pp. 133-143.

Rosenberg, T. (2015, January 15). For Better Crime Prevention, a Dose of Science. *The New York Times,* p. The Opinion Pages.

Rubenstein, E. (1999). *An Awakening from the Trances of Everyday Life: A Journey to Empowerment.* Sages Way Press.

Rubie-Davies, C., Hattie, J., & Hamilton, R. (2003). Great Expectations: Implications for New Zealand Students. *NZARE Conference 2003,* (pp. 1-14). Auckland.

Rubik, B., Muehsam, D., Hammerschlag, R., & Jain, S. (2015). Biofield Science and Healing: History, Terminology, and Concepts. *Global Advances in Health and Medicine,* suppl 8-14.

Rubin, A. (n.d.). Psychological Stress and Immune Function.

Rudy, B. M., David III, T. E., & Matthews, R. A. (2012). The Relationship Among Self-efficacy, Negative Self-referent Cognitions, and Social Anxiety in Children: A Multiple Mediator Model. *Behavior Therapy, 43,* 19-628.

Ryan, R. M., & Deci, E. L. (2008). A Self-Determination Theory Approach to Psychotherapy: The Motivational Basis for Effective Change. *Canadian Psychology, 49*(3), 186-193.

Salami, S. O. (2007). Management of Stress among Trainee-Teachers Through Cognitive-Behavioural Therapy. *Pakistan Journal of Social Sciences, 4*(2), 299-307.

Sandberg, J. (2000). Understanding Human Competence at Work: An Interpretative Approach. *Academy of Management Journal, 43*(1), 9 - 25.

Sarma, K. (2008). *Mental Resilience: The Power of Clarity: how to develop the focus of a warrior and the peace of a monk.* Novato: New World Library.

Sbarra, , D. A., Smith, H. L., & Mehl, M. R. (2001, September 21). Advice to divorcees: Go easy on yourself. *Association for Psychological Science.*

Schnall, S., & Roper, J. (2010). Elevation Puts Moral Values Into Action. *Dept of Social and Developmental Psychology, University of Cambridge, School of Psychology.*

Schnall, S., Roper, J., & Fessler, D. M. (2010). Elevation Leads to Altruistic Behavior. *Psychological Science.* doi:DOI: 10.1177/0956797609359882

Schnall, S., Roper, J., & Fessler, D. M. (2010, February 3). Pay It Forward: Elevation Leads to Altruistic Behavior. *Psychological Science.*

Scoglio, A. A., Rudat, D. A., Garvert, D., Jarmolowski, M., Jackson, C., & Herman, J. L. (2015, December 16). Self-Compassion and Responses to Trauma: The Role of Emotion Regulation. *Journal Interpersonal Violence,* Epub. Retrieved 2016

Segal, Ph.D., J. (1997). *Raising Your Emotional Intelligence: A practical Guide: A Hands-on Program for Harnessing the Power of Your Instincts and Emotions.* New York: Henry Holt and Company.

Seligman, M. &. (1986). Explanatory style as a predictor of productivity and quitting among life insurance sales agents. *Journal of Personality and Social Psychology*, 50: 832-838.

Seligman, M. (2011). *Flourish: A Visionary New Understanding of Happiness and Well-Being.* New York: Free Press.

Seligman,, M. (2006). *Learned Optimism* (Originally published 1991 ed.). New York: Simon & Schuster.

Shahba, S. a. (2013). Comparative Study of Problem-solving and Emotional Intelligence on Decreasing of third Grade Girl Students' Aggression of the Rajaee Guidance School of Tehran. *Procedia--Social and Behavioral Sciences, 84*, 778-780. Retrieved 2014

Shenk, D. (2010). *The Genius in All of Us.* Doubleday.

Sherman, D. K., Bunyan, D. P., Creswell, J. D., & Jaremka, L. M. (2009). Psychological Vulnerability and Stress: The Effects of Self-Affirmation on. *Health Psychology, 28*(5), 554-562. doi:DOI: 10.1037/a0014663

Shifrer, D., & Langenkamp, A. (2012). A Mixed methods Study of How Socioeconomic Status is Associated with Adolescents' Sense of Control. *Unbundling Youth, Family, and Community involvement in College Access,* (pp. 0-8). Austin.

Siebert, A. (2005). *The Resiliency Advantage: Master Change, Thrive under Pressure, and Bounce Back from Setbacks.* San Francisco: Berrett-Koehler Publishers, Inc.

Siegel, D. (2016, 1 23). *Science Says: Listen to Your Gut.* Retrieved from DrDanSiegel.com: http://www.drdansiegel.com/blog/2016/01/23/sciencesayslistentoyourgut/

Silva, P. J. (2002). Self-Awareness and the Regulation of Emotion Intensity. *Self and Identity, 1*, 3-10.

Simmons, A., & Yoder, L. (2013, January - March). Military Resilience: A Concept Analysis. *Nursing Forum, 48*(1), 17-25.

Snyder, C. R. (2002). Hope Theory: Rainbows in the mind. *Psychological Inquiry, 13*, 249-275.

Soper, B., Milford, G. E., & Rosenthal, G. T. (1995). Belief when evidence does not support theory. *Psychology & Marketing, 12*(5), 415-422. doi:DOI: 10.1002/mar.4220120505

Southwick, S. M., Bonanno, G. A., Masten, A. S., Panter-Brick, C., & Yehuda, R. (2014, July). Resilience definitions, theory, and challenges: interdisciplinary perspectives. *European Journal of Psychotraumatology,* Epub 1-14.

Stangier, U. (2016, March). New Developments in Cognitive-Behavioral Therapy for Social Anxiety Disorder. *Current Psychiatry Reports, 18*(3), Epub.

Stutzer, A., & Frey, B. S. (2006, April). Does marriage make people happy, or do happy people get married? *The Journal of Socio-Economics, 35*(2), 326-347. doi:doi:10.1016/j.socec.2005.11.043

Sultan, S., Epel, E., Sachon, C., Vaillant, G., & Hartemann-Heurtier, A. (2008). A longitudinal study of coping, anxiety and glycemic control in adults with type 1 diabetes. *Psychology and Health, 23*(1), 73-89. doi:DOI: 10.1080/14768320701205218

Talbot, M. (1991). *The Holographic Universe.* New York: Harper Collins.

The HeartMath Institute. (2012, November 11). *Coherence.* Retrieved from www.heartmath.com: www.heartmath.com

Trougakos, J. P., Hideg, I., Cheng, B. H., & Beal, D. J. (2013, March 25). Lunch Breaks Unpacked: The Role of Autonomy as a Moderator of Recovery during Lunch. *Academy of Management Journal, 57*(2), 405-421.

Troy, A. S., Shallcross, A. J., Davis, T. S., & Mauss, I. B. (2013, September 1). History of Mindfulness-Based Cognitive Therapy is Associated with Increased Cognitive Reappraisal Ability. *Mindfulness. 4*(3), 213-222.

Tugade, M. M. (2004). Resilient Individuals use positive emotions to bounce back from negative emotional experiences. *Journal of Personality and Social Psychology,* Journal of Personaltiy and Social Psychology.

Vaillant, G. E. (2012). *Triumphs of Experience: The Men of the Harvard Grant Study.*

van Breda, A. D. (2015). A comparison of youth resilience across seven South African sites. *Child and Family Social Work,* Epub.

van der Werff, S. J., van den Berg, S. M., Pannekoek, J. N., Elzinga, B. M., & van der Wee, N. J. (2013, May). Neuroimaging resilience to stress: a review. (R. Rozeske, Ed.) *frontiers in Behavioral Neuroscience, 7.*

Veilleux, J. C., Skinner, K. D., Reese, E. D., & Shaver, J. A. (n.d.). *Negative affect intensity influences drinking to cope through facets of emotion dysregulation,.* University of Arkansas.

Virginia Hill Rice, P. R. (2012). Theories of Stress and its Relationship to Health. In *Handbook of Stress, Coping, and Health, Implications for Nursing Research, Theory, and Practice* (Second Edition ed., p. Chapter 2). Save Publication, Inc.

Visser, C. (n.d.). *Coert Visser's Blog.* Retrieved from http://www.solworld.org/: http://www.solworld.org/

Voss, R. W. (1997, Summer). Beyond the Telescope of Gender-polemics: Need for a Wide Angle Lens in Pastoral Vision. *The Journal of Pastoral Care, 51*(2).

Wakslak, C. J., & Trope, Y. (2009). Cognitive consequences of affirming the self: The relationship between. *Journal of Experimental Social Psychology, 45,* 927-932. doi:doi:10.1016/j.jesp.2009.05.002

Walumbwa, F. O., Luthans, F., Avey, J. B., & Oke, A. (2011). Authentically leading groups: The mediating role of collective psychological capital and trust. *Journal of Organizational Behavior, 32,* 4-24.

Webb, T. L., & Sheeran, P. (2003). Can implementation intentions help to overcome ego-depletion? *Journal of Experimental Social Psychology, 39,* 279-286. doi:doi:10.1016/S0022-1031(02)00527-9

Weijers, D., Jarden, A., Angner, E., Burns, G., Chadwick, E., Jose, P. E., . . . Thin, N. (2013). Review of The Oxford handbook of happiness. (S. A. David, I. Boniwell, & A. C. Ayers, Eds.) *International Journal of Wellbeing, 3*(2), 1097. doi:10.5502/ijw.v3.i2.8

Weissman, D. D. (2005). *The Power of Infinite Love & Gratitude: An Evolutionary Journey to Awakening Your Spirit.* Hay House.

Wellington, S. (2001). *Be Your Own Mentor.* New York: Random House.

Whitney, D., & Trosten-Bloom, A. (2010). *The Power of Appreciative Inquiry: A Practical Guide to Positive Change* (2 ed.). NY: McGraw-Hill.

Wikipedia. (2016). *Executive Function.* Retrieved from Wikipedia: www.wikipedia.com/Executive_Function

Wingo, A. P., Ressler, K. J., & Bradley, B. (2014). Resilience characteristics mitigate tendency for harmful alcohol and illicit drug use in adults wiht a history of childhood abuse: A Cross-sectional study of 2024 inner-city men and women. *Journal of Psychiatric Research.* doi:doi: 10.1016/j.jpsychires.2014.01.007

Wong, E., Tschan, F., Messerli, L., & Semmer, N. K. (2013). Expressing and Amplifying Positive Emotions Facilitate Goal Attainment in Workplace Interactions. *Frontiers in Psychology,* 188. doi:doi: 10.3389/fpsyg.2013.00188

Wood, J. V., Perunovic, W. E., & Lee, J. W. (2009). Positive Self-Statements Power for Some, Peril for Others. *Psychological Science, 20,* 860-866. doi:doi: 10.1111/j.1467-9280.2009.02370.x

Wu, G., Feder, A., Cohen, H., Kim, J. J., Calderon, S., Chamey, D. S., & Mathe, A. A. (2013). Understanding Resilience. *Frontiers in Behavioral Neuroscience, 10.* doi:doi: 10.3389/fnbeh.2013.00010

Zacher, H. (2014). Career adaptability predicts subjective career success above and beyond personality traits and core self-evaluations. *Journal of Vocational Behavior, 84,* 21-30.

Zimmer-Gembeck, M. J., & Skinner, E. A. (2014). The Development of Coping: Implications for Psychopathology and Resilience. In D. Cicchetti (Ed.), *Developmental Psychopathology* (Vol. Resubmission #2, pp. 1-117). Oxford, England: Wiley & Sons. Retrieved January 2016

Zyromski, B., & Joseph, A. E. (n.d.). *Utilizing Cognitive Behavioral Interventions to Positively Impact Achievement in Middle School Students.* Retrieved from http://files.eric.ed.gov/fulltext/EJ894786.pdf

Citations

[1] (Gist, 1997, p. 205)
[2] (Hoffman, 2010, p. 277)
[3] (Quigley & Barrett, 2014 (in press))
[4] (Kilpatrick, et al., 2013)
[5] (Grant & Sonnentag, 2010, p. 13)
[6] (Grant & Sonnentag, 2010, p. 13)
[7] (Baumeister R. F., Vohs, DeWall, & Zhang, 2007)
[8] (EDi, 2016)
[9] (Entrepreneur)
[10] (Business Collective, 2016)
[11] (ANB, 2016)
[12] (Lemelle & Seielzo, 2012, p. 116)
[13] (Lemelle & Seielzo, 2012, p. 116)
[14] (Grant & Sonnentag, 2010, p. 13)
[15] (Pool, Wood, & Leck, 1998)
[16] (Peil, 2014)
[17] (Siegel, 2016)
[18] (Veilleux, Skinner, Reese, & Shaver, p. 96)
[19] (Veilleux, Skinner, Reese, & Shaver, p. 96)
[20] (Petit, et al., 2015, p. 2471)
[21] (Berking, et al., 2011, p. 317)
[22] (Grant, et al., 2015, p. 757)
[23] (Baumeister R. F., Vohs, DeWall, & Zhang, 2007)
[24] (Peil, 2014)
[25] (Campbell, 1975)
[26] (Fredrickson, B.L., et al., 2008)
[27] (Lazarus, 1991)
[28] (Lazarus, 1991)
[29] (Fredrickson B. L., The Science of Happiness, 2009)
[30] (Baumeister R. F., Vohs, DeWall, & Zhang, 2007)
[31] (Rubik, Muehsam, Hammerschlag, & Jain, 2015)
[32] (Muehsam & Ventura, 2014)
[33] (Haidt, 2006)
[34] (Goldberg, 2002)
[35] (Goldberg, 2002)
[36] (Rubenstein, 1999)
[37] (Talbot, 1991)
[38] (Ricard, 2003)
[39] (Eiser & Pahl, 2001)
[40] (Oregon State University , 2012)
[41] (Montgomery, 2012)
[42] (Feldman, Tarr, & Lebrecht, 2012)
[43] (Allison, Uhles, Asuncion, Beggan, & Mackie, 2006)
[44] (Fredrickson B. L., The Science of Happiness, 2009) (Seligman,, 2006) (Seligman M. , 2011) (Fredrickson, B.L., et al., 2008)
(Achor, The Happiness Advantage: Seven Principles of Positive Psychology That Fuel Success and Performance at Work, 2010)
[45] (Barnica, 2014)
[46] (Barnica, 2014)
[47] (Barnica, 2014)
[48] (Nisbett, 2003)

[49] (Achor, The Happiness Advantage: Seven Principles of Positive Psychology That Fuel Success and Performance at Work, 2010, p. 50)

[50] (Kashdan & Jonathan, 2010, p. 883)

[51] (Lemelle & Seielzo, 2012, p. 117)

[52] (Carver, 2015)

[53] (Carver, 2015)

[54] (Creswell, et al., 2005)

[55] (Wood, Perunovic, & Lee, 2009)

[56] (Correll, Spencer, & Zanna, 2004)

[57] (Nelson, Fuller, Choi, & Lyubomirsky, 2014)

[58] (Lindstrom & Eriksson, 2006)

[59] (Diener & Chan, Happy People Live Longer: Subjective Well-Being Contributes to Health and Longevity, 2011)

[60] (Vaillant, 2012)

[61] (Berry, et al., 2014)

[62] (Berry, et al., 2014)

[63] (Limar, 2011)

[64] (Dossey, M.D., 2013)

[65] (Dossey, M.D., 2013)

[66] (Boehm, 2012)

[67] (Parton, 2016)

[68] **(Popp, et al., 1984)**

[69] (The HeartMath Institute, 2012)

[70] (Nisbett, 2003)

[71] (Ornstein, 1977)

[72] (Farr, 1998, p.)

[73] (Ben-Itzhak, Bluvstein, & Maor, 2014, p. 2)

[74] (Kashdan & Jonathan, 2010, p. 865)

[75] (Ben-Itzhak, Bluvstein, & Maor, 2014, p. 2)

[76] (Farr, 1998, p. 6)

[77] (Siebert, 2005, p. 35)

[78] (Visser, p. 2)

[79] (Whitney & Trosten-Bloom, 2010, p. 19)

[80] (Farr, 1998, p. 21)

[81] (American Psychological Association (APA), 2010, p. 15)

[82] (Baumesiter, Vohs, & Tice, 2007, p. 351)

[83] (Hopp, Troy, & Mauss, 2011, p. 543)

[84] (Baumeister, Self-Regulation and Conscientiousness, 2015, p. 3)

[85] (Rollin, Bradley, & Atkinson, 2004)

[86] (Livingston, 2003, p. 4)

[87] (Berlew & Hall, 1966, p. 7)

[88] (Chang, 2011)

[89] (Rubie-Davies, Hattie, & Hamilton, 2003)

[90] (Dudovitz, Li, & Chung, 2013)

[91] (Khanlou & Wray, 2014, p. 65)

[92] (Siegel, 2016, p. 83)

[93] (Achor, The Happiness Advantage: Seven Principles of Positive Psychology That Fuel Success and Performance at Work, 2010, p. 71)

[94] (Paul & Moser, 2009, p. 278)

[95] (Paul & Moser, 2009, p. 280)

[96] (Lyubomirsky, King, & Diener, The benefits of frequent positive affect: Does happiness lead to success?, 2005)

[97] (Parashar, 2015)

[98] (Peterson C. , 2006, pp. 115-116)

[99] (Peterson C. , 2006, pp. 115-116)

[100] (Parashar, 2015)

[101] (Carey, Ph.D. & Forsyth, 2016)

[102] (Bandura, 1986)

[103] (DuBois & Flay, 2004)

[104] (DuBois & Flay, 2004)

[105] (Crocker & Park, Reaping the Benefits of Pursuing Self-Esteem Without the Costs? Reply to DuBois and Flay (2004), SHeldon (2004), and Pyszczynski and Cos (2004), 2004)

[106] (Cheng & Furnham, 2003)

[107] (Leary, Schreindorfer, & Haupt, 1995, p. 297)

[108] (Achor & Gielan, Make Yourself Immune to secondhand Stress, 2015)

[109] (Pyszczynski, Greenberg, Solomon, Arndt, & Schimel, 2004, p. 465)

[110] (Crocker & Park, The Costly Pursuit of Self-Esteem, 2004, p. 392)

[111] (Kramer, 2012, p. 3)

[112] (Crocker & Park, The Costly Pursuit of Self-Esteem, 2004, p. 396)

[113] (Crocker & Park, The Costly Pursuit of Self-Esteem, 2004, p. 404)

[114] (Crocker & Park, The Costly Pursuit of Self-Esteem, 2004, p. 406)

[115] (Crocker & Park, The Costly Pursuit of Self-Esteem, 2004, p. 407)

[116] (Crocker & Park, Reaping the Benefits of Pursuing Self-Esteem Without the Costs? Reply to DuBois and Flay (2004), SHeldon (2004), and Pyszczynski and Cos (2004), 2004, p. 415)

[117] (Crocker & Park, The Costly Pursuit of Self-Esteem, 2004)

[118] (Luthans & Youssef, Emerging Positive Organizational Behavior, 2007, p. 324)

[119] (Barry, Grafeman, Adler, & Pickard, 2007, p. 934)

[120] (Masten & Monn, 2015, p. 10)

[121] (Lemelle & Seielzo, 2012, p. 118)

[122] (Lemelle & Seielzo, 2012, p. 118)

[123] (Porath, 2014)

[124] (Porath, 2014)

[125] (Virginia Hill Rice, 2012)

[126] (Barasch & Hirshberg , 1995)

[127] (Maslach, Jackson, & Leiter)

[128] (Nielsen & Daniels, 2016, p. 193)

[129] (Pool & Qualter, 2012)

[130] (Lemelle & Seielzo, 2012, p. 120)

[131] (Judge & Bono, 2001)

[132] (Lemelle & Seielzo, 2012, p. 128)

[133] (Grant & Sonnentag, 2010, p. 15)

[134] (Larson, Norman, Hughes, & Avey, 2013, p. 29)

[135] (Luthans, Avolio, Avey, & Norman, 2007, p. 566)

[136] (Walumbwa, Luthans, Avey, & Oke, 2011, p. 7)

[137] (Larson, Norman, Hughes, & Avey, 2013, p. 37)

[138] (Larson, Norman, Hughes, & Avey, 2013, p. 38)

[139] (Mason, et al., 2016)

[140] (Mason, et al., 2016)

[141] (Sandberg, 2000, p. 9)

[142] (Walumbwa, Luthans, Avey, & Oke, 2011)

[143] (Nubold, Muck, & Maier, 2013, p. 30)

[144] (Nubold, Muck, & Maier, 2013, p. 30)

[145] (Nubold, Muck, & Maier, 2013, p. 39)

[146] (Nielsen & Daniels, 2016, p. 193)

[147] (Wakslak & Trope, 2009)

[148] (Sherman, Bunyan, Creswell, & Jaremka, 2009)

[149] (Peil, 2014)

[150] (Sbarra, , Smith, & Mehl, 2001)

[151] (Rudy, David III, & Matthews, 2012)

[152] (Longe, et al., 2010)

[153] I've seen this increase income in < 1 year by 60%. It has to do with both expectation and belief in our self and worthiness.

[154] Childhood Verbal Abuse and Risk for Personality Disorders During Adolescence and Early Adulthood

[155] (Regional Research Institute for Human Services, 2005)

[156] (Webb & Sheeran, 2003)

[157] (Legal , Chappe, Coiffard, & Villard-Forest, 2012, p. 358)

[158] (Cooper, Heron, & Heward, 2007)

[159] (van Breda, 2015)

[160] (van der Werff, van den Berg, Pannekoek, Elzinga, & van der Wee, 2013, p. 2)

[161] (Simmons & Yoder, 2013, p. 17)

[162] (Simmons & Yoder, 2013)

[163] (Kimhi & Eshel, 2009)

[164] (Kimhi & Eshel, 2009)

[165] (Lyubomirsky & Porta, Boosting Happiness and Buttressing Resilience: Results from Cognitive and Behavioral Interventions, (in press))

[166] (Southwick, Bonanno, Masten, Panter-Brick, & Yehuda, 2014, p. 12)

[167] (Min, Lee, & Lee, 2013, p. 1196)

[168] (Wingo, Ressler, & Bradley, 2014)

[169] (Khanlou & Wray, 2014, p. 70)

[170] (Kim & Agrusa, 2011)

[171] (Kudinova, et al., 2015)

[172] (Dweck, 2008)

[173] (Fredrickson B. L., 2005)

[174] (Okon-Singer, Hendler, Pessoa, & Shackman, 2015, p. 1)

[175] (Pietrzak & Southwick, 2011)

[176] (Lerner & Keltner, 2000)

[177] (Voss, 1997)

[178] (Zimmer-Gembeck & Skinner, 2014)

[179] (Kilpatrick, et al., 2013)

[180] (Kilpatrick, et al., 2013)

[181] (Bonanno & Diminich, 2013)

[182] (Fredrickson B. L., Positivity, 2010)

[183] (Shifrer & Langenkamp, 2012)

[184] (Shifrer & Langenkamp, 2012, p. 2)

[185] (Snyder, 2002)

[186] (Regional Research Institute for Human Services, 2005)

[187] (Peil, 2012)

[188] (Seligman, 2006)

[189] (Regional Research Institute for Human Services, 2005, p. 1)

[190] (Harvey & Delfabbro, 2004, p. 5)

[191] (Snyder, 2002, p. 16)

[192] (Khanlou & Wray, 2014)

[193] (Wu, et al., 2013)

[194] (Wu, et al., 2013)

[195] (Emery, Heath, & Mills, 2015, p. 612)

[196] (Grant & Sonnentag, 2010, p. 14)

[197] (Deci & Ryan, The "What" and "Why" of Goal Pursuits: Human Needs and the Self-Determination of Behavior, 2000)

[198] (Infurna & Gerstorf, 2014)

[199] (Duke, 2016)

[200] (Deci, Koestner, & Ryan, A Meta-Analytic Review of Experiments Examining the Effect of Extrinsic Rewards on Intrinsic Motivation, 1999, p. 627)

[201] (Gagné & Deci, 2005)

[202] (Trougakos, Hideg, Cheng, & Beal, 2013, p. 405)

[203] (Lloyd, Malek-Ahmadi, Barclay, Fernandez, & Chartrand, 2012)

[204] (Buzinski & Price, 2015, p. 8)

[205] (Buzinski & Price, 2015, p. 9)

[206] (Weijers, et al., 2013, p. 214)

[207] (Deci & Ryan, The "What" and "Why" of Goal Pursuits: Human Needs and the Self-Determination of Behavior, 2000)

[208] (McGonagle, 2015, p. 51)

[209] (Soper, Milford, & Rosenthal, 1995, p. 412)

[210] (Neher, 1991, p. 89)

[211] (Kivetz & Tyler, 2006, p. 207)

[212] (Kashdan & Jonathan, 2010)

[213] (Bond, Lloyd, & Guenole, 2012)

[214] (Zacher, 2014, p. 27)

[215] (Carr & Steele, 2009, p. 854)

[216] (Briscoe, Henagan, Burton, & Murphy, 2012, p. 314)

[217] (Briscoe, Henagan, Burton, & Murphy, 2012, p. 314)

[218] (Briscoe, Henagan, Burton, & Murphy, 2012, p. 314)

[219] (Inkson, 2008)

[220] (Briscoe, Henagan, Burton, & Murphy, 2012, p. 314)

[221] (Zacher, 2014, pp. 21-22)

[222] (Zacher, 2014, pp. 21-22)

[223] (Zacher, 2014)

[224] (Zacher, 2014, pp. 21-22)

[225] (Coetzee & Harry, 2014, p. 90)

[226] (Zacher, 2014)

[227] (Wellington, 2001, p. 87)

[228] (Wellington, 2001, p. 224)

[229] (Farr, 1998, p. xi)

[230] (Farr, 1998, p. 6)

[231] (Farr, 1998, p. 7)

[232] (Atkins & Parker, 2011)

[233] (Bond, Lloyd, & Guenole, 2012)

[234] (Bond, Lloyd, & Guenole, 2012)

[235] (Gable & Harmon-Jones, 2010)

[236] (Carver, 2015)

[237] (Boyce, Wood, Daly, & Sedikides, 2015)

[238] (Costa & McCrae, 1988)

[239] (Mroczek & Spiro III, 2007)

[240] (Helson & Kwan, 2002)

[241] (Dweck, 2008)

[242] (Mroczek & Spiro III, 2007)

[243] (Paulus, Vanwoerden, Norton, & Sharp, 2016)

[244] (Lyubomirsky, The How of Happiness: A Scientific Approach to Getting the Life You Want, 2008, p. 49)

[245] (Lyubomirsky, The How of Happiness: A Scientific Approach to Getting the Life You Want, 2008)

[246] (Lyubomirsky, The How of Happiness: A Scientific Approach to Getting the Life You Want, 2008)

[247] (Lyubomirsky, King, & Diener, The benefits of frequent positive affect: Does happiness lead to success?, 2005, p. 803)

[248] (Garland, et al., 2010, p. 22)

[249] (Shahba, 2013, p. 6)

[250] (Segal, Ph.D., 1997, p. 185)

[251] (Bowling, Eschlerman, & Wang, 2010, p. 924)

[252] (Schnall, Roper, & Fessler, Elevation Leads to Altruistic Behavior, 2010)

[253] (Ito & Urland, 2003)

[254] (Isen A. M., 1991)

[255] (Holden, 2009, p. 96)

[256] (Silva, 2002)

[257] (Fredrickson B. L., Positivity, 2010)

[258] (Bandura, 1986)

[259] (Lyubomirsky, King, & Diener, The benefits of frequent positive affect: Does happiness lead to success?, 2005)

[260] (Broderick, 2013)

261 (McGregor, Haji, & Kang, 2008)

262 (Achor, The Happiness Advantage: Seven Principles of Positive Psychology That Fuel Success and Performance at Work, 2010) (De Neve, Diener, Tay, & Xuereb, 2013) (Greenberg, 2007) (Lyubomirsky, King, & Diener, The Benefits of Frequent Positive Affect: Does Happiness Lead to Success?, 2005) (Mason D. , 2011) (Peterson, Luthans, Avolio, Walumbwa, & Zhang, 2011) (Seligman M. &., 1986) (Oswald, Proto, & Dgroi, 2009)

263 (De Neve, Diener, Tay, & Xuereb, 2013) (Harter, Schmidt, & Hayes, 2002) (Praveen, Dhamodharan, & Chandrasekar, 2015)

264 (Boroujeni, Asadi, & Tabatable, 2012)

265 (Isen A. M., 1972) (Isen A. M., 1976) (Leith & Baumeister, 1996) (Gable S. a., 2004) (Schnall & Roper, Elevation Puts Moral Values Into Action, 2010)

266 (Lyubomirsky, King, & Diener, The Benefits of Frequent Positive Affect: Does Happiness Lead to Success?, 2005)

267 (APA, 2013) (APA, 2014) (Boehm, 2012)

268 (McCarthy & Casey, 2011) (Fredrickson B. L., Positivity, 2010) (Kok, et al., 2012)

269 (Barn & Tan, 2012) (Clark, 2010) (McCarthy & Casey, 2011)

270 (Wingo, Ressler, & Bradley, 2014)

271 (Diener & Tay, A Scientific Review of the Remarkable Benefits of Happiness for Successful and Healthy Living, 2012 (draft)) (Fredrickson B. L., Positivity, 2010) (Stutzer & Frey, 2006)

272 (Fredrickson B. L., 2005) (Fredrickson B. L , 2001) (Fredrickson B. L., Positivity, 2010) (Gable & Harmon-Jones, 2010) (Mansor, Kirmani, Tat, & Azzman, 2012) (Johnson K. J., 2010)

273 (Gouin, Hantsoo, & Kiecolt-Glaser, 2008) (Khansar, Murgo, & Faith, 1990) (Kiecolt-Glaser, 1999) (Padgett & Glaser, 2003) (Rubin) (Achor, The Happiness Advantage: Seven Principles of Positive Psychology That Fuel Success and Performance at Work, 2010)

274 (Black, 2003) (Boehm, 2012) (Danner, 2001) (De Vriendt, Moreno, & De Henauw, 2009) (Diener & Tay, A Scientific Review of the Remarkable Benefits of Happiness for Successful and Healthy Living, 2012 (draft)) (Foss & Dyrstad, 2011) (Gouin, Hantsoo, & Kiecolt-Glaser, 2008) (Hryhorczuk, Sharma, & Fulton, 2013) (Jauch-Chara & Oltmanns, 2014) (Lloyd, Smith, & Weinger, 2005) (Ozier, et al., 2008) (Sultan, Epel, Sachon, Vaillant, & Hartemann-Heurtier, 2008)

275 (Brissette, Scheier, & Carver, 2002) (Cohn, 2009) (Friborg, et al., 2006) (Fredrickson B. L., 2003) (Maston, 2001) (Ong, Bergeman, Bisconti, & Wallace, 2006) (Sarma, 2008) (Tugade, 2004) (Wingo, Ressler, & Bradley, 2014) (Wu, et al., 2013)

276 (Peterson, Luthans, Avolio, Walumbwa, & Zhang, 2011)

277 (Lemelle & Seielzo, 2012, p. 128)

278 (Judge & Bono, 2001)

279 (Laloyaux, Dessart, Van der Linden, Lernaire, & Laroi, 2016)

280 (Compare, Zarbo, Shonin, Van Gordon, & Marconi, 2014)

281 (Compare, Zarbo, Shonin, Van Gordon, & Marconi, 2014)

282 (Vaillant, 2012)

283 (Hopp, Troy, & Mauss, 2011)

284 (Hopp, Troy, & Mauss, 2011)

285 (Hopp, Troy, & Mauss, 2011)

286 (Hu, et al., 2014)

287 (Troy, Shallcross, Davis, & Mauss, 2013)

288 (Scoglio, et al., 2015)

289 (Sbarra, , Smith, & Mehl, 2001)

290 (Kivetz & Tyler, 2006)

291 (Cisler & Olatunji, 2012)

292 (Armstrong, Galligan, & Critchley, 2011)

293 (Kobylinska & Karwowska, 2015)

294 (APA, 2014)

295 (Murphy, Barch, Pagliaccio, Luby, & Belden, 2015 (in press))

296 (Kudinova, et al., 2015)

297 (Zyromski & Joseph)

298 (Ryan & Deci, 2008)

299 (Butler, Chapman, Forman, & Beck, 2006)

300 (Stangier, 2016)

301 (Koerner, Antony, Young, & McCabe, 2013)

[302] (Hofmann, Asnaani, Vonk, Sawyer, & Fang, 2012)
[303] (Lohmann, MS, LPC, 2013)
[304] (Driessen & Hollon, 2010)
[305] (Bujoreanu, PhD, Benhayon, M.D., PhD, & Szigethy, M.D., PhD, 2011 November)
[306] (American Academy of Pediatrics, 2012)
[307] (Butler, Chapman, Forman, & Beck, 2006)
[308] (Butler, Chapman, Forman, & Beck, 2006)
[309] (Hofmann, Asnaani, Vonk, Sawyer, & Fang, 2012)
[310] (Driessen & Hollon, 2010)
[311] (Hofmann, Asnaani, Vonk, Sawyer, & Fang, 2012)
[312] (Driessen & Hollon, 2010)
[313] (Rosenberg, 2015)
[314] (Hofmann, Asnaani, Vonk, Sawyer, & Fang, 2012)
[315] (Clark, 2010)
[316] (McHugh, Hearon, & Otto, 2010)
[317] (Rosenberg, 2015)
[318] (Riccomini, Bost, Katsiyannis, & Zhang, 2005)
[319] (McHugh, Hearon, & Otto, 2010)
[320] (Hofmann, Asnaani, Vonk, Sawyer, & Fang, 2012)
[321] (Morley, Eccleston, & Williams, 1999)
[322] (Hofmann, Asnaani, Vonk, Sawyer, & Fang, 2012)
[323] (Butler, Chapman, Forman, & Beck, 2006)
[324] (Hofmann, Asnaani, Vonk, Sawyer, & Fang, 2012)
[325] (Okunda, Balán , Petry, Oquendo, & Blanco, 2009)
[326] (Rosenberg, 2015)
[327] (Hofmann, Asnaani, Vonk, Sawyer, & Fang, 2012)
[328] (Hofmann, Asnaani, Vonk, Sawyer, & Fang, 2012)
[329] (Butler, Chapman, Forman, & Beck, 2006)
[330] (Hofmann, Asnaani, Vonk, Sawyer, & Fang, 2012)
[331] (Hofmann, Asnaani, Vonk, Sawyer, & Fang, 2012)
[332] (Hofmann, Asnaani, Vonk, Sawyer, & Fang, 2012)
[333] (Murphy, Straebler, Cooper, & Fairburn, 2010)
[334] (Hofmann, Asnaani, Vonk, Sawyer, & Fang, 2012)
[335] (Mohd, 2008)
[336] (Mohd, 2008)
[337] (Boehm, 2012)
[338] (Hofmann, Asnaani, Vonk, Sawyer, & Fang, 2012)
[339] (Beck & Fernandez, 1998)
[340] (Hofmann, Asnaani, Vonk, Sawyer, & Fang, 2012)
[341] (Hofmann, Asnaani, Vonk, Sawyer, & Fang, 2012)
[342] (Hofmann, Asnaani, Vonk, Sawyer, & Fang, 2012)
[343] (Salami, 2007)
[344] (McGregor, et al., 2004)
[345] (Anderson & Taylor, 2011)
[346] (Lansing & Bert, 2014)
[347] (Hofmann, Asnaani, Vonk, Sawyer, & Fang, 2012)
[348] (Deechakawan, PhD, RN, Cain, PhD, Jarrett, PhD, RN, Burr, MSEE, PhD, & Heitkemper, PhD, RN, FAAN, 2012)
[349] (Hofmann, Asnaani, Vonk, Sawyer, & Fang, 2012)
[350] (Dissanayake & Bertouch, 2010)
[351] (Hofmann, Asnaani, Vonk, Sawyer, & Fang, 2012)
[352] (Nettles & Balter, 2011)
[353] (Nettles & Balter, 2011)
[354] (Nettles & Balter, 2011)
[355] (Nettles & Balter, 2011)
[356] (Nettles & Balter, 2011)

[357] (Nettles & Balter, 2011)
[358] (Nettles & Balter, 2011)
[359] (Nettles & Balter, 2011)
[360] (Nettles & Balter, 2011)
[361] (Nettles & Balter, 2011)
[362] (Nettles & Balter, 2011)
[363] (Baumeister R. F., Vohs, DeWall, & Zhang, 2007)
[364] (Clore & Palmer, 2009)
[365] (King, McInerney, & Watkins, 2012) (Perez-De-Albeniz & Holmes, 2000)
[366] (Dan-Glauser & Gross, 2013)
[367] (Kwong, Wong, & Tang, 2013)
[368] (Wong, Tschan, Messerli, & Semmer, 2013)
[369] (Peil, 2014)
[370] (Wikipedia, 2016)
[371] (Shenk, 2010)
[372] (Maguire, 2000)
[373] (Larson, Norman, Hughes, & Avey, 2013, p. 37)
[374] (Johnson, Bertrand, Fermon, & Foley, 2014)
[375] (Kashdan & Jonathan, 2010)
[376] (Bandura, 1986)

www.ingramcontent.com/pod-product-compliance
Lightning Source LLC
Chambersburg PA
CBHW082032230326
41599CB00056B/6260